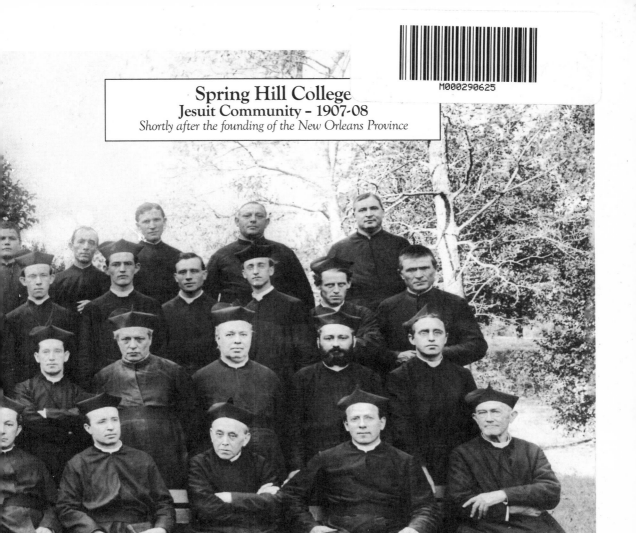

Spring Hill College
Jesuit Community – 1907-08
Shortly after the founding of the New Orleans Province

M000290625

Fr. Alexius de Stockalper, Fr. Joseph O'Reilly, Fr. Thomas Stritch and Fr. Peter Philippe.

Third row: *Bro. Francis Amacker, Mr. Cornelius Leeuwe, Mr. Wallace Burk, Mr. Timothy Cronin, Fr. Alex McLaughlin, Fr. Oscar Wocet, Mr. Patrick Cronin, Mr. William Obering, Mr. Joseph Kearens, Mr. Florence Sullivan, Mr. Jerry Higgins, Mr. Charles King and Bro. Wendolin Locher.*

Fourth row: *Bro. Fritz Melder, Bro. Francis Rickard, Bro. John Dougherty, Bro. William Cohnen, Bro. Pascal Gil, Bro. George Magrath, Bro. Salvador Hellin, Bro. Hilery Castresana, Bro. John Miller, Bro. Henry Rittmeyer and Bro. Richard Black.*

SOUTHERN JESUIT

Biographies

Other Books by
Jerome Neyrey, S.J.

*How Do You Read? Social-Science
Interpretations of the New Testament*
(Co-edited with Eric Stewart)

*Give God the Glory: Prayer and Worship in
Cultural Perspective*

*The Social Science World of the New
Testament: Insights and Models*
(Co-edited with Eric Stewart)

*A Socio-Rhetorical Commentary on the
Gospel of John*

*Render to God: New Testament
Understandings of the Divine*

Honor and Shame: Matthew and the Great Code

*Portraits of Paul: An Archaeology of Ancient
Personality* (With Bruce J. Malina)

2 Peter and Jude

*The Social World of Luke-Acts: Models for
Interpretation* (Editor)

*Paul in Other Words: A Cultural Reading
of His Letters*

*Calling Jesus Names: The Social Value of
Labels in Matthew* (With Bruce J. Malina)

*An Ideology of Revolt: John's Christology in
Social-Science Perspective*

The Resurrection Stories

*Christ Is Community: The Christologies of
the New Testament*

The Passion Narrative in St. Luke

*First Timothy, Second Timothy, Titus, James,
First Peter, Second Peter, Jude*

Other Books by
Thomas Clancy, S.J.

The Conversational Word of God

An Introduction to Jesuit Life

Our Friends (1978, 1989, 1998)

Papist Pamphleteers

*A Literary History of the English Jesuits:
A Century of Books, 1615-1714*

SOUTHERN JESUIT
Biographies

Pastors and Preachers,
Builders and Teachers
of the New Orleans Province

Jerome Neyrey, S.J.

and

Thomas Clancy, S.J.

Jerome Neyrey, SJ

Acadian House
PUBLISHING
Lafayette, Louisiana

ON THE COVER – *Southern Jesuits through the years have served in a wide variety of ministries, leaving a legacy of excellence as pastors, teachers, builders and missionaries.* **Starting with pictures on the back cover, from left to right:** *Fr. Theobald Butler (1829-1916), Bro. Cornelius Otten (1835-1916), Fr. Albert Biever (1858-1934), Fr. Lou Twomey (1905-1969), Bishop Ignatius Glennie (1907-1993), Fr. Youree Watson (1914-1989), Fr. Roy Vollenweider (1914-2005), Fr. Hagema Yamauchi (1920-1976), Fr. Eugene Hebert (1923-1990), Bro. Fillmore Elliot (1930-2004) and Fr. Gerald Fagin (1938-2012).*

Copyright © 2015 by
U.S. Central and Southern Province,
Society of Jesus,
St. Louis, Missouri

All rights reserved, including the right to reproduce this book or portions thereof in any form whatsoever. For information, contact Acadian House Publishing, P.O. Box 52247, Lafayette, Louisiana 70505, or via e-mail: info@acadianhouse.com.

Library of Congress Cataloging-in-Publication Data

Neyrey, Jerome H., 1940-
  Southern Jesuit biographies : pastors and preachers, builders and teachers of the New Orleans Province / Jerome Neyrey, S.J. and Thomas Clancy, S.J. (1923-2009)
      pages cm
  Includes bibliographical references and index.
  ISBN 978-0-925417-92-3 (alk. paper) -- ISBN 0-925417-92-0 (alk. paper) 1. Jesuits. New Orleans Province--Biography. I. Title.
  BX3710.N49N49 2015
  271'.5302276--dc23
  [B]
                        2015011141

◆ Published by Acadian House Publishing, Lafayette, Louisiana
   (Trent Angers and Darlene Smith, co-editors)
◆ Interior design and production by Robert Clements
◆ Cover design and production by Glenn Noya, New Orleans, Louisiana
◆ Printed by Sheridan Books, Chelsea, Michigan

*For all who have supported the Society of Jesus
and labored with us for the sake of the
Kingdom of God and its proclamation*

A narrative history of the Jesuits in the Southern United States

A chronology of the founding and development of the New Orleans Province, showing the historical context in which Southern Jesuits lived and worked over a period of more than three centuries...

At the very beginning of its presence in North America the Society of Jesus sought to labor among and for the Native American people. The Jesuits mastered the various languages and even compiled dictionaries and grammars in order to help others learn these languages. They also served the European and colonial settlers, building churches, establishing schools and aiding the local clergy.

The first Jesuits in the area that would become the New Orleans Province landed in Saint Augustine, Florida, in the sixteenth century. One of them, Pedro Martinez, who had begged for the privilege of serving on the missions, died a martyr. Territorial Indians clubbed him to death on October 6, 1566, on Fort George Island, Florida (near present-day Jacksonville).

While this mission did not endure, other Jesuit missions to various tribes moved north from Mexico into present-day Arizona, New Mexico and Texas. As the native tribes disappeared, either through death or migration, the Jesuits turned their attention to the developing cities and diversifying populations of the South.

French colonization of the central portion of North America was enabled by the explorations made by Jesuit Père Jacques Marquette, who traversed the Mississippi River as far south as Memphis. Louis XIV of France, deciding that establishing settlements in Louisiana would prevent the English from isolating French settlements in Canada, appointed Pierre Le Moyne, Sieur d' Iberville, to explore the mouth of the Mississippi River. His brother, Jean Baptiste Le Moyne, Sieur de Bienville, founded New Orleans in 1718.

Eight years later, Fr. Nicholas Ignace de Beaubois established the first permanent Jesuit foundation in Louisiana. Authorized by the King of France, it would serve as a headquarters where missionaries could rest and conduct business. Six priests were committed to missionary efforts with the local tribes, while the superior remained in the fledgling city of New Orleans. In order to support their missionary efforts the Jesuits acquired land which became a prosperous plantation in what is now the Central Business District of New Orleans.

In 1727, Fr. Paul du Poisson moved upriver to follow the Arkansas tribe. Three Jesuits were stationed among the Choctaw nation, serving some 42 villages. Jesuits also worked among the Yazoo and the Natchez. But some of these tribes rose up against the French colonists and, of course, the French missionaries. Three priests died as martyrs of "devotion and charity": Paul du Poisson, killed by the Natchez; John Souel, killed by the Yazoo; and Antoine Senat, burned at the stake by the Chickasaw.

Impact of the Suppression
of Jesuits in Europe and Louisiana

At a time when Europe was rife with unrest, when absolute monarchy was being challenged by ideas like "independence" and "liberty," the Society of Jesus became the target of hostility and punitive actions that culminated in its suppression in 1763.

Prior to the Suppression, even though the Society had established more than 700 schools and embraced much intellectual activity, the Jesuits were perceived by some as an order engaged in religious deviation and political and economic exploitation. Several European states/nations wanted control of Jesuit assets, and the mid-eighteenth century saw missions, colleges, libraries, churches, and properties of the Jesuit Order confiscated or destroyed by European governments, particularly in France, Spain and Portugal.

With its traditional loyalty to the papacy, the Society of Jesus had become a formidable obstacle to those European monarchies that wanted greater control over their national churches, following the example of the English Reformation. Opponents of the French Jesuits found their advantage when the Society became involved in litigation over Jesuit finances of the Caribbean missions. When loans went unpaid and several banks failed, the various *parlements* sought to determine the Society's liability based on the Jesuit *Constitutions*. As individual regional *parlements* banished Jesuits from their jurisdictions, it became clear that it would be necessary for the king to suppress the Order throughout France and her colonies in 1763. Thus, Jesuit properties were confiscated and the Jesuits were allowed to move into other religious orders or the diocesan clergy, or to leave France.

Meanwhile, in New Orleans the attorney general of the Louisiana colony demanded that the Louisiana Superior Court pronounce its own decision concerning the Jesuits. Within a week of that announcement, the Decree of Suppression of the Society of Jesus in Louisiana was promulgated, on July 9, 1763. Jesuit property was put up for auction and most of the Jesuits returned to France. Those who remained were no longer Jesuits, and no new missionaries were sent to continue the missions to the native tribes.

Development of the New Orleans Mission

After the Napoleonic Wars ended in 1815 and the monarchs who suppressed the Jesuits were no longer in power, the Order was once again welcome in Europe and in Louisiana. Pope Pius VII ordered the Restoration of the Society of Jesus in Europe, and the Jesuits soon re-established schools and regained their reputation as pre-eminent scholars and scientists. The Restoration would have similar effects in Louisiana.

By 1831, priests for Louisiana churches were in great demand but short supply. Louisiana had a total of 26 churches and only 24 priests to minister in those churches. A desperate Leo de Neckere, Bishop of New Orleans, actually detained four Jesuits who had arrived en route to Bardstown, Kentucky. Eventually he allowed three of them to depart, but he kept the fourth, Fr. Pierre Ladavière. When the bishop died, Fr. Ladavière administered the diocese along with the Vicar General, Antoine Blanc, who became bishop in 1835.

Bishop Blanc took Fr. Ladavière with him to Europe to recruit more Jesuits. Refused by the Jesuits of the Paris Province, the bishop traveled to Rome and appealed to Father General Jan Roothaan, who directed French Jesuits to find men in their ranks to help Bishop Blanc establish a college in Louisiana. Four Jesuit priests, a novice and two brothers sailed from Le Havre on Christmas Eve 1836 and arrived in New Orleans in February of 1837. They selected Grand Coteau, Louisiana, as the site for their school and named it St. Charles College; its first students were received in 1838.

In 1847, Bishop Michael Portier of Mobile successfully secured Jesuits from the Lyon Province of France to take over Spring Hill College, located at Mobile, Alabama. It soon became obvious that the Jesuits' colleges and pastoral works in the Southern U.S. should be unified into a single New Orleans Mission entrusted to the Lyon Province.

In July of 1848, the new mission superior, Fr. Jean Baptiste Maisounabe, arrived in New Orleans and began the process of establishing a Jesuit college there. He received a notarial charter for "*La Société Catholique d'education religieuse et littéraire*," which would remain, for more than a century and a half, the corporate title of the New Orleans Province in its English translation, "The Catholic Society of Religious and Literary Education." Sadly, Fr. Maisounabe contracted yellow fever while helping victims of the disease in New Orleans; he died on September 12, 1848.

The middle decades of the 1800s were the worst possible time for Catholic schools. First, a hostile attitude towards Catholics arose throughout the U.S., along with the rise of nativism and the Know-Nothing Party. Second, yellow fever epidemics periodically devastated the population of the Gulf South and wherever else mosquitoes flourished. (In 1853, if New Orleans was one of America's largest cities, with a population of 150,000, it was also unquestionably one of the unhealthiest. In that year, 5 per cent of the population died of yellow fever, and another 30,000 fled the city.) Third, the South experienced the ravages of the Civil War and Reconstruction. Two of the three Jesuit colleges – St. Charles College in Grand Coteau, Spring Hill College in Mobile, and the College of the Immaculate Conception in New Orleans – were in occupied territory during the bulk of the war, which made them difficult to access from other parts of the South. This was especially painful because the colleges in Grand Coteau and Mobile were predominantly boarding schools.

College mission centers

The three Jesuit colleges were much more than educational institutions. All had parishes attached to them and all were centers of missionary activity. Jesuits issued forth from the colleges to serve as chaplains in convents, hospitals and jails. They preached missions, gave retreats all over the South and served in communities without priests.

A dozen church parishes in south Louisiana west of New Orleans trace their origins to the labors of the Grand Coteau Jesuits, most notably Fr. John Abbadie.

In 1899, the Southern Jesuits added a fourth school when Sacred Heart College opened in Tampa, Florida. A church parish and mission trail into west and south Florida soon followed.

From Mission to Province

In 1880, the New Orleans Mission began to detach itself from the Lyon Province and became the Independent Mission of New Orleans – a step toward becoming an autonomous Province of its own. This was a result of growth in local vocations and the increasing use of English rather than French in the region. Fr. Theobald Butler was appointed as the first superior of the independent mission.

The number of Jesuits grew from 132 in 1881 to 222 in 1890 and increased to 246 by 1907. (Its zenith would see some 600 Jesuits in 1960.) This growth, along with the encouragement of the Twenty-Fifth General Congregation, persuaded Father General Franz Xavier Wernz to declare the Mission a Province in 1907. Fr. John F. O'Connor, the last mission superior, became the first provincial of the New Orleans Province.

More than educators

One might think that Jesuits in the South were dedicated primarily to education, but this would ignore the story of their pastoral labors and work with the Spiritual Exercises. With the return of the Jesuits to the South in the nineteenth century following the Suppression, they founded parishes alongside their schools from which priests traveled into the surrounding region ministering to satellite communities.

Some priests were outstanding missionaries, such as Fr. Alfred Latiolais in Florida. After working from 1908 to 1912 among the black Catholics of Macon, Georgia, he took charge of the mission trail from the west coast of Florida and into the interior. While laboring there for 17 years, he established at least 11 churches.

As the numbers of Jesuits in the Province grew, more churches were founded; consequently, in 1960 there were 18 parishes staffed by Jesuits in the South. It should also be noted that most of these parishes served the very poor. Moreover, for many years the Province operated a mission band out of Selma, Alabama, focusing primarily on preaching to poor, predominantly black congregations.

Jesuits in the Southwest

The story of the Jesuits in the Southwest is closely tied to the request for Spanish-speaking Jesuits by Archbishop J.B. Lamy (1814-1888) of Santa Fe, New Mexico. When the Jesuits of the Province of Naples, Italy, were expelled during the *Risorgimento*, many priests and brothers from there were free and eager to be recruited to the missions in the U.S. Archbishop Lamy brought many of them to San Felipe de Neri, the historic church in Old Town Albuquerque in 1868.

Fourteen years later Fr. Donato Gasparri built the original Immaculate Conception Church in Albuquerque. Eventually, the Jesuits cared for several other parishes and missions in the area, going as far as Las Vegas, New Mexico. These Neapolitan Jesuits became the core of the New Mexico-Colorado portion of the Denver Mission.

The story of the Jesuits in Texas began in 1881, when the Naples Province added west Texas to its responsibilities in addition to Colorado and New Mexico. In the El Paso area, Jesuits assumed care of a string of 200-year-old missions and went on to establish and maintain more than 30 parishes, thus laying the foundation for the Diocese of El Paso.

The Jesuits were parish priests for all the churches in the immediate area of El Paso. In 1875 in Las Vegas, New Mexico, they established the *Revista Católica*, for many years the only Spanish weekly journal in the United States. In 1918 the press was relocated to El Paso, where it produced Spanish language Bibles and other religious material until it ceased operation in 1958.

The Jesuits established the College of St. Mary – which was actually a grammar school and high school – in Galveston, Texas, in 1884, but it was heavily damaged by the disastrous hurricane of 1900. It was closed in 1922.

In 1919, the Denver Mission ceased to exist. The Missouri Province acquired responsibility for Oklahoma and Colorado, and the New Orleans Province accepted the same for Texas and New Mexico. The Neapolitan Jesuits working there either returned home or became members of the Missouri or New Orleans province.

Academic growth

From time to time Father General would send a "visitor" with plenary powers to make sure that government of the far flung regions of the Society of Jesus remained in good order. The visitor also observed whether members were living faithfully their vocations and serving the Church in the best way possible.

In 1921, Fr. Norbert de Boynes arrived from France via the Maryland-New York Province to find a healthy New Orleans Province with 305 members. He expressed his admiration for their hard work and apostolic zeal in a province that covered a million square miles with 26 million people of whom 60 per cent had no church affiliation and only 1.6 million were Catholic. He recommended that men be prepared more carefully for school and pastoral work. He also encouraged cutting back on apostolic commitments. He wanted the apostolates of the Southern Jesuits to take a more intellectual turn.

"Why," he asked, "could not Loyola University be the center and focus of this intellectual activity?"

The Province had already been anticipating the visitor's recommendations. The downtown Jesuit college – really a high school with the first year of college added – experienced a profound evolution when college courses were transferred uptown to Loyola College in 1911. Loyola College had been founded in 1904 and was chartered as Loyola University in 1912.

With more and more Jesuit men becoming available, secondary schools were founded in Shreveport (1902), Dallas (1942), El Paso (1959) and Houston (1961). Retreat houses also began to spring up: Manresa in Convent, Louisiana (1931); Our Lady of the Oaks in Grand Coteau, Louisiana (1938); Ignatius House in Atlanta, Georgia (1957); and Montserrat in Lake Dallas, Texas (1959). A minor seminary was opened in the Diocese of Corpus Christi in 1961 as well, though it functioned as a boarding high school by the time the Jesuits left there in 1982.

Foreign missions

Beginning in the mid-1930s, New Orleans Province Jesuits began assisting the Jesuits of the Champagne Province of France with the Trincomalee Mission in Ceylon. The first to arrive from New Orleans was Jesuit scholastic John T. Linehan, on September 17, 1933. Fr. Ignatius Glennie – the only Jesuit from the New Orleans Province to become a bishop – was appointed rector in 1944 and became Bishop of the Trincomalee-Batticaloa Diocese on September 21, 1947. In 1962, the two missions were amalgamated into a Vice Province and eventually became the Jesuit Province of Sri Lanka, in 1984.

During the 1960s the New Orleans Province began sending men to work in the Province of Central Brazil. Southern Jesuits also could be found laboring in Belize, El Salvador, South Africa, Zambia, Zimbabwe, Russia and The Philippines.

Adjusting to modern times

After peaking in the 1960s, the number of vocations declined and departures from the Society of Jesus increased. Vatican II and the Jesuits' Thirty-First and Thirty-Second General Congregations brought new emphasis in ministry and explicit invitations for the laity to become more involved in the work of the Society.

In the Southern U.S., the Jesuits withdrew and closed El Paso Jesuit High School in 1972. Jesuits were withdrawn from the high school in Shreveport in 1982; however, it remained open and and continued to be guided by a lay board as Loyola Academy.

The Province also returned more than 20 parishes to the administration of local dioceses over the course of its history. The average number of Jesuits has decreased in various cities in which Jesuits labor, and communities have consolidated.

With the dawning of the 21st century, Jesuits of the New Orleans Province faced new challenges, as did the Society around the world. In 2004, a strategic discernment process began at a national level in an effort to find more efficient ways of governing in the best interest of the universal mission of the Society. One of the many outcomes of this process was the consolidation of the New Orleans Province with the Missouri Province to form the new Central and Southern Province of the U.S. This new entity came into existence on July 31, 2014, and the two former provinces thus became a part of the long, rich history of the Society of Jesus in North America.

Nevertheless, the story of Jesuits working for the Church in the Southern U.S. continues as a new generation of young Jesuits is being prepared to engage in many of the same ministries as their predecessors. Their future ministries continue to be focused and evaluated for their adherence to the criteria for Jesuit missions as outlined by the Thirty-Second General Congregation and updated in subsequent meetings. The primary criterion is to find the best means to serve "the faith that does justice." This reflects the Church's growing emphasis on showing a preferential option for the poor and – especially in its educational institutions – to prepare young men and women who will live and work in service to others.

Continuing to recognize outstanding Jesuits

For more than three centuries, Southern Jesuits have touched many hearts and souls with a special charism that springs from their formation as sons of St. Ignatius. As pastors, teachers, counselors and retreat directors, they have left an indelible mark on the spiritual and intellectual caliber of many with whom they've come in contact.

Hundreds of Jesuit men have graced the churches, classrooms and retreat centers of the Southern and Southwestern U.S. and the mission fields of Ceylon/Sri Lanka, Brazil and elsewhere around the globe. Of these, many have been top-flight teachers and pastors, inventors and innovators, servants of the poor, and preachers of the Word.

Numerous iconic figures are found among the Jesuits of the South: James Duffo, "the Jubilarian of 50 Plagues;" Carmelo Tranchese, "The Angel of the Slums;" Orie Abell, "Father of WWL" and Lloyd Barry, champion of Jesuit Brothers. Also in these ranks are social justice advocates Anthony Achèe, Cornelius Thensted, Harry Tompson, and Louis Twomey.

Then there were men who were known for their extraordinary intellects, including Ransom Marlow, a master of mathematical physics; Louis Eisele, an inventor of seismograph recording equipment; and Francis Riedinger, who helped build a helium liquefier at Loyola University.

Also gracing the membership of the Southern Jesuits are several men who very well may be saints, such as John Moore and Richard Thomas, founder of "The Lord's Ranch," near El Paso. Those who worked in the mission fields included Bishop Ignatius Glennie; William Moran; Robert Hollingsworth, who taught job skills to the unskilled in Brazil; and Eugene Hebert, who disappeared without a trace in Sri Lanka and is thought of as a martyr for peace.

* * *

In all, this book contains brief biographies of 220 Jesuit priests and brothers. It is divided into three parts, three eras of history, and the men's stories are presented in alphabetical order in their respective eras. The first part is the Mission Era (1700-1907); the second is the Building & Expansion Era (1907-1968), which begins with the creation of the New Orleans Province; and the third is the Modern Era (1968-2014). The bios are placed in the era in which the men did the bulk of their work as Jesuits, and are not necessarily separated by birth or death date.

Like the bios, photos of the men are divided into three sections and are presented in alphabetical order. Pictures of the vast majority of the men featured in the book are present, thanks to the meticulous work of Rev. Vincent Orlando, S.J.

The main author of this book is Rev. Jerome Neyrey, S.J., who researched and wrote the text over a three-year period, beginning in 2009. The book is an outgrowth, a continuation, of a series of three books of Southern Jesuit biographies titled *Our Friends*, authored by Tom Clancy, S.J., and published in 1978, 1989 and 1998. While the lion's share of the work for this new edition was done by Fr. Neyrey, about 30 percent of the bios herein were written by the late Fr. Clancy and edited slightly in preparation for inclusion in this new volume.

The primary source of information for the new biographies is the Jesuit archives in the Monroe Library on the campus of Loyola University in New Orleans.

While this commemorative volume includes considerably more biographies than its predecessors, it does not feature every Jesuit who served in the New Orleans Mission or Province. It does, however, include write-ups on many of the men who made notable contributions to the building of the New Orleans Province into the highly successful entity that it became over the years.

– *Trent Angers, OFS*
Editor

Contents

Jesuits have served in the Southern United States for more than three centuries, many of them for 50 to 60 years or more. Jesuit Fathers of the New Orleans Province celebrating 50 years as members of the Society of Jesus gathered for a picture after concelebrating Mass at Holy Name of Jesus Church in New Orleans on Dec. 12, 1982. **Front row, left to right:** *George Twellmeyer, Alvin Pilie, Bernard Tonnar and George Raywood.* **Back row:** *Frederick Ponder, Thomas Mulcrone, Youree Watson and Sidney Tonsmeire.*

SOUTHERN JESUIT
Biographies

MISSION ERA

1700 - 1907

This broad expanse of time, covering more than 200 years, began with the Jesuits' early efforts to evangelize the Native American people of the Deep South. It continued through the Suppression and Restoration of the Society of Jesus, the founding of several Jesuit churches and educational institutions, and the formal establishment of an autonomous mission, independent of French authority.

This era can be divided into three parts:

• 1700 – 1763 – The **Louisiana Mission** was dedicated to the evangelization of Native Americans and later also to early European settlers.

• 1837 – 1880 – The **New Orleans Mission of Lyon Province** was staffed by French Jesuits who arrived in New Orleans in 1837. They began by building St. Charles College in Grand Coteau, La.

• 1880 – 1907 – The **Independent New Orleans Mission** was formed when the mission separated from the Lyon Province and became an independent entity. This was made possible in part by the increasing number of local, home-grown Jesuit vocations.

Some of the main events of American history that coincided with this period include the founding of New Orleans (1718), the American Revolution against British rule (1775–1783), the Louisiana Purchase (1803) and the Battle of New Orleans (1815). Also occurring in this era were the Civil War (1861-1865) and abolition of slavery, post-war Reconstruction, and the imposition of Jim Crow laws designed to treat blacks in the South as second-class citizens.

The first Jesuit martyr in the New World

Pedro Martinez, SJ (1533-1566) came to America more than a
century before the formal beginnings of any Southern mission.
He had high hopes of evangelizing the native people.

The first Jesuit who attempted to work in the territory that would become the New Orleans Province was also the first Jesuit martyr in the New World.

Born Oct. 26, 1533, in Teruel, Spain, Pedro Martinez studied at Valencia University and received his master's degree at age 19. However, he was more famous as a swordsman than as a student, as noted by his biographer, Michael Kenny, SJ:

"A youth of quick wit but quicker hand, there was rarely a duel in the city in which Martinez was not principal, second or promoter."

Although he had feelings of antipathy toward the new Society of Jesus, in September of 1553, he accompanied four other young men to the Jesuit house to be interviewed for the Society by Fr. Jerome Nadal, an acquaintance of St. Ignatius and one of the first Jesuits. Martinez was very impressed by the Jesuits he encountered there and asked Nadal to be received into the Society.

Ironically, his four companions were turned down, but Pedro was told to think it over for a week and come back. However, a week later he had forgotten about the Jesuits and kept an engagement set for a duel. After the parties failed to show, he remembered his appointment with Nadal.

He went back to his quarters, bundled up his few possessions and made his way to the Jesuit house. When Nadal told him the house was too poor to feed him, he replied that he came to work, not to eat, and demanded to be allowed to dig in the garden. When Nadal objected that there was nowhere for him to sleep, he said, "I did not come here to sleep."

By such tactics the gallant swordsman stormed his way into the Society on Oct. 2, 1553. Even though he was only a scholastic, he won plaudits for his ability to reach the populace through his preaching. After he was ordained in 1558, his talents for preaching and governing were immediately pressed into service and he became a kind of troubleshooter at various Jesuit houses in Spain.

Meanwhile, he kept asking to go on the missions. He was rector at Monterey when the appointment to go on the Florida missions came from Superior General Francis Borgia, who later was canonized.

Fr. Martinez sailed for the New World in June of 1566. As the ship approached the unexplored continent, the captain sent a party ashore in a small boat to *reconnoiter*. Fr. Martinez accompanied them. They landed at Cumberland Island, Ga., but after a storm blew the large ship back out to sea the scouting party had to make their way south in their smaller boat.

At first the Indians were friendly but as the party moved further south into present-day Florida the Indians grew more hostile. Near Fort George, within the present corporate limits of Jacksonville, Fla., the Indians attacked Fr. Martinez, dragged him ashore and clubbed him to death.

It was Oct. 6, 1566, three weeks short of his 33rd birthday.

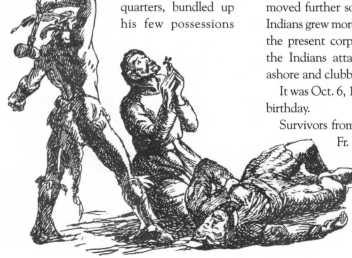

Survivors from the party brought back word of Fr. Martinez's death. He was kneeling with his crucifix in his hand when he received the fatal blow.

It is presumed that he is buried in Florida.

John Francis Abbadie, SJ
1804 – 1890
Tireless apostle
of southwest Louisiana

Fr. Abbadie was one of the first band of French Jesuits who re-established the New Orleans Mission after the Suppression of the Jesuits ended. He is also recognized as the tireless apostle of southwest Louisiana.

Born on the French slopes of the Pyrenees on Dec. 15, 1804, he was educated by a parish priest in his early years before attending college in Auch and seminary at Tarbes.

In August of 1826 he entered the Society of Jesus at Montrouge. His formation took him all over France in considerable hardship because of the poverty of the newly restored French Province. The same year he was ordained he was posted to Louisiana, although he had already volunteered to go to India.

On Christmas Eve 1836 he left from Le Havre with Bishop Blanc, who had convinced Jesuit superior Fr. Jan Philipp Roothaan to send Jesuits to establish a college in his diocese in south Louisiana. Traveling with them were six other Jesuits, five Ursulines, and three Religious of the Sacred Heart. When they arrived in New Orleans at the end of February 1837, their superior, Fr. Nicholas Point, was on hand to meet them. Fr. Point had already scouted the two possible sites for the college, Donaldsonville and Grand Coteau, but the decision had not yet been made. Meanwhile, the Jesuits were dispatched to various parts of south Louisiana to minister to the people. Fr. Abbadie went to Donaldsonville, in Assumption Parish.

The college was opened in Grand Coteau on Jan. 5, 1838, with Fr. Point as president and Fr. Abbadie as vice-president. There was considerable opposition to the college from anti-clericals, especially those from nearby Lafayette, but the townspeople of Grand Coteau protected the Fathers from the vigilantes.

Fr. Abbadie served at the college for ten years. From 1848 on, he was engaged in pastoral work in Louisiana, mostly in Grand Coteau but also in Convent and Baton Rouge. He worked heroically through several yellow fever epidemics and traveled tirelessly by buggy and horseback all over southwest Louisiana to minister to scattered Catholics.

He was a small, wiry man with boundless energy. One of his hobbies was gardening, and in 1837 he planted the original rows of oak trees connecting St. Charles College with the Academy of the Sacred Heart. On Dec. 16, 1890, Fr. Abbadie died, at age 86, and is buried at Grand Coteau.

Joseph Anthonioz, SJ
1822 – 1891
He rolled his church to Rayne
using 60 pair of oxen!

Joseph Anthonioz was born in a country that no longer exists. He was a native of the former Duchy of Savoy, a territory that now spans parts of France and Switzerland.

Born on March 10, 1822, in Les Gets (France), he grew up Catholic and, desirous of becoming a Jesuit, he entered the Lyon Province in 1843. After his ordination in 1855, he departed for the New Orleans Mission. On arrival he was sent to the Jesuit residence at Baton Rouge, but in 1858 he was transferred to Grand Coteau. He spent the rest of his life there except for two brief sojourns at Spring Hill, where he served as treasurer and taught chemistry, physics and mathematics.

He made his Tertianship in Frederick, Md., during the Civil War, and one of his experiences was serving as chaplain in the Union Army. When he returned to New Orleans, the war was still in progress and he had to get permission from the notorious General Benjamin "Beast" Butler to proceed to Grand Coteau. The fact that he had served as a Union chaplain helped his argument, and the general even gave him permission to take two barrels of Mass wine with him. This made his welcome doubly warm because Mass wine was hard to obtain during wartime.

Slowly Fr. Anthonioz shifted his emphasis from teaching to evangelization. Several churches were founded in various towns of southwest Louisiana by the Fathers of Grand Coteau. Fr. Anthonioz' name is especially connected with churches in Arnaudville, Rayne, Point-aux-Loups (Iota) and Mermentau. But he worked longest in Pouppeville, the city now known as Rayne, 15 miles west of modern-day Lafayette.

The church that ended up in Rayne started out several miles away. But when the railroad came through the settlement of Rayne, the little community became a burgeoning population center. So, Fr. Anthonioz decided to move his church to Rayne. He and his parishioners met this logistical challenge by hitching 60 pair of oxen and rolling the building on wooden wheels to the new site. Quite a feat!

In 1891, Fr. Anthonioz suffered a stroke, and after lingering for a week, he died on Aug. 22. He is buried at Grand Coteau.

Michel Baudouin, SJ
1691 – 1768
The last pre-suppression
New Orleans Jesuit

As Fr. Nicholas Ignace de Beaubois was the first Jesuit of the pre-suppression era active in New Orleans, Fr. Michel Baudouin was the last.

Since he was born in Quebec, on March 16, 1691, and was reared there, he had to travel to Bordeaux, France, to enter the Society. It was 1728 when he came to the Louisiana missions, where for nearly two decades he ministered to the Choctaw Indians. He accompanied the chiefs in their annual visit to Mobile to receive their presents from the French.

Fr. Baudouin was aware that life among the Indians could be dangerous. In 1729 Fr. Paul du Poisson, the young apostle of the Arkansas tribe, had been beheaded by an Indian of the Natchez tribe. On Dec. 11, 1730, Fr. Jean Souel was killed by Yazoo Indians near present-day Vicksburg.

In 1751 Fr. Baudouin moved to New Orleans to take up the duties of mission superior, a position to which the bishop of Quebec had attached the office of vicar-general for the lower Louisiana territory. This office was a source of contention for the Jesuits since for years there had been jurisdictional struggles with the Capuchin friars.

The July 9, 1763, Decree of Suppression of the Society of Jesus in Louisiana expelled the Jesuits, allowing for the seizure of their property and the auctioning of their goods. The Jesuit plantation occupied a large part of what is today the central business district of New Orleans. The downriver boundary was Common Street and Tulane Avenue. The upriver boundary was Felicity Street, and the boundary ran from Broad Street to the Mississippi River. All this property was confiscated, and the cattle, tools, slaves and furnishings were sold at auction. From those auction proceeds, the Jesuits, including Fr. Baudouin, were promised pensions; however, it is not clear whether they were ever paid.

Additionally, the missionaries were recalled from the Indian country and ordered to become parish priests upon their return to France. By this time Fr. Baudouin was 72, and since his native Quebec was then in English hands, he was allowed to remain in New Orleans.

He lived in the houses of those who gave him hospitality in New Orleans until Holy Week of 1768. He died on April 1 and was buried in the old parish church of the New Orleans colony of Louisiana.

More than 70 years were to elapse before the Jesuits would be re-established in New Orleans.

George Blackney, SJ
1819 – 1854
A master of rhetoric,
a victim of yellow fever

In the early days of the New Orleans Mission, an appeal went out for English language preachers. Fr. Peter Kenny, who had visited the American Jesuits in New York and Missouri, asked for help from his Province in Ireland. Fr. George Blackney answered the call.

Born in County Carlow on Aug. 23, 1819, George was a member of a prominent Catholic family. His father, Col. Walter Blackney, was a parliamentary lieutenant of Daniel O'Connell, the great Irish Catholic emancipator. Four of George's sisters became nuns.

Young Blackney was educated at home by the family chaplain. When George was 17, his tutor accompanied him to Rome to finish his education. There at the age of 20 George entered the Society. After finishing his theological studies in France he returned to Ireland to teach rhetoric at the Jesuit college of Clonglowes Wood. In 1847 he arrived at Spring Hill College in Alabama, where he was the first professor of rhetoric, prefect of studies, and founder of the literary society.

But after two years, he was transferred to New Orleans, where it was thought there would be broader opportunity for his oratorical talents. At the Jesuit college on Baronne Street, he taught rhetoric and served as spiritual father of the community. He was also in great demand for retreats, missions and sermon courses.

On Dec. 7, 1854, he was preaching the final sermon in a series designed to inform parishioners about the decree regarding the Immaculate Conception that was to be proclaimed by Pope Pius IX the next day. At the end of his sermon, at the old St. Joseph's Parish church in New Orleans, Fr. Blackney collapsed at the pulpit, a victim of yellow fever. According to the account in the New Orleans *Delta*, thousands attended his funeral and burial in New Orleans. He was 35 years old.

He was the twelfth Jesuit to die in the mission since the return of the Jesuits to the South following the suppression. Most of them were victims of yellow fever. Of the first 11 there were six Frenchmen, two Germans, one Italian, a Swiss, and a Belgian. Fr. Blackney was the first Irishman. Many more were to follow him.

Ignatius Boemecke, SJ
1824 – 1912
He was the first of 13 in one family
to serve as a Southern Jesuit

The oldest son of Ignatius and Elisabeth Kaiser Boemecke, Ignatius Boemecke was born near Hanover in Nesselroden, Germany, on Aug. 15, 1824, into an extended family that inspired many vocations.

When he was considered old enough, Ignatius was apprenticed to a joiner to learn the carpenter's trade, after which he traveled throughout Germany, France, Switzerland and Italy plying and perfecting his trade. Eventually he arrived in Rome, where, after an interview with the Jesuit superior general, Jan Roothaan, he entered the Society as a brother on June 19, 1847.

Later that year, Boemecke went to France to join a band of volunteers leaving Marseilles for the New Orleans Mission. It included Darius Hubert, James Duffo and many other pioneers of the South. Bro. Ignatius was sent to the Jesuit church and college on Baronne Street, just two small frame buildings at that time. There he took his vows in June of 1849 and remained for most of his Jesuit life. As porter, he was the face of the Jesuits to the world and the dispenser of charity and advice to the many who came to the door. He was well-known in the city for his piety and humility.

Ignatius was the first of 13 members of his family to serve the New Orleans Mission and Province. The next two recruits were his younger brothers, Andrew and Charles, who both entered the Society as temporal coadjutors in 1850. Four nephews followed: Bro. Herman Hugh (1857-82), Fr. Augustine Hugh (1852-1912), Fr. George Rittmeyer (1859-1925) and Bro. Henry Rittmeyer (1864-1929).

There were six more volunteers, all descendants of Bro. Ignatius' sister, Catherine, who married a Maring. Twelve of the 13 persevered in their vocations; Bro. Edward Maring entered but left the Society in 1889. However, his son William entered the California Province in 1930. The last representative of this remarkable family, William died in 2011. Another notable thing about the members of this family is their longevity; they averaged nearly 50 years in the Society.

After serving 62 years at Baronne Street, Bro. Ignatius Boemecke was retired to Grand Coteau, where he occupied his last years in prayers and devotions and where he is buried. He died there on June 29, 1912, three months shy of his 88th birthday.

Charles Booker, SJ
1822 – 1884
The first English Jesuit missionary
in New Orleans

In 1847 revolutionary fires made things hot for the Jesuits in France. Suddenly, those priests who had resisted the appeals of American Southern bishops were more willing to go to the South.

Thus, in October of 1847, Fr. Aloysius Curioz led a band of 24 Jesuits who sailed from Marseilles to New Orleans. Among that number was Charles Booker, the first of the English missionaries to go to New Orleans.

Born Aug. 7, 1822, the son of a London Catholic publisher, Charles Booker completed the classical course at Stonyhurst College near Lancashire and then entered the Jesuit Novitiate in nearby Hodder. In 1847, while studying philosophy in Belgium, he responded to the appeal for volunteers from New Orleans Mission Superior Fr. Jean-Baptiste Maisounabe.

On arriving in New Orleans he was put to work right away at the Baronne Street college.

In the early days of the school the faculty rarely exceeded three or four. Besides teaching grammar to the boys, Booker also taught English to the other Jesuits and studied theology privately under the direction of Frs. John Cambiaso and Anthony Jourdant. This was the accepted way to learn theology for most scholastics in the early days of the mission.

The college, which stood on the corner of Baronne and Common, was not a very healthy place. Under the complex, there were five cesspools whose odors often invaded the school, church and residence. Needless to say, it lacked up-to-date sanitation standards.

In 1854 Booker was ordained to the priesthood and dispatched to the new Sts. Peter and Paul College in Baton Rouge. However, after yellow fever practically wiped out the community and the college closed, he returned to Baronne Street in 1856.

For the next 21 years he worked in schools: New Orleans, Spring Hill and Grand Coteau. He was minister, prefect of studies, prefect of discipline and preacher, but mainly he taught grammar. From 1876 to 1881, he was a missioner based in Grand Coteau, but he completed his life's work at Baronne Street, teaching the youngest class and looking after the library.

When he died on Jan. 14, 1884, the New Orleans *Morning Star* wrote:

"All who knew Father Booker loved him. Simple as a child, he had the artless power of guilelessness to multiply friends. His boys especially loved him, in and out of class; among young and old 'Daddy Booker' was the fond name given him in affection by his devoted children."

One of Fr. Booker's avocations was photography, and it is probably due to his skill and enterprise that so many photographs of the old Baronne Street college exist.

He is buried at Grand Coteau.

Theobald Butler, SJ
1829 – 1916
First superior of the New Orleans Mission was a great recruiter

Theobald Butler, born in Ballycarron, Ireland, on July 13, 1829, was the first superior of the Independent New Orleans Jesuit Mission and one of the pioneers of the Province, but how he got there is perhaps the most interesting part of his story.

He entered the Irish Province and was sent to Dole in eastern France to make his Novitiate in 1846. But all Jesuits were ordered out of the country by the leaders of the February Revolution of 1848, so Butler attempted to return to Ireland.

He traveled to Paris with Fr. Anthony de Chaignon, who was destined for the New Orleans Mission. There they were supposed to part company, but young Butler discovered he had been robbed. In his confusion he boarded the wrong train and found himself again with the de Chaignon party on the way to Le Havre, where they planned to sail for America.

There he discovered that no one on the ship bound for America spoke English. Because Butler was conversant in English, the captain asked Butler to sail with them as an interpreter. Butler was willing and consulted Fr. de Chaignon, who told him to write to his provincial in Ireland. However, before an answer came back, the ship sailed with Butler on board.

After a voyage of 60 days they landed in New Orleans to find a letter from the Irish provincial recalling the novice. Fr. Jean Baptiste Maisounabe, the mission superior, wanted to keep Butler, so he referred the matter to Father General Jan Roothaan. The reply from Rome stated that the choice was left to Butler, but that if he returned to Ireland he would have to begin his Novitiate over again. Butler chose New Orleans and took his vows on Sept. 24, 1848, at Spring Hill College.

His Novitiate was private as were his other studies, and during this time he was also teaching and working in administration. Finally, in 1864, he was ordained a priest. Only then was he sent to Fourvière in Lyon to study theology in the regular course of the Society. En route he went to the home of his aristocratic family in Tipperary, Ireland. He had been gone for 18 years and was so changed that his mother did not recognize him at first.

Fr. Butler served as superior of the New Orleans Mission from 1880 to 1888 and was stationed at one time or another in almost all of the Jesuit houses in the South. Perhaps his greatest service to the missions was his recruiting trips to Europe; he crossed the ocean 12 times in search of potential novices and laid solid foundations for the future growth of the Province.

On Dec. 8, 1916, Fr. Butler died at the age of 87 in Macon, Ga., and is buried at Spring Hill.

Nicholas Ignace de Beaubois, SJ
1689 – 1770
He played a major role in establishing the New Orleans Mission

Nicholas Ignace de Beaubois was an innovative administrator, negotiator and recruiter who played a major role in establishing the New Orleans Mission.

Since 1700, there had been Jesuits scattered along the Gulf Coast and the Mississippi River regions, but they were part of the Quebec Mission. In 1723, Fr. Joseph Francis de Kereben was named superior of the New Orleans Mission, but his activities were mostly confined to the Illinois country north of the Ohio River. In 1724 Fr. de Beaubois was named to succeed him and to establish and coordinate Jesuit activities farther south.

Born in Orleans, France, on Oct. 15, 1689, Nicholas entered the Society on Oct. 20, 1706. After his theology course, in 1719 he was assigned to Canada to work among the Indians. By the time of his appointment as superior he had worked in the Illinois country for several years. His first move in his new position was a trip to France to work out an agreement with the colonial officials and to recruit for the mission.

He proved a tough negotiator. The Jesuits were to have a house in New Orleans and a plantation near the city for the support of the missionaries. He successfully negotiated government support for the missionaries working among the Indians, the sole object of their ministrations. Fr. de Beaubois was also instrumental in bringing the Ursuline sisters to New Orleans.

A far-sighted and dynamic administrator, he promoted friendly relations with the Indians and managed a model plantation that pioneered in the cultivation of sugarcane. He also proposed building a canal to link nearby Bayou St. John with the city.

But he had one flaw: He lacked tact. He pushed the colonial officials too hard.

This led to two recalls to France. The first was temporary, from 1728 to 1732. However, the second recall in 1735 was permanent. In France he continued to be agent and fund-raiser for the American mission while stationed at the Jesuit college in Bourges. From 1743 until the suppression of the Society in France in 1762, he was in retreat work at Amiens and Vannes.

Fr. de Beaubois died near Avignon on Jan. 13, 1770, and is buried in France.

Philip de Carriere, SJ
1825 – 1913
Father of the Jesuits of Florida

Philip de Carriere was born into a strongly religious family in Toulouse, France, on April 20, 1825, and was destined for a life in service to God. It was a family tradition.

Of his six younger siblings, one became a Trappist prior, another a Visitandine mother superior, and a third – along with Philip – a Jesuit.

Philip entered the Novitiate at Vals on Oct. 4, 1844, but the political and economic upheavals of the Revolution of 1848 interrupted his formation in France. Consequently, he joined a band of 24 Jesuits who left France for New Orleans. To effect his escape, he disguised himself as a man of the world and smoked a cigar, his first and last one.

Spring Hill College was his home for all but four of his next 36 years. He finished his studies privately while teaching the classes of younger boys. Many students came from Central America, and de Carriere's ability to speak Spanish – as well as French, English and Italian – served him well.

He took his last vows in the hands of Jesuit Superior General Pieter Beckx in Rome on Aug. 15, 1867, and returned to Spring Hill, where he became more active in parish and retreat work. In 1884 he was transferred to Immaculate Conception Church in New Orleans, where he served in both the church and school. Then in 1888, when he was 64, he was dispatched on one-day's notice to Tampa. Bishop Moore of St. Augustine had appealed for help when the local pastor fell victim to yellow fever, and Philip was chosen for the job because of his knowledge of Spanish.

It was easier to start for Tampa than to arrive there. En route, quarantine officials stopped him and warned that he was traveling toward certain death. When he finally arrived, he wrote that he was the only priest in Tampa and that he was entrusted with the care of everything in Florida to the south with the exception of Key West.

Fr. de Carriere's work in Tampa and Fr. James Duffo's in Jacksonville moved Bishop Moore to ask the mission superior, John O'Shanahan, to take over southern Florida, at that time a disease-ridden wilderness with few inhabitants. An agreement to do so was signed in 1889 and remained in force until 1921. By that time, south Florida was booming, and, thanks to the discoveries of Army researcher Dr. Walter Reed, yellow fever was under control.

For many years Tampa remained a base of Jesuit missionary activity, and Fr. de Carriere was its benevolent and energetic leader. He truly was the father of the Jesuits in Florida.

At the age of 78 he was retired to the Jesuit Novitiate at Macon. His last 10 years were spent writing letters to his many friends, passing on the missionary tradition to the novices and juniors, and preparing his soul for death.

On Jan. 27, 1913, Fr. de Carriere died at age 87. He is buried at Spring Hill.

James Duffo, SJ
1820 –1900
'Jubilarian of 50 plagues'

Fr. James Duffo is named in the records of the New Orleans Mission as "the jubilarian of 50 plagues." While an exaggeration, he did survive and serve in more than a dozen outbreaks of yellow fever in his 52 years of priestly life.

Fr. Duffo did not have an elaborate formation as a Jesuit. He was ordained six years and three months after entering the Society. There is no record of any Tertianship. He was formed in his apostolate by serving prisoners, both black and white, hospital patients, and yellow fever victims.

Born on Nov. 18, 1820, in Tuzaguet, France, he was admitted to the Jesuit Novitiate at Vals in November 1841. Six years later, he came to America with Anthony Jourdant and was ordained with him by Bishop Portier in February of 1848. Shortly thereafter, the two priests set out for Grand Coteau, where Fr. Duffo taught and served as sub-minister.

By the time of the New Orleans yellow fever epidemic of 1853, he was on hand to take care of the sick and console the dying. Some accounts say he caught the fever, recovered, and was therefore immune to the disease, enabling him to minister to many people afflicted with the fever.

In one summer month, an average of 400 people died daily in the city. Duffo gave the last sacraments to nearly 100 persons daily and also cared for the stricken Jesuits. From that point on, he was considered the designated plague priest of the South. In 1854, he went to Natchitoches when the fever broke out there. In 1855, 1858 and 1867 he was needed in New Orleans again.

When he was in New Orleans, he took care of inmates in the parish prison, then located in the area still known as Tremé. He would accompany condemned prisoners to the gallows and pray with them during their final moments. The *New Orleans Picayune* observed:

> The task which Father Duffo has been fulfilling a long time, that of comforting criminals in their last hour, and reconciling them with a merciful Deity, is a task during which the comforter suffers as much as the comforted.

He also visited hospitals and served as chaplain to the nuns and their school communities. From 1853 to 1886 he was a member of the Baronne Street Jesuit community with the simple notation *operarius* (worker). When he took off for plague-stricken cities he often had to replace pastors laid low by disease.

In 1887 he was posted to the missionary center in Selma, Ala., which the Jesuits had taken over in 1880. His charge was to evangelize 8,000 square miles of central Alabama. Hardly had he arrived in Alabama when a summons came from Bishop Moore of St. Augustine, Fla.; yellow fever had struck Jacksonville and Tampa. Fr. Duffo went to Jacksonville, while Fr. Philip de Carriere went to Tampa. In 1888 he was back in New Orleans, where he celebrated his golden jubilee as a priest in 1898. In 1899 he returned to Selma.

Fr. Duffo died on Feb. 27, 1900, at age 79, and is buried at Spring Hill. Six months later to the day, Dr. Walter Reed and his team of three others identified the mosquito that caused yellow fever.

Darius Hubert, SJ
1823 – 1893
He ministered to Confederate soldiers in the Civil War

The most dangerous, adventurous years of Fr. Darius Hubert's life were from 1861 to 1865 when he served as chaplain in the Confederate Army. He experienced many battles, including Gettysburg, and earned the respect of Confederate leaders, even that of Gen. Robert E. Lee.

Born in Toulon, France, on July 19, 1823, he was educated there and entered the Society in the Lyon Province in Toulouse on Sept. 23, 1843, after experiencing a spiritual conversion. Upon completion of his philosophy at Avignon, he volunteered for the New Orleans Mission and left France in November of 1847.

Hubert reached New Orleans in December and was sent to Grand Coteau, where along with teaching he studied English and theology in private. He was ordained in October of 1850 and taught at the short-lived Jesuit College of Saints Peter and Paul in Baton Rouge.

Fr. Hubert was at Spring Hill when the Civil War broke out in 1861, and when the first Louisiana regiment was organized, its commander, Col. Albert Blanchard, requested him to serve as chaplain. Before leaving for Virginia he traveled to Baton Rouge to bless the flag of the Louisiana Republic.

For the next four years he was in most of the Virginia campaigns, including Gettysburg, where he was wounded. Chaplains in those days did not ordinarily wear military uniforms or hold rank. Fr.

Hippolyte Gache, also a Confederate chaplain in Virginia, made his rounds in cassock, biretta and beads. But Frs. Hubert and Joseph Prachensky, also from Spring Hill, wore natty officers' uniforms for which Fr. Gache teased them.

In the midst of war Fr. Hubert found time to minister to nuns and other civilians in Virginia, but his principal apostolate was with the fighting men. He went aboard the *Merrimac* after her battle with the Union ship *Monitor* to minister to the wounded. His bravery and general devotion to his men won their love and affection, as well as the respect of higher ranks. Even Gen. Robert E. Lee is said to have tipped his hat in respect of Fr. Hubert.

After the Confederate surrender at Appomattox, Frs. Gache and Prachensky worked in New York, but Fr. Hubert came back to New Orleans, to Immaculate Conception Church, where he served as pastor. During the yellow fever epidemics, he went to Savannah in 1876, then to Vicksburg and finally to Jackson in 1878 to minister to victims of the fever. In the last quarter of the 19th century, when Confederate nostalgia was at its height, Fr. Hubert was often the honored guest and featured speaker at Confederate reunions. He even preached at the funeral of former Confederate President Jefferson Davis in 1889.

In 1891, Fr. Hubert went to Macon, Ga., where he died on June 14, 1893, at age 69. He is buried at Spring Hill.

Pierre Ladavière, SJ
1777 – 1858
A man ready for anything,
a true vagabond for Christ

Fr. Pierre Ladavière was part of the band of four Jesuits who arrived in New Orleans on June 21, 1831, on their way to Bardstown, Ky., to work in the newly established center of education at St. Joseph College.

He and the other three – Fr. Pierre Chazelle and Fr. Nicolas Petit plus Bro. Philip Corne – were the first Jesuits to visit New Orleans since the restoration of the Society following its suppression.

Since arrangements were not complete in Kentucky, New Orleans Bishop Leo de Neckere, who had been appealing for Jesuits since his instal-

lation, persuaded the four Jesuits to help him in his diocese. So they went to work in the prisons and hospitals and conducted missions and retreats with great success. Eventually the two other priests departed for Kentucky, but Fr. Ladavière remained in New Orleans to work in various outlying areas, notably St. Michael's Parish (present-day Convent, La., home of Manresa House of Retreats).

Born in *La Chappelle de Condrien [Rhône]* on Sept. 23, 1777, Ladavière was a priest by 1804. One of his early missions was to bring to France the *Bull* of Pius VI, the document excommunicating Napoleon, and to promulgate it. During his first stint in America, he was listed as a professor of Greek at Georgetown in 1812 and as pastor of St. Peter's on Barclay Street in New York.

Before Bishop de Neckere died of yellow fever, in September of 1833, he had persuaded Fr. Ladavière to govern his diocese *sede vacante* (the seat being vacant). But for accepting this charge, Fr. Ladavière was severely censured and recalled to Europe by Superior-General Fr. Jan Roothaan, who was adamant about Jesuits not accepting ecclesiastical dignities.

By the time the order came through for Fr. Ladavière to return to Europe, Antoine Blanc had been consecrated Bishop of New Orleans. Now, Blanc was a close friend of Ladavière, and they departed for Europe together in 1836 on a trip to recruit priests, notably Jesuits, for the diocese.

Bishop Blanc's appeal to the Jesuit provincial of Paris was turned down, so he and Fr. Ladavière set out for Rome to appeal directly to Fr. General Roothaan, who was impressed and told the French provincials to do what they could to help meet the need for manpower in America. Eventually two brothers and five priests departed from Le Havre, in December 1836. The Provincial of Lyon commended Ladavière as "a man *ad omnia* (ready for anything)... because of his career and experience."

Once back in Louisiana, Fr. Nicolas Point took charge of the French Jesuit project to start a college, which was eventually located at Grand Coteau. Fr. Ladavière turned to parish work to help his old friend, Bishop Blanc. In the following years he is listed as pastor of various Louisiana parishes. He seems to have been a true vagabond for Christ.

His last years were spent at Spring Hill College, where Fr. Ladavière died at age 80 on Feb. 1, 1858, and where he is buried.

Jean Baptiste Leon Maisounabe, SJ
1805 – 1848
Courageous pioneer and first superior of the New Orleans Mission of the Lyon Province

Fr. Jean Baptiste Leon Maisounabe was a man of big ideals, big dreams, big plans and big accomplishments. His pioneering spirit in the American South contributed to the vibrant restoration of the Society in New Orleans and to the development of Jesuit mission schools in south Louisiana.

The first organized Jesuit activity in the South after the restoration of the Society started at St. Charles College in Grand Coteau, completing work begun earlier, in 1837, by the French Jesuits. Before the college opened in January of 1838, Father General Jan Roothaan had transferred it to the jurisdiction of the Missouri Mission in 1836. From 1840 Jesuits also worked at St. Michael's Parish (present-day Convent) in Louisiana, and in 1847 the Province of Lyon took over the direction of Spring Hill College. After Father General assigned these three houses to the New Orleans Mission of the Lyon Province, Fr. Maisounabe was appointed superior of the new mission, on May 30, 1847.

Maisounabe, born in Bayonne, France, on May 10, 1805, was already a priest and professor of theology when he entered the Society in 1832. He was serving as rector of the scholasticate at Vals when he was made New Orleans Mission superior. His Provincial wrote:

"This is our first (contribution) to your mission. Our Fr. Rector of Vals, who would have been Provincial of Lyon, has now been given to you."

When Fr. Maisounabe arrived in New York, he tried to soak up as much advice as possible from American Jesuits. He wanted the New Orleans Mission to be American and he worked to ensure that its schools would not simply be transplanted French colleges. He also began to write furiously to France requesting more men and more money. He battled other mission superiors and even provincials for more men for his mission. It was he who engineered the transfer of Fr. Theobald Butler to his mission.

Despite his lack of men and resources, he had big plans. After arriving in Louisiana he planned to incorporate Jefferson College in Convent and to start a new college in Baton Rouge. But his first priority was to put down roots in New Orleans. By De-

cember of 1847 he received a State charter for "*La Société Catholique d'éducation religieuse et littéraire*," which remained in its English form the corporate title of the Province through July of 2014, when the New Orleans Province joined with the Missouri Province to form the U.S. Central and Southern Province. On June 10, 1848, he bought land on the corner of Baronne and Common streets as a site for a future Jesuit college and church. Realizing he would need public support for this endeavor, he issued an appeal for aid, requesting sums as large as $40, $50 and even $100 or more.

In all his dealings with communities in the Mission, Fr. Maisounabe kept in close contact and consultation with the ordinaries, especially Bishop Antoine Blanc of Louisiana.

In only one thing did he fail to follow the bishop's advice. In the summer of 1848 yellow fever was ravaging New Orleans. Bishop Blanc advised him to stay in the country. However, Fr. Maisounabe felt called to aid Fr. Joseph Soller, the only Jesuit in New Orleans devoting himself to the plague-stricken, and who himself would succumb to the fever five years later. In August Fr. Maisounabe joined him in this work of charity.

Less than a month later, Fr. Maisounabe caught the fever and died, on Sept. 12, 1848, having received the Last Sacraments from Bishop Blanc. He was a mere 43 years old and only 16 years a Jesuit. He was buried in New Orleans and in 1915 his remains were moved to Spring Hill.

William Stack Murphy, SJ
1803 – 1875
A 19th century travelin' man

One of those intrepid pioneering Jesuits, Fr. William Stack Murphy had a long career in various Jesuit provinces and missions before settling in New Orleans to spend his declining years.

A native of Cork, Ireland, born April 29, 1803, he was educated by the Jesuits in France and entered the Society on Aug. 27, 1823. One of his original responsibilities was to teach, and among his pupils was J. B. Lamy, who later became the first Archbishop of Santa Fe.

In 1835 Fr. Murphy was sent to the Kentucky Mission of the French Jesuits and served as superior of that mission from 1839 to 1846.

He was teaching at Fordham when he was sent

by Father General Jan Roothaan to St. Louis with the powers of acting vice-provincial of the Missouri Vice-Province. His mandate was to limit the commitments and improve the formation of the young vice-province. Fr. Murphy's work from 1851 to 1856 is generally regarded as a turning point in the history of the Missouri Province.

In 1861 Fr. Murphy was summoned again from New Orleans to be vice-provincial of the Missouri Vice-Province – which would become a full-fledged, independent province just two years later. But this time he served only one year before his release, and he returned to New Orleans by way of steamboat.

It is uncertain whether Fr. Murphy had Confederate sympathies, of which he was accused in St. Louis, but it is certain that he did find the Southern climate more congenial to his health. Consequently, he worked in the pastoral ministry in New Orleans during the last years of his life.

Fr. Murphy, who was fluent in Italian and French, was an excellent classicist. He knew many of the early American bishops and impressed them with his learning and zeal. His talks and sermons were lively with wit, and he was unusually well-liked by his fellow Jesuits. He gave "a touch of class" to every group of American Jesuits with whom he worked.

Fr. Walter Hill, SJ, said of him:

He was a keen observer both of men and things, and he was remarkable for his knowledge of human nature…. Extensive and varied reading of the best authors… had cultivated his taste… which made his conversation … instructive and interesting, never tiresome, and always fresh, even to those who had lived with him for many years.

On Oct. 23, 1875, Fr. Murphy died in New Orleans at age 72. He is buried at Spring Hill.

John Francis O'Connor, SJ
1848 – 1911
First New Orleans Provincial
was a multilingual preacher

Fr. John Francis O'Connor was the first native Southerner to be mission superior and the first provincial of the New Orleans Province. He is said to be the first Spring Hill College alumnus to be ordained to the priesthood.

He was born in Savannah, Ga., on Sept. 17, 1848, and went to Spring Hill at age 15, in the middle of the Civil War. As the war progressed, O'Connor tried to enlist, but his parents sent him back to Spring Hill.

It was only after the surrender at Appomattox in 1865 that he was able to join the Society. He made his Novitiate in France and his philosophy at Stonyhurst in England. Tutored by Fr. William Stack Murphy during his Regency, he studied theology privately while continuing his teaching. He was ordained in 1875.

In 1884 he was appointed the first rector at Galveston. Three years later he was rector in New Orleans, followed by his appointment as the first rector at Shreveport.

From 1891 to 1902 he was the director of the Mission Band of the Province. He initiated Fr. William Power in the technique of evangelization through sermons, confessions and visits, just as Fr. Power later trained Fr. Albert Biever in the same work. Two priests usually gave a mission together and Power and O'Connor were a perfect combination since the former appealed to the intellect of the audience whereas the latter used illustrations and anecdotes that appealed to their imagination and heart.

Fr. O'Connor's great apostolic work was preaching, and like most of the early members of the Province, he was multilingual, able to preach in French, Spanish and Italian as well as English. He travelled the length and breadth of the South, becoming one of the best known priests of the region.

He was appointed superior of the flourishing New Orleans Mission in 1906. A year later, the mission was given the status of a province, the third in America, and Fr. O'Connor became its first provincial.

A few years later, while attending a planning meeting for the 1911 Mobile bicentennial celebration, he suffered a deterioration of health that led to his death.

Fr. O'Connor died at Spring Hill on March 27, 1911, at age 62, and is buried there.

Cornelius Otten, SJ
1835 – 1916
Builder of St. Charles College
and several Southern churches

Brother Cornelius Otten's great fame in the Province derives from his activities as a builder. He was instrumental in the design and construction of many churches throughout the South where Jesuits ministered.

Born in Ginneken, a town in North Brabant, a province of Holland, on March 12, 1835, Cornelius entered the Society on Aug. 14, 1855, and received further instruction in carpentry.

His first major project was the parish church at Grand Coteau, La. The plans were drawn up by the famous New Orleans architect, James Freret, in 1875, and Brothers Otten and Joseph Brinkhaus began the construction in 1879. The church was blessed in 1880.

In 1884 Bro. Otten was transferred from Grand Coteau to Galveston, where the Society had received a church and school (St. Mary's University) that same year. In this new foundation he did about everything. He is listed as sacristan, buyer, carpenter and "*ad omnia.*" In the early years he supervised the conversion of a school building into a chapel.

The Society engaged the services of Nicholas J. Clayton, still famous as one of Victorian Galveston's greatest architects, to design a new church. Beginning in 1889, Bro. Otten directed the construction of the French Romanesque structure.

In 1897 Bro. Otten was transferred to Augusta, Ga., where he began a new church similar to the one in Galveston, but smaller. That same design was followed loosely in Macon and Tampa, where he also constructed churches in 1899 and 1902. After some years in Key West and at Spring Hill College in Mobile, Bro. Otten was recalled to Grand Coteau in 1907 to supervise the rebuilding of St. Charles College, which had burned down in 1900. The job was completed in 1909. Bro. Otten was 74 then.

Cornelius Otten was a skillful builder who worked alongside the construction crews and arranged treats for them as an incentive for sound craftsmanship and Christian living. He impressed all with his piety and, though his skills were of a high professional level, he never shrank from the humblest tasks.

He died on June 6, 1916, at age 81. He is buried at Grand Coteau, close to the church he built.

Nicholas Point, SJ
1799 – 1868
The founder of St. Charles College

Fr. Nicholas Point, while never a member of the New Orleans Mission, deserves to be remembered as the founder of St. Charles College in Grand Coteau.

He established the institution that grew from a log cabin to today's sprawling campus with its massive, newly renovated multi-purpose buildings, magnificent trees and expansive grounds.

Born in Rocroi in northern France on Dec. 10, 1799, Nicholas grew up during the Napoleonic Wars, which ended in 1815 with Napoleon's defeat at Waterloo. This instability in Europe delayed Nicholas's entrance to the Society until 1822, and his bad health delayed his vows until 1827. All through his short period of formation he longed for the missionary life.

Finally, after working in Switzerland and Spain, he was sent to Kentucky, where he was teaching when Bishop Leo De Neckere of New Orleans proposed a college in his diocese. In 1836, Superior-General Jan Roothaan entrusted the mission of establishing the Louisiana college to Fr. Francis Renault, the provincial of Lyon, who in turn suggested Fr. Point as rector. St. Charles College was opened in a log cabin under Fr. Point's direction on Jan. 5, 1838.

In 1840 Fr. Point was replaced as rector of the college. Later that same year he went to work evangelizing the inhabitants of Westport, Kan., the staging area for wagon trains travelling west. In 1841 he went with Fr. Pierre De Smet on his first expedition to the Rocky Mountains, where Fr. Point established missions among the Flathead, *Coeur d'Alene* and Blackfeet Indians in Montana and Idaho. Fr. De Smet described Fr. Point as "zealous and courageous for the salvation of souls…."

In 1847 Fr. Point was sent to Canada, where for the next 18 years he labored among the Indians around Windsor. There he composed his *Recollections of the Rocky Mountains*, which together with his exquisite paintings of Indian life were edited by Joseph P. Donnelly, SJ, and published in 1967 with the title of *Wilderness Kingdom* (Holt, Rinehart and Winston).

Fr. Point lived his last three years in Quebec, where he died on July 4, 1868, at age 68. He is buried in the cathedral there.

William Power, SJ
1855 – 1934
Superior of the New Orleans Mission, outstanding multilingual preacher

Fr. William Power was one of the great marvels of the New Orleans Mission.

Even as a child, he had a prodigious memory, which he cultivated further because of the weakness of his eyes. He memorized much of the work of several Latin and Greek authors as well as large portions of Milton, Shakespeare, Scripture and *Following of Christ.* He was also an accomplished linguist in modern languages, and he spoke and preached in French, German, Spanish and Italian.

His greatest skills were exercised in the pulpit in a day when the parish mission was one of the chief means of evangelizing the people. He excelled in the spellbinding oratory popular in his day and could touch the coldest hearts in his missions and retreats. He was in demand all over the country, but spent most of his active Jesuit life preaching and hearing confessions in the towns and cities of the South.

William Power was born on April 19, 1855, in Dublin and educated there. An apprentice engineer when Fr. Theobald Butler recruited him for the New Orleans Mission, he entered the Society in 1873 at Clermont, France, where he made his Novitiate. After a year of Juniorate he departed for America to teach at New Orleans. He studied philosophy and theology at Woodstock and did his Tertianship at Manresa, Spain.

From 1897 to 1906 he served as superior of the New Orleans Mission. In 1915 he attended the 26th General Congregation, when Fr. Wlodimir Ledochowski was elected General, and three years later that same Fr. Ledochowski appointed him Visitor to Canada. In 1919 he was sent in the same capacity to post-war Belgium, then to Ireland and Australia. He returned to New Orleans to celebrate his Golden Jubilee in 1923.

His health was never strong, though he had a lifelong faith in the ability of long walks to cure any bodily ill. His strength declined steadily during his last ten years.

Fr. Power died on March 28, 1934, in Key West, Fla., at age 78. He is buried at Spring Hill.

Albert Wagner, SJ
1846 – 1924
Revered as a holy man and possibly a saint

Even during his lifetime and especially after his death, Fr. Albert Wagner was thought of as a saint. Some of the nuns who repaired his clothes often kept snippets of them as relics.

There were frequent mentions of him in the personal columns of the New Orleans newspapers when prayers for his intercession were answered:

"Thanks to Fr. Wagner and the Blessed Mother for a special favor."

Born in Lafourche Parish (county) in the small town of Cut Off, La., on April 18, 1846, Albert was the son of a veteran of the Napoleonic Wars who had come to America to seek his fortune by farming the rich soil of the Bayou Country. But when Albert was two, his father died. His newly widowed mother first moved with the children to New Orleans and then returned to France. They settled in Toulouse, where Albert attended a Jesuit school.

At age 16, Albert entered the Society of Jesus. Five years later he heard Fr. Francis de Sales Gautrelet, a French Jesuit who had been president of Spring Hill College in Mobile, make an appeal for volunteers for the New Orleans mission. Wagner volunteered and was soon teaching in New Orleans and then at Spring Hill.

When he was 28, he made the difficult Atlantic crossing for the third time to study theology in England. Ordained a priest in 1876, Fr. Wagner had to spend three more years in study and Tertianship before returning to America.

On his return to the South he taught science once more, sometimes with the assistance of Albert Biever, who was then a scholastic. On weekends Fr. Wagner worked as a rural missionary among the un-churched who lived in the hill settlements west of Mobile. He was also a valued spiritual guide for his students, who revered him as a holy man.

His next assignment was Florida. Fluent in Spanish, he worked longest in Tampa in a parish for Cuban immigrants, among the poorest of the poor. He was most esteemed by his parishioners for his devotion to their well-being, and they helped him celebrate his 50 years as a Jesuit.

The same year as his Jubilee he was transferred to New Orleans, where he spent the last years of his life, mostly in the confessional, often walking or riding the streetcars to visit the convents of the nuns to hear their confessions.

Fr. Wagner died on Sept. 2, 1924, and is buried at Spring Hill.

Richard White, SJ
1863 – 1912
With a zeal for souls,
he converted even
the train's conductor

Although some members of the New Orleans Mission who lived into the 20th century made it to a venerable old age, many were cut off in the prime of life. Two of the great killers were yellow fever and tuberculosis. Fr. Richard White died of the latter disease, cutting short a promising priestly career.

Richard was born July 19, 1863, into an Irish-Catholic family in Dublin. After finishing his schooling, he went into business with his father as a pawnbroker and became betrothed to a young woman. He decided to prepare for this new state in life by making an eight-day retreat at Milltown Park on the campus of Dublin's Trinity College. There, after prayer and reflection, he decided not to go through with the marriage but instead to study for the priesthood.

He was accepted into the Society by the New Orleans Mission. With the idea of preparing himself better for the apostolic life by learning French, he asked for and was granted permission to make his Novitiate in Belgium. After his arrival in America he took care to spend his vacations in Cuba to learn Spanish.

He was on fire with zeal for souls, and all during his short formation he collected clippings and notes for use in sermons and apostolic conversations. He used to talk about "angling for souls" and was heard to exclaim:

"Turn me loose in Georgia. I want to save some of those people."

On railroad journeys and streetcar rides he engaged his fellow passengers in godly conversations. In this manner he converted the conductor who was in charge of the run to the Macon Novitiate.

After his ordination in 1903 he worked mainly in the Florida cities of Tampa, Ybor City and Miami, as well as in Georgia at Macon and Augusta. He had an excess of nervous energy and was always hurrying about fishing for souls. He was especially proud of the improvements he helped bring about in the religious practices of his Ybor City parishioners.

His lungs were always weak and, stricken with tuberculosis, he finally had to retire to the Novitiate in Macon. He died there five months later, on Sept. 9, 1912, at age 49. He is buried at Spring Hill.

John Abbadie
1804 - 1890

Joseph Anthonioz
1822 - 1891

St. Charles College, built in Grand Coteau, La., in 1837-38, opened as an educational institution for Catholic boys in 1838. In 1872, part of the facility was converted into a Jesuit novitiate, which later moved its operation to St. Stanislaus College in Macon, Ga., in 1879. The novitiate returned to St. Charles College for the long term in 1922, shortly after fire destroyed the Macon facility.

Ignatius Boemecke
1824 - 1912

Charles Booker
1822 - 1884

Spring Hill College was built at Mobile, Ala., in 1830 and taken over by the Jesuits of the New Orleans Mission in 1847.

Theobald Butler
1829 - 1916

Philip de Carriere
1825 - 1913

Nicholas Ignace de Beaubois
1689 - 1770

Fr. Nicholas de Beaubois (second man from the left in the foreground) greets Catholic nuns on their arrival in Louisiana in the early 1700s. In 1724, Fr. de Beaubois was named superior of the Indian missions in the South. He negotiated local government support for the missionaries working among the Indians, played a major role in bringing the Ursuline sisters from France to New Orleans, and managed a plantation that pioneered in the cultivation of sugarcane in Louisiana.

James Duffo
1820 - 1900

Darius Hubert
1823 - 1893

Immaculate Conception College in New Orleans was founded in 1849 and went through a number of renovations and expansions over the years. Immaculate Conception Chapel, sometimes called the Baronne Street church, was adjacent to the college. Jesuit High School and Loyola University had their origins in this pioneering educational facility in uptown New Orleans.

Jean Baptiste Maisounabe
1805 - 1848

William Murphy
1803 - 1875

Cornelius Otten
1835 - 1916

John F. O'Connor
1848 - 1911

St. Stanislaus College in Macon, Ga., served as the novitiate for the New Orleans Mission and Province from 1879 until 1921, when it was destroyed by fire. In 1922 St. Charles College in Grand Coteau, La., resumed its former role as Jesuit novitiate.

Albert Wagner
1846 - 1924

Conrad Widman
1833 - 1906

St. John's College in Shreveport, La., was founded by the Jesuits of the New Orleans Mission in 1902. Its name was changed to St. John's High School in 1941, Jesuit High School in 1960, and Loyola College Prep in 1982. The Jesuits relinquished control of the school to the Diocese of Alexandria-Shreveport in 1988.

Conrad Widman, SJ
1833 – 1906

*From the winter snow
of Germany to the heat
of Florida and Louisiana*

Conrad Widman's Jesuit vocation reads like a story from the *Lives of the Saints*. On Jan. 24, 1850, a devout, bright country boy in the south of Germany thought he heard God calling him to become a Jesuit. The problem was that he had never seen or met one.

So one cold dawn he began walking 15 miles in the snow to the city of Weingarten to talk with some Jesuits. Although he was encouraged to apply for the Society, his two attempts to enter ended in failure. He was told to finish his studies first.

Months later, for days he walked the considerable distance to the city of Strasbourg to plead his case in person with the provincial. Then he waited for three days, wandering in the streets and subsisting on practically nothing. When the provincial met him for the second time, he told the young man he didn't think he was cut out to be a Jesuit. But on the following morning, as Conrad was leaving to return home, the provincial spotted him and announced that he had changed his mind.

Young Conrad, who had been born Aug. 22, 1833, in Württemberg, Germany, entered the Novitiate near Münster, on Dec. 20, 1851. As a novice he experienced violent fits of coughing and began to spit up blood. Eventually he lost one lung. He became so weak that he was sent to the Lyon Province in hope that his health might improve. From there he sailed in 1859 for the still warmer climate of New Orleans. Not expected to live very long, he was ordained at Natchitoches, La., in 1861.

Despite his delicate health, he never missed a day's work. Zestful and cheerful, he was also gifted intellectually and fluent in the major European languages, as well as in Greek, Latin and Hebrew. After Spring Hill College reopened following the disastrous fire of 1868, Fr. Widman was sent to organize the new college.

When the New Orleans Mission opened its own Novitiate at Grand Coteau, he was named novice master. Albert Biever, Joseph Brinkhaus, James De Potter and Edgar Bernard were among his novices. In all, he spent 30 years at Grand Coteau, primarily as a teacher of science.

His most remarkable work was done in the south Florida mission from 1890 to 1894. He was the first priest to visit many towns, and he even visited and celebrated Mass for the Seminole Indians in the heart of the Everglades. After his years in Florida, he returned to Grand Coteau, where he became spiritual father to the scholastics there.

His last assignment was to Immaculate Conception Church and College in New Orleans. There on Feb. 16, 1906, Fr. Widman died as his community gathered to recite the prayers for the dying. Despite a lifetime of poor health, he lived to the age of 72. He is buried at Spring Hill.

Fr. Widman had a lifelong interest in the history of the New Orleans Mission and wrote several articles of historical interest for *Woodstock Letters*, a publication of the Society of Jesus from 1872 to 1969. He also left behind a manuscript of the history of the early days of the Mission.

BUILDING & EXPANSION ERA

1907 - 1968

This progressive era began with the formal establishment of the New Orleans Province. It was a period of explosive growth in membership in the Society of Jesus as the number of Jesuits grew from 246 in 1907 to approximately 600 in 1960.

During this time, Southern Jesuits opened 11 churches in Florida, mission band preachers brought the word of God to far flung places, Loyola University of New Orleans was founded, and three high schools were opened (in Dallas, El Paso and Houston). Also, four retreat houses began operating (in Convent, La.; Grand Coteau, La.; Lake Dallas, Tex.; and Atlanta, Ga.) as Jesuits introduced retreatants to the life-altering influences of the Spiritual Exercises of St. Ignatius. By 1960, 21 Jesuit-staffed parishes dotted the landscape of the South and Southwest.

Responding to the Gospel's clarion call to lift up the poor and the powerless, many Southern Jesuits were crusaders for social justice and participants in the Civil Rights Movement of the time. They led the way in the desegregation of educational institutions that were under their control, beginning with Spring Hill College in the early 1950s and followed by Loyola University.

Additionally, Southern Jesuits responded affirmatively to appeals to work in the foreign missions of Ceylon, Brazil and elsewhere around the world, beginning in the 1930s. Likewise, numerous Jesuits of the New Orleans Province heeded their country's call to duty as chaplains in the two World Wars and the Korean Conflict.

Other prominent events occurring in this day and age included the Stock Market Crash of 1929, the Great Depression, escalation of U.S. involvement in the Vietnam War, and the assassinations of President John F. Kennedy, Robert Kennedy and Dr. Martin Luther King.

The letter establishing the New Orleans Province of the Society of Jesus

(An excerpt)

...It is indeed marvelous but true that God our Lord is not wont to work spiritual good through the instrumentality of men unless these instruments are themselves spiritual.

Hence, you must be spiritual men, and spiritual precisely in that character which is proper to our Society – by self-denial which springs forth from un-wavering obedience and great charity.

And so I invite you, bound together and strengthened by obedience and charity, to the task of cultivating this broad field of the Lord with new strength and renewed spirit. For now an easy-going type of living and working will not suffice.

The opportunity at hand demands active men such as will undertake great, even outstanding endeavors with bold and ardent mind such as, not content with the work of some few days or years, will constantly strive to do and to suffer more, with only one desire: that from their efforts the greater glory of God shall result.

– Father General Franz X. Wernz
June 7, 1907

Orie Leo Abell, SJ
1888 – 1971
Father of WWL radio

Orie Abell is best known for his work in building WWL in New Orleans into a formidable Southern radio station.

Born in Kansas in 1888, his Jesuit education was typical: Novitiate at Florissant, Mo.; philosophy and theology at Woodstock, Md. Immediately after Tertianship, he was assigned to Loyola in New Orleans in the physics department and as director of its radio station; he was also custodian of its seismological station (1924-38). He considered himself a "jack of all trades."

His work at the radio station stands out as his chief labor and his greatest success. Although WWL existed before Fr. Abell arrived, he became the energetic source of ideas and dedication which built the radio station into a giant in the South.

In a statement dated Nov. 23, 1948, he tells the story of his labors for WWL. At his arrival, WWL was "... a 10-watt weatherbeaten transmitter that had not been on the air for over 12 months."

But when he left, WWL was operating full-time with a power of 10,000 watts and with full membership in the Columbia Broadcasting System. He obtained a permit from the Federal Communications Commission authorizing the construction of a 50,000-watt transmitter on the shores of Lake Pontchartrain. In short order, he progressively acquired seven different operator licenses in his first five years at WWL.

But he literally built WWL, begging funds for this or that improvement, whether radio tubes or microphones. At his death, in 1971, Abell's contribution was duly acknowledged by Phil Johnson in a WWL-TV commentary:

"He was a simple, logical, earnest man with a soaring imagination and hardheaded energy to make his dreams come true."

As is often the case, the person who begins a work is not necessarily the one who can structure it in its next stage. So it was with Abell, when a new rector at Loyola University wanted to advance beyond the progress Abell had made with WWL. Abell left the radio station with great trepidation, and his staff was gradually replaced with more qualified personnel.

He experienced a sea change in his ministry: from czar of a major radio station to the minister of Jesuit High of New Orleans. Building on his mathematical and organizational skills, he later became the treasurer of the high schools in Dallas and New Orleans and of Loyola University and Spring Hill College (1940-1971).

The writer of Abell's obituary spoke highly of him:

"He liked to putter, to tinker, to play and to build. And like most tinkers, he was a man of wild vision and enormous faith. He saw in radio a means of communication for Loyola University unequaled in history."

From another source in the Jesuit archives, we gain a description of this man:

". . .imagination radiates from his face; solid, but medium (in stature), clear face, determination, but no wrinkles; a man who envisions the future and grabs every opportunity that comes by."

Fr. Abell died on Feb. 14, 1971, and is buried at Spring Hill.

Anthony Joseph Achèe, SJ
1900 – 1962
He spoke up for racial equality in the 1940s

The birth of Anthony Achèe in Houma, La., on Nov. 19, 1900, coincided with the new century. He was to witness the growth of industry, invention, and war during six decades of the 20th century while teaching and guiding many young Jesuits.

He entered the Novitiate in 1918 in Macon, Ga., and was present when that structure burned down in 1921. He studied philosophy in Spokane, Wash., and then traveled to Naples, Italy, to study theology.

Fr. Achèe was named master of novices at Grand Coteau in October 1936, a ministry he continued until 1945, when he became the tertian master there, until 1949. He continued in that position at Pass Christian, Miss., from 1949 to 1953. His acumen being recognized, he was appointed tertian instructor in Hiroshima, Japan, in 1957, and he traveled to work in that city, devastated 12 years earlier by the atomic bomb.

A simple fact tells much about Fr. Achèe: He enjoyed the confidence of the New Orleans Province to hold two of its most delicate and important jobs, master of novices (1936-45) and tertian instructor (1946-53 and 1957-62). Judged to be informed about Jesuit life and spirituality, he became a mentor and companion to those entrusted to his care.

Comments by those he helped shape describe

well the stature of this man. He was appraised as a man of "urbane manners, absolute lack of touchiness, wide practical matter-of-fact knowledge…. His warm humanity wrapped us up with respect and made us feel at ease with a man who took us seriously."

Another said, "One of the hidden reasons of this liking for him was the gratitude for the respect he always showed for us."

When assigned to Grand Coteau, Fr. Achèe developed an unwavering interest in the segregated South. In his files are found dozens of articles, such as "The Social Order," "The Catholic Church and Negroes," and "Race Relations as Seen by a Catholic." Besides reading and studying about segregation, he had occasional radio broadcasts on KVOL in Lafayette, La., and on WGMC in Mobile, where he could address the racial equality issue so prevalent in mid-century America.

One 1949 address coincided with the feast of Peter Claver, who was known as the apostle of the Negro slave and was the patron of the African-American church in Grand Coteau.

Fr. Achèe said to his listeners:

We do not have slaves among us anymore, but we do have the descendants of slaves, who in many places and in many respects are subject to contempt and ridicule and labor under great difficulties, and are looked upon as second-class citizens, and are discriminated against for no other reason than their race.

The labors of Fr. Achèe were many and constant; his humanity and respect for others were always recognizable in his formation of young Jesuits. He spoke his own epitaph in a radio broadcast in 1947:

"The Christian shows contempt for no one – no class of people, no race, no individual – for all are children of the same Father."

On the day of his death, Oct. 26, 1962, Fr. Achèe suffered three heart attacks within 12 hours. He was being transported in a helicopter to the hospital when he died of heart failure – far from home, in Iwakuni, Japan. He is buried there.

Gerald Anthony Armstrong, SJ
1909 – 1996
Vocation to the priesthood
replaced his partying ways

In their early twenties, twin brothers Gerald and Bernard Armstrong, born June 15, 1909, in Augusta, Ga., fancied nothing more than playing bridge and partying. Hoping to provide spiritual stability, their parents arranged for them to make a retreat, during which Gerald received a grace that gradually grew into a calling to the priesthood.

Leaving his partying days behind, he began a regular formation as a member of the Society of Jesus and was ordained in 1944.

Fr. Armstrong served in more than 20 different Jesuit enterprises over the space of his 52 years as a priest. His first assignment was to Our Lady of the Oaks Retreat House in Grand Coteau, first as assistant and then as director (1947-52). Now his whirlwind career began in earnest: In 1953, Jerry was minister of Xavier Hall Retreat House in Pass Christian, Miss., followed by two years during which he taught religion and speech at Jesuit High in New Orleans (1955-57).

Then he moved from education to parochial ministry, spending a year at St. Joseph's Church in Macon, Ga. (1958), followed by a year at Immaculate Conception Church in El Paso (1959). He went east to Sacred Heart in Augusta, Ga. (1960-62), followed by a return to El Paso, this time to the new Jesuit High School (1963-65). Following a year in Houston, he was posted to Immaculate Conception Church in Albuquerque (1967-68), after which he spent a year at Ignatius Retreat House in Atlanta (1969); in 1970 he returned to Albuquerque for one year. He became part of Jesuit High in Tampa (1971-75), and then went to Immaculate Conception Church in New Orleans and to Jesuit High School to serve as a spiritual father.

He began a series of assignments in South Carolina, beginning as an assistant available to the Diocese of Charleston (1978). He served at Our Lady of the Hills in Lexington (1979) and also St. Mary

Help of Christians in Aiken (1980-81). Fr. Jerry was back in Charleston to serve for two years at Sacred Heart Church (1984-85), then at St. Mary's Church in Edgefield (1986) and finally back to St. John the Baptist Church in Charleston (1987).

From there, he went to Dallas and became the parochial vicar of All Saints Church (1989-90), and then the assistant pastor at St. Rita's Church (1991-94).

Now in his mid-eighties, showing signs that he needed to retire for appropriate care, he spent his last two years at Ignatius Residence in New Orleans. During his last four months, he was overwhelmed by the number of people who telephoned to recall their relationship with him and to thank him for his long and faithful service to God's people.

On April 16, 1996, Fr. Armstrong died at age 86. He is buried in Grand Coteau.

Who was this man? A relative commented, "He was a very human person, with human flaws." Those flaws made him a great confessor to broken and distraught people.

One obituary states: "St. Rita Parish greatly admired and loved him. His kindness, good humor, and homiletic skills were marvelous gifts.... His simple down-to-earth style was most attractive. As he shuffled down the aisle, his smile and guarded wave to the people became his trademark."

Manuel Arrizabalaga, SJ
1879 – 1965
'Bro. ABC' born near
St. Ignatius' birthplace

It may have been predestined that Manuel Arrizabalaga Olaizola, born on April 20, 1879, would become a Jesuit, since he was born in the Basque country near where St. Ignatius was born.

After he entered the Novitiate at San Sebastian in Spain, he demonstrated distinctive culinary talents. So, when the theologate needed a cook, Bro. Manuel was sent to them. In 1902 he volunteered to work in America and took a steamer to the United States.

Bro. Arrizabalaga was first assigned the job of cook for the Novitiate in Macon, Ga. (1903-04), and then he moved to Loyola University for nearly a decade (1904-14). After one of its many hurricanes, he went to Galveston to assist in the reconstruction of St. Mary's College (1914-19). He returned to Spring Hill College as manager of the

kitchen (1919-21), a job he also performed at St. John's College in Shreveport (1921-23).

"Go West" he did, first as cook for Immaculate Conception Parish in Albuquerque (1923-26) and then for the Church of the Holy Family (1926-29).

Switching gears, he returned to Spring Hill College in the capacity of horticulturist (1929-30). He was attached to the Missouri Province for five years: one year in St. Louis and four in St. Marys, Kan. (1931-35).

In time he settled on calling himself "Brother ABC" because he wasn't able to get his American brothers to say "Arrizabalaga."

Bro. ABC moved to Grand Coteau as the groundskeeper for a few years (1936-42), and then he was posted to El Paso, where he served in different Jesuit establishments. His chief work was cook for the House of Writers (1942-44), but he also served as the parish's receptionist (1944-46) and as sacristan. He returned as cook for two years at the House of Writers (1948-50) and then to Sacred Heart Church, this time in retirement (1950-54).

Bro. Arrizabalaga was eventually retired to Grand Coteau because of his poor health, but he lived another 11 years, serving as the groundskeeper (1954-65). On his second day of "retirement" he got a hoe to prepare a playing field for the local children, and from that day on all of his efforts were for them. He sold marbles to make money to buy basketballs. He begged old bats and torn balls from the novices and juniors and repaired them for further service.

Bro. Arrizabalaga died of a heart attack on Dec. 13, 1965, at the age of 86. He is buried at Grand Coteau.

His obituary read:

"The New Orleans Province was deprived of the earthly presence of one of its truly unique religious. With no fanfare and as quietly as he had lived his dedicated 68 years of service, Brother ABC passed to his eternal reward."

Thomas Aloysius Atherton, SJ
1901 – 1992
One of the longest-serving Jesuits

Thomas Aloysius Atherton's first contact with a Southern Province Jesuit occurred when he encountered Fr. William Frederick Obering, SJ, who was studying theology in England. It is thought that perhaps that encounter piqued his interest in a vocation as a Jesuit.

Born in Preston, England, on June 22, 1901, Thomas took his primary schooling at St. Walburge's School in his hometown from 1904 to 1914. He then studied at the Catholic Day College – a Jesuit institution – from 1915 to 1918.

At the end of World War I, trans-Atlantic transportation was not readily available, so he was unable to enter the Society in the U.S. Therefore, he entered on Nov. 21, 1918, at Manresa House, the Jesuit college in Roehampton, London, taking his vows two years later.

He made his way to the Juniorate at St. Stanislaus College in Macon, Ga., and after the 1921 fire that destroyed much of the campus, he traveled to Grand Coteau, La. (1922-23). He studied philosophy at Mount St. Michael's in Spokane (1923-26) and returned to the Province to do his Regency at Spring Hill High School (1926-29). He began his theology studies in St. Louis, but moved to Oña, Spain, for further study and later was ordained at Heythrop College in England, in 1932.

During World War II and the post-war years (1942-49), he was an auxiliary military chaplain for all service branches in Key West and West Palm Beach, Fla. After that post, all of Fr. Atherton's priestly work was in parish ministry, serving as an associate pastor in New Orleans, El Paso, Miami, Key West, West Palm Beach and Tampa. He served two stints at Holy Name of Jesus Church in New Orleans (1949-54, 1956-67), and he also ministered at Immaculate Conception Church in New Orleans (1955-56, 1969-70). From 1970 to 1980, Fr. Atherton was in residence at Jesuit High School in New Orleans.

Because of ill health, he retired to Ignatius Residence in 1980. Twelve years later, he suffered a stroke that hastened his death, on Jan. 23, 1992. At the time of his death, Fr. Atherton had the distinction of being the oldest Jesuit in the Province: He was 90 years old, 73 years a Jesuit and 59 years a priest. He is buried at Grand Coteau.

Gabriel Joseph Barras, SJ
1901 – 1968
Wartime chaplain, peacetime teacher

From the American Revolution through the Twentieth Century, more than 3,000 priests and ministers have served as U.S. Navy chaplains, promoting religious and personal well-being for the officers and enlisted men and women of the Navy. Fr. Gabriel Joseph Barras was one of those men, providing comfort and support during not just one but two wars. He devoted his life to serving God, his country, his students, and his parishioners.

Growing up speaking French, Fr. Barras, one of a family of eight children, was born June 12, 1901, in St. Martinville, La.

He studied with the Sisters of Mercy until he was 12 years old, then took his high school education at St. Charles College in Grand Coteau (1913-16), which offered secondary and college diplomas at the time. He entered the Novitiate at St. Stanislaus College in Macon, Ga., in 1916, spending two obligatory years in the Novitiate and two in the Juniorate. He left the warm South for the cold of Spokane, where he studied philosophy at Mount St. Michael's (1920-23). "Gabe" spent his three years of Regency at Jesuit High in New Orleans (1923-26) and studied theology at Woodstock College in Maryland (1926-30).

Ordained on June 23, 1929, he received a typical Jesuit education with an A.B. and M.A. in philosophy and an M.A. in education from St. Louis University, which sounds like a recipe for high school teaching.

His first assignment was to St. John's College (now called Loyola College Prep) in Shreveport, where he taught for two years and served as principal from 1931 to 1935. He then studied at St. Louis University doing graduate work in education and earning an M.A. before returning to Shreveport as rector and principal (1937-40). Because of his expertise in education he was assigned to Spring Hill College as instructor in education and assistant dean (1940-42).

His career in education was interrupted by World War II. Gabe was one of 18 Jesuit priests from the Province who served as chaplains in the military; another 30 served part-time on bases close to their apostolates. Gabe served in the U.S. Navy as a chaplain during the height of the war until its conclusion (Sept. 1942 – Dec. 1945), sharing chaplainship duties with some of his contemporaries (Fr. Sam Hill Ray and Fr. Ed Goss).

At the end of WW II, he resumed his high school work in Shreveport as a teacher and student counselor (1946-47). Perhaps Navy chaplaincy brought out the pastoral side of him, for he was named pastor of Holy Name of Jesus Church in New Orleans (1947-50). With the outbreak of the Korean War, he was back in uniform, this time with the rank of commander, for nearly a decade (1950-59).

When he returned to the Province, he spent a

brief transition period at Immaculate Conception Parish in Albuquerque, N.M., before becoming the inaugural pastor of St. Rita Parish in Dallas. Except for the Navy, his stay in this parish was the longest assignment he ever had (1960-1968).

While on a visit to New Orleans, Fr. Barras died of a heart attack on June 21, 1968. He is buried at Grand Coteau.

Ronald Joseph Barrilleaux, SJ
1897 – 1976
Grand Coteau was the epicenter of his priestly career

Born in the small south Louisiana town of Chacahoula, in Terrebonne Parish, on Aug. 8, 1897, Ronald Joseph Barrilleaux embraced ministries as a pastor and as a director of retreats.

Little of his early education is known except that he spent seven years in Grand Coteau, first at St. Charles High School and then at the college. He entered the Novitiate in 1925, progressing through the standard years of formation and education.

In 1936, as a young priest, he was minister of St. Charles College for a year and then served as prefect of discipline at Jesuit High in Tampa (1937-38). Following these assignments, he began a long tenure as pastor of Sacred Heart Church in Grand Coteau in 1938, a position he held for 12 years, until 1950. He was next appointed assistant pastor to Gesù Church in Miami, followed by service at St. John's Church in Shreveport, Holy Name of Jesus in New Orleans and Immaculate Conception in downtown New Orleans. He had three more assignments as assistant pastor: a return to Gesù Church in Miami in 1962, then to St. Joseph Church in Mobile in 1966 and St. Aloysius Church in Baton Rouge in 1968.

His other ministry involved the retreat houses of the Province. He was the assistant director of retreats at three places: Our Lady of the Oaks in Grand Coteau, Montserrat Retreat House in Lake Dallas and Xavier Hall in Pass Christian, Miss. All of these were public ministries, but he also was assigned to an internal ministry as Father Minister to his brother Jesuits in Grand Coteau for the majority of the time between 1934 and 1950.

A large, bulky man, Fr. Barrilleaux enjoyed walking. People said that he strode rather than walked. It was noted that twice daily he sprang out of the house, twirling his knob-headed cane as he set out on his walks. His junkets continued even in cities like Cleveland, which prepared him for downtown walks in Miami and New Orleans.

It was observed that despite the fact that his default mode was rather gruff and his manner of speech was abrupt, many considered him shy and reserved. However, once he was at the lecture podium, he became assertive, direct and forceful.

The epicenter of the priestly career of Fr. Barrilleaux was Grand Coteau, where he worked for just over one-third of his 78 years. As pastor of Sacred Heart Church in Grand Coteau, he seemed most successful, not only in leading souls to God, but in cajoling his parishioners to replace the wooden grade school with a brick one and to convert the former Mother Connelly house into the parish rectory.

He eventually slowed down and in his last two years ventured into pastoral ministry on just a few occasions. His daily walks became leisure walks, not his former charging down the streets.

Fr. Barrilleaux died of a heart attack on June 19, 1976, a death that was a shock to the parish, for all considered him fit and healthy, despite his being 78 years old. He is buried at Grand Coteau.

Peter C. Beach, SJ
1918 – 1955
A high achiever, a saintly man

When his contemporaries discussed Fr. Peter Beach they compared him to St. Aloysius, who was highly intelligent and deeply devout, and St. Francis Xavier, one of the greatest missionaries of the Church.

Born in New Orleans on Sept. 24, 1918, Peter attended Holy Cross School, where he had a brilliant record as a student and athlete, graduating as valedictorian in 1935.

At Loyola he was equally distinguished. He took every honor in sight and was president of the Student Council. Before his senior year he entered the Society of Jesus, on Aug. 14, 1938. He impressed everyone with his charm, his spirit of prayer, his fraternal charity, and his devotion to poverty. The only fault ever found in him was a certain carelessness in his personal appearance.

After his Novitiate and one year of Juniorate he studied philosophy at Spring Hill. There, despite wearing thick glasses due to poor eyesight and being of medium build, he was an enthusiastic, well-coordinated athlete. He loved competition and never lost his temper in those famous intramurals which were more hotly contested than any Super Bowl.

Sent to Catholic University for a Master's degree in economics, he was often teased about the neighborhood children hanging around the house plaintively asking the superior "if Mr. Beach could come out and play."

In 1947 his petition to serve in Ceylon was granted, and once there he spent two years teaching at St. Michael's in Batticaloa before he was ordained in Kurseong, India, in 1950. In 1953 he returned to Ceylon as principal of St. Joseph's College in Trincomalee. As always, he was a model of dedication and zeal. He had a special gift for helping his students develop their skills and talents.

St. Joseph's in those days was in the throes of reconstruction since its physical facilities were totally inadequate. Still Fr. Beach carried on with good grace. He had a way with the government authorities in Ceylon that enabled him to cut the red tape that had hindered other educators.

It was his custom to rise at 4:30 each morning in order to pray his breviary, make his daily prayer, and celebrate Mass before the busy day began. It was while he was shaving on May 12, 1955, that he suffered a cerebral thrombosis, a blood clot in his brain. His brethren found him paralyzed and nauseated on the floor. On the way to the hospital, ever aware of the needs of his school, he gave detailed instructions about its daily operations.

Despite the best efforts of the British doctors at the Royal Naval Hospital in Trincomalee, he died two days later, on May 14, 1955, and is buried in Sri Lanka. He was 36.

Joseph Francis Beaver, SJ
1918 – 1982
A 'people's priest,'
a practitioner of ecumenism

Affable, fatherly and patient, Fr. Joseph Francis Beaver practiced ecumenism long before it became a goal of the Catholic Church starting with the Second Vatican Council.

Born in Key West, Fla., on Dec. 23, 1918, he completed his elementary schooling at St. Mary's School in Key West in 1931, and then attended Spring Hill High School in Alabama (1931-35). Upon graduation, he entered the Novitiate in Grand Coteau.

He studied philosophy at Spring Hill (1939-42)

and earned a B.A. in French (1941) and a B.S. in biology (1942). Like many Regencies, his was spent in two different places: Jesuit High School in New Orleans (1942-43) and Jesuit High in Dallas (1944-45). Another year was spent in special studies at Fordham University, where he earned an M.S. in biology (1943-44). He went to St. Marys, Kan., for theology (1945-49), and was ordained on June 14, 1948.

Joe spent his entire priestly life in Florida, mostly in Tampa. After his formation, he was assigned to Jesuit High in Tampa as a student counselor (1950-56). Then he returned to Key West as pastor of St. Mary Star of the Sea Church and remained there for nearly a decade, 1956-65. Besides officiating at the weddings of much of Key West's population, he spearheaded construction of St. Mary Star of the Sea Elementary School, Mary Immaculate High School and St. Mary's Church and its adjoining rectory and convent.

Of this good man it was said that he was a "people's priest.... He had tremendous drive, boundless energy.... Very fatherly, patient and sympathetic." He was an ecumenicist long before the word became part of the Catholic vernacular. One could go to a bar mitzvah and there would be Fr. Joe Beaver. A Baptist minister said of him: "He has the personal touch. That was his calling card."

He returned to the high school in Tampa as its rector for a short term (1965-67) and then became alumni director and development director (1967-74). Finally, he moved across town to Sacred Heart Church, where he served as associate pastor (1974-81) until his poor health intervened.

Toward the end of his service, he suffered a stroke, which so incapacitated him that others had to care for him. Because he required nursing care, he was transferred to Ignatius Residence in New Orleans, where he lived for six months, until his final illness overcame him.

Fr. Joe died on June 25, 1982, and is buried at Spring Hill.

Carmine Cyro Benanti, SJ
1901 – 1968
He chose the priesthood
over a career in business

A native Long Islander, Carmine Cyro Benanti, born on Jan. 6, 1901, in West Slip, N.Y., went to work in the secular world after he completed his schooling and became a successful assistant sales manager for a large New York firm. However, the winds of change were blowing him from a promising business career to the challenges and joys of the priesthood.

He moved to Grand Coteau when he entered the Society of Jesus on Oct. 2, 1924, and began his Jesuit formation there. After returning to the North for philosophy at the seminary in Weston, Mass., he spent his four years of Regency at Jesuit High in New Orleans. Upon completion of theology studies in St. Marys, Kan., he was ordained on June 22, 1938.

His first priestly assignment was to Jesuit High in New Orleans as a counselor of students for three years. He served as pastor at Holy Name of Jesus Church until he was appointed pastor of St. Joseph Church in Mobile in 1947. In 1952 he became the pastor of St. Joseph Church in Macon, Ga., serving as the last Jesuit pastor at that church. He then moved back to Mobile, where he served as pastor at St. Joseph Chapel at Spring Hill. He is considered the founder of St. Ignatius Parish in Mobile.

He was a man of service and gratitude; his Christmas cards were expressions of gratitude for help given him in his ministry. He had a deep commitment to validating marriages and returning people to the faith. One of his last Days of Recollection was an address on the "Spirit of Renewal," demonstrating his openness to the contemporary changes in the Church. His years as pastor of so many churches stand as testimony to the strength of his faith and his commitment to others.

After many years of missing family celebrations, Fr. Benanti traveled home to New York for the Christmas holidays, where he suffered a fatal heart attack on Jan. 2, 1968. Jesuits from the area gathered to pray him home, and the president of Fordham University said the funeral Mass. Fr. Benanti is buried in the Jesuit cemetery at Spring Hill College.

Arnold J. Benedetto, SJ
1916 – 1966
A master teacher
and prolific scholar

Perhaps because of his enthusiasm for teaching and a few endearing eccentricities, Fr. Arnold J. "Benny" Benedetto was one of the best-loved professors of many Jesuit seminarians.

In the classroom he was a master teacher, but one prone to exclaiming "Eek!" when he was surprised or disapproved of some behavior. Capturing the interest of his students, he gave outstanding witness to the joys and sacrifices of the intellectual life.

He also worked hard. Because there were no texts for some of the courses he taught, he regularly handed out to his students numerous mimeographed pages for which he himself had cut the stencils the night before. Additionally, he translated and transcribed articles and appropriate chapters from a wide variety of authors.

Benny was born in Macon, Ga., on Jan. 13, 1916, into a large, religious family. Two of his sisters became nuns, and in 1932, after finishing high school at Spring Hill, he followed his older brother, Frank, into the Society. He started philosophy at St. Louis but transferred after one year to the newly opened Philosophate at Spring Hill. After Regency and theology at St. Marys, he was one of six Missourians and eight Southerners who pioneered the Grand Coteau Tertianship (1945-46). Immediately afterwards, he and fellow Jesuit scholar Youree Watson were sent to Rome to do a two-year program in philosophy. In 1948 he returned to take over the theodicy class at the Philosophate on the campus of Spring Hill College. He taught this course for the rest of his life.

In addition to teaching, he was engaged in three principal "extra-curricular activities." He was in charge of the mission church at Sandtown, near Spring Hill College. He took care of the philosophate villa at Battles Wharf on Mobile Bay, where he served as summer superior. He also maintained and built up the Philosophate library. He began acquiring relevant books during his time in Europe, and his enthusiasm for the huge tomes he imported even infected some of the philosophers.

His work ethic was extraordinary. Few of his students and colleagues had ever seen a man who worked harder or typed faster. A steady flow of articles, book reviews and class notes issued from his typewriter. In 1963 Macmillan published his *Fundamentals in the Philosophy of God*, which exhibited his enormous erudition and penetrating analysis, although little of his lively wit shines through in the book. But his published output was only the tip of the iceberg. He left behind dozens of translations and articles on which he was still working or for which he could not find an outlet.

In 1960 he was afflicted with melanoma in his right arm, which was treated successfully. Then in 1965 he developed heart disease that slowed him down and finally stopped him entirely.

On Feb. 14, 1966, Fr. Benedetto died at age 50. He is buried at Spring Hill.

Edgar J. Bernard, SJ
1862 – 1940
An Apostle of the Sacred Heart

For most of the Jesuits who knew him, Fr. Edgar J. Bernard was the closest the New Orleans Province ever came to producing a saint in the traditional mold. His pious mother dedicated him to the Sacred Heart, and even as a boy his penances and prayers remind one of the practices of St. Aloysius.

Born in New Orleans on March 9, 1862, in the midst of the Civil War, he grew up in turbulent and dangerous times. After finishing his course of studies at the College of the Immaculate Conception in New Orleans, he presented himself at Grand Coteau in August 1877 as a candidate for the Society. But because of his youth he was enrolled in St. Charles College until the following year. He finished his Novitiate in Florissant, Mo., under the direction of Fr. Isidore Boudreaux, a Louisianian who had joined the Missouri Province.

Some of his penances as a scholastic left him weak in health, notably his attempt to weather the winter at Woodstock College in Maryland without heat, which ultimately left his hearing impaired. As this infirmity grew worse it was thought that he should not be trained for life in the classroom. Therefore, as a young priest in 1898, he was made minister at the Macon Novitiate. It was a post he would retain for most of the rest of his life, first at Macon and then, after the 1921 fire at the Georgia school, in Grand Coteau.

Besides his humble service to his brethren as minister-treasurer, his great apostolate was the propagation of devotion to the Sacred Heart among his fellow Jesuits and various priests and religious and the laity. He wrote many articles and pamphlets on the subject and was highly regarded as a spiritual director and retreat master for priests.

Because of his deafness, Fr. Bernard carried a horn hooked up to a hose which he inserted into his ear. He made many novenas to St. John Berchmans seeking a cure of his deafness, but without success. Once he offered his horn to a picture of Berchmans and said, "Here, St. John, you seem to need it more than I do!"

On April 30, 1940, Fr. Bernard died at age 78. He is buried at Grand Coteau, where for years some townspeople venerated him as a saint. He was truly a "Hidden Apostle of the Sacred Heart."

Albert H. Biever, SJ
1859 – 1934
A giant of the Province

Albert H. Biever is most celebrated as the Jesuit called in by Provincial Fr. John O'Shanahan, given a nickel for carfare, and told to go uptown and start a university. While this incident is not documented, it is true that Fr. Biever helped establish Loyola University.

However, Fr. Biever himself seems to have thought that his greatest work was the preaching of missions and retreats during the middle years of his tenure as a Jesuit.

At any rate, he was surely one of the giants of the Province.

Born April 24, 1858, in Luxembourg, he immigrated to America with his family, and in December 1875 he began his Novitiate at Grand Coteau. All of his formation was regular except for six years of Regency. He studied philosophy and theology at Stonyhurst and St. Beuno's in Wales, where he developed an interest in science, which he was to use in the classroom and at the pulpit for the rest of his life. He was gifted in languages and preached in French and German as well as English.

Tireless in his pursuit of souls, Fr. Biever, as a young priest, risked his life in the yellow fever epidemics to minister to the sick.

In 1897, Fr. Biever was sent to the Jesuit college on Baronne Street, where he taught and preached until 1904, when he was appointed to start a school in uptown New Orleans. At first this was supposed to be another Jesuit school like the college on Baronne Street encompassing both high school and college. Because of an inauspicious beginning, it was decided to concentrate the college department uptown and the secondary school on Baronne Street. On April 15, 1912, Loyola University's charter was signed by the Jesuit governing corporation, and on July 10 the State approved it. By the time Fr. Biever, the college's first president, left the university in 1914, he had raised the money for Marquette and Thomas Halls as well as for the new church, Most Holy Name of Jesus.

His next assignment was the mission band on which he labored for eight years (1913-21). As part of this evangelizing group, he preached missions and retreats throughout the South and was well-known and loved by many priests and bishops. One of his techniques to draw a crowd was to perform a chemical experiment with appropriate sounds and colors. He also used "magic" lantern slides to introduce and illustrate his discourses. He himself related how he sometimes got a bigger explosion than he bargained for.

Another of his accomplishments that benefitted the community was his supervision of the 1928 construction of the current church on Baronne Street. Fr. Biever worked tirelessly to maintain the architectural integrity and beauty of the original Immaculate Conception Church.

He was revered by many who knew him, and some considered him a saint. Fr. Biever died on Nov. 14, 1934, at the age of 76. He is buried at Spring Hill.

Robert Le Duc Boggs, SJ
1916 – 1990
The congressman's brother, the abassador's brother-in-law

Robert Le Duc Boggs was born into a family that not only nurtured a future Jesuit, but also reared a son who became a U. S. congressman.

Born in Long Beach, Miss., on Nov. 1, 1916, Robert and his family later moved to New Orleans, where he attended Jesuit High School (1930-34). After a year at Loyola, he entered the Society of Jesus in 1935, staying at Grand Coteau, La., for his Novitiate. His formation was regular: philosophy at Spring Hill College, Regency at Jesuit High in Tampa, then theology at St. Marys, Kan., and ordination in 1948.

At this point Robert Boggs had earned three degrees: a B.A. in English from Spring Hill, an STL from St. Louis University, and an M.A. in education from Loyola of New Orleans. Later in his ministry he attended school at LSU for five straight summers.

His first six years after ordination were spent in administration and teaching in high schools. He was the prefect of discipline for two years each at the Jesuit high schools in New Orleans and Tampa (1950-54); similarly, he taught at Jesuit High in El Paso and then at Jesuit High in Dallas (1954-56). He returned to Loyola in New Orleans as Dean of Students (1956-63) and then served at Jesuit High in El Paso as guidance counselor (1963-65). Then it was back to college, this time at Spring Hill, where he was both a teacher and a counselor (1965-69). He remained in Mobile as assistant pastor of St. Ignatius Parish (1969-71) and then returned to New

Orleans in the same role at Holy Name of Jesus.

Robert's brother, Hale Boggs, was a congressman in the U.S. House of Representatives for many years, until his death in 1972. His widow, Corinne "Lindy" Boggs, who died in 2013, finished his term and later became the U.S. Ambassador to the Holy See.

Perhaps it was inevitable that Fr. Boggs would follow his brother into the halls of government. Shortly after his ordination, he delivered an invocation in the House of Representatives. He also served as chairman of the Jesuit Student Personnel Administrators of the Central Provinces of the United States (1962-63). At the same time, he was a member of the Executive Committee on Student Financial Aid of the Southwestern Association (1962-63). He was in great demand to give graduation talks and political invocations.

When he was 73, Fr. Boggs entered the hospital for prostate surgery, but several hours later he suffered cardiac arrest and died. It was on May 25, 1990. He is buried at Spring Hill.

Joseph S. Bogue, SJ
1900 – 1978
'The Boss' of the Philosophate at Spring Hill College

Believing in a balance between physical and mental strength, Fr. Joseph Smarius Bogue emphasized activities involving sports as well as serious academic work.

Born Nov. 22, 1900, in Mobile, Joseph entered the Society at Macon, Ga., in 1919 after a year at Spring Hill College. A junior when the Macon fire occurred, Joe finished his studies at Augusta and Grand Coteau. Then he studied philosophy at Mount St. Michael's in Spokane, did his Regency at Spring Hill and Jesuit High in New Orleans, and studied theology at St. Louis University and St. Mary's College in Kansas.

In 1935, he went to Rome to do a *biennium* (two-year study) and prepare for his life's work: teaching philosophy, particularly ethics. In 1937, he came back to Spring Hill College to open the new Philosophate. The next year he succeeded Fr. William O'Leary as superior, and from 1938 to 1951 he ruled over the Philosophate as "the Boss."

Fr. Bogue's unique approach was to treat each philosopher individually. Fr. Tom Clancy once said to Joe:

"I think the greatest contribution that you

made during this time when you were superior in the Philosophate (was to) treat each one individually. There was no set of rules that governed all cases. Everyone was treated individually."

Joe's response explains his notion of *cura personalis* (care for the entire person):

"Along the way I learned what I liked and did not like in superiors. I continued to do the things I liked in superiors and tried to avoid the things I didn't like. I was interested in those young men personally and individually, so that would be the reason for my treating them personally and individually. I was truly interested in them."

"The Boss" insisted on sports in the Philosophate. Some of the most memorable nights during that time occurred when he came down to the recreation room to present prizes to the winners of the various intramural leagues. On these occasions he would discourse on the scholastics' success and how they had the best Philosophate in the country, indeed in the world. The young Jesuits cheered him heartily.

Eventually Fr. Bogue went to Loyola, where he served as chairman of the Philosophy Department from 1951 to 1958. He then returned to Spring Hill for eight more years, and he spent some years at St. Joseph's in Mobile before retiring to Grand Coteau in 1972. While there, he helped out by directing Ignatian retreats at the newly founded Jesuit Spirituality Center.

Fr. Bogue suffered from a series of debilitating illnesses: diseased joints, severe arthritis, broken bones, a compressed disk, and other conditions. By then emphysema had deflated him, but he continued going to the nearby Academy of the Sacred Heart for Mass and confessions. On Feb. 27, 1978, Joe had a severe bout of emphysema and was rushed to Lafayette General Hospital. Fellow Jesuits sat with him around the clock during his painful last agony as he desperately tried to breathe.

Fr. Bogue died on March 2, 1978, and was buried the following day at Grand Coteau.

Joseph Armand Brinkhaus, SJ
1859 – 1944
A native son of Grand Coteau

Joseph Armand Brinkhaus was born in Grand Coteau on June 22, 1859, in sight of St. Charles College, where he was to spend nearly his entire life. First an honor student in the college, he transferred to the Novitiate in 1875, shortly before his

sixteenth birthday, to begin his training as a Jesuit brother.

One of his first assignments was to help the field hands at the college's huge farm. It turned out, however, that their rough language and manner were not exactly conducive to a young novice's spiritual growth, and he was sent instead to work with Bro. Cornelius Otten at various jobs. "Brother Joe," as he was affectionately called, was only 19 when he assisted Bro. Otten in the challenging work of building Sacred Heart Church (later renamed St. Charles Borromeo) in Grand Coteau. They completed the structure in one year's time.

Six years later, in 1886, Bro. Joe was assigned the task of building the bell tower at the back of the church. It stands today as one of the most interesting and unique structures in church architecture in this part of the country.

Although Bro. Joe was most widely known for his work in construction, he spent his 69 years at the college in numerous other capacities. According to one record, he was a jack of all trades and master of them all. Whatever he did, he did well. When given charge of the sugar mill, he turned out the best sugar the college had ever produced. As manager of the college farm for more than 60 years, he corresponded regularly with Louisiana State University and the U.S. Department of Agriculture in Washington to acquaint himself with the most scientific, up-to-date methods of farming.

So proficient was he, in fact, that some local old-timers who had farmed many years more than he came to Grand Coteau to seek his advice and learn what he had been bold enough to try. Long before Gulf States Utilities supplied the countryside with electricity, Bro. Joe installed a carbide gas system and later an electric dynamo (a generator) and storage batteries to provide much-needed illumination. He was also an innovator in the areas of plumbing, corn-crushing, corn-milling, wood-sawing and pumping water.

Bro. Joe was away from Grand Coteau for only one year of his life. In 1891, he and three other brothers went to New Orleans, where they constructed a beautiful wooden church on St. Charles Avenue. Characteristic of everything he had done previously, the church was a solid and masterful piece of work. Thirty-one years after it was erected, it survived a trip across the Mississippi River to Westwego, where it was reassembled and remained in use for approximately 30 more years.

In August of 1939, at age 80, Bro. Joe turned over the management of the farm to Bro. Martial Lapeyre. He continued in his last years to help in whatever way he could. On March 7, 1944, he died peacefully in his room at St. Charles College, in the quiet little town where he had been born 84 years earlier. Attending him at the time was his nephew, Dr. Armand Brinkhaus.

The totality of his contribution was vast and the quality of his work always of the highest caliber. He may not have traveled far from the place of his birth, but he certainly mastered the art of blooming where he was planted.

Halcott Terrell Burges, SJ
1875 – 1968
*'The Kid' started late
and never looked back*

Bro. Halcott Terrell Burges' favorite appellation for others was "Kid," a nickname he himself acquired – and aptly so, for he was forever young at heart.

Born on Sept. 25, 1875, in Alexandria La., he attended the local parochial school and finished his schooling at Jefferson College in Convent, La., in 1893.

Shortly thereafter "The Kid" embarked on a rover's life. He worked in Louisiana and the Rocky Mountain states as a salesman, hotel clerk, carpenter, streetcar conductor, short-order cook and waiter. He had his share of scrapes and was fond of showing his hands to people.

"Look at those knuckles, kid! They did not get that way from playing the piano," he said.

In February of 1925, when he was 49, he began his postulancy at Shreveport, La., moving to Grand Coteau in July to start his Novitiate under Fr. John Salter, the novice master. Fr. Edgar Bernard was minister there, and "The Kid" learned from him an ardent devotion to the Sacred Heart, which he passed on to others.

Bro. Burges spent most of his Jesuit life at Grand Coteau and at the church on Baronne Street in New Orleans, with shorter stays elsewhere. He could do almost anything, especially repairing watches, one of his specialties. He was a good cook, an inventive repairman and a caring nurse.

He had a great interest in horse racing, and he tried to use it to advance the interests of the Jesuits. When the Province was in financial difficulties in the 1930s, he approached his ex-novice master, Fr. Salter, who was then the Provincial, with the idea of increasing the Province's assets with a series of wise investments at the Fairgrounds Race Track in New Orleans. Needless to say, his offer was refused.

"The Kid" had that special grace which St. Ignatius in the Constitutions demands of all candidates to the Society, *gratia sermonis*, the ability to deal with people. He was a fascinating conversationalist with people of all stations of life. He could talk about anything from Scripture and faraway places to sports, machinery, the mercy of God and great men of the past. He was an outstanding apostle at Baronne Street and an even greater influence on younger brothers and scholastics at Grand Coteau. He had a zest for life and a joy in serving God that changed many hearts.

Perhaps one of the reasons why he kept so young at heart was the advice he gave to so many people and followed himself: "Kid, never look back."

Bro. Burges died at age 93 on Oct. 17, 1968, and is buried at Grand Coteau.

Martin P. Burke, SJ
1886 – 1960
Ministering in a time of racial turmoil

Martin P. Burke, born in New Orleans on Jan. 24, 1886, spent his early years at St. Francis de Sales School, and at age 11 he entered the College of the Immaculate Conception on Baronne Street.

Encouraged by a Jesuit teacher, he sought to enter the Order at a mere 14 years old. He was accepted into the Novitiate, but his superiors did not approve him for vows because of his youth. Nevertheless, he moved on to the Juniorate, pronouncing his vows the next year (1904) while still a teenager.

He studied philosophy at St. Louis (1904-06), returning to New Orleans for the start of his Regency, which at that time was generally five years long. He went to Woodstock, Md., for theology, with ordination in 1915. Along the way he earned an A.B. and an M.A. from St. Louis University, an S.T.D. from Georgetown (via Woodstock), and a PhD from the Gregorian University in Rome.

Martin was a teacher all of his ministerial life. This accolade by one of his students celebrates his stature, mannerisms, voice and message:

"Father Burke was a brilliant and understanding teacher whose stimulating, conversation-like lectures, pronounced in that deep, sonorous voice of his, never failed to arouse our lagging interest."

And indeed he was a very influential teacher.

All went swimmingly until the 1950s and the advent of desegregation. Fr. Burke was teaching side-by-side with Fr. Joseph Fichter, another Jesuit. While the latter relentlessly championed desegregation in general and especially at Loyola University, Fr. Burke served as the mind and voice of the opposition. Loyola's dearest wish was to contain all discourse on this subject within the Jesuit faculty. To this end, the administration drafted a policy statement that "should be followed by all in public utterances" requiring … "that differing doctrines ought not be permitted either orally in sermon or in public lectures and in books." While Fr. Burke was a member of the community drafting the policy, Fr. Fichter was not. The conflict raged for several years, with Fr. Burke asserting philosophical arguments for segregation.

With the Supreme Court's 1954 ruling on *Brown vs. the Board of Education*, the Archbishop's demand that Catholic schools in New Orleans be desegregated, and a final policy statement on the matter by the New Orleans Province, pro-segregationists were left with little to stand on.

In the aftermath of all this, Fr. Burke vacated the battlefield; he left Loyola after 15 years of teaching (1942-57) and was transferred to Spring Hill College, which had desegregated much earlier.

This was a very brief stay, for Fr. Burke died on May 6, 1960, at age 74. He is buried at Spring Hill.

Joseph Toulmin Burleigh, SJ
1898 – 1989
A country boy from Grand Coteau

Joseph Toulmin Burleigh was born on April 12, 1898, on a working farm in Grand Coteau, just a stone's throw from St. Charles College.

He attended the college from 1911 to 1916 and entered the Society in Macon, Ga., in 1916. Everything then was by the book: college studies at Macon (1918-21), philosophy at Mount St. Michael's in Spokane (1921-24), Regency at Spring Hill College (1924-26) and Jesuit High in New Orleans (1926-27), and theology at St. Louis (1927-31). He was ordained on June 26, 1930.

Except for a year of teaching at Spring Hill College (1932-33), his entire ministry was spent serving in various parishes staffed by the New Orleans Province. He was the assistant pastor at Gesù in Miami for a decade (1933-43). He was then transferred from the Atlantic to the Rockies, serving at Immaculate Conception Parish in Albuquerque (1943-46), but he returned to Florida as the associate pastor at Sacred Heart Parish in Tampa (1946-

47). From there, he went back to Grand Coteau as pastor of Sacred Heart Parish, (1948-55). He would return to this parish in 1959 to serve until 1967. After time at St. Joseph's in Mobile (1955-59), he moved to New Orleans to be pastor of Immaculate Conception Parish (1967-75), finally returning to Miami for three years.

Also known as "Doc," when Fr. Burleigh left Miami, the *Gesù Star* saluted him in a feature article, which provides the best source of information about him.

> He likes to hunt, especially ducks, rabbits and quail. As Fr. Burleigh says, "I am a country boy".… When asked what was his most rewarding duty he said he found hearing confessions to be the most consoling work he has done throughout his entire life as a priest. He likes to help individuals who have problems, worry a lot and are disturbed.… When asked what he thought of taking Communion in the hand, Fr. Burleigh said: "If people would only remember Jesus as a little boy, they would understand why it is right and beautiful to take Communion in the hand. As a baby, Jesus was most certainly picked up and loved by many people."

In the same vein, he enthusiastically endorsed the Lay Ministers Program, saying it was impossible for the first apostles to share the Eucharist in the early church without a network of lay associates. "Doc" sounds like a man of good common sense.

Toward the end of his work in Miami, "Doc" Burleigh was exhausted, so he was assigned to Ignatius Residence for recuperation. This break restored his body so well that he was sent back to Gesù in Miami (1979-83) and Sacred Heart in Tampa (1983-85). But now it was time for a true and complete retirement, and so he returned to Ignatius Residence. On Aug. 5, 1989, Fr. Burleigh died at the age of 91. He is buried at Grand Coteau.

Ernest Joseph Burrus, SJ
1907 – 1991
Holocaust hero, eminent scholar

Ernest Joseph Burrus was a modern-day hero and a man of God. Risking his life, he helped to rescue Austrian Jews and to preserve the word of God, despite Nazi efforts to stop him.

Born in El Paso on April 20, 1907, he decided early on to become a Jesuit and received a Waysider Scholarship for candidates for the Society to study at Spring Hill College. He entered the Novitiate in 1925. His training was typical: philosophy at Mount St. Michael's, where he earned an M.A.; Regency at Grand Coteau (1932-35); an M.A. in classics from Loyola of New Orleans (1933); and additional studies during the summers of 1933 and 1934 at Catholic University in Washington, D.C. Theology took him to Valkenburg, Holland, for two years, but the austerity of the theologate forced him to continue in Innsbruck, Austria. He was ordained on July 17, 1938, just a few months after Adolf Hitler announced the *Anschluss* (union) with Austria in March.

Repulsed by the ideology and practices of the Nazis, Fr. Burrus took an active role in fighting against them, earning him *persona non grata* status from the National Socialists. The Gestapo expelled him in 1939 for helping Jews escape Austria, as well as for smuggling out a sermon of Fr. Rupert Mayer's and for carrying Pope Pius XI's encyclical "With Burning Concern" from Italy into Switzerland for publication.

Returning safely to the U.S., he ministered to German prisoners-of-war in southern Louisiana and was assigned to teach Greek, Latin, German, Spanish and history in the Juniorate at Grand Coteau for nine years (1941-50). In 1949 he published a critical edition of Fr. Andrés Calvo, SJ's, history of colonial Mexico. In 1950 Félix Zubillaga, SJ, urged Father General to assign Fr. Burrus to the Jesuit Historical Institute in Rome, where he spent 38 years researching documents in Spanish, German, Italian, French, Dutch, Portuguese, Latin and Greek.

In 1957 he received a Guggenheim Foundation Award, and in 1961 St. Louis University awarded him an honorary LL.D. for microfilming documents in the Vatican Library. His work of microfilming Spanish documents for Loyola University in New Orleans merited him an honorary PhD in 1987. That same year the *American Historical Review* named him Historian of the Year. Leaving Rome, he did research from 1975 to 1978 at the University of Arizona at Tucson. From 1978 to 1988 he exercised pastoral ministry at Sacred Heart Church in El Paso.

His ministry also included teaching hundreds of Jesuits, mostly in the Juniorate, and by 1983 he had authored and/or edited some 174 books, articles and reviews, the majority on Jesuit history. He appeared on Vatican TV and commercial TV in El Paso; he taught catechism in Rome; and he visited the sick in hospitals in El Paso.

Earlier, in 1956, official records noted his weak physical health and "psychic worry." After a severe heart attack hindered his work and other major health problems mounted, he retired to Ignatius Residence in New Orleans in 1989.

Based on comments of many religious of the New Orleans Province, it is clear that he enjoyed the respect of his peers, who often had a good word to say about him.

Fr. Burrus died on Dec. 11, 1991, at age 84, truly a hero and God's scholar. He is buried at Grand Coteau.

Paul Louis Callens, SJ
1895 – 1970
Muscian, poet, playwright, he was a master of languages

Fr. Paul Louis Callens, SJ, was well-known for his innate command of languages and for his numerous contributions to scholarly journals.

His work appeared in *The Classical Outlook*, the *Classical Bulletin* and *Via Latina*, which published his Latin comedy verse-play, *Bubo et Cubo*. One of his major works, the book *Tata Vasco*, tells the story of a great Mexican reformer of the 16th century. It was published in Spanish and English in 1959 in Mexico, where he had done extensive research in Mexican history, one of his lifelong interests.

Born on Aug. 25, 1895, in Tourcoing, France, Callens began his early training with the De La Salle Christian Brothers and at the Apostolic School in Thieu, Belgium. His records say that on Oct. 6, 1914, he entered the Novitiate in Macon, Ga., "as a volunteer missionary."

After the typical Novitiate, he atypically spent only one year in the Juniorate. He studied philosophy at Mount St. Michael's, earning an M.A. in the process. Regency was spent at Immaculate Conception College in New Orleans. His study of theology was divided between the Spanish theologate at Oña and then at Valkenburg, Holland, from which he earned an STL. He was ordained on Aug. 29, 1926, in Enghien, Belgium.

Because of his exceptional command of languages, both ancient and modern, Fr. Callens taught languages to the young Jesuits at Grand Coteau for many years. He also taught at Loyola University, Spring Hill College and St. Charles College, as well as the Jesuit high schools of New Orleans, Shreveport and Tampa. While at Loyola, where he was the head of the classics department, he became the chaplain for the local Poor Clares, a ministry that lasted 15 years.

He was also a poet and a musician, and it is his words that are inscribed over the entrance to the former library at Loyola: *"The monuments which learned men have built for us throughout the ages you will find accumulated in these books."* Talented musically, he worked zealously to implement Pius X's *Motu Proprio* of Nov. 22, 1903, for the reform and elevation of church music. His contribution as director of choirs and composer of many successful hymns is one of his great legacies.

He was long associated with the famous Pius X School of Liturgical Music at Manhattanville, N.Y., where each summer he introduced young seminarians to the best in church music. He also attended the Solesmes School for church music study in France. His last assignment was to the Corpus Christi Minor Seminary, beginning his tenure there with the founding of the school.

At age 74, Fr. Callens, worn out in body but never in creativity nor imagination, died in Waterbury, Conn., on Dec. 1, 1970. He is buried at Grand Coteau.

James Devine Carroll, SJ
1905 – 1992
The work of the archivist

It is somewhat ironic that the data surrounding the life of Fr. James Devine Carroll are skimpy and lack facts about his birth, parentage, family and early life. The irony lies in the fact that Fr. Carroll devoted much of his life to the collection and organization of the history of the Jesuit Province in the Southern region.

Little is known of him from his birth on April 30, 1905, until he attended Boston College High School and then entered the Jesuit Order at Grand Coteau in 1923. He took his philosophy at Hillyard in Washington state and his theology at St. Mary's College in Kansas.

For eight years he served as a member of the provincial staff, and he worked for several years at retreat houses, mainly in Atlanta and Dallas. However, his main service to his Jesuit brethren was as the Province archivist.

In 1971, Father Provincial John Edwards, SJ, asked Fr. Carroll to draw up a job description for a Province archivist. Fr. Carroll described such a person as a "manager of all the stored information which can be of service to the major superiors of the Province…; (one who should) distinguish between Archivist's present task and future task…. His present task is to reduce the body of stored material to what should be permanently retained, and to systemize it for ease of recall…."

In March of that same year, Fr. Carroll described to the Provincial a major problem confronting the archivist:

"My organization of the records and archives on 'local departmentalizing by year, by subject, etc.' is less effective, and often enough an impossibility, because of the fact that so many letters that come to the Provincial's office are omnibuses: treating various subjects, confounding personnel and (causing) operational problems."

Carroll also expressed his desire to stimulate historians "by getting them hooked early on." He suggested a division of labor concerning the documents pertaining to the South. Since the houses in El Paso were closing at the time, Carroll suggested there was enough information available in Albuquerque for a dissertation on the Jesuits. Whoever would tackle that project "would need both Spanish and Italian, besides Latin – Did I say a dirty word? – for the early records are in those languages," Carroll noted.

Fr. Carroll labored for 20 years as the Province archivist. He died on March 15, 1992, at age 86. A Jesuit for 69 years, he is buried at Grand Coteau.

Felix Leo Clarkson, SJ
1908 – 1980
He promoted devotion to the Blessed Mother and Sacred Heart on two continents

Fr. Felix Leo Clarkson nurtured a lifelong devotion to Mary, the mother of God, and inspired many others to pray for her intercession.

Born on Aug. 9, 1908, in Lebanon, Ky., he received his primary schooling at St. Augustine in Lebanon (1915-25) and finished his secondary education at St. Mary's High School in St. Marys, Kan. Upon graduation, like many other young Jesuits, he immediately entered the Novitiate at Grand Coteau. After two years, he began first studies in the Juniorate (1928-30), and then studied philosophy at Mount St. Michael's in Spokane (1930-33). From Gonzaga University he earned an M.A. in philosophy and in English. He spent his Regency at Jesuit High in New Orleans (1933-36) and returned to St. Marys, Kan., to study theology (1936-40).

He was ordained June 21, 1939.

His first assignment was parochial work at St. John Berchmans Church in Shreveport, focusing especially on the promotion and care of Sodalities (1940-47), and he eventually became the diocesan director of Sodalities.

The New Orleans Province had just recently established a mission in Ceylon and interested persons were asked to volunteer. Fr. Clarkson was quick to respond. Upon arrival in Ceylon, he embraced the work of minister of the Jesuit community at St. Michael's College (1947-51) while also serving for a year as director of the minor seminary in the Diocese of Trincomalee (1949).

Progress in preaching the gospel depended on proficiency in Tamil, a very difficult language, and to that end Felix moved to a language school at Kamala, where he labored for two years (1951-53). Felix himself said that he "persevered with great tenacity of purpose in studying and learning the Tamil language."

He returned to Batticaloa to serve as assistant pastor of St. Sebastian's Church for two years (1953-55); he then did the same ministry in Thalankudah for 12 years (1955-67).

He was known as one who embraced popular devotions: He was a promoter of the Sacred Heart devotion, spiritual director of both the Legion of Mary and the St. Vincent de Paul Society, and advocate of praying the Rosary.

He returned to the New Orleans Province and was assigned as chaplain at Lafayette General Hospital (1970-72). He moved back to Grand Coteau as assistant pastor of St. Charles Borromeo Parish. His health weakened during this ministry and he had to retire to the infirmary at Grand Coteau.

Fr. Clarkson died on Aug. 13, 1980, at age 72, and is buried at Grand Coteau.

Raymond John Cody, SJ
1905 – 1974
The indispensable brother socius

Raymond John Cody's Jesuit priesthood preparation was nearly complete, but in his third year of theology he decided against being ordained.

Born in Minneapolis on Jan. 23, 1905, Cody entered the Society after graduating from Spring Hill College in 1924. He studied philosophy, taught in Tampa, New Orleans and Shreveport and then studied theology in St. Marys, Kan. Because he

was conflicted about the vocational direction he wanted to take, he was sent to Tertianship in the hope that he would choose the priesthood.

Eventually, however, Cody went to Florissant, Mo., to begin his Brother Novitiate. Years later he explained his decision in a letter to the Provincial. The following is an excerpt from that letter of Jan. 2, 1945:

> I am convinced that I should not go on to the priesthood, to priestly work, but rather ask to spend the rest of my life in the Society as a temporal coadjutor.... To me the brother's life holds no special attraction, naturally speaking. What appeals to me in the lay brotherhood of the Society is religious life in the Society, the life that I have been living happily for the past 20 years.

He went to Rome to be secretary to the American assistant. Upon his return to New Orleans, he served as the brother *socius* to several provincials (1946-69) and became indispensable to them.

Several generations of Jesuits had dealings with Bro. Cody because of his lengthy stint in the Province office. He read most of the incoming letters and typed the replies. Seldom did anyone speak ill of him and his work. All were spoken to or written to with respect, a respect which was reciprocated.

The last years of his life became difficult because of his declining health and memory. At one point the Province decided to hire lay typists, which meant nudging Bro. Cody aside. His perfectionism, which had served him well earlier, later became the concrete into which he had set his way.

His worst fear was to become useless, so he took on many jobs, such as making three trips daily to the post office and doing refectory chores. He would clean up breakfast dishes, set the supper table, serve coffee and later do the dishes. His service included giving rides to neighbors who were waiting for the bus and often chatting up the kids in the neighborhood. They responded by waving to him on his trips and even brought him flowers. They always wanted to tell him how their schoolwork and activities went.

As Fr. Tom Clancy said of him in his obituary: "Raymond John Cody, SJ, had all the virtues of an old-fashioned Jesuit. Many Jesuits to whom I owed a great deal are dead, but I don't remember any Jesuit death affecting me as much as Lew's."

Bro. Cody – nicknamed "Lew" because of his resemblance to a 1920s comedian named Lew – died on Christmas Eve 1974. He is buried at Grand Coteau.

Godfrey Joseph Cook, SJ
1902 – 1995
*From the U.S. to Spain to Ceylon,
he served with true devotion*

Fr. Godfrey Joseph Cook traveled the world in long and devoted service to God, teaching and leading retreats, ministering to the poorest of the poor in Ceylon, and adding to the legacy of a large, devout Jesuit family.

Godfrey Koch (later changed to "Cook") was born on Jan. 13, 1902, in Witten, Westphalia, Germany. Through his mother, he belonged to the Boemecke-Maring clan which produced 13 members of the New Orleans Province of the Society of Jesus, starting with Brother Ignatius Boemecke (1847). In 1913, at age 11 he went off with his cousin, Karl Maring, who was only 15 himself, to join the Jesuits of the South.

Upon entering the USA, Godfrey, as many immigrants did, changed his name from its German form, "Koch," to its English equivalent, "Cook." He attended St. Charles College in Grand Coteau, starting in 1913. Then, in 1917, at age 15, he entered St. Stanislaus Novitiate in Macon, Ga. But the Novitiate was destroyed by fire in 1921, so he continued his studies at St. Michael's in Spokane.

He later went to Cuba to learn Spanish and teach there. His fluency in that language allowed him to study theology in Spain.

Ordained in 1930, his ministry was varied. He taught at Spring Hill College and also worked in Grand Coteau as *socius* to the novice master. He served in various parishes, in San Antonio, Shreveport and Miami.

With the end of World War II, new windows opened for him. During the war, the mission of Trincomalee in Ceylon (which became known as Sri Lanka in 1972) became the responsibility of the New Orleans Province. Godfrey Cook was the first to volunteer to go there, although he waited until 1946 to travel with colleague Claude Daly.

His first work there was in schools, but he was most effective as a traveling missionary ministering to the people of eastern Ceylon in small towns and villages. He became an assistant to Fr. Henry Ponniah in Kalmunai caring for the churches down the coast, Akkaraipattu to Pottuvil.

Fr. Cook is noted for the care he gave to the Kuravars. If Ceylon had a caste system, the Kuravars would be the lowest of the low and the poorest of the poor. They were the country's gypsies, who lived on the fringes of society.

Harry Miller, SJ, commented on Fr. Cook and the Kuravars:

(He approached slack officials) he needed to approve his development work, initiating the whole Kuravar community to the church and building them into a fixed human community, fighting the fight in whatever form it rose before him, building churches … transforming a placid rural lot of people into a force for God under the banner of St. Michael Fighting.

With his hearing and vision impeded, he withdrew from his labors in 1988. He told his community that to his end he was committed to an active prayer life for his brother missionaries.

Fr. Cook died on June 15, 1995, at age 93. He is buried in Sri Lanka.

Auguste Dessommes Coyle, SJ
1910 – 1978
The man loved Shakespeare!

Auguste Dessommes Coyle was a servant of "the Word." He preached various *Tre Ore* services, gave commencement addresses, and conducted preached retreats. He kept boxes of notes for future speeches: homilies, retreat talks, commentary for special feast days.

His dramatic, rhetorical speech strove to move the hearts as well as the minds of his audience. He was a master of gestures; his head was crammed with illustrative stories; Shakespeare quotes were never far from his tongue. All were memorized, of course, so he could eye-ball his audience.

A native New Orleanian born on March 16, 1910, Coyle was privately tutored, but later matriculated at Jesuit High School and graduated from Spring Hill High School. He spent a year each at Spring Hill College and the University of Detroit (1928), after which he entered the Novitiate.

But he left the Novitiate after six weeks. He explained later:

I entered the Society in April, 1928, left the Novitiate within six weeks because of homesickness. The Master of Novices was absent from Novitiate most of that time because of illness. Readmitted into the Society by Fr. General Ledochowski at request of Fr. J. Salter, then provincial, who had been master of novices when I first entered.

Unlike that of many of his colleagues, his Jesuit formation was irregular: first year of philosophy at

Grand Coteau (1933-34) with the rest completed in St. Louis (1934-36). He taught one year at College Jean-de-Brébeuf in Montreal and two at Grand Coteau as a member of the Juniorate faculty. He studied theology at St. Marys, Kan. The record says he began Tertianship at Auriesville, N.Y., but did not finish the program.

"Gus" returned to the Juniorate, where he was a long-term Juniorate teacher (1944-67) and Juniorate dean (1950-67).

From 1967 to 1971 Fr. Coyle served as Rector-President of Jesuit High School in Tampa. In 1971 he was named pastor of Holy Name of Jesus Church in New Orleans, and he continued as associate pastor from 1974 until his death in 1978.

Fr. Coyle is remembered as an especially effective teacher of Shakespeare. He loved the language and the larger-than-life characters.

His second love was Vergil's *Aeneid*. He so desired that his students feel the drama and pathos of the epic that he scheduled readings of the Dido-Aeneas story at the grotto behind St. Charles College.

When things would go awry, he would sweep into the classroom with a new plan to do this or read that. He was the consummate monitor of oral readings in the college dining room. Generally, he pressed a yellow button to signal to the reader to slow down, but if he heard garbled sentences or mispronounced words, he hit the red button and called out "Repeat! Do it over, only correctly!"

Fr. Coyle was also the chaplain and senior religion teacher at the Academy of the Sacred Heart in Grand Coteau for nearly 20 years. Upon his death, to honor the work he had done for them, the alumnae established an annual scholarship in his name to be given to an incoming freshman with an ASH alumna relative.

Fr. Coyle died on Sept. 9, 1978, and is buried at Grand Coteau.

Harry Louis Crane, SJ
1906 – 1982
'A prodigious builder' and financial wiz

Fr. Harry Louis Crane's career lends credence to the idea that each person has certain strengths and gifts. His were the gifts of envisioning, planning and constructing much-needed buildings and for managing the finances for these projects as well as for the Province in general.

Born on April 28, 1906, Crane had the classic Catholic education of a native New Orleanian: Holy Name of Jesus School (1912-20) and then Jesuit High School (1920-24). He entered the Society at Grand Coteau in 1924, passing through the traditional stages of formation with ease: two years in the Juniorate, philosophy at Spokane, and Regency at Spring Hill College (1931-35). He began his study of theology in Valkenburg, Holland (1935-37) then transferred to St. Marys, Kan. (1937-39).

Harry was a true peripatetic. After two years teaching in the Juniorate, he served as assistant dean at Loyola in New Orleans and then as *socius* to the provincial. At 38, he began a six-year stint as the provincial of the New Orleans Province, beginning in 1944. Afterwards he served as spiritual father at Jesuit High in New Orleans (1951-53), then the rector of the school (1953-59). He returned to Grand Coteau to teach Latin; he also served as rector of the college (1962-67).

Because Fr. Crane was observed to have strong skills in finance, he served as Province treasurer (1967-72). He greatly improved the finances of the Province by establishing the Retirement Fund and creating a Financial Advisory Board.

Fr. Crane's own provincial, Thomas H. Stahel, preaching at Harry's funeral, cited from the Gospel of Luke (14:28-33) the parable about beginning to build but first sitting down to estimate the cost. Of Harry, he said, "He was a prodigious builder; he laid foundations and erected towers."

As a fundraiser and supervisor, he built the House of Studies at Spring Hill. While at Jesuit High in New Orleans, he raised the money needed to fund and construct the Recreation Center (1953-54). As rector of St. Charles College, he laid the foundation for the new wing housing the new chapel, kitchen and dining room (1963-64). But he was hardly finished; he also supervised the building of St. Ignatius Church in Mobile (1977-81). Fr. Crane knew how to solicit funds and how to use them for needed, quality structures.

He was a pleasant person with a modest demeanor. Like many Jesuits, he had a keen, dry wit and an eye for humor. Few, if any, thought his wit cruel or unkind. His correspondence is full of flashes of wit, a readiness to laugh, often at his own expense. Those who lived with Harry remember him as a wise person whose opinions were regularly sought, who was deeply solicitous of the welfare of those in his care, and who was just fun to be with.

On Sept. 8, 1982, Fr. Crane died at age 76. He is buried at Grand Coteau.

Michael J. Cronin, SJ
1878 – 1962
'Truck Driver Mike'

In 1889, when Fr. John Whitney, SJ, visited the village of Darrindaffe near Listowel in County Kerry, Ireland, in search of vocations for the New Orleans Mission, he hit a gold mine.

Living there were two Cronin brothers married to two sisters. One had 12 children and the other had 13.

These two families contributed six vocations to the missions. They were Michael F. (1871-1936), Dan (1877-1957), Timothy (1881-1940), Michael J. (1878-1962), John (1873-1939), and Patrick (1883-1958). There were other Cronins in the Province – Patrick (d. 1951), Jack (d. 1972) and John (d. 1891) – who were not related to the above families. (Fr. Thomas J. Cronin, SJ, 1920-2005, was a nephew of the first family mentioned above.)

Fr. Mike, sometimes called "Truck Driver Mike," was the last of the Cronin cousins to die, and his life is a good example of the service these two families rendered to the Church. He entered the Society in Macon, Ga., in January of 1898. After his ordination and Tertianship he was engaged almost exclusively in pastoral work in Texas, Louisiana, Alabama, Georgia and Florida.

He always showed a divine preference for the poor and the downtrodden. They knew where his heart was and learned to call for him when they came to the rectory for help. The poor Cubans of Florida called him "El Santo."

Some of his best work was done in Miami, where he labored from 1936 to 1948 to develop the mission among African-Americans. His efforts resulted in St. Mary of the Missions and St. Francis Xavier Church. He was an ardent beggar for his flock and was tireless in presenting their needs to the Church and to the civic community.

In his seventies, Fr. Cronin worked in Key West, where he heard confessions, took door duty and helped the people. He celebrated his Diamond Jubilee there in 1958 and was honored by the City three years later upon his departure for Spring Hill.

Fr. Cronin died there on Aug. 9, 1962, and was laid to rest alongside his brothers John (d. 1939) and Patrick (d. 1958) at Spring Hill.

John Edward Curley, SJ
1909 – 1984
An abiding love of rhetoric

People who knew John Edward Curley said that from his earliest Jesuit education he already knew exactly what he wanted to do when ordained: to preach the word of God effectively and to as many people as possible.

Born in Baltimore, Md., on Oct. 2, 1909, he graduated from the local Loyola High School (1929), followed by one year at Loyola University of Baltimore. On Aug. 26, 1930, John arrived at the Novitiate in Grand Coteau, where he began the traditional course of priestly formation: Juniorate (1932-34), philosophy at St. Louis University (1934-37), Regency at St. John's College in Shreveport (1937-40), and theology at St. Mary's College (1940-44). He was ordained on June 22, 1943.

As a preaching Jesuit, he downplayed certain aspects of his intellectual training, namely, Greek, Latin and philosophy, in favor of rhetoric. It seems that any opportunity to speak was heaven to him. Jack loved reading orally at table, debating and performing in the Juniorate's plays. Indeed, he enjoyed every form of verbal expression.

It came as no surprise that immediately after ordination Fr. Curley was assigned to the Jesuit Mission Band. Since the Mission Band was not located in one place, its members traveled to towns and villages giving missions, retreats, sermons, etc. It was exhausting work but also a labor of love. It probably did not hurt Jack's command of his audience that he looked like the popular actor Humphrey Bogart and spoke with the same throaty voice.

He labored in the Mission Band for 24 years, from 1946 to 1970. During this period he became a zealous champion for the Apostleship of Prayer. An advocate of the devotion to the Sacred Heart, Jack became a regular speaker on Sacred Heart Radio and local TV in St. Louis, beginning his broadcasting in 1956.

He gravitated toward preaching retreats. He eventually served as director of Montserrat Retreat House (1972-75), then as assistant director at Manresa House of Retreats (1983).

In the late '70s, he suffered a debilitating stroke

and recovered slowly at Ignatius Residence in New Orleans. When Jack seemed ready to resume his ministry, he was assigned to Manresa. But after another stroke, he retired permanently to the Province's infirmary.

Fr. Curley died on May 8, 1984, and is buried at Grand Coteau.

He is described in an obituary written by a close friend:

"Many of us will always remember Jack as a pleasant companion, an enthusiastic storyteller, a practical prankster, an outstanding orator, an effective retreat director and tireless promoter of the Apostleship of Prayer throughout the South....

"I hope that all of us will try to realize what good one man was able to accomplish for time and eternity, for God and his fellow men."

Edward P. Curry, SJ
1914 – 1963
An excellent principal,
a master raconteur

In a religious order committed to education, high school principals are precious resources. Many excellent principals have served in the New Orleans Province, but none was more successful than Fr. Edward P. Curry.

The function of a Jesuit principal is to be the leader of an educational team and the ruler of adolescent and often unruly boys. He also has to form the young scholastics sent to teach in his school. So, succeeding at the job requires a wide range of skills, including teaching, personnel management and diplomacy.

Fr. Curry's preferred place of instruction was the *haustus*, or break room. He loved to tell stories and was a master raconteur. One of his companions wrote at his death:

[Ed had] a seemingly endless repertory of anecdotes. And through all his stories there was a sameness, a pattern, a common denominator which, once understood by his hearers, intrigued them. This thread which knitted together all the incidents he related was his simple fascination for the sheer joy of living and working with his brother Jesuits.

Edward Curry was born in New Orleans on Jan. 18, 1914. During his student years at Jesuit High he was strongly influenced by another great principal, Fr. Percy Roy. Upon his graduation in 1931 he entered the Society and made the regular course of

studies in the Society at Grand Coteau, St. Louis and St. Marys. In his Regency at Shreveport he showed great promise, and his first assignment was to be assistant principal in Dallas. He was there for six years (1946-52), moving up to the role of principal for the last three.

In 1954 he was sent to Jesuit High in Tampa, where he reorganized the curriculum during the time when the school was departing from its downtown location and moving to new facilities. Jesuit High in Tampa grew and flourished under his leadership.

Fr. Curry was among the group of 14 priests who pioneered the short-lived Tertianship at Grand Coteau in 1945. Strangely enough, four tertians in that class died at age 50 or younger. In Ed's case it was a heart attack. He had become obese in his later years, probably because all his pastimes were indoor, sedentary ones.

On June 27, 1963, Fr. Curry died in Tampa at the age of 49, having enriched the lives of many a young man. He is buried at Spring Hill.

Joseph Michael Dardis, SJ
1912 – 1977
Mentor and director of Jesuits
in their early formation

Despite ill health, Fr. Joseph Michael Dardis spent his life in service to the young men in his classroom, to his many parishioners, and to the seminarians he mentored.

Born into a large New Orleans family on Dec. 21, 1912, he was schooled locally and graduated from Jesuit High. He entered the Novitiate at Grand Coteau on July 30, 1929, and began his road to ordination: Juniorate (1931-34), philosophy in St. Louis (1934-36), and Regency at Jesuit High in New Orleans.

However, he became ill and spent his next and final year of preparation convalescing in El Paso (1937-38). Respecting his illness, he forewent the winters of Kansas for the perpetual spring of Alma, Calif. Even so, he remained in poor health, so in 1939 he was sent to Montezuma Seminary in Montezuma, N.M. He was ordained with his class at St. Mary's College on June 18, 1941.

His ministry extended across three different apostolates. He served as assistant pastor at St. Francis Xavier Church in Albuquerque (1944-45) and a decade later he was pastor of San Felipe

Church in Old Town Albuquerque (1954-55). He taught briefly at St. John's High School in Shreveport (1949-50) and Jesuit High in New Orleans (1966-67). Although Joe was not at his best in the classroom, he did teach many young men. Records are scarce, but most novices and juniors at Grand Coteau learned Latin from him.

However, his most significant ministry was related to seminary formation, both for various dioceses and for the Society of Jesus. Right after ordination and coinciding with his ministry at St. Francis Xavier, he served at Lourdes Seminary in Albuquerque (1944-46) and then at Immaculate Heart of Mary in Santa Fe (1946-49). He was one of the founding fathers who established Corpus Christi Minor Seminary and served on the Novitiate staff 1960-63 and 1967-72. He also worked at the Novitiate in Grand Coteau for a dozen years, 1950-54, 1955-60 and 1963-65.

In every place he served it is noted that he was a dedicated and appreciated "spiritual father" and counselor. He was trusted by the Society of Jesus to be a mentor and director of Jesuits in their early formation. The following remarks, taken from an obituary for Fr. Dardis, come from a colleague at Corpus Christi Minor Seminary:

> *Father Dardis was a community man. Any room he walked into brightened as he would begin his routine of corn-ball jokes and imitations, all full of delight and wry comment. As a religious he was faithful to his calling as well as his routine. As a priest he was zealous, having spent most of his years here at the Seminary on regular Sunday supply at the same small Spanish mission. As a confessor he was always gentle....*

The death of Fr. Dardis came abruptly. While taking his daily jog, he suffered a heart attack and died on April 30, 1977, in Corpus Christi. He is buried at Grand Coteau.

All in all, Joe Dardis was a "spiritual father" for 32 years, 29 of them in seminaries or novitiates.

Emmanuel de la Moriniere, SJ
1856 – 1930
The greatest preacher of his day

By the mid-twentieth century the apostolic gift most prized by Jesuits was learning. But for the first century of the New Orleans Mission the highest prestige was attached to pulpit eloquence. Many Jesuit priests were celebrated preachers, but arguably the greatest of all was Emmanuel de la Moriniere, known familiarly as "Fr. DeLam."

Born in Belle Terre, the capital of the island of Guadeloupe, he immigrated with his family to New Orleans, where he was enrolled in the Jesuit college. Early on, he expressed a desire to be a priest and so he entered the Novitiate at Grand Coteau on Sept. 8, 1873. In Regency at Spring Hill, he became acquainted with Fr. Abram Ryan, the renowned priest-poet of the Confederacy, who had been ordained the year Fr. de la Moriniere was born.

Fr. de la Moriniere studied philosophy and theology at Woodstock, Md., and was ordained in Baltimore in 1888. As a teacher and preacher, from 1890 to 1918 he served at Galveston, Macon, Spring Hill, Immaculate Conception Church in New Orleans, and Grand Coteau. Everywhere he went, he won the reputation of an outstanding pulpit orator.

When Spring Hill burned in 1909 he traveled through the cities of the North raising funds for the reconstruction of the college by giving lectures on Shakespeare. Professional actors came to hear him so they could imitate his art.

It was the heyday of the Chautauqua societies, when audiences flocked to hear the florid oratory of men such as William Jennings Bryan, Fr. DeLam's contemporary. The adult-education and entertainment events were long and the language was lush, but it was very much a style reflecting the tastes of the day. For example:

> *...You might as well try to shear the sun of his beams, to strip the moon of her silver mantle, to pluck by the roots yon Rocky Mountains, to check the flow or drain the basin of the Mississippi River, as to sever the tie which binds the Catholic Church to Louisiana from the very moment when the settler's axe cleared her tangled forests, and the navigator's sail opened to the traffic of the world her countless water courses.*

His discourses, some of which lasted nearly three hours, were written out beforehand, but he never used a paper in the pulpit or on the speaker's stand. At the height of his powers, Fr. DeLam was in great demand for grand occasional discourses, such as for the Centennial of the Louisiana Purchase in New Orleans (1903), and at the dedication of the Bienville monument (1906) and the statue of Fr. Abram Ryan (1913). These talks were published by Dr. James Nix in 1927 under the title *Discourses*.

On Oct. 21, 1930, Fr. de la Moriniere, a celebrated and gifted man who dedicated his life in service to God's people, died in New Orleans at age 64. He is buried at Grand Coteau.

James De Potter, SJ
1855 – 1933
Teacher of metaphysics and ethics

Born in Belgium on July 12, 1855, James De Potter attended the famous apostolic school at Turnhout that was founded by Peter De Nef, a devout layman, shortly after the Restoration of the Society. Many of the Belgian and Dutch recruits who worked with the American Jesuits in the 19th century were graduates of this school for aspiring missionaries.

He entered the Society at Grand Coteau in April of 1875 and early on showed a lively intellect and a flair for teaching. He was master of many subjects but most of his life he taught metaphysics and ethics. Many of the Jesuits who entered the Province in the late 19th and early 20th century received their philosophical formation from Fr. "De Pot."

From 1907 to 1918 he was *socius* to the provincial in New Orleans, while often continuing his teaching on a part-time basis at the old Jesuit College on Baronne Street. At various times in his life he also gave lectures on education to the scholastics.

Fr. De Potter was rector at St. Stanislaus College in Macon, Ga., when the disastrous fire struck in early November of 1921. The fire destroyed the buildings and consumed thousands of priceless volumes. After barely escaping the flames, Fr. De Potter shepherded his flock of novices and juniors into makeshift quarters until they were installed at Grand Coteau to begin the 1922 school year.

Fr. De Potter's tertian instructor was the famous Jesuit Venerable Adolph Petit, and there were great similarities between their temperaments and spiritualities. He was a quiet, gentle man who was never known to utter an unkind word and who dealt with souls with a suavity born of love.

He was an active teacher right up to the time when he succumbed to a fatal illness. At the age of 78, Fr. De Potter died, on Nov. 5, 1933, in New Orleans and is buried at Grand Coteau.

John Vincent Deignan, SJ
1891 – 1966
Doctor of chemistry

Although he spent most of his life in the United States, Fr. John Vincent Deignan never became a citizen. He was, however, a prominent chemist and member of various professional groups in the American science community.

John's record of his schooling begins with his graduation in 1905 from Presentation Seminary in Birr, Ireland, near his hometown of Bailieborough. He got his secondary education at Mungret College (1905-08) and The National University (1908-10).

Much of his schooling in Ireland was with the Jesuits, and when he chose to enter the Society he traveled from Ireland to Macon, Ga., to begin his Novitiate. His formation was traditional: at Macon two years each in the Novitiate and the Juniorate (1910-14) and three years at Woodstock College studying philosophy (1914-17). His Regency was spent at Spring Hill College (1917-22), a place to which he would return to teach chemistry for 37 years. He studied theology at Montreal and was ordained on June 30, 1924.

Showing an affinity for science, Fr. Deignan did special studies in chemistry at Fordham (1927-29), earning a PhD. With doctorate in hand, he returned to Spring Hill to teach chemistry and to build and promote the chemistry department. In 1929, he was made chairman of the department. Although chemistry was a poor sibling to the physics and biology departments, he became one of the most influential professors and helped advance well-qualified students into medical school and doctoral studies.

As one would expect, he was prominent in various professional societies. Fr. Deignan was a Fellow of the American Association for the Advancement of Science (A.A.A.S.), a member of the Chemical Society and a Fellow of the group Organic Chemists. In time, Fr. Deignan became emeritus professor of chemistry (1958).

He lived to celebrate his Golden Jubilee, the 50th anniversary of his entrance into the Society. Eventually his strength weakened and he was forced to slow down.

Fr. Deignan died on June 19, 1966, and is buried at Spring Hill.

Jean Delanglez, SJ
1896 – 1949
Renowned scholar
of American Jesuit history

Jean Delanglez had a brilliant, though short-lived career as a scholar of American Jesuit history.

An author of renown, he was passionate about chronicling the American colonial history of the Jesuits, particularly that of the Society in the South before the Suppression.

He was born Jan. 14, 1896, to Jean-Baptiste and Marie-Louise Deinze Delanglez in Mouscron, a little Belgian town right across the border from Lille, France. He finished his schooling under the clouds of World War I and came to America in 1921 to enter the Society.

He completed his Novitiate in Grand Coteau in 1923. He took his philosophy in Spokane at Mount St. Michaels's, and then made a year of Regency. This was followed by theology in Dublin, where he was ordained in 1931.

His first priestly assignment was graduate studies in history at Catholic University of America in Washington, D.C. The famed Dr. Peter Guilday, the preeminent authority on the history of American Catholicism, directed his doctoral thesis, *The French Jesuits in Lower Louisiana, 1700-1763*, which was published in 1935. It is the definitive study of the Louisiana Jesuits before the Suppression.

Toward the end of his Tertianship he suffered a severe heart attack. Because of his health and an Assistancy commitment to the Institute of Jesuit History – which had recently been established at Loyola of Chicago – superiors assigned him exclusively to research for the Institute. He never did any teaching except for one semester of a graduate seminar.

At the time there was a great deal of interest in American Jesuit history. Fr. Gilbert Garraghan, SJ, had just brought out his 3-volume *Jesuits of the Middle United States* (1938). Fr. Delanglez later helped to get *Garraghan's Guide to Historical Method* through the presses.

Jean Delanglez worked on colonial history with a passion. He haunted the halls of the Newberry Library in Chicago and soon came to be recognized as an authority on the French colonial period not only in the U.S. but in Canada and France as well. The Canadian government so admired him that they even named a peninsula after him, *Presqu'ile Delanglez*.

He is the renowned author of dozens of scholarly articles and several weighty books, including *Some La Salle Journeys* (1938), *Frontenac and the Jesuits* (1940), and *Life and Voyages of Louis Joliet, 1645-1700* (1948).

Fr. Delanglez died on May 9, 1949, at Loyola University in Chicago and is buried in Chicago.

W. Patrick Donnelly, SJ
1908 – 1967
The legendary optimist

Fr. W. Patrick Donnelly is one of the Jesuits of the Province around whom legends cluster, most of them having to do with his penchant for saying the wrong thing at the wrong time.

One example concerns his conversation with a group of men in the parlor car on the L & N railroad. The talk turned to football and Pat announced that he had it on good authority that Henry Frnka, then coach at Tulane, would soon be fired. One of the gentlemen contested his statement, and it was only when Pat was well into his rebuttal that it was pointed out to him that he was arguing with Mr. Frnka himself.

But he must have done something right because he was beloved by thousands of people and is considered one of the first truly successful fund-raisers in the history of the Province.

Born in Augusta, Ga., on March 12, 1908, Pat finished school and worked for a year before entering the Society in September of 1927. During his philosophy at St. Louis University he developed a keen interest in history and wrote as his master's thesis an excellent monograph on Jesuit explorer Pierre Jean De Smet, the founder of many American missions.

However, he was not destined to pursue this interest. After teaching at Spring Hill College, taking theology at St. Mary's College and doing his Tertianship at Pomfret Center in Connecticut he worked in administration with hardly a letup from 1942 until his death 25 years later.

He was principal of Jesuit High in New Orleans from 1942 to 1946, rector-president of Spring Hill College from 1946 to 1952, rector-president at Loyola University from 1952 to 1961 and then, after a respite in the Tampa parish, served as rector-president of Jesuit High in El Paso from 1962 until his death.

Pat was the soul of optimism. He was full of projects, dreams and plans, and he had the infectious enthusiasm to get laymen interested in those plans.

It is no discredit to his predecessors in Mobile and New Orleans to say that he was the first Jesuit to make those communities really sensitive to their obligations to support Catholic higher education.

Nor in his zeal for support did he temper Catholic social teachings. When people at Loyola complained to him about Fr. Lou Twomey's social justice efforts, he would launch into a sales pitch about their obligation to support the University.

He had a charm that people found difficult to resist. He used to give a talk at Loyola, at the beginning of every year, in which he compared the Jesuit community to a team. He always emphasized that he was the quarterback.

His death came as a surprise since he was a sparely built, tall man, full of energy. Fr. Donnelly died on Sept. 2, 1967, at only 59 years old, and is buried at Spring Hill.

Leo Thomas Dowling, SJ
1873 – 1956
He excelled in service to the sick and reclaiming neglectful Catholics

Fr. Leo Thomas Dowling had a keen interest in literature and a refined taste for poetry. He was a charming man with a fine sense of humor and unfailing affability.

A native of New Orleans, he was born on April 19, 1873, and received his education at the Jesuit college in his hometown. After entering the Society at Macon, Ga., in 1889, his progress in formation was straightforward: philosophy at Grand Coteau, Regency at St. Mary's University in Galveston, theology at Woodstock, and ordination on June 28, 1903. He then taught for five years in Galveston before his Tertianship.

Fr. Dowling taught the juniors at Macon for nine years, utilizing his own love of literature and sense of humor to succeed in building their interest in books and love of reading. He enjoyed the company of young Jesuits and retained an openness to new and novel ideas. He left Macon in 1917 and taught poetry at Loyola, was assistant pastor in Mobile, and then returned to Loyola, where he taught until 1926.

After many fruitful years in the classroom, he devoted the rest of his life to pastoral duties – at Augusta, Selma, New Orleans, El Paso, Albuquerque, Grand Coteau, Shreveport, West Palm Beach and Macon. In his pastoral work, Leo excelled in service to the sick and had an unusual gift for re-

claiming neglectful Catholics. He seldom "talked religion." He brought people things to read; by his humor he brightened many days of those who suffered. In a disarming way, he would leave a Sacred Heart badge with the sick. When the time came to hear confessions, he always said the right thing most amiably. He was by no means an orator, but he had an informal, personal appeal and a happy smile to go with it.

Colleagues remembered Leo as an ideal community man who was interested in the work of his fellow Jesuits. His conversation had the light touch of humor. With a bit of banter and even a song, Leo would enliven the recreation of his brother Jesuits.

In May 1955, Leo suffered a partial stroke. All admired his patience and cheerfulness in the face of this disability and his remarkable determination to return to his former activities. However, only rarely could he say Mass, and he needed special help to attend daily Mass as his health failed. He was hospitalized first in Gulfport, Miss., then taken to Mercy Hospital in New Orleans.

On Aug. 7, 1956, Fr. Dowling died at age 83. He is buried at Grand Coteau.

Edward Allen Doyle, SJ
1914 – 1979
Vice president of Loyola, president of Jesuit High

Because Edward Allen Doyle's father was in the military service, the Doyle family moved constantly. Edward, who was born in Columbia, S.C., on July 14, 1914, began his education at Ft. Benning, Ga.

The family moved to Honolulu, where he attended the prestigious Punahou School (1922-25), then it was off to Xavier Prep in Manhattan (1925-27), followed by graduation from Aquinas High in Columbus, Ohio (1931). He took his college diploma with honors from Georgetown University (1931-35). He himself served as a second lieutenant in the Reserve Corps of the U.S. Army and made a striking first impression: military, athletic and handsome.

Although it was an odd time of year to enter the Novitiate, Ed arrived at Grand Coteau on Nov. 16, 1935. The course of his studies was irregular because Ed already had a college degree. Therefore, he had one year in the Juniorate, two years studying philosophy, Regency first at Grand Coteau and then at Jesuit High in New Orleans (1941-43), and theology at St. Marys, Kan. He earned a PhD in education at Catholic University, graduating in 1953.

In 1951 Fr. Doyle became the dean of the faculty of Loyola University, a position he would hold for 15 years. At the same time, he was vice-president of the university, a member of the board of directors, dean of the College of Arts and Sciences, a member of the Executive Committee of the Graduate Division of Education, and an associate professor of education.

He was quickly made a full professor, a rise in rank solely based on publications. In addition to his published dissertation, *Status and Function of the Departmental Chairman*, he was the author of subsequent publications, including the proceedings of the *Deans' Institute in Santa Clara University* and *Changing the Trend of Jesuit High School Graduates to Attend Non-Catholic Colleges* (1955).

The provincial asked him to be the director of higher education for the Province (1959-61). Soon he was asked to be the principal of Jesuit High in New Orleans and then its president (1967-74).

Life for Fr. Ed Doyle was more than teaching and administration: He also excelled at priestly and pastoral ministry. For a brief time, he served as pastor of Immaculate Conception Church in New Orleans (1974-75).

Many spoke of him as a "courteous priest," a humble man, who loved his friends and was loved in return. He had a marvelous sense of humor and delighted in combing obituaries for curious and surprising nicknames. He reveled in author Damon Runyon and his characters; Ed especially delighted in "Hot Horse Herbie," "Nicely Nicely" and "Miss Cutie Singleton."

Fr. Doyle died on Dec. 29, 1979, at age 65 and is buried at Grand Coteau.

David Ross Druhan, SJ
1899 – 1968
A great Christian gentleman

In his lifetime Fr. David Ross Druhan's geniality was proverbial. He was a most likeable fellow who got along well with virtually everyone, all of the time.

Although prematurely gray, he had the trim physique and springy step of an athlete and used to join the novices and juniors in their ball games.

He and his brother, John, entered the Society at Macon, Ga., John in 1914 and Ross two years later. Since Ross was destined to teach in the Juniorate he had only one year of Regency in New Orleans

and then went to theology with the French Jesuits in Enghien, Belgium. A superb athlete and a joyful companion, he made lifelong friends in his seminary years.

Eventually Fr. Druhan arrived at the Juniorate in Grand Coteau, where he taught for five years. After a year in Tampa he matriculated at Catholic University for a doctorate in classics. He didn't really relish the scholarly life and was reticent to discuss his thesis concerning Venerable Bede's *Ecclesiastical History*. In 1938, he returned to Grand Coteau as rector and soon added the duties of classics professor and dean.

In 1945 he went to the newly established Jesuit High in Dallas where he served a six-year term as rector-principal at the downtown school. During these years he became a Province consultor, following in the footsteps of his brother John, who had served from 1939 to 1948. From 1952 to 1959 he served as Province prefect of studies. In 1957 he was elected by the Provincial Congregation as a delegate from the Province to the 30th General Congregation in Rome.

His last major charge was to join a team of Jesuits beginning a new work of the Society at Corpus Christi Minor Seminary, where he served as rector from 1960 to 1966. His forte had always been fostering good relations with the diocesan clergy, and this assignment gave full play to this grace. He also held together his community in the very difficult pioneering days.

Perhaps his greatest apostolate was the help he gave the priests and religious of the diocese. He was, to cite one example, very helpful to the Sisters of the Most Holy Sacrament in revising their rule. It is hard to find anyone who did not love him or who had ever heard another Jesuit say a harsh word about him. He was a great Christian gentleman.

At age 68, on Nov. 22, 1968, Fr. Druhan died at Spring Hill College, where he is buried.

Gabino Evaristo Egana, SJ
1891 – 1969

A spirit of generosity:
He gave without counting the cost

Gabino Evaristo Egana was a missionary of the "old school," a generous soul who worked tirelessly on behalf of those entrusted to his care.

Born at Deusto, Vizcaya, Spain, on June 12, 1891, he entered the Society of Jesus at Loyola,

Guipúzcoa, on July 2, 1909, and pronounced his vows in Naples, Italy, on July 3, 1911.

After coming to the United States, he was assigned to the Denver Mission. But needing to complete his formation, he went to Woodstock, Md., for philosophy. His Regency was conducted at Xavier High in New York, Regis College in Denver and Rockhurst College in Kansas City. He studied theology in St. Louis and was ordained on June 26, 1921.

When the Denver Mission was dissolved, in 1919, Fr. Egana became a member of the New Orleans Province. He spent the majority of his active life in parish work in the Southwest, particularly in Texas and New Mexico: Sacred Heart and Holy Family in El Paso; and St. Ignatius, Immaculate Conception, San Felipe and St. Francis Xavier in Albuquerque.

In the last years of his ministry, he served in other Jesuit apostolates. He worked for two years as a religion and English teacher, as well as spiritual father for the Jesuit community at Arbusto, Puerto Rico. Then he spent two years at Canisius House in El Paso (1959-61) and two years at Jesuit High in New Orleans (1963-65).

His last few active years were spent at Guadalupe Church in San Antonio. Though he could no longer drive or hear very well, he volunteered to handle all the funerals, a service greatly appreciated by the other Jesuits. Despite his physical ailments, his mind was razor sharp, and he brought lively conversation to the community in which he lived.

He worked without counting the cost. He never thought of himself first and was always apologetic when he needed something or could not perform some task. A man of sensitive and refined feelings often exposed to the crudities of human nature, he treated all as children of God.

Especially in his long, last illness did he show the courage of his life. When asked how he felt, he would tell the truth, but without any sign of complaint. He accepted his death as he accepted his priestly life – from God's hands.

When his poor health finally became too much of a burden for him to carry out his ministry, he moved to Grand Coteau, where he could be cared for better in the infirmary. On Sept. 5, 1969, Fr. Egana died peacefully at age 78. He is buried at Grand Coteau.

Louis John Eisele, SJ
1912 – 1988
The creative mind of 'Father Earthquake'

Earthquakes, science and engineering held the attention of Fr. Louis John Eisele through much of his industrious and productive lifetime.

Born Aug. 1, 1912, in Tampa, Fr. Eisele graduated in 1929 from Sacred Heart College, now known as Jesuit High, in Tampa, and then entered the Novitiate in 1930. He followed a regular formation path with philosophy in St. Louis, special studies for an M.A. in physics, Regency at Spring Hill College and then theology at St. Marys, Kan.

After ordination in 1944, Fr. Eisele taught at Spring Hill, where for the next 40 years he was a general instructor in physics and electronics.

However, Lou is most celebrated for his directorship of the Spring Hill College Seismograph Station. He was continually improving the seismograph and recorders at the Spring Hill Station. He invented the "Eisele AC Transducer" pen-and-ink seismic station. He installed a new seismographic electronic recording unit at Spring Hill, the first in the nation. The new machine could record the progress of a quake, indicating its duration and severity, thus giving meteorologists potentially life-saving information.

Seismologists were wont to contact Fr. Eisele for more precise data on the location and magnitude of a quake anywhere in North America. A colleague in Panama City, Fla., once asked him to find out if an earthquake was north or south of his position, and Lou nailed the location with pinpoint accuracy.

Fr. Eisele was the first person in the world to record an 8.5 earthquake in Alaska in 1964. Colleagues and students called him "Father Earthquake," an accurate nickname.

Besides the universal respect he earned as an inventor of seismograph recording equipment and the renown he enjoyed for the accuracy of his recordings, Fr. Eisele also had the acclaim of his peers in Alabama. In 1959 he was named an honorary-lifetime member in the Mobile Engineers Club, and he served as president of the Alabama Academy of Science in 1962-63. He was voted membership in the South Alabama Chapter of the National Safety

Council and subsequently elected to its board of directors and executive committee.

Fr. Eisele was not the easiest Jesuit on the faculty to live with or to have as a teacher. He was a private person, saying a private Mass in a very orderly way. When the mandates of the Second Vatican Council reached Mobile, young Jesuits found it difficult to converse with him because he was critical of the Council.

Ultimately, though, he was known as a superior craftsman. An associate once commented, "He was mechanically knowledgeable in many ways."

And Lou constantly said, "Man made it, I can fix it."

Fr. Eisele died on Dec. 3, 1988, and is buried at his beloved Spring Hill College.

Joseph Marie Paul Emile Elfer, SJ
1873 – 1958
*More than just a teacher
of physics and chemistry,
he even made some
of the lab equipment*

The ingenious and eccentric Joseph Marie Paul Emile Elfer, SJ, had the capacity to make violins, popcorn machines and telescopes, to bind books and to write commentaries on St. John of the Cross, which he printed in his room – somehow.

Beginning in 1941, Paul Emile wore a linen smock and rarely cut his hair. A friend once commented:

"He struck me as odd because he wore his hair long, almost to his shoulders, and also sported rimless crescent-shaped glasses…. He lived in a room with all kinds of stuff in it; he roasted green coffee beans, ground them, and dripped his coffee, very strong indeed, in his room."

Born in New Orleans on Aug. 17, 1873, Paul Emile entered the Society on Oct. 1, 1890, at Macon and followed the usual course of studies, eventually being ordained on June 29, 1903. He labored primarily in the high schools of the Province and began teaching at Spring Hill High School, before moving to Jesuit High in Tampa, then to Jesuit High in New Orleans (1916-17), and later to Galveston (1917-22). He returned to Spring Hill for four years (1922-26) and then went to Jesuit High in New Orleans (1926-30).

Following a four-year stint at Manresa House of Retreats (1930-34), he was the pastor at Immaculate Conception Parish in New Orleans (1934-41) and then assistant pastor at St. Charles Borromeo in Grand Coteau (1941-48). He concluded his labors with a decade at Jesuit High in New Orleans (1948-58).

Fr. Elfer was colorful and ingenious. In Regency he taught "stenog-typewriting," which he continued at Spring Hill. Primarily he was a professor of physics and chemistry; for six years he supervised the laboratories and classrooms dedicated to chemistry and physics in Jesuit schools. And he manufactured much of the laboratory equipment himself.

Sometime in the mid-1950s, his health began to fail and he was eventually hospitalized – for the first time in his life. Fr. Elfer suffered a fatal stroke and died at age 84, on April 18, 1958, and is buried at Grand Coteau.

The provincial wrote posthumously:

Now a teacher, now an associate, this father will be remembered as a confessor to externs and to ours. He was a man of great and diverse enterprises…. He possessed childlike simplicity and the spirit of charity. On earth he marveled at all he made; in heaven he will marvel at all the heavenly wonders which will be in his care…. (translated from the Latin)

Clyde Joseph Elliot, SJ
1915 – 1977
*He was one of five religious
from the same New Orleans home*

Clyde Joseph Elliot was born in New Orleans on Sept. 25, 1915, into that wonderful, prolifically Catholic Elliot household that produced five religious.

After graduation from Jesuit High School in 1933, he attended Loyola for a year, then entered the Novitiate in 1934 and began the typical course of study for Jesuit priests: philosophy at Spring Hill College (1938-41), a year at St. Louis University doing graduate studies in mathematics (1941-42), Regency at Spring Hill (1942-44), and theology at St. Mary's College (1944-48). He was ordained on June 18, 1947.

He spent the traditional *biennium* (two years of

course work in philosophy prior to a dissertation) at Gregorian University in Rome (1949-51), earning his doctorate in 1952. He was also a member of the philosophy faculty of the Jesuit House of Studies, a part of Spring Hill College, from 1951 to 1966. Thus, he was responsible for the intellectual formation of young Jesuits. Next, he spent a year at Loyola University and returned to Spring Hill in 1968. He was assigned to live at the provincial's residence in New Orleans in 1969 to begin the important work of Province planning. Considered a man of good judgment, he was sent back once more to Spring Hill to serve as the rector of the Jesuit community, which he did from 1973 to 1976.

In a desire to help with the renovation of the Jesuit quarters, Fr. Elliot began to tear out plaster. But he breathed in so much of it that it caused his lungs to fail. Medicine was no help for him at this point, so he returned to the provincial's residence to await his death, which came on Jan. 19, 1977. Fr. Elliot is buried at Spring Hill.

The best description of Fr. Elliot was composed by his younger sibling, Bro. Fillmore Elliot, SJ, then working in Brazil:

Clyde was a gentle breeze, whose efficiency and thoroughness with humility... affected many Jesuit lives.... The many virtues and quiet efficiency of his life sometimes hid a very deep heart. He loved Spring Hill with a passion, but it was a quiet love.

Francis X. Entz, SJ
1883 – 1954
Doctor of ancient letters

The European Province of Alsace gave many vocations to the Southern Jesuits, and among the most notable was Charles Xavier Entz, born near Strasbourg on April 20, 1883.

His early ambition to become a doctor was supplanted by his desire to be a missionary to the American Indians. When he entered the Novitiate at Macon on Sept. 2, 1903, the novice master changed his first name to Francis. For the rest of his life he was FXE.

Entz's field of missionary work turned out to be in the classroom. He was bilingual in French and German and became an accomplished Latinist, also speaking and writing English and Spanish faultlessly. Along with Florence Sullivan and John

Hynes, SJ, he revised Fr. Dominic Yenni's classic grammar, reissued in 1920 as *The New Yenni Latin Grammar*. Because of this and other contributions to knowledge of the classics, Gregorian University awarded him a doctorate in ancient letters.

FXE began and ended his teaching career in New Orleans, completing 26 years in the classroom at Jesuit High. In 1943 at the age of 60 he took over the honors class, 4-A. Its motto became "4-A leads the way every day in every way," although FXE would add sometimes, "So they say."

Humor was a feature of FXE's classroom manner. Although his English was correct, he often encountered unfamiliar phrases that he would unintentionally mispronounce in a rich, full, confident voice that brought many to laughter. He was mischievous in class and given to little rhymes and pitiful puns. Moreover, Fr. Entz looked funny. He was solidly built like a big cylinder and capped by a tremendous bald head, which brought his height to about 5' 7".

Referring to his baldness, he would say, "No grass grows on a busy street." And his students were quick to respond, "Nor in a barren desert!"

Of course, he had a serious side, too. He was serious about learning and even more serious about God. He impressed most of his admiring students as a zealous priest. Among his best services to the Church is the number of religious vocations he inspired. In each of his classes he had prospects to whom he devoted special attention. He would talk to them of the glories and happiness of the priestly life. Many of them were thus prompted to consider lives of service to God.

On Aug. 18, 1954, Fr. Entz died at age 71. He is buried at Grand Coteau.

Joseph Hermann Fengler, SJ
1910 – 1984
Missionary to Ceylon,
master storyteller

Fr. Joseph Hermann Fengler, SJ, born in Philadelphia, Pa., on Jan. 3, 1910, entered the Novitiate on Nov. 11, 1929, and was ordained on March 25, 1941. A few years before his ordination, he volunteered and was accepted for the Province mission in Ceylon.

In 1936 he sailed to a country where he was to spend 32 years ministering to the needs of its people.

He studied theology in Poona, India, and struggled to learn Tamil, the language of eastern Ceylon. He spent many months studying at Saragunnai in southern India, but he never achieved fluency in Tamil.

Returning to Ceylon, he taught, acted as prefect of discipline, oversaw parish schools and even managed a school's farm. He served in the flagship institutions: St. Joseph College in Trincomalee (1943-46) and St. Michael's College in Batticaloa (1946-51, 1958-62).

During World War II, he also served as auxiliary chaplain to the Royal Air Force (1943-45). After his first stint at St. Michael's, he exercised pastoral ministry as a parish priest in Thalankudah (1951-52), then as pastor at Ampara (1952-53) and at Muthur (1953-58). Joe completed his stay in Ceylon by preaching retreats for three years, first in Batticaloa and then in Lewella.

He returned to the States in 1968, serving as associate pastor of Our Lady of Guadalupe in San Antonio (1969-77) and then of Immaculate Conception in Albuquerque (1977-83). Although he suffered several heart attacks, he vowed never to be "put on the shelf."

Worn out with labors and ill health, he joined the community at Ignatius Residence in New Orleans. Sensing his imminent death, he asked Fr. Thomas Atherton, SJ, to come and perform the Last Rites of the Church for him.

He died on Feb. 21, 1984, and is buried at Grand Coteau.

After Joe's funeral, stories circulated about him illustrative of his Jesuit character. For example, he had taken in a little boy whose father was hanged. A mother, unable to afford life-saving surgery, received her surgery because Joe gave her all the money he had collected to paint his village church.

Joe appeared daily with neat cassock, hair slicked, recent shave and polished shoes.

His provincial said at his funeral:

"He was a great storyteller. He could through his words, gestures, wonderful memory and vivid imagination, take you to the places he had been and introduce you to the people he had known.... I have never actually been to Sri Lanka (known as Ceylon until 1972), but I think I have some feel for the village of Muthur, for the road from Batticaloa to Trincomalee."

His stories were testaments to his own unwavering faith, his deep spirit of poverty, his love of the poor and the dispossessed, his enjoyment of human friendship, and his deep compassion.

Joseph H. Fichter, SJ
1908 – 1994
Advocate for Mother Henriette Delille and champion of social justice

Fr. Joseph Fichter had an unparalleled intellectual career achieved by few American Jesuits.

A native of Union City, N.J., born on June 10, 1908, Joseph started his Jesuit training at Grand Coteau in 1930. He hit the ground running. By the time he had finished his priestly studies in 1945 he had already published four books, mostly biographies and texts in theology, and had authored 50 articles in various national magazines such as *America*, *Commonweal*, *The Catholic World*, and *Interracial Review*.

After completing his studies for his PhD in sociology at Harvard in 1947 – and believing sociology should be applied to the identification, understanding and solving of human problems – he came to Loyola University in New Orleans to teach.

His first major research project was a study on the sociology of the parish. He had signed a contract with the University of Chicago to publish his findings in four volumes. Volume 1 was titled *Southern Parish: Dynamics of a City Church*, but after it came out and caused a stir about desegregation in the archdiocese, he was forbidden to publish any more. The first volume was translated into six languages.

Continuing his study of parishes, he also researched varied topics such as parochial schools, religion as a profession, high schools, the charismatic movement, alcoholism, health care, and clerical celibacy. Of his 40 scholarly works, his two professional autobiographies – *One Man Research* [1973] and *The Sociology of Good Works* [1994] – are perhaps the most accessible.

Fr. Fichter was a champion of social justice and often was embroiled in controversy and conflict, particularly in areas of race relations and the sociology of religion. He explored sensitive issues and was usually at odds with those who preferred for such issues to remain unexamined.

Fr. Fichter spent half his professional life at Loyola University. The other half he served as guest professor at distinguished universities in America and abroad, including such universities as Münster in Germany, Southern Methodist, Tulane, Santiago, State University of New York, Chicago, and others. His most important appointment was to the Stillman Chair of Catholic Studies at Harvard; he was the first American named to this chair and the first to serve the maximum term of five years.

But perhaps he should be remembered for two things he did, one at the beginning and the other at the end of his long career. In his early years at Loyola he had an enormous influence on his students, including the future long-time mayor of New Orleans, "Moon" Landrieu, Mike O'Keefe, Jack Nelson and Xavier University president Norman Francis – men who were to change the political face of New Orleans. In his last years he devoted himself to doing research to promote the cause for the canonization of Mother Henriette Delille, the free woman of color who founded the first congregation of African-American nuns, Sisters of the Holy Family, in 1842 in New Orleans.

Fr. Fichter died on Feb. 23, 1994, at age 85, and is buried at Grand Coteau.

John David Foulkes, SJ
1867 – 1941
An exemplary preacher and a fine teacher

John David Foulkes was born in Widnes, England, on Dec. 1, 1867, to a non-Catholic father and an Irish Catholic mother. The family moved to Wicklow, Ireland, and ten years later another sibling, David John, was born; he would eventually follow his older brother into the Jesuit Order.

John David entered the Apostolic School of Little Hampton, England, to prepare for the priesthood, and in 1887 he decided to become a Jesuit. He traveled to Macon, Ga., where he entered the Novitiate on Sept. 13, 1887. In time he studied philosophy at Spring Hill College in Alabama and theology at Woodstock College in Maryland. He was ordained in June of 1905.

He spent his first years of ministry in Tampa, followed by teaching in various places from 1909 to 1911. He was then appointed the vice-rector of the College of the Immaculate Conception in New Orleans and made rector the following year, an office he held until 1919.

For five years he served with the Province Mission Band, a group of priests who spread out to preach retreats, give catechetical instruction, and extend pastoral care to Catholics with scant resources. All agreed that this was a very good appointment. One auditor commented:

"I heard some of his sermons and well do I remember his distinctive posture and presence,

his perfect pronunciation, and his power to drive home a point."

He returned to the educational apostolate in 1927 when he was appointed to Loyola University as regent of the Law School and professor of some of its courses. Because of his somewhat lengthy tenure in that position (1927-36), one may conclude that he did it to the satisfaction of his superiors and students. In 1939, he was appointed rector of Jesuit High in New Orleans.

About two years later, he was making his annual retreat at Spring Hill College when he failed to show up for meals. He was found dead on the floor of his room on Dec. 14, 1941.

Who was John David Foulkes? What type of Jesuit was he? Not much information is available, but it is known that when Fr. Foulkes was buried at Grand Coteau, he was enthusiastically honored by his Jesuit community. They knew his "sincerity and singularity of aim."

The author of his obituary stated:

He had perfect control over his students. Never once did we ever see him lose his temper; but when he told the boys that something had to stop, they knew what he meant and that was the end of it…. He was a kind man. If you went to his room for courage or advice, he kindly gave you all the time you needed and spoke to you words of understanding and encouragement.

Francis Fox, SJ
1895 – 1949
A talented bilingual teacher and preacher

A gifted speaker, Fr. Francis Fox was also a top-notch educator who often went beyond the classroom to teach.

Born in New Orleans on Aug. 30, 1895, he graduated from Jesuit High School. After a brief stay at Loyola University, he entered the Novitiate in 1913. His early Jesuit training was routine: Novitiate and Juniorate, philosophy at Mount St. Michael's in Spokane, Regency at Jesuit High in New Orleans, and theology in Sarrià, Barcelona, Spain. He was ordained in 1927.

His first ministerial assignments were traditional: teaching at St. John's College in Shreveport and Jesuit High in New Orleans.

It would seem that his studies in Spain richly equipped him with fluency in Spanish, and so many of his later assignments were in Spanish-speaking parishes in the Southwest. Moving from the classroom to the pulpit, Francis served as assistant pastor of Our Lady of Guadalupe Church in San Antonio and Sacred Heart Church in El Paso. He became the assistant pastor of San Felipe in Old Town in Albuquerque.

Even here his work was education, since he so often worked with the children of the parish and those in the parish school. One could see him at school going from class to class to teach religion. And after school, he would usually work with the children from the public schools.

Often he was called upon to address the students of St. Mary's High School, as well as the local chapter of the Columbian Squires. Furthermore, he delivered lectures on Religion in Education over the local radio station, KVER. The Archbishop of Santa Fe commended him in a personal letter for the excellent quality of his talks.

Fr. Francis was, as might be expected, regular as a clock: He arose at 5:45 a.m. and heard confessions until he celebrated the Liturgy at 6:45 a.m. His Sunday sermons were renowned for their careful preparation and convincing delivery.

Early one morning, he was taken to the hospital for an illness which seemed routine, and he was about to be released when he died suddenly and unexpectedly. It was Jan. 23, 1949. Across the hall was another hospitalized priest; he had heard the commotion and rushed over to anoint Fr. Francis as he breathed his last.

Fr. Francis is buried at Grand Coteau.

J. Cruz Maria Garde, SJ
1874 – 1945
He shepherded Spanish-speaking flock in Southwestern U.S.

Although Cruz Maria Garde was born in Valle del Roncal in the Spanish Province of Navarre (July 16, 1874), he spent most of his life and his ministry in the American Southwest.

After his family moved to Durango, Mexico, he was sent to the Jesuit College of the Sacred Heart in Las Vegas, N.M., where the seeds of his vocation were planted. He wanted to be a priest, and in July of 1893 he entered the Jesuit Novitiate at Florissant, Mo.

He spent five years as a regent at Sacred Heart College in Denver, to which he returned after theology to serve as vice-president and prefect of studies. During this time, in 1921, the school was

renamed Regis College in honor of the Jesuit saint, John Francis Regis.

In 1916 he was named editor of the *Revista Catolica*, an international weekly Spanish language Catholic newspaper. During his tenure as editor the paper improved its coverage of Latin America and considerably increased its subscriptions. In 1918, its headquarters in Las Vegas, N.M., were transferred to El Paso, where Fr. Garde was to spend the rest of his life. He became a member of the New Orleans Province when the Denver Mission of the Province of Naples was split between the New Orleans and Missouri provinces in 1919.

From 1918 to 1929 he was the pastor of Sacred Heart Parish and, beginning in 1928, he supervised the building of a much larger church. The bigger facility was needed to accommodate the influx of refugees fleeing Mexico during the religious persecution there. Fr. Garde was a devoted shepherd to his flock, which numbered about 20,000, most of whom lived in poverty.

In 1922 he took on the office of vicar-general of the diocese – in addition to his jobs as pastor and editor. He was relieved of the latter post in 1923.

After 1929 he served as pastor of both Immaculate Conception and Holy Family parishes in El Paso.

Besides his work for the poor and his service to the new Diocese of El Paso, Fr. Garde was famous for his aid and assistance to the priests and religious driven from Mexico by the government-sponsored religious persecution.

When Fr. Garde died, on April 11, 1945, four parishes claimed his remains; his body lay in state at each of them in turn while thousands came to pay their final respects. He is buried in El Paso.

John Augustine Gasson, SJ
1904 – 1988
Author and Doctor of Psychology

John Augustine Gasson was a scholar with a PhD, a teacher for nearly 50 years, and co-author of a book that became a basic text used in college psychology courses.

Born on Nov. 26, 1904, in Pittsfield, Mass., he attended the local grammar and high schools, graduating in 1921. He entered the Novitiate in Pittsfield in 1921, but took his vows in Grand Coteau.

Pursuing an extensive course of studies, he first attended Weston College in Massachusetts for his college studies and his philosophy (1925-28). He earned an A.B and an M.A. in philosophy from Boston College, which accredited all his courses at Weston College. He spent his Regency teaching at Spring Hill College (1928-30), returned to Weston College for theology (1930-34), and was ordained on June 22, 1933. His studies earned him an STL degree, after which he went to Gregorian University in Rome for psychology, returning in 1937 with his doctorate.

The first assignment for this new PhD was Spring Hill College, where he taught in the Jesuit House of Studies as professor of rational psychology from 1937 until 1966. He moved to the regular faculty of Spring Hill College as professor of psychology (1966-75), during which time he served as director of the division of social sciences. In 1975 he was proclaimed professor emeritus of Spring Hill College and retired from teaching completely.

Little else is known of the professional career of Professor Gasson, but he did co-author with his colleague Magda B. Arnold a noteworthy book, published in 1954, *The Human Person: An Approach to an Integral Theory of Personality.*

Fr. Gasson died on May 29, 1988, at age 83. He is buried at Spring Hill.

Harold A. Gaudin, SJ
1898 – 1983
Rector of St. John's High in Shreveport

Fr. Harold A. Gaudin's dedication to the pastoral ministry took him to places all over the South and touched the lives of his many parishioners and fellow Jesuits.

On June 15, 1898, Harold Gaudin was born in New Orleans, where he attended the Jesuit grammar school and high school, then known as Immaculate Conception College (1912-17), after which he entered St. Stanislaus Novitiate in Macon. His formation was predictable: philosophy at Mount St. Michael's in Spokane, Regency at Jesuit High in New Orleans and Spring Hill College, theology at Weston College in Massachusetts, and an M.A. followed by ordination on June 26, 1930.

His first assignment was as teacher in the Juniorate at Grand Coteau (1933-34). Then he matriculated at Gregorian University for a *biennium* in philosophy (1934-35), soon earning a doctorate. In 1936 he was appointed president and rector of Loyola University, a position he held until 1939.

Although he returned to Macon as pastor of St. Joseph's Church (1942-46), he soon became vice-rector then rector of Jesuit High (then known as St. John's High School) in Shreveport, as well as rector of the Jesuit community and pastor of St. John's Church (1946-53). Then he was named pastor of the Gesù Church in Miami (1953-59). For the next eight years he was the director of the Montserrat Retreat House at Lake Dallas, Tex. (1959-67). After two years at Jesuit High in Dallas (1967-69), he returned to Montserrat (1969-71). His dedication to pastoral ministry was completed when he became pastor, first at St. Charles Borromeo in Grand Coteau (1971-73), then at St. Ignatius in Mobile (1973-75), and finally assistant pastor at St. Jude's Cathedral in St. Petersburg, Fla. (1975).

He moved then to the Jesuit retirement community in New Orleans, and from 1976 until his death he helped with requests for priests to say Mass and hear confessions in the neighboring parishes. His hearing weakened, his pace slackened, his words did not flow easily, and distractions seemed to take over, but his character and his ideals were as noble as ever.

Fr. Gaudin died on April 8, 1983, at the age of 84. He is buried at Grand Coteau.

This is how one of his friends described him:

"He was the most charming man I ever knew, consistently jolly, least subject to moodiness, the easiest to live with, and, in spite of his well-known shortcomings, one of the most spiritual."

Another friend observed:

"In my long life I have known many Jesuits, but I have never met any more loyal to the Church and the Society than Harold. He rejoiced in their work and progress, especially in their evidence of sanctity. He suffered deeply on learning about the weakness of some of their sons. He adapted quickly to the demands and recommendations of Vatican II."

When the announcement of Harold's death was posted on his community's bulletin board, someone penned this: "Another giant has gone to God." Most who knew him would have agreed that this was no exaggeration.

New Orleans Province

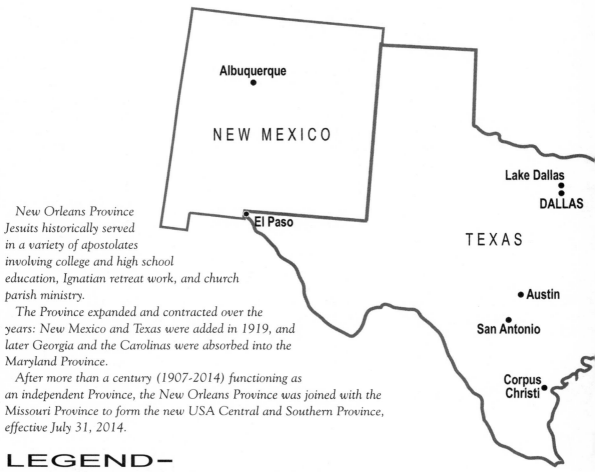

New Orleans Province Jesuits historically served in a variety of apostolates involving college and high school education, Ignatian retreat work, and church parish ministry.

The Province expanded and contracted over the years: New Mexico and Texas were added in 1919, and later Georgia and the Carolinas were absorbed into the Maryland Province.

After more than a century (1907-2014) functioning as an independent Province, the New Orleans Province was joined with the Missouri Province to form the new USA Central and Southern Province, effective July 31, 2014.

LEGEND–

Towns and cities where Southern Jesuits operated various institutions

ALABAMA

Mobile: Spring Hill College; Assumption Hall-Jesuit House of Studies; St. Ignatius Church; St. Joseph Church

Selma: Assumption of the BVM Church

FLORIDA

Key West: St. Mary Star of the Sea

Miami: The Gesù Church; St. Francis Xavier Church

Palm Beach: St. Edward Church

Stuart: St. Francis Borgia Convalescent Home

Tampa: Jesuit High School; Sacred Heart Church

West Palm Beach: St. Ann Church

GEORGIA

Atlanta: Ignatius Retreat House

Augusta: College of the Sacred Heart; Sacred Heart Church

Dublin: Immaculate Conception Church

Macon: St. Joseph's Church; St. Stanislaus Novitiate

LOUISIANA

Baton Rouge: Church of the Immaculate Conception; College of Sts. Peter and Paul; St. Joseph's Church

Convent: Manresa House of Retreats

Grand Coteau: Christ the King Church; Our Lady of the Oaks Retreat House; St. Charles Borromeo Church; St. Charles College and Jesuit Novitiate; St. Peter Claver School

The 3 states shaded in grey were at one time included in the New Orleans Province but eventually were absorbed into the Maryland Province – Georgia and South Carolina in 2013 and North Carolina earlier.

New Orleans: Holy Name of Jesus Church; Ignatius Residence; Immaculate Conception Church and College; Jesuit High School; Jesuit House of Studies; Loyola University; Good Shepherd Nativity School

Shreveport: St. John's Church; St. John's College/Jesuit High School

MISSISSIPPI

Pass Christian: Xavier Hall

NEW MEXICO

Albuquerque: Church of the Immaculate Conception; St. Francis Xavier Church; St. Ignatius Church; San Felipe Church; Sacred Heart Church

Las Vegas: St. Ignatius Residence

NORTH CAROLINA

Hot Springs: Church of the Little Flower; St. John Berchmans Mission

TEXAS

Austin: Xavier Hall

Corpus Christi: Corpus Christi Minor Seminary

Dallas: Jesuit College Prep; St. Rita's Church

El Paso: Church of the Immaculate Conception; Holy Family Church; Jesuit High School; Sacred Heart Church; St. Joseph Church; St. Peter Canisius Church; St. Ignatius Church; St. Patrick Church; *Revista Catolica Press*

Galveston: College of St. Mary; Sacred Heart Church

Houston: St. Joseph's Church; Strake Jesuit College Prep.; Cristo Rey Jesuit College Prep.

Lake Dallas: Montserrat Retreat House

San Antonio: Our Lady of Guadalupe Church

Spring: St. Ignatius Loyola Church

Richard Thomas Gaul, SJ
1903 – 1993
A fisher of men

In his day, Fr. Richard Thomas Gaul was venerated by his students as a holy man; some even thought he had the gift of reading hearts.

He was born on Nov. 13, 1903, in Pittsfield, Mass. After Boston College, he entered the Jesuit Novitiate in Macon on Aug. 13, 1921. His education as a Jesuit was totally traditional: Novitiate, Juniorate, philosophy, Regency and then theology. He was ordained on June 22, 1934.

His initial ministry was counseling, first at Jesuit High in New Orleans and then at Loyola University and Spring Hill College, where Tom Clancy, a future provincial, encountered him. Fr. Gaul thought Tom too frivolous and utterly unserious about a vocation to the priesthood, but Tom showed him!

In 1944, Fr. Gaul became pastor of Immaculate Conception Parish in El Paso; at the same time he served as superintendent of all the El Paso diocesan schools. He was later posted to the parishes of the New Orleans Province in Miami, Augusta and Albuquerque. When he returned to El Paso in 1959, he worked at Jesuit High until it closed in 1972 and remained in El Paso as the chaplain for Providence Hospital for 17 years.

Fr. Clancy described Fr. Gaul as a man who fished for Jesus, referring to the practice of early Jesuits hanging around outside their churches or in the marketplace to engage people in conversation and so evangelize by meeting people and mixing with them.

"Fr. Gaul was an expert fisherman. I should know. He hooked me," Fr. Clancy noted.

Testimonies to his "fishing" skills poured into the Province office from people whose lives he touched when he was in El Paso; most had the impression he was a man close to God.

When his health began to fail, Fr. Gaul was taken to Ignatius Residence in New Orleans. He was miserable there. He believed he was still in El Paso; for the rest of his life, he never accepted the fact that he was in Ignatius Residence.

Just weeks before his 90th birthday, Fr. Gaul died, on Oct. 11, 1993, and is buried at Grand Coteau. At the time, he was critically ill with sepsis, pneumonia and dementia. It might also be said that he died of apostolic exhaustion.

Bishop Ignatius Philip Trigueros Glennie, SJ
1907 – 1993
The Province's only bishop served in Ceylon for 27 years

Ignatius Glennie was truly a man on the move. From Mexico to the eastern half of the United States to New Orleans and most notably to Ceylon, he spread the love of God wherever he went.

He was also the only Jesuit from the New Orleans Province to become a bishop.

Born in Durango, Mexico, on Feb. 5, 1907, Ignatius resided there until the Mexican Revolution broke out and bandits like Pancho Villa and Emilio Zapata were terrorizing the country. The small family of four moved to San Antonio, Tex., where his father was placed in charge of a branch of the bank where he previously worked in Durango. His father died a year later, and Ignatius and his sister, Ines, moved with their mother to New Jersey. There Ignatius attended Bailey Hall, the short-lived grammar school now known as Seton Hall Prep School (1916-23).

The family later moved to St. Leo, Fla., and from there Ignatius entered the Society of Jesus on Aug. 14, 1924. After philosophy in Spokane and Regency in New Orleans, he moved halfway around the world, to Ceylon, in the company of three other Jesuits posted to the Ceylon mission.

After a short while in Ceylon, he went north into India to Kurseong, in the shadow of the great Himalayas, to study theology. Ignatius was ordained on Nov. 21, 1938, and remained in Kurseong to study for a doctorate in theology, which he was awarded in 1941. Still on the move, he returned to Ceylon and was posted as a newly minted DD to teach at the Papal Seminary in Kandy. Truly he had the right stuff, for soon after arriving at the seminary, he was moved up to the position of rector of the seminary. He was very well liked and respected.

But it was time for a move to a position where such apostolic talent was going to be put to even greater use. On Sept. 21, 1947, Fr. Glennie was consecrated Bishop of Trincomalee-Batticaloa, the part of the island with most of Ceylon's Catholics, the region where a second generation of Jesuits was already laboring.

One of Bishop Glennie's first projects was to institute a minor seminary in the diocese, which was established in Batticaloa and later transferred to Uppuveli. A graduate of this seminary noted: "Bishop Glennie considered the seminary as the apple of his eye."

Similarly, the bishop built a house in Batticaloa for the refreshment of his clergy, which was interpreted as a sign of appreciation for his priests. And they appreciated him. One of these clergy observed:

"A remarkable quality of Bishop Glennie was that he knew each of his priests and seminarians on a personal level…. He told us that Jesus liked the title 'I am the Good Shepherd' more than all his other titles. The Good Shepherd is a provider, protector and defender. He knows his sheep by name."

Bishop Glennie was called to preach and to build. His diocese was very extensive, and to accommodate the Catholic population scattered all over it, he built many new parishes and mission stations. His was the task of opening orphanages and charitable institutions in the two large cities of his diocese, Batticaloa and Trincomalee. It is said that the young had a special place in his heart; in order to help them he established the Social Service Center and the Boys' Town and Vocational Training Institute.

Several times he sought to resign from his position, only to be turned down by Rome. Bishop Glennie wrote in a 1973 letter to Larion Elliot, SJ:

"The fact is that the Holy Father himself wrote to me refusing my request [to resign] and I wrote again explaining my reasons more fully and that it was refused again."

But the time did come in 1974 for him to resign and return to the New Orleans Province. Because of his background in seminary education, he was sent to the Minor Seminary in Corpus Christi staffed by Southern Jesuits. After that he was at the Mary-Joseph Residence in New Orleans, run by the Little Sisters of the Poor.

On April 27, 1993, Bishop Glennie died at Ignatius Residence in New Orleans. He was 86 years old, 54 years a priest and 45 years a bishop. He is buried at Grand Coteau.

Aloysius Berchmans Goodspeed, SJ
1901 – 1980
Director of WWL TV and Radio recognized by President Kennedy

Aloysius Berchmans Goodspeed was a Jesuit to the core. His first name was borrowed from St. Aloysius Gonzaga and his second from St. John Berchmans, through whose intercession the renowned Miracle of Grand Coteau was worked.

Born in New Orleans on Oct. 30, 1901, Aloysius attended Immaculate Conception College and graduated in 1918. On Aug. 14 of that year, he entered the Jesuit Order at St. Stanislaus Novitiate in Macon, Ga., where his traditional path of studies was disrupted by the fire which destroyed the college in November of 1921. He was ordained in St. Louis, Mo., on June 25, 1931.

He began his priestly ministry in 1935 as principal and prefect of discipline at the school that would later be known as Jesuit High in Shreveport. Returning to New Orleans in 1937, he served as *socius* to the provincial and then to the vice-provincial during the General Congregation that began in 1938. Having demonstrated leadership in that position, he was then assigned to be the rector and treasurer of Jesuit High in Tampa (1943-48).

He tasted parochial ministry for the first time when he was appointed assistant pastor and treasurer at Immaculate Conception Parish in New Orleans (1949-53). Competent and trustworthy with funds, he was sent to Loyola University as treasurer (1954-65) and was also appointed auditor of the Province's finances (1954-69).

From 1956 until 1966, Fr. Goodspeed was the faculty director of Loyola's radio and TV stations and supervised the opening of WWL-TV in New Orleans. He served in two more parishes, St. Ann's and St. Joseph's, then returned to Loyola one more time as treasurer of the Jesuit community (1977-80).

Fr. Goodspeed participated in several civic organizations, including the local chapter of the American Red Cross. A descendant of an old English-American family, he was a member of four patriotic organizations, including Sons of the American Revolution and the Society of Colonial Wars.

Representing WWL radio, he accepted a Citation of Special Merit from President John F. Kennedy

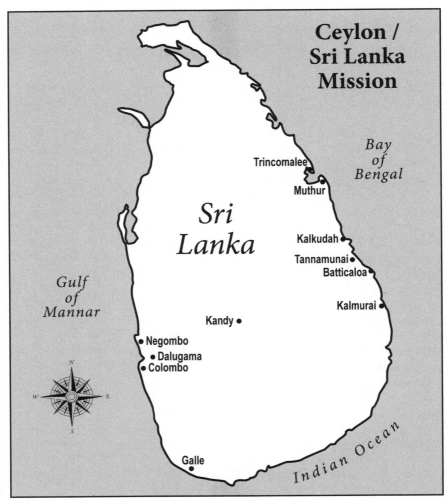

New Orleans Province Jesuits helped to staff the Ceylon/Sri Lanka Mission for more than three decades, from the mid-1930s through the 1960s. Others contributing in this regard were Jesuits of the Naples (Italy) Province, and earlier the Jesuits of Champagne (France) and Belgium.

Formerly known as Ceylon, the name of the island-nation – located off India's eastern coast – was changed to Sri Lanka in 1972.

For many years, there were two Jesuit missions on the island – the Trincomalee-Batticaloa Mission and the Galle Mission. In 1962, these two missions were combined into one Vice Province, which eventually became the Jesuit Province of Sri Lanka.

LEGEND

Towns and cities with Jesuit-operated institutions

Batticaloa: St. Michael's College; Manresa Retreat Center; Candidates House; Jesuit school

Colombo: Jesuit House

Dalugama: House of Formation

Galle: Bishop's House; St. Aloysius College; St. Xavier's Seminary

Kalkudah: Kalkudah Estate

Kandy: Fatima Retreat Center; Minor Seminary

Negombo: Candidates House

Trincomalee: St. Joseph's College; Jesuit Academy; Jesuit Residence; Jesuit Pre Novitiate of St. Stanislaus Kostka at the White House on Dec. 5, 1962. The award was given for the work the station did during the Cuban Missile Crisis, when it sent broadcasts into Cuba. He even had the distinction of being on a plane that was hijacked to Havana on Nov. 4, 1968.

All considered him a master of anecdotes, which served as icebreakers with guests and as entertainment for fellow Jesuits. He was known as an older Jesuit who fostered younger ones, thus bridging a gap. One Jesuit described him in this manner:

"(He brought) with him a twinkle and a chuckle and a thousand amusing stories to entertain us. He was a joyful man, strong-willed, yet kind, concerned, thoughtful, always caring."

One day in June 1980, as Fr. Goodspeed left work at WWL-TV, he was involved in an auto accident and sustained serious head and neck injuries. He remained in the hospital for a month and died at age 78, on July 31, 1980, the feast of St. Ignatius. He is buried at Spring Hill.

Edward Francis Goss, SJ
1909 – 1979
He never wanted to leave
Our Lady of the Oaks

Fr. Edward Francis Goss was never happier than when he was doing retreat work. It's what he apparently believed he was put on this earth to do.

Little is known of his early life, except that he was born in New York City on May 16, 1909, entered the Society on July 30, 1927, and with an M.A. in history, began teaching in the Juniorate (1942-44) and at Jesuit High in Tampa (1946-50).

In 1953 his apostolic labors shifted from the classroom to the retreat house. Fr. Goss was assigned successively to Our Lady of the Oaks in Grand Coteau (1953-59), Xavier Hall in Pass Christian, Miss. (1959-61), Manresa House of Retreats in Convent, La. (1961-65) and Ignatius House in Atlanta (1965-67). In 1972, he returned to Grand Coteau, where he remained preaching retreats until he died in 1979.

Many knew Fr. Goss for his distinctive military bearing, refined by two stints as chaplain in the Air Force (1944-46 and 1950-52). A tall, stout man, he retained many of the mannerisms and styles learned while in the service – a brush cut, for example. A tremolo of low timbre with frequent vocal punctuation marks characterized his unforgettable voice and style of speaking.

When asked how Fr. Goss's retreat impressed them, his retreatants all praised him. One said of him, "Fr. Goss's obvious great love for Jesus… Also the fact that Fr. Goss is like aged wine – he gets better all the time. After 28 retreats, I can only say that he is the very best that I have ever heard."

Fr. Goss had a two-pronged wish: not to retire in his old age and never to leave the Oaks. His ministry included adults at the Oaks and young boys in the neighborhood, whom he befriended, took swimming at the nearest pool, and took camping.

Despite his diabetes, he baked cakes and cookies after retreats, often eating most of what he baked. It is rumored that he had dozens and dozens of candy bars squirreled away in his chest of drawers and between his mattress and box springs. On the walls of his office were three posters: "I've definitely got to get myself organized!" and "Today I need all the help I can get" and "Every good diet allows you to cheat a little."

The death of Fr. Goss occurred on Nov. 18, 1979, while he was in a conference with a retreatant. Fr. Goss bowed his head, leading the penitent to think he was napping. But something was wrong. As though jolted by electricity, Fr. Goss cast back his head and began his rapid descent into death. All the retreatants gathered in the courtyard and prayed the rosary for his swift passage into the hands of God.

Thus his two wishes came to pass: He never retired nor left the Oaks. He is buried at Grand Coteau in the Jesuit cemetery adjacent to the retreat house.

Lester Francis Xavier Guterl, SJ
1907 – 1968
From the New York Stock Exchange
to the quiet of Grand Coteau

Lester Francis Xavier Guterl, though named for a Jesuit saint, did not always plan to become a Jesuit. Instead, he began his post-graduate life with a career that took him to notable companies and provided him with business experience and skills.

Born on June 6, 1907, in Jersey City, N.J., Lester completed his elementary schooling at St. Aedan's Parish School (1914-22), after which he attended St. Peter's Prep, a Jesuit high school in Jersey City, graduating in 1926. He attended Fordham University for two years (1926-28) and transferred to Villanova College in Villanova, Penn., where he earned a B.A. in 1929. He worked at various jobs in the following years, including the New York Stock

Exchange, Western Electric and other companies.

Pursuing a different path, he entered the Novitiate of the New Orleans Province on Sept. 13, 1931. After two years of Novitiate, he spent only one year in the Juniorate because of his previous college education. Similarly, he had only two years of philosophy at St. Louis University and graduated from there with a master's degree in English (1934-36). Continuing the pattern, he had two years of Regency at Spring Hill College (1936-38) and then returned to the East for theology at Woodstock College in Maryland (1939-42). He was ordained on June 22, 1941.

Fr. Guterl's ministry followed the double helix typical of Jesuits: education and pastoral work. His first educational assignment was to Loyola University in New Orleans as dean of men (1943-50). He moved to Spring Hill College for two years (1950-52), serving as chairman of the Department of Education, among other duties. He would return to Spring Hill in 1962 as a teacher of Scripture until 1965. He served as acting principal at St. John's High School in Shreveport for two years (1953-55).

The next several years of his ministry were spent in six parishes: Gesù in Miami (1955-56), St. Joseph's in Macon (1956-58), Sacred Heart in Augusta (1958-59), St. Mary's in Key West (1959-61), Sacred Heart in Tampa (1965-66), St. Ann's in West Palm Beach (1966-67), and back to St. Mary's in Key West (1967-68).

On Feb. 3, 1968, Fr. Guterl died in Key West at age 60. He is buried at Spring Hill.

Louis C. Hahn, SJ
1915 – 1977
*Prison ministry brought
him closer to Christ*

Louis C. Hahn was born into a deeply religious Protestant family in Beaumont, Texas, on Aug. 25, 1915. He went to public schools there and to college at Lamar Tech and the University of Texas. He was converted to the Catholic faith as a young man and entered the Novitiate in 1939.

After the regular course of studies at Grand Coteau, Spring Hill, St. Mary's and Pass Christian, he was assigned to retreat work at Manresa. He

worked there from 1952 to 1957, when he was sent to Atlanta. Great apostolic success blessed these first years of priestly ministry. People seemed to love him.

He was a skilled piano player and an entertaining singer. He loved music; he loved people; he loved his work. In 1959, he went to Georgetown to teach theology, and he was there until 1966 with the exception of a two-year stint at Loyola. He enjoyed his time at Georgetown and had great success there. His convivial presence was much appreciated by his students and his fellow Jesuits.

After that he served as an associate pastor in Dallas and Albuquerque. But, during these years he did not seem to have his old zest for life. He had always been plagued by an explosive temper and it flared more frequently during these assignments. Nevertheless, he was still a good priest.

In 1972, Fr. Hahn experienced a second conversion. It was occasioned by his part-time work as a prison chaplain in Albuquerque and triggered by a directed retreat he made in Grand Coteau. After this, he asked to go into prison work full-time. A short time before he died he was asked by the Ignatian Center of Spirituality to write an account of his ministry. It is evident from his candid words how his prison ministry brought him closer to Christ.

There are certainly difficulties in the work with prisoners. For example, I have to have a great deal of patience when dealing with some of the most immature inmates, and that makes me very emotional. It doesn't show up while I am with the prisoners, but later at my apartment when I see a TV show – or listen to some music – that is the least bit emotional, I can easily break down in tears. Maybe some of this is brought on by loneliness.

There are other disadvantages, too.... What I miss most of all is the liturgy found in the typical Jesuit community, plus the recreation room, the friendships, and even the card games.

On the whole, though, this work has been an enormous blessing for me. It brings me closer to Christ, as I realize more and more that working with the poorest of the poor is pleasing to him. Moreover, I have developed a definitely greater ability to empathize with people. The love and friendship shown to me by the prisoners and staff are very rewarding.

Fr. Hahn died in Galveston, Texas, on June 20, 1977, at age 61. He is buried at Grand Coteau.

George Bernard Hamilton, SJ
1905 – 1995
He treated rich and poor alike as lovable children of God

George Bernard Hamilton was one of eight children, two of whom became Jesuits.

The other was his brother, Walter, who labored and died in the Philippines.

Born in New York City on Jan. 23, 1905, George attended the prestigious Regis High School in his hometown and graduated in 1923. He took employment in the New York Stock Exchange and remembered that he was there on Black Tuesday, Oct. 29, 1929, the day the stock market crashed. At various times, he was employed by Consolidated Edison and other companies.

The vocation seed sown at Regis grew to the point that on Dec. 7, 1930, George entered the Novitiate at Grand Coteau. The next steps of his formation were predictable. However, for his Regency he traveled to Ceylon (1937), testing the waters to see if he could be a missionary there. The decision was affirmative and so George went to Poona in the south of India for his theology studies (1937-41), and was ordained on March 25, 1940. Along the way he learned to speak Tamil, that language so difficult for many Jesuits to master.

"Missionary" is a job description of considerable flexibility. Fr. Hamilton was first assigned to St. Michael's College in Batticaloa, where he was the treasurer, spiritual father, editor of school publications, parish priest, teacher, moderator of the Sodality, and both hospital and military chaplain. He served at St. Joseph's College in Trincomalee with much the same duties.

His longest stay was the five years when he lived and labored alone at Muthur, one of the poorest mission stations, which was across the harbor from Trincomalee. He supplied himself by crossing the harbor once a week to visit St. Joseph's for food and provisions.

It is in his ministry that spanned from elite colleges to the lowest of the lowly that much can be learned about the heart and soul of George Bernard, who is said to have treated all as lovable children of God.

It was his second, and very serious, motorcycle accident in Ceylon that occasioned his return to the U.S. Fr. George's ministry had always been parochial, and when he recovered from the accident he served as associate pastor at Gesù Parish in Miami (1953-57), and then at Immaculate Conception Parish in El Paso (1958-60). He served at St. John's Church in Shreveport from 1961 to 1989.

Following these appointments, Fr. George had light pastoral duties in Grand Coteau at St. Charles Borromeo Church, until he became increasingly disoriented. It was then that he moved to Ignatius Residence, the Jesuit retirement facility in New Orleans, where he lived for five more years.

On Jan. 24, 1995, he died at age 90. He is buried at Grand Coteau.

The closing words of his obituary were: "... zealous missionary, faithful priest, loyal Jesuit."

Elwood Paul Hecker, SJ
1914 – 1989
A counselor's ministry

Elwood Paul Hecker was a man gifted with a warm and affable personality coupled with an insight into human suffering and frailty. These characteristics contributed greatly to his long ministry as counselor to many students in various Jesuit schools.

Elwood Hecker (known as "Woody" to his friends), born in New Orleans on Aug. 9, 1914, attended Jesuit High in New Orleans and Loyola University. He entered the Society on Aug. 1, 1934, at Grand Coteau, and his formation was regular: Juniorate, philosophy at Spring Hill College, Regency at Jesuit High in Tampa and Jesuit High in Dallas, and theology in Kansas. He was ordained June 18, 1947. He earned several degrees, including a B.A. in chemistry at Spring Hill College, MEd at Loyola University and an M.A. in psychology at the University of Texas at El Paso.

For quite a while in the Southern Jesuit world, Fr. Hecker's name was nearly synonymous with counseling. With a brief exception, his ministry was devoted to the practice of or instruction in counseling. He spent 10 years as student counselor at Jesuit High in New Orleans (1951-61); then followed with five years of counseling at Jesuit High in El Paso (1965-70) and 12 years in his profession at Spring Hill College (1970-82). His ministry concluded with another stint as counselor at Jesuit High in New Orleans.

In 1982, when he was 68, he took one unit of clinical pastoral education at Hotel Dieu Hospital in New Orleans. His mentors wrote up a final evaluation of him which provides a window into his person:

He is easy to engage in conversation.

He has a very pleasant manner and gives a definite impression of calm and serenity.... Father proved patient, kind, and generous with his time, even with resistant patients.... Father Hecker developed excellent working rapport with his patients. They definitely felt cherished by him and were open to his counsel. Warmth and sincerity stand out as great assets in Father Hecker. Summation: Hecker is a very likeable man. He has an even temperament, calm and collected.

On March 21, 1989, Fr. Hecker died of cardiac arrest at age 74. He is buried at Grand Coteau.

Louis John Hiegel, SJ
1915 – 1969
Loyola Law School graduate and teacher

Louis John Hiegel's Jesuit ministry revolved around a career in law, his knowledge and enthusiasm contributing to his success as a teacher and as an advisor.

Louis was born on Nov. 14, 1915, in Conway, Ark. After schooling in the local St. Joseph's School, he entered the Novitiate in Grand Coteau on Oct. 2, 1934, and spent two years of spiritual formation there (1934-36), followed by two years of collegiate studies (1936-38). Like most Jesuits of his day, he traveled to Spring Hill College for the study of philosophy (1938-41). He spent the World War II years teaching at Jesuit High in New Orleans (1941-44). And like many others, he studied theology at St. Mary's (1944-48). He was ordained on June 18, 1947.

Fr. Hiegel studied Canon Law at Gregorian University in Rome and earned his doctorate in 1955. But that was not enough of a credential for the career that was opening before him. Upon his return to New Orleans, Louis began work on a J.D. at Loyola Law School and graduated in 1960.

During this time he was working at Loyola in various capacities. He served as procurator advocate of the Archdiocesan Tribunal of New Orleans, dealing with marriage annulment cases. He was the national moderator of Alpha Delta Gamma social fraternity and a member of the American Bar Association and the Blue Key National Honor Society, as well as a number of religious and professional societies.

For several years, Fr. Hiegel served as an associate professor in the Loyola Law School and chaplain of the same.

He was stricken with a blood clot in the lung and died suddenly on Jan. 14, 1969, at age 53. He is buried at Grand Coteau.

Johannes Hofinger, SJ
1905 – 1984
'The catechetical sputnik' brought the Word to 6 continents

The ministry of Fr. Johannes Hofinger remains a generous gift to God and to the people whose lives he touched. Not only did he challenge people to pray, he also challenged them to become authentic witnesses to a message *of* life and *for* life.

He was so renowned for his work in religious education that the Archdiocese of New Orleans named its major annual catechetical gathering the Johannes Hofinger Conference, honoring the man who was an inspiration to catechists everywhere.

Few records of his youth are available except to note that Hofinger was born on March 21, 1905, in St. Johann in Tirol, Austria, and he entered the Society on Sept. 7, 1925. He made his priestly studies in Berchmanskolleg in Pullach, a suburb of Munich, and was ordained in Innsbruck, Austria, on July 26, 1935. He eventually pronounced his final vows in Hopeh, China, in 1942. Fr. Hofinger returned to Innsbruck to complete a doctorate under the great Jesuit liturgist, Joseph Jungmann, SJ.

He then resumed his earlier work in China, where from 1939 to 1949 he was a professor of theology. After the Chinese revolution in the early 1950s, he continued his work with Chinese seminarians in Manila, Philippines. In 1953, he founded the East Asian Pastoral Institute of Manila, which greatly contributed to the renewal of religious education and preaching in the missions.

It is estimated that Johannes made 16 trips around the world, organizing and directing catechetical conferences on six continents. Thus, this evangelizing globetrotter aptly nicknamed himself "the catechetical sputnik."

Johannes Hofinger moved to New Orleans, and in 1976 he joined the Crescent City's archdiocesan Office of Religious Education staff and served as associate director until his death.

In the early 1980s, people began to recognize and celebrate his contributions. In 1981 he received the William Rainey Harper Award of the Religious Education Association of the U.S. and

Canada. Within the same year, Johannes was presented the F. Sadlier Dinger Award for spearheading the catechetical movement in the United States. This citation noted Hofinger's three principal catechetical works: *The Art of Teaching Christian Doctrine*, *The ABCs of Modern Catechetics*, and *Pastoral Renewal in the Power of the Spirit.*

Fr. Hofinger died on Feb. 14, 1984, at age 78 – the day before he was to have become a naturalized U.S. citizen. He is buried at Grand Coteau.

John W. Hynes, SJ
1886 –1953
Manresa retreat attendance grew dramatically when he took charge

Among the older Jesuits of the Province, Fr. John W. Hynes is considered one of the greatest Jesuits in its history. He was by no means a textbook saint: His language was salty; his temper would flare. He was plain-spoken and restive under superiors who peered too closely over his shoulder. He passionately loved God and possessed a portion of apostolic charm reminiscent of St. Ignatius Loyola himself.

Born in El Paso on June 24, 1886, he entered the Novitiate at Macon in 1901 shortly before his 15th birthday. Early on he was recognized as a man of unusual intelligence and promise.

His apostolic life after ordination is divided roughly into three periods, the first as a student and professor of theology. After receiving his doctorate from Gregorian University, he taught theology for several years at Mundelein Seminary outside Chicago.

His second career began in 1927 at Loyola University, where, in sequence, he became Director of Athletics, Dean of the College of Arts and Sciences, and finally Loyola's president (1931-36). He worked with other American Jesuits to form the Jesuit Educational Association, which evolved into the Association of Jesuit Colleges and Universities and the Jesuit Secondary Eduction Association. He is recognized as one of its principal founders.

When the Great Depression throttled the economy Fr. Hynes responded by expanding Loyola's night and summer schools. That meant he had to call on the largely Jesuit faculty to work overtime. As compensation for their hard work, he arranged for a Florida villa to be available for the community between regular session and summer school.

Fr. Hynes also served as Province prefect of studies and director of WWL Radio, but his most famous career was his third and last, from 1940 to 1952, when he was in charge of the Manresa Retreat League.

Since 1924, retreats had been given in Suburban Acres, a former night club in Jefferson Parish, just outside of New Orleans. Then in 1930 Jefferson College at Convent, La., was purchased by the Province and turned into a retreat house. By 1938 the number of laymen who made weekend retreats stood at 229. By 1952 there were 2,700 retreatants, and Manresa was open all year long.

It was difficult to resist the Hynes charm on the telephone and almost impossible if he caught someone at lunch or in the office. He had a fabulous memory for names – a trait that only added to his charm. When he celebrated his Golden Jubilee as a Jesuit in 1951, there was a standing-room-only crowd at the Saturday morning Mass at Baronne Street.

Fr. Hynes died on Feb. 4, 1953, at age 66. His work lives on and he lives on in the hearts of the people whose lives he touched. He is buried at Spring Hill.

Albert J. Jung, SJ
1938 – 1964
The short, happy life of a New Orleans Jesuit

Albert J. Jung, born in New Orleans on March 23, 1938, had a deep love for academia. He attended parochial school, was a student in Fr. Frank Coco's 4-A Honors class at Jesuit High in New Orleans and was the valedictorian of his class in 1955.

Immediately upon graduation, Al entered the Novitiate at Grand Coteau, where his contemporaries remember how close he was to his parents and to his brothers and sisters. It was a great occasion when he got a letter from home, and the mutual love of his family was evident when they visited him at Grand Coteau and Spring Hill.

A dedicated, excellent student, Al developed his own speed-reading technique and usually had a room full of books, which he read avidly. In the Juniorate his superiors appointed him sub-beadle to provide him with opportunities for practical experience. He begrudged the time he had to spend dispensing soap and other sundries and would sometimes hand them out without taking his nose out of the book he happened to be reading. When he went to Spring Hill for philosophy his passion for study only intensified, and he obtained an exception to the rule about the maximum number of books which could be checked out at one time from Byrne Library.

And yet he was also a boon companion. He loved sports and was an enthusiastic and skillful competitor in the Philosophers' Intramural Leagues, despite the fact that he had an enlarged heart – which made it necessary for him to rest more often when participating in sports or climbing stairs.

Al's talent for and interest in academics marked him for graduate school. When he took the Graduate Record Examination in 1962 he scored in the top one percentile. But first he was to teach in Dallas. He had an honors class which he loved, but he was also a very effective teacher for the slower students and athletes, to whom he communicated his love of poetry and literature. He worked them hard, worked himself harder, and his heart showed the strain.

In his second year at Dallas he had open-heart surgery, and he spent the first semester recuperating. But he was anxious to return to his responsibilities in the classroom. Finally, on Jan. 7, 1964, his doctor approved his return to the classroom.

However, Jung did not show up for his first class, so a colleague went to his room and found him sprawled over his typewriter. Al had been typing materials for his Latin class when the fatal attack came.

It was difficult for his community and the student body to believe that such a loving and energetic heart was stilled forever.

On Jan. 8, 1964, Jung died at age 25 during his second year of Regency. He is buried at Grand Coteau.

George Patrick Kelleher, SJ
1900 – 1968
*A Yankee by birth, he felt
at home in the Southwest*

It is not clear how he came to be associated with the United Service Organizations (USO), but while in New Orleans George Patrick Kelleher served as its assistant moderator from mid-World War II to the end of the decade (1942-49).

When he was assigned to Albuquerque, he continued his involvement and served as spiritual director for the local USO for most of the 1950s.

An Irish-Catholic, George Patrick Kelleher,

born in Richmond Hill, N.Y., on April 7, 1900, was educated locally in public elementary schools (1907-14). There was a hiatus in his schooling, for after grade school he worked for P. J. Kennedy Advertising Co. from 1914 to 1916. When a more reliable job with the Long Island Railroad opened up for him, he took it and worked there for 12 years (1916-28), even while he attended high school (1923-27). He studied at City College in New York for a year (1927-28).

The Spirit of God led George to enter the Jesuit Order at Grand Coteau on Sept. 7, 1928. After two years in the Novitiate and two in the Juniorate, he traveled to St. Louis for three years of philosophy (1932-35). Probably because of his age – he was in his thirties – his Regency lasted only one year at Jesuit High School in New Orleans (1936-37), after which he went to St. Marys, Kan., for theology. He was ordained on June 21, 1939.

Fr. Kelleher's entire priestly ministry was spent in parishes staffed by the Southern Jesuits. Moreover, three of these parishes were under the patronage of the Immaculate Conception. From 1941 to 1949 he was an associate at Immaculate Conception in New Orleans. Then he was posted to Immaculate Conception Church in Albuquerque for eight years (1949-57) and he returned there to serve for 11 years after a short posting in El Paso.

Even though he spent less than half a year at Immaculate Conception Church in El Paso, from August to December in 1957, El Paso must have made a deep impression on George, because when he retired he moved back there.

On Feb. 17, 1968, Fr. Kelleher died in El Paso at age 67. He is buried in Albuquerque.

Stephen Keller, SJ
1859 – 1941
*His occupation and disposition were
reminiscent of 16th century Jesuit saint*

Bro. Stephen Keller, in the opinion of those who knew him, ranked along with Fr. Edgar Bernard as being among the closest approximations to classical sanctity produced in the Province.

The fact that he was the doorkeeper, as well as the tailor, made it easy for Jesuits to think of him as another Alphonsus Rodriguez, the 16th century Jesuit saint who served as the porter for his community.

Born in Marenweiler, Germany, on Dec. 14, 1859, Keller entered the Novitiate at Macon, Ga., on Feb. 12, 1887. He was stationed at the Novitiate for the rest of his life, first at Macon, then at Grand Coteau.

Bro. Keller's job never changed: He was always the doorkeeper and tailor. He was not only responsible for the manufacture of cassocks and birettas, but also for the repair and care of clothing in general. At this time a Jesuit's wardrobe, which included underwear, shirts, trousers, socks, suits and coats, was deposited in the clothes room. A Jesuit kept in his room only a cassock, a pair of trousers, and a change of linen that was dispensed each week. When it was necessary to go out of the house, one called at the clothes room to pick up clothing and a hat roughly one's own size.

Bro. Keller thus had frequent business with the members of the community, and he impressed them all with his kindness and patience. He was a cheerful little man who received the nickname of "*Schneider*" (i.e. "tailor" in German) from the other brothers. One of his good friends was Bro. Aloysius Imsand (d. 1935), who was a huge man of herculean strength. When they walked in funeral processions together, it was a source of great merriment to the novices to see the bulky Imsand and the little Keller side by side.

Bro. Keller greatly influenced the novices and especially the younger brothers, many of whom were sent to work under his instruction in the tailor shop. In his time it was the custom for those brothers approved for last vows to spend six months at Grand Coteau. Many of them worked under little "*Schneider*," who was their Tertian instructor in example if not in title.

Next to charity Bro. Keller's most striking quality was his devotion to prayer. Besides the daily prescribed exercises of piety, he devoted much of his free time to contemplation in the chapel and to the recitation of his Rosary, especially while he walked about the beautiful grounds. His simple candor about the favors he received in prayer only inspired reverence on the part of even his crustiest brethren. He continued working in the tailor shop until just a short time before his death.

On Dec. 30, 1941, Bro. Keller died at age 82. He is buried at Grand Coteau.

Emil Cecil Lang, SJ
1909 – 1989
Twice the socius, *once the provincial*

Emil Cecil Lang was a chaplain in the U. S. Army from 1942 to 1946, serving in the Mediterranean Theater with an engineering group.

Lang, born in New Orleans on July 27, 1909, and baptized in Holy Name Church, attended its grade school (1915-22). The Jesuit connection continued with his attendance at Jesuit High in New Orleans (1922-26), and upon graduation he entered the Novitiate and spent two years of spiritual training in Grand Coteau (1926-28), followed by college studies in the Juniorate (1928-30). He was sent to study philosophy at Spokane (1930-33), earning an M.A. in philosophy. All three years of his Regency were spent at Spring Hill College (1933-36).

He began his theology studies in Valkenburg, Holland, but with the threat of war, Cecil returned to the States and finished his theology at St. Mary's (1937-40), earning an STL degree. He was assigned to teach in the Juniorate at Grand Coteau and to serve as chaplain at the nearby Academy of the Sacred Heart (1941-42).

His first position after the war was to act as *socius* to the provincial (1946-49). He taught religion and mathematics at Loyola University (1949-51), but then returned to his former job as *socius* (1951-53). Subsequently, Cecil filled three different administrative positions: rector of St. Charles College (1953-58), rector of the Jesuit House of Studies at Spring Hill College (1958-61) and Provincial of the New Orleans Province (1961-65).

Perhaps exhausted by administration, E. Cecil Lang was thereafter assigned as assistant pastor to several of the parishes in the Province: St. Ann's Church, West Palm Beach, Fla. (1965-68 and 1975-79); St. Joseph Church, Mobile (1968-70 and 1979-83); Gesù Church, Miami (1971-75); Immaculate Conception Church, New Orleans (1983-84); and Immaculate Conception Church, Albuquerque (1987-89).

Fr. Lang died on Oct. 14, 1989, and is buried at Grand Coteau. He was 80 years old and 63 years a Jesuit.

John William Lange, SJ
1909 – 1977
*He labored in the mission fields
of Ceylon/Sri Lanka for 43 years*

John W. Lange was a member of the New Orleans Province most of his life, but he died a member of the Vice-Province of Sri Lanka (Ceylon), having labored in that mission field for more than four decades.

Born on Jan. 20, 1909, he entered the Society at Grand Coteau on July 30, 1927. While he was studying philosophy, an appeal went out for Jesuits to go to Ceylon. Jack volunteered and departed for the mission in 1934.

For the next two years more Southern Jesuits were sent over. Fr. Wlodimir Ledochowski, the Superior General of the Society, wanted the New Orleans Province to take over this mission from the Champagne (France) Province. But New Orleans Province leaders were not enthusiastic over the prospects of diluting their ranks, for the needs at home were great. Southern Jesuits would have to deal with a new climate, culture and language, as well as older European Jesuits who were mystified by the "American ways" of the newcomers.

Fr. Jack Lange endured it all. He matured as an educator in Trincomalee; he studied and became proficient in Tamil, and eventually made his theology studies and Tertianship in India.

Only after World War II did any new recruits arrive from the South. By this time Fr. Lange was a seasoned missionary. He worked as a pastor, managed an orphanage, started a vocational school, and from 1952 to 1960 served as mission superior. It was during this period that he built, practically with his bare hands, the new college at Trincomalee, although he wore out himself and his Jesuit associates in doing so.

He was a friendly man but very austere, and he found it difficult to understand why anyone would complain after laying cement blocks for 60 hours a week. He had a great mechanical knack. He designed a keyboard for a Tamil typewriter in 1937, as well as a machine to record the famous "singing fish" of Batticaloa.

In the 1960s Superior General Fr. Pedro Arrupe asked every Jesuit province to submit a sociological survey of its area. By this time Sri Lanka was an independent vice-province embracing the whole of the island. Fr. Lange was asked to do the survey, despite a total lack of training. Almost single-handedly, he produced a survey that won special praise from Father General.

In his last years he undertook to manage Kalkudah Estate, whose principal product was coconuts. Alone, he was able to live with the austere poverty he had come to love. But he failed to take care of his health. His body, which he had driven so relentlessly in the pursuit of God's glory, finally gave out on him.

At 68, Fr. Lange died, on Feb. 16, 1977, in Colombo, Sri Lanka. He is buried in Sri Lanka.

Martial Octave Lapeyre, SJ
1908 – 1989
The man could fix anything!

Born on Sept. 16, 1908, into a socially prominent New Orleans family, Martial Octave Lapeyre was one of four children who chose religious vocations. Two went into the sisterhood, one became a Jesuit priest, and Martial became a Jesuit brother.

After he graduated from Jesuit High School, he entered the Novitiate at Grand Coteau on Aug. 14, 1926.

From 1927 to 1963, he applied his considerable talent in the field of mechanics, even spending two years in aviation in Alaska. Bro. Martial might as well have embroidered on his shirts: "Mechanic: If it's metal and it moves, it's mine." Because he possessed such useful skills, he was always on the move to a variety of communities, mostly traveling between Spring Hill College and Grand Coteau.

Because he was a master of making machines work, especially canning machines, and possessed other valuable skills such as carpentry and remodeling rooms, his talent was used in a special project: the Brothers' Training Program. This innovative program allowed brothers to learn new skills. Thus, Bro. Martial was a key figure in shaping the education and capabilities of the brothers from 1949 to 1955.

In 1957 he was made the press manager of the Jesuit publication *Revista Católica Press*, which unfortunately closed in 1963. He remained a whiz at institutional maintenance, and his organizational skills qualified him as a good house minister. He alternated these skills in his eight years at the new Jesuit High School in Dallas (1966-73) and at Montserrat Retreat House in Lake Dallas (1973-77).

Bro. Lapeyre is immortalized in the lore of the Province for his plane crash in Alaska. Early in his Jesuit life he had expressed a desire to go to the Alaska mission as a pilot, so he set out to accomplish that goal. He took a correspondence course in flying, took flying lessons, and went to New York in 1931 to pick up a plane paid for in part by one of his sisters. Then he went to Alaska.

During the ill-fated trip, he and Bro. George Feltes were forced to make a crash landing on an icy mountain. They survived the crash but nearly froze to death, enduring six days of minus-40-degree weather with very little food. After they were rescued, the superior sold the plane and Bro. Martial returned to Grand Coteau.

Colleagues remembered him with fondness. Fr. Tom Clancy, SJ, wrote in *Our Friends, 1st Edition:*

"In his lifetime there was probably no other Jesuit in the Province more in demand than Lap. It was easy to see why. He was a hard worker who could fix anything. He lived poorly, never complained, and got along with everyone. He had a shy self-deprecating sense of humor and great patience with those less blessed with talent and energy."

Bro. Lapeyre died on April 18, 1989, at age 80. He is buried at Grand Coteau.

Everett Henry Larguier, SJ
1910 – 2000
The extraordinary mathematician

Everett Larguier's progress through Jesuit High School was studded with gold medals in mathematics, algebra and Latin, and he graduated first in his class. This stellar student could have gone anywhere, done anything – and he chose to give his life in service to God.

Born in New Orleans on Jan. 25, 1910, he entered the Novitiate in 1929, but afterwards went to St. Louis to complete an undergraduate degree in mathematics and to satisfy his philosophy requirements. At the same time he worked on a master's degree in mathematics. As an undergraduate, Everett's articles were published in the *Annals of Mathematical Statistics 6 & 7.* After a semester at the University of Chicago, he published more articles in journals such as *Thought* and *Duke Mathematical Journal.*

While studying theology at St. Mary's (1938-42), he wrote a book on the foundations of mathematics, which publishers deemed too dense, so "Wimpy" (as his friends called him) salvaged two chapters and published them in *Scripta Mathematica.* He began doctoral studies in mathematics at the University of Michigan, a difficult program that

he completed in four years (1943-47). His director sent this letter to his provincial:

Larguier has impressed us very favorably with his interest in mathematics and with his ability to do really first class work in this subject. If he were a layman, we should at the present time be trying to obtain for him an opportunity of doing instruction of mathematics at a university of some standing. . .[with possibilities] to do graduate work.

But his superiors in the South exerted pressure on Everett to finish his degree and return. Excerpts from Everett's letter to the provincial are both touching and characteristically understated:

It is with regret that I say this, but persistent inquiries concerning finishing date are not conducive to academic peace of mind – an important factor in the proper pursuit of the final phases of this work... [concerning his return to Spring Hill that summer]. From a scholastic viewpoint, this is at best a tolerable, not a desirable, procedure. But in any event, Father, a renewal of confidence from you would be greatly appreciated. It is most disconcerting, after doing all that is in my power, to feel that there possibly exists some question of my earnestness . . . it is distressing.

On Memorial Day 1947, he defended his dissertation: *Homology Bases with Applications to Local Connectedness,* subsequently published in the *Pacific Journal of Mathematics.*

When Fr. Larguier returned to Spring Hill College to teach mathematics, he resurrected the college press and became its director. Important publications followed, including his own *Fundamental Concepts in Mathematics* (1953) and two small books on calculus (1954, 1956), one of which the students called *Calculus for Jerks.* He was retired as professor emeritus in 1975.

Very intelligent, yes. But what kind of person was he? Always at the head of his class, he was bright, imaginative, clever and disciplined. He said of himself that he was "a vulnerable man who thrived when watered with appreciation." He readily submitted his judgment to his superiors, not, however, without expressing his concerns with clarity and tongue-in-cheek humor.

His health was never robust, and he was often rushed to the hospital, first for a ruptured appendix, later for ulcers, recurring kidney stones, and pneumonia.

On Sept. 19, 2000, Fr. Larguier died at age 90 – 71 years a Jesuit. He is buried at Spring Hill.

Alfred Latiolais, SJ
1869 – 1959
Tampa area trailblazer,
founder of 11 Florida churches

Fr. Alfred Latiolais is one of the fabled figures of the Province. Since he lived 90 years, he was able to hand on by oral tradition what missionary life was like in pre-boom Florida, in the years before World War I.

This man who was to become a major contributor to the history of the Church in Florida was born in Breaux Bridge, La., on April 16, 1869. He was a farm boy who until he was 15 did not know English or even how to write his native French. He did, however, know how to read his French catechism.

His real schooling began when he enrolled in St. Charles College in Grand Coteau. He grew fond of the Jesuits and asked to enter the Society as a lay brother. The fathers persuaded him to study for the priesthood.

With all of five years of schooling behind him, he entered the Novitiate at Macon, Ga., in 1889. He made up for some of his deficiencies in a third year of Juniorate and then proceeded through the regular course of studies in the Society. In 1903, he was ordained at Woodstock in Baltimore.

Instead of returning for a fourth year of theology, he was sent to Key West, where he worked as an assistant for four years. His Tertianship was spent at Macon, serving as *socius* to the master of novices. Then from 1908 to 1912 he worked among the African-Americans in and around Macon.

In 1912 he was sent to Tampa to take charge of the missions on the west coast of Florida. Tampa would remain his headquarters for the next 36 years. His greatest period of apostolic activity was his first 17 years in Florida, when he established at least 11 churches in the area around Tampa.

Transportation was difficult in those days and there were certainly no Holiday Inns in this sparsely settled country. Fr. Latiolais travelled by horseback, by buggy, by train, by boat, by foot and towards the end of his tenure, by car, which was made necessary by his occasional back trouble. The roads were poor, and it was difficult to find a place to eat or sleep. It was sometimes hard even to find a Catholic. The missionary said Mass in private homes, in hotels, in theaters and in railway stations.

As Florida grew, many of the missionary stations became parishes. Fr. Latiolais lived to see this transformation, much of which occurred between 1938 and 1948, the years during which he served

as minister and spiritual father of the Jesuit high school in Tampa.

At the age of 79 he retired to Grand Coteau. He attributed whatever success he had as a missionary to his physical strength rather than to his apostolic gifts. But it was evident from his life's work that he had plenty of both.

Fr. Latiolais died on Aug. 3, 1959, at age 90. He is buried at Grand Coteau.

Guy J. Lemieux, SJ
1908 – 1966
A master storyteller, he taught
philosophy for many years at Loyola

A bout with polio had left Guy Lemieux with a shortened left arm. This, combined with a rolling walk, a droll manner, a cultivated drawl and a touch of cynicism unusual in a Juniorate professor, made him a memorable figure for the novices and juniors.

He was already a master raconteur, and, though the point of his stories was usually subtle, he became a prized companion at recreation.

Born in New Orleans on July 1, 1908, Lemieux graduated from Jesuit High and Loyola before entering the Society at age 22 in October of 1930. Because he already had his B.A. from Loyola, he was sent to Florissant, Mo., with the idea of combining his Juniorate and study of philosophy. He was ordained at St. Marys, Kan., in 1941.

His first assignment was teaching in the Juniorate, then he moved to Spring Hill for two years. He then settled down at Loyola to teach philosophy for the rest of his life. His specialty was ethics and he was an excellent moralist, consulted often by his Jesuit brethren and other priests on cases of conscience.

With his students he was always accommodating. His tiny office was usually crowded by day, and at night there were long counseling sessions. Women of all ages were called "darling," male students and ex-students were all "son." His influence with them was multiplied by the fact that in most cases he knew their parents and in some cases their grandparents.

Fr. Lemieux was a leader in the Province. His gripes and *bon mots* were rapidly repeated. Many times superiors were the object of his pleasantries. Because of this he was an excellent choice in 1966 to be the superior of the Loyola community. He took a lot of ribbing about the appointment, but he was very conscientious in his care for the men of the community.

Because of his wit he was a formidable adversary in the recreation room. Early on he formed the conviction that segregation was wrong and gently exposed the folly and sophisms of racism in his classes, with his friends and in the Jesuit residence.

Many Jesuits and laymen were adamantly opposed to Lou Twomey, SJ, who forthrightly condemned racism. Their social attitudes were often corrected by the quieter and – be it noted – the more sarcastic approach of Guy Lemieux.

His easy exterior manner made him appear the least likely candidate for heart trouble, but Fr. Lemieux was felled by a coronary while on a visit to Spring Hill on Sept. 27, 1966. He was 58 years old and 25 years a priest. He is buried at Grand Coteau.

Robert Mary Libertini, SJ
1885 – 1973
A multi-lingual
Army chaplain from Italy

Robert Mary Libertini, a noted U.S. Army chaplain, was born in Lecce, Italy, on June 8, 1885, took his early education in his hometown from 1893 to 1904, and entered the Naples Province on Sept. 26, 1904.

In 1909, he went to Tortosa, Spain, to study philosophy for two years, but did not do the usual Regency. Instead, in 1911 he traveled to the United States to work in the Denver Mission.

Upon arrival in the U.S., he studied theology at Woodstock College, Md., and then was ordained on June 28, 1914. Soon after ordination, he traveled west and pronounced his final vows at Sacred Heart Church in El Paso. He became a U.S. citizen in 1925.

Having grown up in Europe, he was fluent in five languages: Italian, Spanish, English, French and Portuguese; this helped him to better serve many non-English-speaking immigrant parishioners. His priestly ministry began as pastor in San Elizario, Texas (1916-21), followed by service at San Ignacio in El Paso (1921-23) and then at Sacred Heart in Albuquerque (1923-25).

In 1925 he was sent by the Apostolic Delegate "all over the U.S. to preach to Italian colonies and bring Italian peoples to church, sacraments, and social good living." This mission had been preceded by a commission from the Missouri Pro-

vincial to preach missions in British Honduras, an assignment that lasted five months. Eventually he returned to pastoral work in Old Albuquerque for six years (1931-37) and became pastor in Alameda, N.M., from 1937 to 1942.

With the outbreak of World War II, he volunteered to be an Army chaplain, a service which lasted from 1942 to 1945. He was posted in Texas to Fort Bliss, Fort Sam Houston and Fort Russell, and assumed various duties in New Mexico, as well. He retired with the rank of Major.

He returned to Albuquerque to be pastor of San Felipe in Old Town (1946-52) and to El Paso to be assistant at Sacred Heart (1952-67). He then went to St. Charles Borromeo in Grand Coteau to be a parish priest in 1967. It was an easy lateral move to join the retired and infirm Jesuits at St. Charles College.

Andrew Rosenberger, M.D., served with Fr. Libertini during the war, and this is what he wrote in a note dated May 14, 1957:

> I am writing you concerning an old friend, a man who served with me in the Army for four years during World War II. During these years Father Roberto Libertini and I became more than friends. I learned to know him as one of the most saintly, the most selfless men I ever knew. He is a man who made many converts and was instrumental in bringing back to God many who had been away for years. This was done solely by his good example.

Fr. Libertini died on May 29, 1973, at age 87. He is buried at Grand Coteau.

Whitmel Horne Macnair, SJ
1920 – 1973
Ceylon missionary: precise,
charitable – and moody

Whitmel Horne Macnair was a man with no formal training in money matters, though he acquired this talent through practice and determination. The beneficiary of this newfound ability was the Ceylon Mission.

Whitmel was born on Nov. 2, 1920, in Tarboro, N.C. His family moved to Tampa, and Whitmel eventually attended the local Jesuit high school (1933-38). During this time he worked on a farm, which he listed as his labor experience before he entered the Society.

On Aug. 14, 1938, he entered the Novitiate, spending two years in spiritual formation and two years in the Juniorate. In 1947 he was posted to St. Joseph's College in Trincomalee, Ceylon. Soon after that appointment, he traveled to Poona and Kurseong, India, for theology (1948-50) and was ordained on Nov. 21, 1950.

Fr. Macnair went back to Ceylon, this time to St. Michael's College in Batticaloa, where he wore many hats: prefect of discipline, bursar, teacher and minister, among other duties (1953-56). From 1957 till 1959, he labored at St. Joseph's College, performing the same tasks, only now he was also the treasurer of the Trincomalee mission.

He had no prior training in accounting and bookkeeping, so he taught himself these skills. Also, he was celebrated as a solicitor of funds. Moreover, he assisted many of the lay staff of the college – for instance, helping one staff member buy some Society land for a reasonable amount of money, and providing a loan for the education of the brother of a Jesuit scholastic.

And he was witty. He was famous for his mimicry, his satirical songs, and his imitations of well-known people. Fr. Macnair was an accomplished preacher whose short sermons were gems remembered with admiration by those attending his Masses. After his death his homilies were found to have been carefully written out and filed.

The obituary for Whitmel Macnair provides rich details about his personality. For one thing, he had a difficult streak: "He was known as a man subject to moods which had to be watched before you approached him." Care, precision and a certain level of stubbornness most characterized him.

The day he received a diagnosis of cancer, his life nearly came to a halt. His obituary records:

When we heard that he had been sentenced to an imminent death of cancer, we all wondered how he would take it. We were all edified and overjoyed that he accepted the sentence not only with resignation, but with positive joy.... Once he knew he was to die, he made up his mind to carry on in the art of dying (with the same) order and precision he had maintained in his life.

He tried but was barely able to concelebrate Mass with the community on Jan. 18, 1973. Returning to his sick room, he asked for help to sit up, but his breathing quickly deteriorated so he was laid down on the bed, where he soon died. Fr. Macnair, only 52 years old, died with his Jesuit brothers praying at his side. He is buried in Sri Lanka.

Joseph William Malloy, SJ
1907 – 1994
He experienced the Normandy Invasion and Battle of the Bulge in WWII

Joseph William Malloy was the last Jesuit to attend St. Charles College as a layman; the school closed in 1922 and was simultaneously reborn as the Jesuit Novitiate. He was also the first Jesuit priest to come from Lake Charles, La., where he was born May 17, 1907.

His earliest education was at St. Charles Academy in his hometown (1913-20), but his secondary education was divided between St. Charles College in Grand Coteau (1920-22) and Spring Hill High School in Mobile (1922-24).

He returned to Grand Coteau, where he entered the Novitiate in 1924 and began his college studies in the Juniorate in 1926. As was the custom, he went to Spokane to study philosophy (1928-31), and then spent his Regency at Spring Hill High School (1931-35). His formation was complete after the study of theology at St. Marys, Kan. (1935-39).

As World War II approached, Fr. Malloy received U.S. Army chaplain training at Harvard University and was commissioned into the 179th Field Artillery. He landed in Normandy with his unit just weeks after D-Day (June 6, 1944), and then accompanied his unit across western France and into Belgium. He was involved in the bitterly cold and snowy Battle of the Bulge in December of 1944. In March, his unit plowed through Germany to Frankenberg in central Germany. Fr. Malloy remained with his unit while the Army occupied the land of the defeated enemy.

His discharge states that he served at "Normandy, Northern France, the Ardennes and Central Europe." For his service and heroism, he was awarded the European Campaign Medal with 5 bronze stars, the American Defense Service Medal, the American Campaign Medal, the Victory Medal of World War II, and a testimonial from the U. S. President.

Discharged in 1946, Fr. Malloy began a new campaign, namely, parochial care in Albuquerque. His first assignment was to St. Francis Xavier, initially as associate and then as pastor (1946-55).

For ten years, he served at San Felipe de Neri of Old Town Albuquerque, a parish established in 1706 and a much-prized assignment (1955-65). He became pastor of the downtown church, Immaculate Conception (1965-77), and then served as pastor of Santa Clara Parish in Wagon Mound, N.M. (1977-82).

After retiring, he offered his services to parishes needing assistance. His labors were duly acknowledged with the award of the Archbishop Lamy Medal, named for the first archbishop of Santa Fe. He spent one year at Immaculate Conception Church in New Orleans before joining the parochial staff of St. Charles College in Grand Coteau (1984-89), serving primarily the African-American population at Christ the King mission in Bellevue, La., just a few miles west of Grand Coteau. He finished his priestly labors as chaplain for a nursing/retirement home in Opelousas, La., just north of Grand Coteau.

His last years were spent at Ignatius Residence, the Province's house for retired and ailing Jesuits. Indicating where his heart really was, he refused to change his watch from Mountain Standard Time to Central.

On Feb. 7, 1994, Fr. Malloy died, at age 86, a Jesuit for 70 years. He is buried at Grand Coteau.

Anthony Francis Mangiaracina, SJ
1907 – 1976
A master of novices who modeled warmth and humility

Fr. Anthony Francis Mangiaracina was an innovative master of novices who trained many young men on their way to becoming Jesuits. His lengthy tenure preceded the changes brought about by the Second Vatican Council, changes that he had foreseen years before.

Born in New Orleans on Aug. 17, 1907, Mangiaracina entered the Novitiate at Grand Coteau and followed the traditional course of priestly formation until he was ordained in 1941. His first assignment was to Grand Coteau as *socius* to the master of novices (1943-45). He quickly became the master of novices himself, a position he held for 16 years.

His years as master of novices were characterized by unveiled piety – he wept when praying – and his continued concern for his novices who had moved on, as well as his "relaxed" approach to

training of his novices. Some criticized his manner of structuring the Novitiate, calling it "Mangiaracina's kindergarten." He shocked many whom he trained by asking them candidly to "criticize" his performance as master, a habit he integrated into his training strategies.

Fr. Tony was assiduous in developing vocations. He seemed always to be encouraging a high school senior or talking to young men about Jesuit life – a novel thing in those days. His tenure in the Novitiate, therefore, was one of care and concern. One provincial commented:

"Tony's greatest contribution to the New Orleans Province was the example he gave to his novices and to others about how a Jesuit could be a warm and loving person."

As master of novices, he was expected to continue the usual, traditional practices for training novices even as change was in the air. Current formation practices were pre-Vatican II in nature, but years earlier Tony could see that revisions would have to be made. However, he had been required to hold to the old traditions, which were often contrary to the ways he trained novices. This conflict surely contributed to his high blood pressure.

A colleague remarked:

"Often in conversation with others, he would inevitably talk about life in the Church today and life in the Society and the changes that were taking place. As long as Tony was in the Society and as old as he was, there was still a freshness and youthfulness about him in his approach to modern problems."

Fr. Mangiaracina, who "made" Jesuits, was also an accomplished cabinetmaker. It was his hobby and a direct way of helping others, e.g., furniture for the novices' chapel. His output included a greenhouse, a fish tank, and a fleet of flat-bottom boats, which he constructed for the novices' villa at Kinder, La.

When he departed Grand Coteau, his physician reported he was "under considerable pressure and somewhat tired." His next jobs were of moderate stress: minister at Loyola (1961-64), at Strake Jesuit College Prep (1964-67), at Grand Coteau (1967-69) and at the Provincial's residence (1969-70). As a man with an eye for details, he served admirably in these jobs.

Aging and infirm, he returned to Grand Coteau and offered his services as spiritual director at the new Spirituality Center. To the novices of that era, he was a fine example of the older Jesuit with a youthful outlook. After his fifth heart attack, it was clear Fr. Mangiaracina was dying. He asked the community for their pardon for his faults and offenses. Then he embraced his vow crucifix.

He died on May 1, 1976, and is buried at Grand Coteau.

Warren Stone Martin, SJ
1901 – 2002
*At age 100, 'Chief' was
the oldest Jesuit in the U.S.*

Warren Stone Martin lived to be 100 years old, making him the oldest Jesuit in the United States at that time. In his long career, he was spiritual father, or "Chief," to generations of Jesuits in training.

He got the nickname "Chief" because, as one Jesuit quipped, he had a face that led some to think of the Cigar Store Indian.

Born in New Orleans on Nov. 27, 1901, Warren had a somewhat unusual primary education for a future Jesuit: He attended two private schools named for and administered by women – Mrs. Maguire's School (1908-12) and Miss Finney's School (1912-15).

After he graduated from Immaculate Conception College in New Orleans in 1919, he entered the Novitiate in Macon, Ga., where he divided his Juniorate between Macon and the school at Augusta, Ga. (1921-23), followed by philosophy at Mount St. Michael's in Spokane (1923-26).

During the summers from 1926 to 1929 he took education courses in Spokane and Mobile – an indication of his future ministry. After teaching at Jesuit High in New Orleans and Spring Hill High School in Mobile, he traveled to St. Mary's College in Kansas for theology (1929-1931) and was ordained on June 22, 1932.

Initially, Fr. Martin served as a high school teacher and student advisor at Jesuit High in Tampa (1934-1944) and then at the Jesuit school in Shreveport (1944-45). The Province moved him to the House of Studies at Spring Hill College in Mobile to be spiritual father to the Jesuit philosophy students. He stayed there for 20 years.

Changing course, he resumed high school teaching at Jesuit High in Shreveport for seven years before it was discerned that his teaching and directing skills were needed at a minor seminary which the Province had begun to staff. Thus, he worked for ten years at Corpus Christi Minor Seminary.

After nearly a lifetime of service, Fr. Martin returned to Jesuit High in Tampa for a few more years before he fully retired in 1996.

At the age of 92 he came to live in the Province retirement community in New Orleans. His body failing, he suffered a series of strokes and died on May 24, 2002, at a cool 100 years of age. He is buried at Spring Hill, which had benefitted from his service for many years.

His full century of life meant that he was part of many major changes. In 1921, early in his Jesuit life, the Novitiate at Macon, Ga., burned down, which forced a move to Grand Coteau, La. Jesuit High in New Orleans, his *alma mater*, moved in 1926 from downtown to its current campus on Carrollton Avenue. He taught at Spring Hill High School, which closed in 1935, and also taught in Tampa at the old downtown school next to Sacred Heart Church and then at the new school on Himes Avenue. Like many, he experienced Vatican II, which changed how Catholics thought about God and how the faithful expressed that in sacraments.

Emile Mattern, SJ
1865 – 1935
*American Assistant
to Superior General*

Fr. Emile Mattern spent the last 12 years of his life as American Assistant, a trusted advisor of Father General as well as his Admonitor.

The 26th Superior General of the Society, Fr. Wlodimir Ledochowski, wrote of him, "He won the hearts of all by his admirable gentleness and humble charity... a truly simple and virtuous man...."

Born an Alsatian in Andlau on Oct. 2, 1865, he enrolled at an apostolic school and entered the Society of Jesus in October of 1884. Recruited by Fr. John F. O'Connor, the mission superior in New Orleans, Mattern started his Novitiate in New York and finished it at Florissant, Mo. His philosophy studies were made at Grand Coteau and his theology at Woodstock, Md. His Tertian instructor was the renowned Venerable Adolph Petit.

One year after his Tertianship he began his long career in administrative government. He became rector at Grand Coteau in 1901, and he was there when the college burned down in 1907. He also served as rector in New Orleans when Loyola University was begun in 1912. He was the novice master at Macon when a typhoid epidemic hit in 1914, and in 1918 he was provincial when west Texas and New Mexico were added to the Province at the dissolution of the Denver Mission. He made the decision to relocate the Novitiate to Grand Coteau after the Macon fire of 1921.

In 1923, as provincial, he went to Rome to be a delegate to the 27th General Congregation. His linguistic abilities, vision and religious spirit impressed the delegates who elected him by a large majority to be the third American Assistant since the establishment of the American Assistancy – the first non-European Assistancy – in 1915. Acting as an advisor to the general, he handled matters involving the American Jesuit provinces and houses, reading their letters and making recommendations about his region.

He was a quiet man, much loved by all who knew him. From boyhood his health was shaky, but he showed great energy all his life. He is remembered as one of the most distinguished of American Jesuits, one who constantly advanced to positions of even greater distinction.

Fr. Mattern died in Rome on the feast of St. Ignatius, July 31, 1935, at age 69. His funeral was attended by Superior General Ledochowski, members of the General Curia, and his brother, Paul, who was also a Jesuit and rector of the Maronite College in Rome. Fr. Mattern is buried in Italy.

Julius James May, SJ
1916 – 1985
Born to teach, he spent 3 decades in the classroom

A cheerful man and a good listener who was encouraging and supportive, Julius James May was born to teach.

Born in New Orleans on Aug. 31, 1916, "Jay" attended Jesuit High School (1929-33), studied one year at Loyola University, then entered the Novitiate at Grand Coteau on July 3, 1934. His trajectory was traditional: two years of Juniorate, three years of philosophy at Spring Hill and the requisite three years of Regency. He studied theology at St. Marys, Kan. (1944-48), and was ordained on June 18, 1947.

Having already earned a B.S. degree in chemistry from Spring Hill, Jay worked summer after summer to achieve an M.S. in chemistry/physics from the University of Texas. He accomplished that goal in 1958.

Fr. May's apostolic ministry was spent entirely in the classrooms of the high schools of the Province. Fr. May began teaching chemistry at Jesuit High in Dallas, remaining there nearly two decades (1949-67). Then he transferred to Jesuit High in Tampa, where he taught chemistry for a decade (1967-76). A third high school, Jesuit High in Shreveport, awaited him (1976-80) and next he taught at Corpus Christi Minor Seminary (1980-82). Finally, he was assigned to Jesuit High in New Orleans as both tutor and teacher.

His health had been in decline for several years, and after just months back in New Orleans he retired to Ignatius Residence. Fr. May died on Dec. 12, 1985, at age 69. He is buried at Grand Coteau.

It is fortunate to have Fr. May's obituary written by Mike Majoli, SJ, one of his close friends throughout high school, 13 years of formation and many years of ministry. Fr. Majoli lauded Jay's virtues, especially his loyalty:

"Nothing caused him to lose heart when a friend was involved."

Of his compassion, Fr. Majoli wrote:

"Jay was untiring in helping the slow-witted, the poor, the discouraged."

John Patrick McFarland, SJ
1908 – 1990
Philosophy teacher for 46 years

John Patrick McFarland was destined to teach philosophy, and he did so for nearly half a century.

A Northerner by birth, he was transparent, intelligent, dedicated and simply decent. Rare was the day when he appeared angry or depressed or confounded. In short, he was a very supportive priest and a pleasure to be around.

After John was born on Feb. 17, 1908, in Napoleon, Ohio, his family eventually moved to Lima, Ohio, where he took his primary and secondary education at St. Rose School. After he graduated, he immediately entered the Jesuit Order on Sept. 2, 1926, at the Novitiate in Milford, Ohio. There he did his spiritual formation and his first college studies, leaving Milford in 1931.

His destiny was to teach philosophy and so his education was tailored to this end. For decades, he pursued degrees at several institutions, earning a B.A. from Loyola University of Chicago (1932-33) and an M.A. and a PhL from St. Louis University

(1945-46). He also studied at Laval University in Quebec City (summers of 1950-53), Oxford University in England (1967-68), and Ottawa University for doctoral studies (1969-70).

Although he earned multiple degrees in philosophy, the doctorate eluded him. Ultimately, it seemed not to have mattered, as he had a grand career of teaching philosophy to seminarians. He taught first at the Chicago diocesan seminary, St. Mary of the Lake, in Mundelein, Ill. (1946-69). He moved to the South to teach the Jesuit scholastics at Spring Hill College (1970-75), transcribing from the Detroit Province to the New Orleans Province, where he spent the rest of his ministerial life. He concluded his career at City College, Loyola's evening division school (1975-90). In all, Fr. Mc-Farland devoted nearly 46 years of his life to the teaching of philosophy.

Fr. McFarland had to retire because of a cancer which ultimately took his life. He moved to the Jesuit infirmary, where on April 14, 1990, he died at age 82. He is buried at Grand Coteau.

Alexis Clifford McLaughlin, SJ
1867 – 1964
The 'grand old man'
of the Province

For many members of the Province, Cliff McLaughlin will always be its "grand old man."

Born in New York City on Nov. 29, 1867, he entered the Society at the old West Park Novitiate in 1886, but completed his Novitiate at Frederick, Maryland. During his Juniorate his health deteriorated and there was serious question of whether he would be able to continue in the Society. Even a sojourn at home did not seem to bring about any improvement.

Then he ran into a Jesuit guest, Fr. John O'Shanahan, superior of the New Orleans Mission, and it was to him the young junior told his story. Fr. O'Shanahan made arrangements to take the sickly McLaughlin back to the South with him, but with one proviso: "If I cure him, I keep him."

Although Cliff was never really cured, he found a way to survive by devising his own exercise program: long walks and calisthenics. They must have helped because he was still able to do chin-ups into his eighties.

There were two health issues that bothered him most: his very poor eyesight and a faulty sense of balance. Yet he would walk with the best

of the younger Jesuits well into his old age.

He was ordained in Mobile in 1901 and for the next 43 years with few intermissions he was an *operarius* in many Southern parishes and missions. His specialty was the one-on-one encounter. After a few words of greeting he would often engage anyone he met in a dialogue about salvation. When the topic of absolution was brought up, he frequently would bring out the stole considered necessary for sacramental use and proceed to hear a confession.

His preferred prospects were the poor. In his later years, on arriving at Spring Hill, he would get one of the philosophers to drive him down to the "boondocks," where he would inevitably discover the son or granddaughter of someone he knew and urge them to make their peace with God or have their marriage blessed or their children baptized.

Once, in 1945, he went with the juniors on an excursion from Grand Coteau to Baton Rouge. He used the opportunity during the ride to the top of the State Capitol to engage the elevator operator in a conversation about religion and salvation. While the juniors were admiring the view, he was hearing the confession of his new friend.

Fr. McLaughlin was a poet and, in 1944, he published *Songs from the Vineyard*, a collection of more than 100 sonnets and poems he wrote over a period of 50 years. His poetry reflected the rotund writing style he learned in the Victorian age. There was something of that same style in his community exhortations, which were filled with sublime thoughts and unconscious humor.

Everyone loved Cliff and the feeling seemed to be mutual. While he was never heard to say an uncharitable word, it was his restless zeal and his joyful zest in loving the Lord that impressed people most.

Fr. McLaughlin died on Dec. 28, 1964, at age 97, and is buried at Grand Coteau.

John F. Moore, SJ
1922 – 1968
A saintly man: meek,
kind, gentle and humble

John F. Moore was one of the most unforgettable characters of the New Orleans Province. He was also one of the few Jesuits whom most of his Jesuit brethren considered a saint.

He was always the same in physical appearance: a meek, soft-spoken, gentle, slightly built man with a shy smile. His practice of poverty was evident in his clothing and shoes. His simple way of talking about the Lord was disarming, but very effective. He was never known to say an unkind word about anyone.

Johnny was born in Mobile, Ala., on May 2, 1922, of Irish parents. After graduating from McGill Institute he followed his older brother, Michael, into the Society. He pursued the formation course of his day: Grand Coteau, Spring Hill, Regency at Jesuit High in New Orleans, and St. Marys, Kan.

Because of his exceptional intellectual gifts, he was sent to do a *biennium* in philosophy in Rome and another year in Germany studying modern logic. His dissertation was on Bertrand Russell, the British philosopher and social critic. Starting in 1958 he taught in the Philosophate and college at Spring Hill.

He also served as chaplain to the Brothers of the Sacred Heart, whose house of studies was adjacent to the Spring Hill campus. With the help of the scholastics, he ministered to the black faithful of Sandtown. In his last years, he was active in the interracial apostolate.

There are many Johnny Moore stories, some centering on his poor health in his last years. He had ulcers and then cancer was diagnosed. In the summer of 1967, he had part of his lung removed. A fellow Jesuit visited him in the hospital and asked him if he was in much pain. His laconic reply was, "Only when I breathe."

Dr. Charles Boyle, who was both John's student and faculty colleague at Spring Hill, wrote of "the awe we felt in the presence of his truly Christian humility and charity; and the inspiration we received from his relentless academic demands upon himself."

He gave an extraordinary Christian witness to doctors, nurses and visitors during his last months at Providence Hospital. Youree Watson, SJ, said at his funeral:

"Some declared what all probably felt, they had never known a patient like him: so resigned, so obedient to orders, so cheerful, so desirous not to be a burden, so devout."

On Jan. 29, 1968, at age 45, Fr. Moore died of a brain tumor. He is buried at Spring Hill.

John Henry Mullahy, SJ
1914 – 1978
Even his science-minded students got a well-rounded education

In his many years as a professor at Loyola University, John Henry Mullahy was recognized by colleagues and students alike for his seriousness of purpose and strong sense of duty.

Fr. Mullahy tried to make his students both professionally excellent and morally good persons with faith and concern for others. He had a robust work ethic motivated by love of God and neighbor.

Born in Baltimore on June 26, 1914, John entered the Novitiate at Grand Coteau on Aug. 30, 1932, and took vows in 1934. He studied philosophy at St. Louis University and Spring Hill College. He stayed at Spring Hill for his Regency (1939-41) and spent 1941 and 1942 at Fordham University, where he taught and took courses in preparation for graduate studies in biology, achieving an M.S. in cytogenetics.

He then moved to St. Marys, Kan., for theology (1942-46), and was ordained June 17, 1945. In 1955, after evaluating his spirituality, obedience, discipline and zeal, his Jesuit superiors admitted him to final vows.

His first assignment was for a year at Spring Hill College teaching biology. During this time, he was also prefect of students in Quinlan Hall.

In 1951, he received his doctorate in biology from Vanderbilt, where he also served as an instructor. While there he found time to be associate pastor of the Cathedral of the Incarnation in Nashville. A Fulbright grant sent him to the University of Manchester in 1952. He received another grant that same year to the *Stazione Zoologica* in Naples, Italy.

Later, he was sent to Loyola University, where he spent his ministerial life teaching biology. Wanting his scientific-minded students to have a broad approach to their field of study, he taught – and insisted on – a humanistic education.

He was also pre-med advisor, head of the Beta Beta Beta National Biological Honor Society fraternity, and department chairman (1955-78). Some said his scholarly work was hindered – colleagues said "sacrificed" – by his devotion to teaching and promoting his students into the medical profession.

Beginning in 1956 he celebrated Masses daily at the convent of the Poor Clares and later at St. Vincent's Home for Unwed Mothers and Infant Asylum.

For a short time, he was at the University of Washington as a visiting professor.

Fr. Mullahy was a member of the British Phycological Society, the International Phycological Society of Plant Morphologists, the Lund Botany Society, and the Albertus Magnus Guild. He published papers in general biology, cytology, and phycology, also known as algology (the study of algae).

He had a heart attack in 1970, but he continued working until 1978. The day before his death, he had attended the university's graduation Mass. The next day, on the way to graduation, in the company of Loyola's senior Jesuits, his heart failed.

Fr. Mullahy died on May 16, 1978, at age 63. He is buried at Grand Coteau.

William Frederick Obering, SJ
1886 – 1953
He said 'no' loudly to expansion of Alabama's sterilization law

William Frederick Obering remains the youngest candidate to enter Jesuit life in the history of the New Orleans Mission and Province.

Named for his father – who was himself named for Kaiser Wilhelm I – William was born in Tuscaloosa, Ala., on Sept. 18, 1886, and grew up in Demopolis, a mission of the Jesuit parish in Selma. The oldest of six children, at age 13 he prevailed upon his widowed mother to allow him to travel to the Macon, Ga., Novitiate in 1899.

His studies were often interrupted by health problems, but he was known to be a determined and hard-working scholar. He studied theology in England, where he met Thomas Atherton, a future Jesuit of the New Orleans Province.

In 1930 he received his doctorate in political science from the Catholic University of America after writing his dissertation, *The Philosophy of Law of James Harrison Wilson, Associate Justice of the United States Supreme Court*. Fr. Obering then spent the majority of his teaching years at Spring Hill College.

Fr. Obering left his most distinguishing mark when he joined the fight against a 1935 attempt by the Alabama Legislature to expand the state's existing therapeutic sterilization law. Targets of the legislation would be "those suffering from perversions, constitutional psychopathic personalities or marked departures from normal mentality." This included inmates of penal institutions or insane asylums whose "physical, mental or moral condition" would not be improved, as well as all who were "a sexual pervert, sadist, homosexualist, masochist, sodomist, or any other grave form of sexual perversion."

Fr. Obering wrote letters against the bill to members of the Mobile County legislative delegation and to newspapers as well. He testified before a state senate committee in Montgomery and persuaded others to raise their voices as well. Fr. Obering even wrote to Alabama Chief Justice Charles Hughes, whom he had known when they were boys.

The bill passed both houses of the legislature. Governor Bibb Graves, though sympathetic to the Ku Klux Klan, asked the Alabama Supreme Court for an opinion. The unanimous *per curiam* opinion stated that sterilization was a major procedure and so could be carried out constitutionally only with due process guarantee of notice and hearing, something that the bill did not authorize. The legislature reenacted a nearly identical bill, with procedural safeguards included. The governor vetoed that bill as well.

Because of his poor respiratory health, no doubt exacerbated by the cigars that he often enjoyed, Fr. Obering spent his last 13 years in the drier environment of the West. In Albuquerque, he taught at St. Joseph's University and served at Immaculate Conception Church. He then moved to El Paso and joined the staff of *Revista Católica*, a leading Catholic Spanish-language newspaper, and served at Immaculate Conception Church.

A fall down the steps of the residence, resulting in a broken hip and consequent pneumonia, led to Fr. Obering's death on Sept. 2, 1953, at age 66.

He is buried at Spring Hill.

Eugene J. O'Connor, SJ
1887 – 1968
A towering figure
with an ordinary manner

It was Fr. Eugene O'Connor's trademark to emphasize personal relationships with his many students. He took a page from Socrates, for his manner of teaching was "constantly conversing with and questioning the students."

As any accomplished teacher might say, "This shows your students that you are interested in them and want them to do well."

Born in Augusta, Ga., on Sept. 4, 1887, Gene began his life as a Jesuit on May 1, 1905, with his entry into the Macon Novitiate. He would remain there three years doing his first college studies, followed by philosophy at Woodstock, Md., and theology in St. Louis. Along the way he earned a B.A. in Latin, an M.A. in English and a doctorate in theology from Gregorian University.

It was shortly after his ordination in 1921, that Gene O'Connor arrived at Loyola University. Although learned in English, he did not teach it; instead, he taught Latin, a subject familiar to Jesuit-educated men. His stay at Loyola covered the decade of the Roaring Twenties, when Loyola's football teams often went undefeated.

Fr. O'Connor saw his students attain success in nearly every field imaginable: law, medicine, science and other professions. Some even belonged to the cryptology team that broke the Japanese secret code in World War II. Three of Fr. O'Connor's former students eventually joined the Loyola faculty: Guy Lemieux, SJ, Jacques Yenni, SJ, and Dr. Lawrence Bourgeois.

While teaching was his apostolic work, which he did for years, under nine presidents of Loyola, it should be noted that he also contributed 40 years of pastoral service to the nuns at Holy Name Convent (1926-66).

After suffering a debilitating stroke, Fr. O'Connor struggled futilely to remain at Loyola. He died on Sept. 22, 1968, a Jesuit for 63 years. He is buried at Spring Hill.

An excerpt from Fr. John Lafarge's book, *The Manner is Ordinary*, provides a window into the soul and mind of Eugene O'Connor.

The externals of his life all indicate the ordinary manner. He studied; he taught and prepared classes; he met with people who came to seek his counsel. Every morning he celebrated the Eucharist, and he was devoted to the Divine Office and the rosary.

Yet in many ways he towered above his fellows. He was brilliant, possessing a quick wit and keen mind. His Irish good humor and affable, smiling manner were above ordinary. He was "a gifted man, devoted priest and a true friend," wrote a colleague.

A relevant passage from Shakespeare best characterizes Fr. O'Connor:

His life was gentle, and the elements so mixed in him that Nature might stand up and say to all the world, this was a man.

John J. O'Connor, SJ
1905 – 1937
Ceylon missionary,
'another John Berchmans'

The grandson of an Irish immigrant, John J. O'Connor, gifted both athletically and academically, could have chosen any professional career. Instead, he devoted his life to serving God's people, particularly in Ceylon.

One of nine children, John was born on March 4, 1905, in Augusta, Ga., where he attended Catholic schools. A high achiever at Richmond Academy, he was a star shortstop on the baseball team, an outstanding quarterback on the football team, and the valedictorian of his class.

Although he was offered a scholarship to Villanova University, he chose to enter the Society at Grand Coteau on Oct. 27, 1924. He had come to know and respect the Jesuits who had the care of Sacred Heart Parish in Augusta.

In the Novitiate under the guidance of his fellow Georgian, Fr. John Salter, O'Connor developed further the deep piety of his boyhood, and many of his contemporaries thought of him as another John Berchmans, the young Jesuit saint. His spirit of prayer and practice of charity were especially outstanding. In addition he was handsome, athletic and endowed with real gifts of leadership.

During his Regency, he taught math and served as athletic director for three years at Jesuit High in New Orleans. It was during this time that the New Orleans Province was asked to help in the mission of Trincomalee, Ceylon. John volunteered and was one of the first New Orleans men sent over.

His first year and a half were spent in Batticaloa teaching in St. Michael's College and learning Tamil, the difficult native language. Meanwhile, his already-poor health declined further, especially after he caught malaria. It was thought that the cooler climate of Kurseong in the foothills of the Himalayas would work an improvement. While he was there, in 1936, he studied theology.

In April of the following year he caught a bad cold while walking in the rain to teach catechism at a nearby school. It was two days before he took to his bed and the doctor was called. Pneumonia was diagnosed. He died a week later, on April 16, 1937, after having turned 32 just the month before. He is buried in India.

Bishop Ignatius Glennie, who had been with Fr. O'Connor since their Novitiate days, reported that his last words were:

"Jesus, have mercy on us."

Peter F. O'Donnell, SJ
1905 – 1968
His fearsome exterior
belied his charming personality

Even though Fr. Peter F. O'Donnell had a somewhat fearsome appearance and was often intimidating, he was indeed one of the best-loved Jesuits of the Province.

Born in Algiers, La., Oct. 6, 1905, he was schooled in Morgan City. After finishing at Jesuit High in New Orleans, he promptly entered the Novitiate at Grand Coteau in 1923. He made the regular course of studies in three Jesuit institutions: Mt. St. Michael's, near Spokane; St. Mary's College in St. Marys, Kan.; and Manresa Hall in Port Townsend, Wash. His Regency was prolonged due to his poor health and attendant problems.

His first assignment was to Grand Coteau, where he served from 1939 to 1943 as *socius* to Novice Master Fr. Anthony Achèe. They made a peerless pair: the *socius* being the tough guy while the master was more paternal.

When he was still in his thirties, his bad health continued to work its rigors on his frail body. Although he was of medium height, his emaciated frame made him appear to be taller. His thick glasses and cadaverous visage made him a fearsome figure indeed. It was a brave novice who faced an interview with Fr. *Socius* calmly, since he was known to be ruthless in correcting his novices' uncouth habits.

And yet underneath that forbidding exterior there was a nice guy struggling to get out. He charmed the parents of novices and juniors when they came to visit and he was greeted lovingly by Jesuit visitors and the diocesan clergy who dropped in. As a matter of fact, he was one of the best-loved Jesuits of the Province.

He left Grand Coteau to spend a number of years as Spring Hill's minister in the internal apostolate of the Society. He was *socius* to the new provincial, Fr. Harry Crane, for two years and then returned to Grand Coteau as rector. For 11 years he served as a province consultor. The last 15 years of his life were spent as pastor in Augusta, Ga., and West Palm Beach, Fla.

Wherever he went he was famous for certain things: his charm and affability, and his good relations and fast friendships with the clergy of the diocese even as he continued to be plagued by ill health. After undergoing two major operations, he went back to Grand Coteau in late 1967 to try to regain his strength.

On the evening of March 11, 1968, he was returning from Opelousas on the new Highway 167. As he approached the Grand Coteau exit, another car entered the wrong lane and there was a head-on collision, killing all four occupants of the two cars. Fr. O'Donnell was 62.

He is buried at Grand Coteau.

Louis Aimé Paris, SJ
1863 – 1955
A multilingual teacher
of the humanities

A classicist, a linguist, a priest – Louis Aimé Paris was all these things, but perhaps the best descriptor of him is teacher. He devoted his long apostolic ministry to teaching his students the humanities: literature, music and languages.

Born on May 16, 1863, in Hesdigneul, France, he was educated at Littlehampton, England, in classical languages and rhetoric (1880-84). He crossed the Atlantic to enter the Novitiate in West Park, N.Y. on Sept. 3, 1884, but for reasons unknown he traveled to Florissant, Mo., where he took his vows on Sept. 12, 1886, and studied one year in the Juniorate. Louis studied philosophy at Spring Hill and then at Grand Coteau (1890-93).

His Regency spanned three schools: Jesuit High in New Orleans (1887-88), Juniorate in

Grand Coteau (1888-90) and finally Spring Hill College (1893-94). He returned to Europe for theology, spending four years at Milltown Park in Dublin (1894-98) and was ordained there on Aug. 1, 1897.

Teaching was his major apostolic endeavor, and it took him all over the South, first to Spring Hill College. He was then assigned to the Jesuit school in Galveston, Texas, where he taught all four strata of students. His musical talent led to his becoming the director of the choir and the band (1906-18).

His love for literature occasioned his appointment to the faculty in Macon, Ga., where he taught poetry (1918-21). Because of the 1921 fire at Macon, he and the Juniorate moved to Augusta for one year (1921-22) and then to Grand Coteau (1922-28). The scope of his teaching broadened to take advantage of his talents. From 1928 to 1939, Louis taught Latin, Greek and French.

While at Grand Coteau, he experienced several disabling health problems, suffering from a cancer that lingered but did not kill him. He remained there, but was able only to give private lessons and tutoring.

On Dec. 5, 1955, Fr. Paris died at age 92 and is buried at Grand Coteau.

Ferdinand Peter, SJ
1863 – 1939
Devoted to his duty
as sacristan – for 54 years!

According to an informal 1974 poll taken in the Province, the name of Bro. Ferdinand Peter was among those most frequently mentioned as being one of the outstanding men of the Province. Certainly his longevity and dedication to his responsibilities inspired his colleagues' choice.

Born in Tisis, Austria, on April 26, 1863, he entered the Society at Florissant, Mo., on April 10, 1884, but finished his Novitiate at Baronne Street in New Orleans, where he arrived on July 10, 1885. Fifty-four years later, he was still at the same post, that of sacristan.

When he first came to Baronne Street, the church there had been in existence for a little more than a quarter century. Attached to it was the Jesuit college on the corner of Baronne and Com-

mon. During Bro. Peter's time, he saw the church rebuilt in 1928, the college grow with its move to St. Charles Avenue, and the high school department transferred to Carrollton Avenue.

He had many duties as sacristan, but among the most important was the formation of altar boys. Bro. Peter trained them, marshaled them, corrected them and listened to them. Many of them eventually joined the Society of Jesus. Even to these boys, Bro. Peter had an aura of sanctity. As soon as the priest and acolytes left the sacristy, he retired to a corner to continue his meditation, usually relying on his copy of *Vercruysse's Practical Meditations*.

Bro. Peter never took a vacation. His longest absence from his duties occurred when, after an operation, he was sent to the home of his sister in North Carolina to recuperate for a few weeks.

Bro. Peter died on July 10, 1939, at age 76. He is buried at Grand Coteau.

Samuel Hill Ray, SJ
1894 – 1983
Founder of Our Lady of the Oaks
Retreat House

Fr. Sam Hill Ray was a man who envisioned things and then saw them through to fruition.

Because he spoke fluent French, he preached in neighboring towns, encouraging men to come to Grand Coteau for a spiritual retreat. This helped to persuade Bishop Jeanmard to approve the building of Our Lady of the Oaks Retreat House. Fr. Ray was its founder and director.

While teaching in the Juniorate, Fr. Ray imagined a newsletter for the Province, so the Juniors wrote to various houses for news and anecdotes, resulting in *The Southern Jesuit*. The newsletter evolved into a *bona fide* and popular magazine.

He also left a tangible and humane legacy to his students: First he begged funds to build a villa on the coteau near the Academy of the Sacred Heart and then he secured permission for his students to walk there for some leisure time.

Born on Jan. 11, 1894, in Titusville, Fla., Sam Hill Ray entered the Jesuit Novitiate at Macon, Ga., on Aug. 15, 1910, at age 16. His course of formation was typical: philosophy at Mt. St. Michael's Philosophate in Spokane, Wash. (1915-18), four years of Regency at Grand Coteau (1918-22), and theology in Montreal (1922-24).

Fr. Ray was assigned to St. Charles College in Grand Coteau as the dean of the Juniorate (1927-29). A stickler for the proper use of language, he was determined to root out "defective pronunciation and marked regionalisms." He demanded that all juniors "read more and cultivate a high standard of English in speaking and writing."

As the first retreat director at Our Lady of the Oaks, he became significant to many young men in the 1930s, since at that time Catholic school policy made it compulsory for all boys to go on a spiritual retreat.

"He was very influential in the molding of young men in those days," former retreatant Paul Fournet said of him on the occasion of Fr. Ray's fiftieth anniversary as a member of the Jesuit Order.

After serving as dean of men at Loyola, he served in World War II as a Navy chaplain on the *U.S.S. Hamlin*. Once home, he wrote a book, *A Chaplain Afloat and Ashore*, utilizing material from the letters he sent to his mother and sister, letters they had been commanded to save. They are chatty and playful, especially in the ways he signed off: "*Hamlin* Sam," "Tokyo Ray," and "Sam Hill among the Buddhas."

After serving in the Navy, Ray returned to Loyola as a spiritual counselor (1946-55). During this period, the civil rights movement emerged, which put great pressure on Loyola to integrate. Unfortunately, Fr. Ray strongly opposed the idea. Wherever possible he defended the tradition of segregation, sometimes in letters to other Jesuits and other times at public forums. The 1954 desegregation policy of the New Orleans Province did nothing to silence him, and Ray continued to fight integration, a position which proved to be a genuine scandal.

Fr. Ray was a colorful character, an inveterate entertainer and a lover of the spotlight. At least nine awards were bestowed on him, including "Military Order of the World War" (1960); "Honorary Brew Master of Falstaff Brewery" (1954); and "Mayoralty of New Orleans Certificate of Merit for Outstanding Service" (1955).

He also published two Western novels. While in El Paso he wrote *Border Tales: The Fabulous Southwest* and *Picture-History of the Pass to the North*. He could be found often selling his books at a table in the foyer of a New Orleans department store.

Fr. Ray had a stroke and died Nov. 22, 1983, at age 89. He is buried at Grand Coteau.

George Henry Raywood, SJ
1914 – 1988
A compassionate minister to fellow alcoholics

George Henry Raywood was an alcoholic who – with God's help and that of his Jesuit colleagues – didn't allow his drinking problem to ruin his life. Instead he turned it into a ministry of recovery and grace, helping many others who suffered with the same addiction.

Born in Cincinnati on Feb. 22, 1914, George graduated from Spring Hill College High School in Mobile and entered the Novitiate in Grand Coteau in 1932. His formation was typical: Novitiate, Juniorate, philosophy, Regency, and theology. He was ordained in 1945.

In September of 1948, he traveled to Ceylon (now called Sri Lanka) and was assigned to the Papal Seminary in Kandy. He taught at St. Michael's College in Batticaloa, where for six years he served as teacher, assistant principal, and then as rector-principal. He returned to the U.S. in 1960 to be the assistant to the Ceylon Mission procurator and to the director of the Jesuit Seminary Fund.

After those assignments, Fr. Raywood turned to parish ministry, first at Holy Name of Jesus (1963-66, 1971-73), and at Immaculate Conception (1966-69), both in New Orleans. After working at St. Rita Parish in Dallas from 1969 to 1971, he eventually arrived in Grand Coteau to labor in three ministries, first at St. Charles Borromeo Parish, then at Our Lady of the Oaks Retreat House, where he served as director (1975-78). Finally, he was assigned to St. Charles College, where he began his most important ministry as retreat director and spiritual guide at the Jesuit Spirituality Center. He labored there for nine years.

George's frequent moves deserve comment. He said of himself: "In 1960 I returned to the States for three months and quickly became a full-fledged professional indoor drinker." His community confronted George and put in his hand a ticket to Southdown, a quality rehabilitation center in Toronto.

He took his last drink in 1973.

George bluntly described this period of recovery as a new birth.

At age 59, an alcoholic, I learned about God and me.... I learned that God loves me, warts and all. I stopped hiding and running

and let Him catch me. This was much more
than a turning point, though; this was death
and new life.... From Michael Buckley, SJ,
I learned the unique question for priests, for
Jesuits, "Is this man weak enough?" The Pas-
chal Mystery has literally happened to me. I
have peace, serenity, and yet another career.

When Fr. Raywood encountered retreatants,
people observed his compassion and ability to
accept them where they were on their spiritual
journey. His alcoholism was a *felix culpa*, a disas-
ter which metamorphosed into recovery and a
grace-filled ministry.

"In my old age I have come alive," he said.

Fr. Raywood was most successful and influential with retreatants who were recovering alcoholics. The number of his friends and the affection in
which they held him were considerable, but
not altogether surprising, for, like Jesus, he was
a compassionate healer. He became a local and
national prophet for Alcoholics Anonymous.

Fr. Raywood died on July 14, 1988, and is buried
at Grand Coteau.

Harvey W. Rockwood, SJ
1901 – 1964
His fundraising helped
keep the Province going
in lean times

In the 1940s and '50s, Fr. Harvey "Rocky"
Rockwood was held up to young Jesuits as an example of the good a Jesuit can do, even though
he is not particularly academically accomplished.

Born in Vicksburg, Miss., on Aug. 1, 1901, he
dropped out of high school at age 16 to work in
a bank. The secular world did not hold much
attraction for him, and he entered the Society
at Grand Coteau at what was then the advanced
age of 22.

Three years in the Juniorate did something
to repair his academic shortcomings, but he was
still behind his fellow novices during philosophy studies in Spokane. He had just one year
of Regency at Spring Hill. His heroes during his
formation period were the great preachers and
mission-band men of the Province. He had an
especially deep admiration for Fr. John Hynes,
who seemed to be the first to recognize Rocky's
burning zeal and his special gifts for dealing with
people.

After theology at St. Mary's, he came back in
1936 to a Province that was suffering from the
ravages of the Depression. Put in charge of the
Jesuit Seminary Fund, he worked as a fund-raiser for
the next 21 years. After Fr. Rockwood's death,
Fr. Tom Shields wrote of him:

> Only those who can recall the Depression
> days can fully appreciate what Fr. Rockwood
> did for the Province. Day by day he worked at
> raffles, cake sales, rummage sales, card parties,
> and every other means of gathering funds. Each
> function... brought in only small amounts, but
> in the aggregate they kept the Province going.

He even used to exhort nuns to give him their
"idols," namely, statues or pictures or rosaries to
which they had a strong attachment. He would
then take these items home and raffle them off
for the Jesuit Seminary Fund.

It should be noted that fundraising in his day
involved mingling with ordinary people and
not so much with cultivating the well-to-do.
Fr. Rockwood used to motivate himself and the
scholastics to a more austere life by frequent
reminders that they were all living on "the pennies
of the poor."

During that time he gave many retreats. He
was a popular retreat master, partly because of
his sense of humor and easy compatibility with
retreatants. His last years were spent in Miami,
helping out at the Gesù and serving as both
hospital and prison chaplain.

On May 25, 1964, Fr. Rockwood died of a
heart attack while serving as chaplain on a
seven-day Caribbean cruise. There was an out-
pouring of sympathy at his final rites in the Gesù;
more than 6,000 people filed by to pay their
respects. He is buried at Spring Hill.

Patrick Michael Rosenblath, SJ
1928 – 1973
The man in charge
of the kitchen

Little is known of Bro. Patrick Michael
Rosenblath's life prior to his becoming a Jesuit.
However, it is known that his short tenure in the
Society was marked by his service and adaptability.

Born in Shreveport, La., on Aug. 6, 1928, to
Quinlan and Mildred Rosenblath, Patrick entered the Society of Jesus on Oct. 27, 1945, as
a Brother novice and took his vows on May 16,
1948. He remained at Grand Coteau, presumably learning his trade and craft.

His first assignment was at the Jesuit House of Studies in Mobile, Ala., where for four years he was in charge of the kitchen with duties as refectorian, supervisor of the kitchen, and cook. He was then sent to Jesuit High in El Paso to fill the positions of school registrar and moderator of both the Radio Club and Photography Club.

"Rosey," as his peers called him, spent a year in Shreveport (1967-68), again as supervisor of the kitchen while performing other jobs as well. He served at Lake Dallas Retreat House as its minister and treasurer from 1968 to 1969, and then he returned to El Paso for three years as minister and part of the team for CCD (Confraternity of Christian Doctrine) and CYO (Catholic Youth Organization).

He returned to Spring Hill College in 1973 but died that same year, on May 19, at age 44. He is buried at Spring Hill.

Murphy William Ross, SJ
1903 – 1983
Apostle of the 'Little Way to God'

Murphy William Ross was a letterman on the Jesuit High of New Orleans football team, a fact that would later impact his life when he became an athletic director in Dallas.

Born in New Orleans on Dec. 18, 1903, he was intensely proud of his father, who began newspaper work as a typesetter but rose through the ranks to become the editor of the newspaper *The New Orleans States*. Murphy could surely have found employment at the paper, but he took a different path for his life. After his 1923 high school graduation, he decided to become a Jesuit.

Entering the Novitiate at Grand Coteau on Aug. 24, 1923, Mike, as he was called, spent the traditional two years in spiritual formation. However, he ended up spending three years in the Juniorate because the Great Depression left the Order without adequate finances for his further education and also because he became ill.

In 1928 he began his philosophy studies in Spokane, but they were interrupted because he was again temporarily sidelined by illness. He spent four years of Regency at Spring Hill College (1931-35), after which he did his theology studies at St. Mary's in Kansas. He was ordained June 22, 1938. It should be noted that all through his training he was subject to debilitating headaches and stomach problems.

Fr. Ross's ministerial career began with assignments to teach in the Province's high schools. During World War II, he taught at Jesuit High in New Orleans and in 1944 he traveled to Jesuit High in Dallas, where he served for five years, the first two as assistant principal.

He was also that school's athletic director, which was a factor in an accident which nearly killed him. In the process of placing football equipment on top of a stack of shelves near the ceiling of the athletic room, he fell headlong onto the concrete floor and was unconscious for many days, in danger of his life. Ultimately he was able to withstand an operation which inserted a permanent metal plate into his skull.

In recuperation, he undertook parish work in West Palm Beach, Fla. (1949-53); Augusta, Ga. (1953-56 and 1959); Miami (1956-59) and finally New Orleans. He felt that his best work was done in the confessionals of Holy Name of Jesus (1959-71) and the Immaculate Conception Church (1971-75), both in New Orleans. He kept detailed records of his time in the confessional and was justly proud of the many hours he spent dispersing the healing forgiveness of the Lord. His last assignment was a return to Jesuit High in Dallas, where he both taught and counseled. He stayed there from 1975 until the fall of 1983 when illness forced him to retire.

Occasionally he expressed disappointment that he had never been a priest of reputation, such as one who gave convocations or delivered graduation speeches. His vocation instead was to be an apostle of the "Little Way to God."

He retired to Ignatius Residence in New Orleans in the fall of 1983 and died at age 80 on the last day of December of that same year. He is buried at Grand Coteau.

Orie Abell
1888 - 1971

Anthony Achèe
1900 - 1962

Gerald Armstrong
1909 - 1996

Thomas Atherton
1901 - 1992

Manuel Arrizabalaga
1879 - 1965

Gabriel Barras
1901 - 1968

Ronald Barrilleaux
1897 - 1976

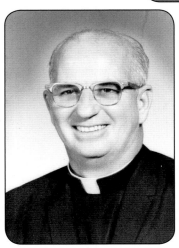

Joseph Beaver
1918 - 1982

Peter Beach
1918 - 1955

Carmine Benanti
(1901 - 1968), at left,
with a fellow Jesuit

Arnold Benedetto
1916 - 1966

Edgar Bernard
1862 - 1940

Albert Biever
1858 - 1934

Loyola University of New Orleans began operating as a Jesuit-run facility in 1904, with Fr. Albert Biever as its first president. In 1912, Loyola was authorized by the State of Louisiana to begin granting university degrees.

Robert Boggs
1916 - 1990

Joseph Bogue
1900 - 1978

Halcott Burges
1875 - 1968

Martin Burke
1886 - 1960

Joseph Burleigh
1898 - 1989

Ernest Burrus
1907 - 1991

Paul Callens
1895 - 1970

Felix Clarkson
1908 - 1980

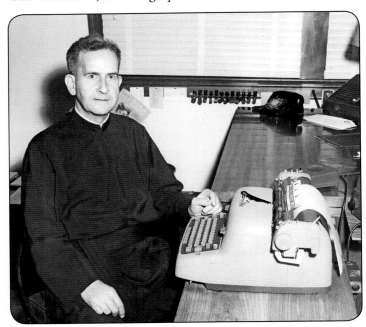

Auguste Coyle
1910 - 1978

Raymond Cody
1905 - 1974

Godfrey Cook
1902 - 1995

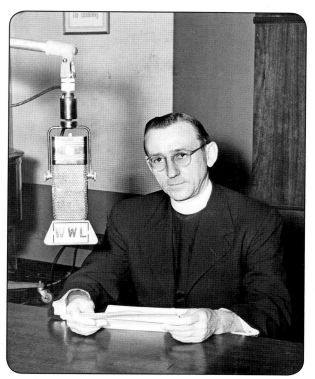

Harry Crane
1906 - 1982

Michael Cronin
1878 - 1962

John Curley
1909 - 1984

Edward Curry
1914 - 1963

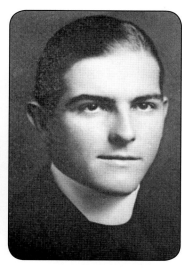

Joseph Dardis
1912 - 1977

Spring Hill College, founded in 1830 by the Diocese of Mobile and taken over in 1847 by the Jesuits, is Alabama's oldest institution of higher learning. In 1954 it became the first racially desegregated college in the Deep South.

Emmanuel de la Moriniere
1856 - 1930

James de Potter
1855 - 1933

John Deignan
1891 - 1966

Patrick Donnelly
1908 - 1967

Leo Dowling
1873 - 1956

Edward Doyle
1914 - 1979

Ross Druhan
1899 - 1968

Gabino Egana
1891 - 1969

Paul Elfer
1873 - 1958

Louis Eisele
1912 - 1988

Clyde Elliot
1915 - 1977

Francis Entz
1883 - 1954

Joseph Fengler
1910 - 1984

Joseph Fichter
1908 - 1994

J. Cruz Garde
1874 - 1945

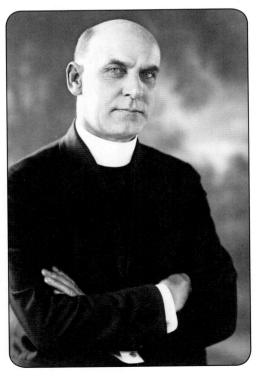

John Foulkes
1867 - 1941

John Gasson
1904 - 1988

Harold Gaudin
1898 - 1983

Richard Gaul
1903 - 1993

Aloysius Goodspeed
1901 - 1980

Bishop Ignatius Glennie
1907 - 1993

Lester Guterl
1907 - 1968

Louis Hahn
1915 - 1977

Edward Goss
1909 - 1979

George Hamilton
1905 - 1995

Manresa House of Retreats, located in Convent, La., on the banks of the Mississippi River midway between Baton Rouge and New Orleans, occupies the site of the former Jefferson College, a private school for the sons of plantation owners. The Jesuits of the New Orleans Province purchased the property in 1931 and soon began offering men's retreats here based on the Spiritual Exercises of St. Ignatius.

Elwood Hecker
1914 - 1989

Louis Hiegel
1915 - 1969

Johannes Hofinger
1905 – 1984

John Hynes
1886 - 1953

Our Lady of the Oaks Retreat House in Grand Coteau, La., was built by the Diocese of Lafayette in 1938 and donated to the Jesuits of the New Orleans Province. Group retreats for men, women and couples are made here year-round.

The retreat house is next door to St. Charles Borromeo Church, which is pastored by the Jesuits, and just a stone's throw from St. Charles College, which houses the Jesuit Novitiate and Spirituality Center.

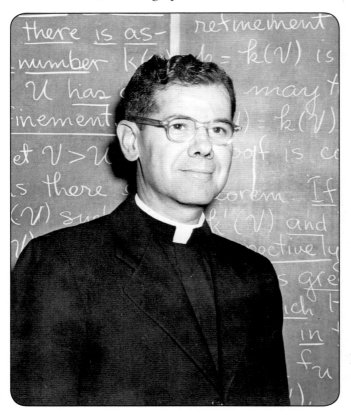

Alfred Latiolais
1869 - 1959

Everett Larguier
1910 - 2000

Robert Libertini
1885 - 1973

Guy Lemieux
1908 - 1966

Whitmel Macnair
1920 - 1973

Joseph Malloy
1907 - 1994

Tony Mangiaracina
1907 - 1976

Warren Martin
1901 - 2002

Julius May
1916 - 1985

John McFarland
1908 - 1990

Emile Mattern
1865 - 1935

Montserrat Retreat House in Lake Dallas was founded in 1959 as a Catholic men's facility. Now, men, women and Christians of all denominations are welcomed for weekend retreats and days of prayer and recollection.

Alexis McLaughlin
1867 - 1964

John Moore
1922 - 1968

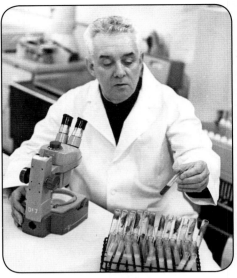

John Mullahy
1914 - 1978

Eugene O'Connor
1887 - 1968

Peter O'Donnell
1905 - 1968

Louis Paris
1863 - 1955

Ferdinand Peter
1863 - 1936

Samuel Ray
1894 - 1983

George Raywood
1914 - 1988

Harvey Rockwood
1901 - 1964

Patrick Rosenblath
1928 - 1973

Murphy Ross
1903 - 1983

Roy Schilling
1928 - 1974

Edmund Roth (1904 - 1981), at left,
with fellow Jesuit Brother
Joseph Eaton

John Schwing
1911 - 1983

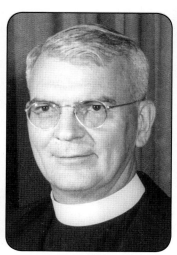

Thomas Shields
1900 - 1975

Louis Soniat
1900 - 1973

Lucien Soniat
1897 - 1943

Cornelius Thensted
(1903 - 1981), at left,
and **John Salter**
(1877 - 1933)

George St. Paul
1897 - 1977

Carmelo Tranchese
1880 - 1956

Cornelius Thensted
1903 - 1981

Louis Twomey (1905 - 1969), at left, with **Fr. Gen. Pedro Arrupe**

Ignatius House Retreat Center in Atlanta was established in 1960 by the Jesuits of the New Orleans Province, offering silent weekend retreats, days of reflection, and spiritual direction to individuals and groups of all faiths. The property that the retreat center sits on was donated by Suzanne Spalding Schroder and her son, Fr. John Schroder, S.J. In 2013 the adminis-tration of the center was assumed by the Jesuits of the Maryland Province.

Austin Wagner
1887 - 1956

John Walsh
1915 - 1989

Robert Walet
1910 - 1988

Joseph Walsh
1912 – 1990

Youree Watson
1914 - 1989

Michael Watters
1891 - 1969

James Yamauchi
1920 - 1976

Patrick Yancey
1896 - 1969

Edmund Walsh Roth, SJ
1904 – 1981
The humble infirmarian

Before Edmund Walsh Roth entered the Novitiate and after he had attended Loyola University for two years, he worked for a while as a registered pharmacist. That experience was a prelude to his ministry as a Jesuit infirmarian.

A native New Orleanian born on April 17, 1904, Edmund Roth attended both Jesuit High (1918-24) and Loyola University (1925-27), then became a registered pharmacist (1927-33). After working in the secular business world, he entered the Novitiate at Grand Coteau, La., on Aug. 16, 1933, to become a Brother. Thus, he was not obligated to follow the long educational process required of priests.

Much of his apostolic ministry was spent as infirmarian to various Jesuit communities. He began at Grand Coteau, where he stayed from 1933 until 1937. He was moved to Jesuit High in New Orleans as both infirmarian and kitchen manager (1937-39), followed by a few years at Spring Hill College in Mobile in the same capacity (1939-43). He returned to Grand Coteau for four years (1943-47), and then moved back to New Orleans to be sacristan at Loyola University (1947-53).

He returned to Spring Hill as infirmarian at the Jesuit House of Studies (1954-56), and beginning in 1959 he served the Jesuit High community in El Paso for a number of years.

He was an undemanding person who seemed not to ask for much nor require much. Although he had serious arthritis and limped in his gait, he spoke about it only when asked. He would not eat spicy foods, but in El Paso one could hardly avoid it.

Marty Elsner, SJ, who delivered the homily at Bro. Roth's funeral, described him as a quiet and shy man who was slow to make friends. Clearly he wanted friendships, but a person approaching him had to give a bit of himself to strike up a friendship. This shy man seemed unable to invite himself to go with a group from the community. Even if he wanted to go to athletic contests, he needed an invitation. But invite him they did, and he went with them.

On April 6, 1981, Bro. Roth died at age 76 in New Orleans. He is buried at Grand Coteau.

John M. Salter, SJ
1877 – 1933
Relative of vice president of the Confederacy; Depression era Provincial

A member of prestigious American families, John Mary Salter, born in Sparta, Ga., on June 23, 1877, was the grandnephew of Alexander H. Stephens, who served as vice president of the Confederate States of America.

John was also a member of the noted Williams, Edwards and Stoddard families of New England, which produced many renowned members, including the founder of the Protestant Church of the Advent in Boston and two aunts who were members of the Society of the Sacred Heart. With such a pedigree he could have done anything he wanted; he chose service to God.

Salter entered the Society of Jesus when he was 17. Finishing his Novitiate and classical studies in Macon, he studied philosophy at St. Charles College in Grand Coteau and St. Louis University, followed by four years of teaching at Sacred Heart College in Augusta, Ga.

He did his theology studies at Woodstock College in Maryland, in "Yankee country," where he distinguished himself by doing "the Grand Act," a public defense of theses in theology and philosophy before a group of professors.

In 1910 he began teaching at Loyola, and when he was 36 he was appointed rector of Sacred Heart College in Augusta. At this time, Georgia was very much the center of the Province with several parishes, the Novitiate and the young college at Augusta, which was begun in 1900. As a scholastic, John had taught there from 1901 to 1906; and he served there again as rector from 1913 until he oversaw its closing in 1918.

His next assignment was to be master of novices and rector of St. Stanislaus College at Macon, succeeding Fr. Emile Mattern. He was still there when the Novitiate burned down in November of 1921, forcing the juniors to transfer to Augusta, while the novices had to make do in the Novitiate villa. The following year the Province's Novitiate was transferred to Grand Coteau, where Fr. Salter continued as novice master until 1928.

As novice master John Salter was popular;

although demanding, he had a greater tolerance for human weakness than some of his European-born predecessors. Many who knew him appreciated that while he was a man of rare scholarship and outstanding ability as an executive, he was also a modest and self-effacing man.

He was made provincial in 1928, right on the brink of a tumultuous time in American history. In his new position he had to deal with the disastrous consequences that the Great Depression had on Province finances as well as on the people served by the Jesuits.

He also oversaw changes in some of the Society's missions and parishes. It was Fr. Salter who returned the Selma residence to the Bishop of Mobile in 1931, relinquishing that long-held institution. Since 1880, Selma had been a hub of Jesuit home mission activity.

On the other hand, he accepted Guadalupe Church in San Antonio and sent Carmelo Tranchese, SJ, there as pastor. In 1931, he also purchased Jefferson College in Convent, La., which metamorphosed into Manresa House of Retreats. Up to that time laymen's retreats were conducted in Jefferson Parish.

Fr. Salter became ill in Augusta on March 19, 1933, and remained in University Hospital a few weeks before returning to New Orleans. On May 2, 1933, Fr. Salter died at age 55.

Interestingly, he is buried at Grand Coteau next to Thomas Sherman, SJ, the son of Union General William Tecumseh Sherman. This was merely a coincidence since the two Jesuits died closely together, Fr. Sherman on April 29, 1933, and Fr. Salter just a few days later. Thus, the grandnephew of the vice-president of the Confederacy lies in death alongside the son of the Union Army general.

Roy E. Schilling, SJ
1928 – 1974
'Mr. 5-by-5' ruled the classroom with high energy and rapid wit

Roy E. Schilling was a master teacher certified in English, French, Latin, Greek, German and humor. Additionally, he was an administrator whose skills were very much needed and appreciated in the Province.

Born in New Orleans on Nov. 5, 1928, he graduated from Jesuit High in 1945 and worked there as assistant registrar for two years before entering the Society in 1947. He was an excellent student throughout his studies at Grand Coteau, Spring Hill and St. Mary's.

After Tertianship, there was a problem of where to assign him. He was a skilled classicist and a good linguist, as well as being gifted with a prodigious musical talent as an organist, pianist and vocalist. He would have done credit to any school to which he was appointed.

It was decided that he would serve at Jesuit High in New Orleans. During his Regency he had great success moderating the Philelectic Society – the drama department – at Jesuit High. As part of the initiation to the group, a candidate was asked "How many pounds in a Schilling?" Fr. Schilling was good-natured about it and would call a halt to the response only after many minutes of laughter.

His talent as a teacher was obvious, but his talent as an administrator was more critically needed. After a year teaching in the Juniorate he became the assistant principal at Jesuit High in New Orleans and then became principal at Jesuit High in Shreveport from 1965 to 1971. Although he was an able and effective principal, he really longed to return to the classroom, and so he was content to spend his last years teaching once more in New Orleans.

Fr. Schilling loved his students and had an obvious gift in dealing with them, particularly with athletes. He was surely not the athletic type; in fact, his contemporaries called him "Mr. Five-by-Five," a reference to his rotund physique.

This high-energy teacher was all over the classroom talking with a rapid wit that a disc jockey would have envied and with the intelligence of a born educator and highly cultured man. Students flocked to him after class and on weekends and even came back to see him after they graduated.

On Nov. 18, 1974, just days after his 46th birthday, Fr. Schilling died suddenly of a heart attack. It was touching to see the devotion of current and former students who thronged to his funeral Mass and the gratitude of parents whose sons he had influenced.

He is buried at Grand Coteau.

John Elmer Schwing, SJ
1911 – 1983
Latinist, teacher, stamp-collector

John Elmer Schwing is remembered as a Latinist and natural-born teacher. And many also recall he was a master stamp-collector with a remarkable and extensive collection.

Johnny Schwing was born on July 22, 1911, in New Iberia, La., one of 11 children. His early education was with the Christian Brothers, who staffed St. Peter's College in New Iberia (1917-26). He then spent two years at Spring Hill High School in Mobile (1926-28).

He returned to Louisiana and entered the Order on Aug. 14, 1928. His path was very traditional from then on: two years of Juniorate (1930-32), three years of philosophy at St. Louis University (1932-35), one year of Regency at Spring Hill College (1935-36) and three years at Jesuit High School in New Orleans (1936-39). As was the custom, Schwing studied theology at St. Marys, Kan. He was ordained June 17, 1942. He had two degrees in Latin: an A.B. and an M.A., both from St. Louis.

Fr. Schwing was born to teach. He spent six years at St. John's High School in Shreveport as teacher, athletic director and occasionally as the community minister (1944-49). He stepped across the Texas-Louisiana line to teach and coach for a few years at Jesuit High in Dallas (1949-52) before he was sent to Spring Hill College, where he taught for 20 years (1952-72) and coached tennis for 12 years (1960-72).

In 1972 Fr. Schwing was re-assigned as a teacher to Jesuit College Prep in Dallas. And it is there that one could find his remarkable stamp collection.

Fr. Schwing died on Sept. 12, 1983, at age 72. He is buried at Grand Coteau.

Thomas J. Shields, SJ
1900 – 1975
'The Silver Sage of Banks Street'

From the Jesuits' vantage point, Fr. Thomas Shields, born in New Orleans on Aug. 16, 1900, was one of the most important provincials in the history of the Province.

After World War I the Province showed steady growth, but the Depression found the Jesuits over-extended and with a Seminary Fund too poor to educate the increasing number of scholastics. There were tensions in leadership, and the younger men in the Province had not been trained to take over positions of responsibility.

Thus, Father General Wlodimir Ledochowski appointed the English Jesuit, Fr. Joseph Bolland, to conduct a visitation of the Province in March of 1936, with Fr. Thomas Shields as his *socius*. At the conclusion of the visitation young Shields was appointed Provincial in January of 1937.

Fr. Shields was only 36, but he had the unmistakable bearing and character of a leader. A tall, slender man with prematurely gray hair, he was an excellent speaker with a deep and sonorous voice.

The Province rallied behind the new provincial. Fr. Shields started the Philosophate at Spring Hill and guided Loyola and Jesuit High in New Orleans in the stabilization and better use of the radio station WWL and the Père Marquette building. He appointed a set of younger superiors and worked with Fathers Jean Lapeyre and Harvey Rockwood to build up the Seminary Fund.

He was also a pioneer in sending Jesuits off for special studies. Perhaps his greatest service as provincial was his excellent rapport with the younger men. His visitation at Spring Hill was spent largely on a raft in Mirror Lake getting to know the philosophers better.

After his term as provincial, Fr. Shields served as rector-president of Loyola (1945-52) and of Jesuit High in Dallas (1953-59). He also served as pastor in Miami from 1959 to 1967 and then helped out as treasurer at the Spring Hill Jesuit House of Studies and at Jesuit High in New Orleans. He lived under six provincials after his own term of office.

To the end of his days he remained vital and young at heart. Reflecting on Fr. Shields' years of service at Jesuit High in New Orleans, an interested observer of the Jesuit scene called him "The Silver Sage of Banks Street." His peers elected him several times to the Provincial Congregation, where he always gave reasoned advice. He usually had something interesting and humorous to add to Province deliberations and community recreations. He democratized the government of the Province, in the sense that many Jesuits found it easy to talk naturally and openly with him.

Fr. Shields died on July 27, 1975, at age 74. He is buried at Grand Coteau.

Andrew Cannon Smith, SJ
1898 – 1984
*Under his leadership,
Spring Hill and Loyola
were integrated*

Under the leadership of Fr. Andrew Cannon Smith at Spring Hill College in Mobile and at Loyola University in New Orleans, many cultural changes were made. Most significantly, he integrated Spring Hill, admitting non-white and female students. Later he helped integrate Loyola.

Born in Natchez, Miss., on July 27, 1898, Andy was educated locally until he attended Spring Hill College for two years. In 1916 he traveled to Macon to join the Jesuits. After his Novitiate, he progressed through the traditional Jesuit course of studies, except for theology, which he studied at Enghien, Belgium (1925-28).

Upon his return Andy earned an M.A. in English at the Catholic University of America and promptly began a doctorate in the same discipline at the University of Chicago, successfully defending his dissertation, *Theories of Literary Taste.* With these degrees, he stepped out to a career of teaching and administration, spent mostly at Spring Hill College.

He was at Spring Hill College, not to teach high school students in "the little yard" but college students in "the big yard." He was professor and chair of the English Department and later academic dean (1934-52).

Still more appointments came his way. Probably because of his extensive academic experience, he became the Province prefect of studies for two terms (1935-36 and 1940-52).

Fr. Smith then became the rector-president of Spring Hill College (1952-59). It was on his watch that women were admitted to the Hill. With his leadership the college adopted a non-discrimination policy in student admissions (1952 and 1954), making Spring Hill College the first traditionally white educational institution in the South to open its doors to non-white students.

Several other far-reaching developments resulted from his labors, including establishing the night school at Spring Hill in 1935. He showed remarkable leadership for the college during the World War II years, including the direction of the Army Air Corps training program held on the campus.

Fr. Smith spent a few years away from Mobile, serving some time as the vice-provincial for the New Orleans Province. He returned to academic administration as the rector-president of Loyola in New Orleans (1961-66). Although the Law School at Loyola now accepted black applicants, the rest of the college was painfully hesitant. Fr. Smith proceeded to integrate the other departments.

Elected as the delegate of the New Orleans Province, he attended the Jesuits' General Congregation 31 in Rome (1965-66). Spring Hill also honored him at his retirement with an honorary doctorate and the Gautrelet Award, given for integrity and outstanding professional achievement.

Ernest Burrus, SJ, provided an excellent cameo of Fr. Smith:

> He was a diminutive, smiling, even jovial man who greeted me cordially, welcomed me heartily, kindly asked me my name and tactfully inquired about my home. Height was not the measure of his stature; but all would remember his smile, which one knew instinctively was genuine. His smile was part impish, part magnetic, and part contagious. Inside the circle of wagons known as the Jesuit community recreation room, Andy presided over the conversation, goading it on with his wit and playfulness....
>
> He stood out in the affectionate and grateful memory of everyone who met him as an exceptionally brilliant and gifted scholar, quick-witted, a warm-hearted friend and a most edifying religious.

Fr. Smith died Feb. 25, 1984, and is buried at Spring Hill.

Louis Gustave Soniat, SJ
1900 – 1973
*His 'Thought for the Day'
ran 23 years on WWL Radio*

Fr. Louis Gustave Soniat's provincial once described him as one of the "crustier members of a very crusty community." But, for all his bark, he was for years one of the more popular house confessors at Loyola.

Soniat was born in New Orleans on Oct. 7, 1900. After primary schooling at St. Stephen's, he graduated in 1919 from Jesuit High in its downtown New Orleans location. He entered St. Stanislaus Novitiate in Macon on Aug. 14,

1919. The destruction by fire of the Macon building compelled him to finish his formation at Grand Coteau. His academic formation was traditional, and he was ordained on June 25, 1933.

Fr. Soniat was a proficient linguist. French was his first language, and along the way he picked up Spanish, Portuguese and Italian. It came as no surprise that he was first sent to Loyola in New Orleans to be the chair of the department of modern languages, from 1939 to 1951. He was then appointed chair of the department of theology, a position he held until 1956.

It was at Loyola's radio station that Louis did his finest preaching. In 1941 he took over and further developed a popular early morning radio program called "Thought for the Day," which was begun in 1939 by Fr. Edward Cassidy, SJ. With Fr. Soniat at the mic, the program continued for 23 years, until 1964. As a one-man show, he spoke inspirationally on subjects such as the Christian family and supernatural life. He even delivered an on-air eulogy on the death of President Franklin Roosevelt. He was regarded as a pioneer in the field of religious communications.

After he injured himself playing tennis – and incurred a painful handicap that he endured for the rest of his life – WWL brought its radio equipment to his residence at Loyola to facilitate his broadcast.

He served Loyola for 22 years before he was retired in 1965 to the Jesuit House of Studies on the Spring Hill campus. From there he was taken to the Province infirmary at Grand Coteau.

A colleague from Grand Coteau commented on the intense pain Louis endured when he was completely bedridden:

"The monotony and suffering must have been intense. For a period of the last five or six years he was completely bedridden and condemned to spend his whole time on his back. He gave an example to the community of heroic patience."

Fr. Tom Clancy, SJ, observed that Fr. Soniat also enjoyed a regularly occurring peace during his last years. He loved the Psalms and, like the psalmist, used to argue with God, but his grumblings and his joy alike rested on the firm foundation of a deep faith in his Savior.

At age 72, on July 12, 1973, Fr. Soniat died at Lafayette General Hospital in nearby Lafayette, La. He is buried at Grand Coteau.

Lucien Ignatius Soniat, SJ
1897 – 1943
*A short, simple life
with a quiet ministry*

Lucien Ignatius Soniat enlisted as a soldier in the U.S. Army during World War I and honorably served his country before humbly and completely serving his God.

Soniat was auspiciously born on the feast of St. Ignatius, July 31, 1897, in New Orleans. His primary education was in the parochial schools of New Orleans, then at Jesuit High and finally at Spring Hill College. Afterwards, he was employed in a hardware store (1917-18) until he entered the Army toward the end of the Great War, during which he became adept in hospital and stenographic work. He worked in real estate until the call to the Society became clear and loud.

He entered the Novitiate at Macon, Ga., on Sept. 7, 1921, but because of the fire there two months later, he was transferred to the new Novitiate at Grand Coteau. Typically, he spent two years in spiritual formation and the first two years of college studies there. In 1925 he was sent to Spokane, Wash., for studies in philosophy, and returned to New Orleans for a year of Regency at Jesuit High School. He began his study of theology in St. Louis, but when St. Mary's in Kansas was opened, he finished his studies there. He was ordained on June 25, 1931.

He was assigned to Sacred Heart Church in Tampa, where he served as assistant pastor for two years. He returned to Jesuit High School in New Orleans for a brief stay as minister of the community. He was then transferred to Immaculate Conception Church in downtown New Orleans in 1938.

During his last six years, Fr. Soniat knew no relief from physical suffering. Pain associated with his heart and lungs became so insistent that he was advised to seek rest at Grand Coteau.

In March of 1943, Fr. Soniat received Viaticum and a few months later he died in a Lafayette, La., hospital on July 3, 1943, at age 45. Although he lived but a brief life, it was a good one – a simple one with a quiet ministry and a faithful vocation.

He is buried at Grand Coteau.

George Aloysius St. Paul, SJ
1897 – 1977
Author of Here and Hereafter, *translator of old house diaries*

A notable New Orleans Catholic family, the St. Pauls fostered three religious vocations: George and his brother, Henry Allain, to the Society of Jesus and Zita Marie to the Religious of the Sacred Heart.

George Aloysius St. Paul was born in New Orleans on Aug. 22, 1897. After only three years of school, he entered Immaculate Conception College (now known as Jesuit High School) at age ten in 1907. He graduated in 1912 at age 14, attended Loyola University for two years and entered the Society on Aug. 13, 1913. He proceeded to pass through the typical course of studies.

George's health was precarious. He suffered with depression and a nervous condition, contracted typhoid fever early in his life, in 1914, and then experienced the virulent Spanish influenza raging in 1918.

Eventually, George studied theology with the French Jesuits, who had been in exile at Ore Place in Hastings, England, since 1906. When the Jesuits returned to Fouvière in Lyon in 1926, he went with them.

Back in the States, George was given the job of *socius* to the master of novices. Next, he went to Jesuit High in New Orleans, first as teacher, then as preacher and retreat director. In 1943 he joined the Mission Band, first at the new Jesuit high school in Dallas to foster retreats and then at Pass Christian in Mississippi.

In 1952 he left this ministry and returned to Grand Coteau, where he spent the last 25 years of his life as part-time teacher and assistant treasurer. He gathered materials from his ministry in parish missions and published them in 1956 using the title *Here and Hereafter* (2nd edition, 1963). At the urging of his superiors he began translating the old house diaries of St. Charles College from French to English.

Fr. St. Paul was an educated Jesuit, an accomplished classicist and stylist, who wrote in the best rhetorical style of the day. He wrote poetry, which frequently appeared in his sermons and conferences. His occasional sermons were his specialty: They were long and flowery, laced with Scripture passages, and focused on classical audiences – to whom he preached without a microphone.

The depression that had plagued him in his early life returned to haunt him later. He suffered from mental torments, especially worrying about his performance of the daily liturgy. It seemed as though the only prayer he was capable of enjoying was the rosary. His provincial said of him: "He probably holds the Province record for rosaries worn out."

Other health-related problems began to appear, such as falling down at night, bodily weakness and trouble with his lungs.

Fr. St. Paul died on Nov. 22, 1977, at age 80. The novices just out of their long retreat sang beautifully at his funeral. Retreatants and friends from the town filled the chapel. He is buried at Grand Coteau.

Claude Joseph Stallworth, SJ
1908 – 1984
An exceptional educator, administrator and recruiter

Claude Joseph Stallworth was blessed with enviable administrative skills, which he used to the advantage of the students and families he served for 20 years at Jesuit High in New Orleans.

Born in Mobile on July 12, 1908, he attended local elementary and secondary schools, followed by a year at Mt. St. Mary's University in Maryland. He matriculated at the North American College in Rome, earning a PhL (1927-28). After he returned to the States, he attended Spring Hill College, graduating in 1931 with an A.B.

A year later Claude entered the Novitiate in Grand Coteau, on June 15, 1932, going through two years of spiritual formation and only one year of Juniorate. He spent two years in St. Louis studying more philosophy, earning two more degrees, and then two years of Regency at Jesuit High in New Orleans. His four years of theology were done at St. Marys, Kan., where he earned an STL. He was ordained on June 17, 1943.

Fr. Stallworth served in only one school in all the years of his ministry, first as assistant principal (1945-46) and then as principal of Jesuit High School in New Orleans until 1965. He was an excellent administrator and the school hummed under his guidance.

He was also recognized by educational institutions as an exceptional educator and served in various capacities in many organizations: State Committee of the Southern Association of Colleges and Secondary Schools – seven years; Standards Committee of the Southern Association of Colleges and Secondary Schools – three years; Executive Committee of the same organization – three years; Executive Committee of Louisiana High School Athletic Association – seven years; Chairman of the Southern Regional Unit of the N.C.E.A. – one year; and President of the Southern Association of Independent Schools – one year.

He was also a great recruiter of Jesuit vocations, inspiring many men to become members of the Society. When he stepped down from being principal, he remained at the high school for three years, continuing to teach.

At this point in his life, Fr. Stallworth suffered several debilitating illnesses, which required him to enter a nursing home. His choice was Villa Mercy, just across the bay from his Mobile home. The severe stroke which left his right side paralyzed also deprived him of the ability to speak. Additionally, he suffered from gout and arthritis, had several heart attacks and many bouts of arrhythmia, and he developed a cancer of the stomach.

Although close to Mobile, he lived some distance from the Jesuits with whom he had a special bond of companionship. Superiors visited him often, taking him on short excursions or out for a meal. In a letter to Claude, Father Provincial Edmundo Rodriguez wrote:

"I have always been deeply impressed by the love that the men have for you, especially people like Harry Tompson, John Condry and others from Jesuit High."

He was able to celebrate his fiftieth anniversary as a member of the Society of Jesus in 1982. Fr. Stallworth had spent nearly 19 years at Villa Mercy when he died on Feb. 1, 1984, at age 75. He is buried at Spring Hill.

Cornelius J. Thensted, SJ
1903 – 1981
He worked untiringly for blacks of the Grand Coteau area

In the history of Grand Coteau, La., few names are remembered more than that of Fr. Cornelius J. Thensted.

The town's Thensted Center, named in honor of his many years of ministry, opened in 1982 to provide much-needed community services.

These include home visits to the elderly and ill, a thrift store, an emergency food pantry, after-school tutoring, counseling services, social activities for senior citizens, and classes for money-management, budgeting and career choices.

Fr. Thensted was fondly remembered by several of the town's mayors, including two black women: Mary Murray and Jean Coco. Many consider him one of the area's quintessential movers and shakers for the many ways he labored to make better the lives of its citizens, especially African-Americans.

Born in New Orleans on Aug. 13, 1903, Cornelius graduated from Immaculate Conception College in downtown New Orleans in 1920, and then studied at Loyola University for two years. He entered the Novitiate at Grand Coteau on Aug. 14, 1924. His was the typical course of formation and studies, which included philosophy, Regency at Spring Hill High School, and theology at St. Mary's in Kansas. After ordination in 1935, he did his Tertianship in Cleveland, Ohio, and returned to Grand Coteau.

He began a long tenure in Grand Coteau in ministry to the African-American population in pre-desegregation Louisiana. At first he had two concurrent jobs (1937-41): assistant pastor of St. Peter Claver in Grand Coteau, working with the revered Fr. Julius Oberholzer, and as pastor of Christ the King Mission in nearby Bellevue. In 1941, he and Fr. Oberholzer swapped places, and Fr. Thensted became pastor in Grand Coteau (1941-58).

His ministry was centered on liturgy and the sacraments, but he was also architect of a substantial educational compound for his black parishioners. He is credited with building two schools, a new church, and living quarters for the Sisters of the Holy Family who taught in his schools.

At that time in the American South, blacks were excluded from white schools; hence no help was offered by the State. Fr. Thensted labored to beg monies from white people to build schools for black Catholics, even publishing a quarterly newsletter entitled *Please...* and sending it to donors across the United States.

Following are excerpts from a typical Thensted solicitation letter:

The Negro needs Christian leadership from his own ranks; if we cannot produce Christian leaders, then the Negro will be lost to Christianity.... Not only must we teach everything essential for human living, we must provide facilities at least equal to the facilities of those who would compete with us for the souls of these children.

I am pleading with you to help us with alms and even to interest others to help us with alms in our work for the temporal and eternal welfare of our Negro children. Perhaps you could interest some friend to sponsor a child for a week (50 cents) or for a month ($2.00).

Fr. Thensted was quite successful. He did more than build: He served as an advocate, even restraining local whites who occasionally threatened blacks walking down the street at night. A close associate of his was also threatened. This good shepherd prevailed.

Jesuits rarely remain in an assignment for long, but Fr. Thensted worked in the black parishes from 1937 to 1958. These years, which spanned the Great Depression and World War II, were times of scarcity, an especially heavy burden borne by poor blacks laboring mostly in agriculture. Fr. Thensted returned for a brief assignment from 1960 to 1964.

Eventually Fr. Thensted labored in three additional parishes: Sacred Heart in Tampa (1958-60 and 1968-70), St. Joseph in Mobile (1964-68) and Immaculate Conception in New Orleans (1970-74).

Growing confused and disoriented with age, he was retired at age 71. Fr. Thensted died on Feb. 15, 1981, at age 77 and is buried at Grand Coteau.

Himself a frugal Jesuit, Fr. Thensted worked constantly with the truly impoverished of the Grand Coteau/Bellevue area. He sought alms, not for himself but for his flock. He established a compound where food and education were available to the poor and to those rejected by the white world. He was a most determined and energetic laborer, often visiting parishioners who were accessible only via unpaved roads. Thomas Jenniskens, SJ, a colleague who knew him well, said of him:

"Fr. Thensted was gruff-sounding. He didn't sound like a gentleman, but he was truly a gentle man."

If ever the grace of generosity has been given to a Jesuit, Fr. Thensted had a double portion.

Carmelo A. Tranchese, SJ
1880 – 1956
Angel of the slums

"The Rumpled Angel of the Slums," a 1948 article on Fr. Carmelo A. Tranchese in the *Saturday Evening Post*, shone a light on the work of this holy, compassionate man.

More than any other priest in the country he called the attention of the American church and nation to the plight of Mexican-Americans. From 1932 to 1953 he was indeed God's messenger to and for the poor parishioners of Our Lady of Guadalupe in San Antonio.

Born on Aug. 29, 1880, he was proud to be a native of Naples, Italy, and he had a happy, though mischievous, boyhood there. Although he never attended a Jesuit school, he recounts that he was drawn to the Society through his friendship with a local Jesuit, Fr. Melecrinis. He admits that he was also fascinated with the beards of the Jesuit missionaries he knew.

He liked to recall how his ignorance of Latin nearly kept him out of the Society. He had followed the science curriculum in college but had never studied Latin. Even though an intensive cram course still left him deficient, he was admitted to the Order at the age of 16.

However, in the Juniorate he became an accomplished classicist, and later in his life he liked to compose Latin odes. He even sent one of his Latin poems to President Franklin Roosevelt.

He made his theology studies with the English Jesuits at St. Beuno's College in North Wales and was sent for what was supposed to be just one year to the old Denver Mission. Thus, he began in 1912 a missionary career that lasted 45 years. In all that time, he never grew a beard like those of the Jesuits missionaries that had so intrigued him as a youngster.

Fluent in Spanish and Portuguese as well as in English and his native Italian, he worked in New Mexico, Colorado, west Texas and California as a pastor and a missionary. After the breakup of the Denver Mission, Carmelo became a member of the New Orleans Province.

In 1932 Fr. John Mary Salter, SJ, accepted Our Lady of Guadalupe Parish in San Antonio into the New Orleans Province and named Fr. Tranchese as pastor. He arrived just as the worst effects of the Depression were being felt by his poor parishioners.

Fr. Tranchese thus began the work that helped transform their lives. He organized a relief program and soon began to lobby for public housing. In his struggle to help his people he became a close friend of First Lady Eleanor Roosevelt, and it was her intercession that saved his housing project. He founded *La Voz*, the Spanish diocesan paper, and organized schools for his flock. He was always ready to intercede with police or creditors on behalf of his people. It is no wonder that for years after his departure some of his parishioners still spoke of him as "the Pastor." He was greatly loved.

He retired to Grand Coteau and continued to help out in the local parish right up to the final days of his illness. He occupied his spare moments reading Dante and classical literature.

Fr. Tranchese died on July 13, 1956, at age 75. He is buried at Grand Coteau.

Ferdinand Troy, SJ
1869 – 1936
The lone wolf of the rugged Southwest missions

Fr. Ferdinand Troy was probably born in Irkutsk, Siberia, on Jan. 6, 1869, thus making him the only member of the New Orleans Province born in Russia.

His birthplace is also listed as Bohemia, and his true name was Troyaneck or Trojaneck.

At any rate, he went to the apostolic school in Turnhout, Belgium, an institution devoted to the preparation of future foreign missionaries. There he chose the Jesuit mission of Colorado-New Mexico, which at that time was the charge of the Naples Province.

He entered the Society on April 30, 1887, probably in Italy, but finished his Novitiate at Florissant, Mo. After further studies in St. Louis, Regency in Denver, and theology at Woodstock, he returned to Denver to work among the Hispanics of Colorado. He could communicate easily since he had already acquired a good knowledge of English and Spanish. Even more important, he knew his people; his sermons and instructions were simple and well-adapted to his flock.

In 1919 the Denver Mission was divided. The northern portion, Colorado, went to the Missouri Province, and the southern portion, New Mexico and west Texas, went to the New Orleans Province.

By that time, Fr. Troy was working outside of Albuquerque, N.M., in Alameda, Armijo, and the missions of the Sandia Mountains. He continued to do so for the rest of his life. He was the pastor of Nativity of Our Lady Parish in Alameda, and he built churches in Alameda and Armijo and had started a third in San José.

Like many of the old *operarii* – that is, missionaries who fanned out from a central house to work – Fr. Troy was pretty much a lone wolf. He had little to say, but his companions testified to his solid and rugged piety. He also had the physical constitution that enabled him to sustain the rigorous life of the mission and the hard physical work it entailed.

His only leisure pursuit was an interest in the early history of the Italian Jesuits in New Mexico. He loved to pore over the old records of the mission. The history he had begun to write was interrupted by his untimely death.

Tragically, shortly before Christmas in 1936, he was hit by a reckless driver in front of his Alameda church. On Dec. 23, 1936, Fr. Troy died at age 67. He is buried in Albuquerque.

Louis J. Twomey, SJ
1905 – 1969
A social activist, he 'awakened the conscience of the South'

Fr. Louis Twomey was surely one of the greatest social apostles the New Orleans Province ever produced. Influential, controversial and passionate, he championed the rights of workers and helped to end racial segregation in the South.

Born Oct. 5, 1905, in Tampa, Fla., Lou attended the local Jesuit high school and then studied at Georgetown University. A skilled athlete, he turned down a baseball contract with the Washington Senators to enter the Jesuit Novitiate at Grand Coteau in September of 1926, a month short of his 21st birthday.

He made the regular course of studies in the Society at St. Louis, St. Marys, Kan., and Cleveland. He was studying theology when the 28th General Congregation (1937) called for Jesuits to put special emphasis on the struggle for social justice. He volunteered for that work, but the wartime needs of the Province were pressing and his first assignment (1941-45) was to be principal of Jesuit High in Tampa. The stories of those days are legion, and the scholastics who taught for him never forgot his dynamic leadership and his novel ideas of organization.

In 1945 he was sent to the Institute of Social Studies at Erasmus University at Rotterdam in The Hague to prepare himself for his real life's work: social justice. In 1947 he arrived at Loyola University, where he taught for nearly 30 years. With an M.A. in economics and an iron determination, he set up the Institute of Industrial Relations, an organization that worked to improve labor-management relations. There he promoted vocational training, community development and race relations.

Fr. Twomey lectured on ethics and jurisprudence in the Law School and won many converts to his mostly unpopular doctrines of racial equality, the rights of the working man, and international justice. He also lectured in the Sodality Summer Schools of Catholic Action and was increasingly invited to talk to national groups and write for national publications. He soon became a trusted advisor of labor groups, and his office in the attic of Cummings Hall became a meeting place for Southerners struggling against segregation and economic injustice.

In 1948 he began to publish a mimeographed monthly, *Christ's Blueprint for the South*, and this increased his influence with Jesuits all over the world and among priests and seminarians. He was a trusted collaborator of New Orleans Archbishop Joseph Rummel in the latter's effort to desegregate the schools and other institutions of the archdiocese.

Some of his most vigorous critics were to be found among his Jesuit brethren, but he was not known to say an uncharitable word against any of them. He had a deep prayer life and a strong devotion to Our Lady. All through those difficult days, his obedience and devotion to the Church and the Society were unwavering.

In his last years he continued his social activist work and started an international institute to train Central American social activists. He was called to Rome in the 1960s to aid Father General Pedro Arrupe in drawing up his 1967 letter on racism, "The Interracial Apostolate," an important step in the history of the Jesuits in the United States.

Toward the end of Fr. Twomey's life the recognition that he had not yet received came to him in waves. It was evident at the time of his death that not only had he been one of the most influential priests of his time but also one of the most loved.

Fr. Twomey died on Oct. 8, 1969, just three days after his 64th birthday. He is buried at Grand Coteau.

After his death, renowned Louisiana novelist Walker Percy said of him:

"He was a good man to have around, and there were too few like him. As much as anyone he pricked and awakened the conscience of the South."

Austin L. Wagner, SJ
1887 – 1956
Half a century on the job

Details of the life of Austin L. Wagner before his entrance into the Society are few, and little outside of his ministry is known about this man who served half a century as a Jesuit. However, the records do show that his priesthood was typically productive.

Wagner was born in Mobile, Ala., on July 3, 1887. Details about his early education are scarce, but it is known that he attended Spring Hill High School for four years (1901-05). In 1905, he entered the Order in Macon, Ga., spending two years in the Novitiate and two more in the Juniorate. Instead of studying philosophy, he was sent to the Juniorate in Grand Coteau to teach English literature (1911-14), which counted for part of his Regency.

He eventually made his philosophy studies at Immaculate Conception College in Montreal (1915-17), and returned to Grand Coteau to finish his Regency (1917-19). Typical of regents, he was always loaded with extracurricular activities, whether skilled in them or not: dramatics, Sodality moderating, athletics and debating. He was sent to St. Louis University for theology and was ordained on June 27, 1921.

Fr. Wagner's ministry reflects the typical apostolates of the New Orleans Province. He was sent to Jesuit High in Tampa, where he worked from 1927 to 1935. He taught at St. John's College in Shreveport (1937-40), and in 1943 he became minister of the community at Jesuit High in Dallas.

Fr. Wagner's ministry then turned to serving in parishes, first at the Jesuit parish in Macon, then at Sacred Heart in Augusta, Ga. He was posted to Immaculate Conception Parish in El Paso, where he remained from 1949 until his death in 1956.

He had two periods of directing retreats. With no apparent previous training, Fr. Wagner was made director of Our Lady of the Oaks Retreat House in Grand Coteau (1944-48), and he directed retreats at the Xavier Hall Retreat House in Pass Christian,

Miss. He also had an internal ministry to Jesuits, serving as minister of several Jesuit communities at various times in his career.

Fr. Wagner, age 68, died in El Paso, on June 15, 1956. He is buried at Spring Hill.

Robert Edmund Walet, SJ
1910 – 1988
Teacher, principal, pastor – and winner of the Bronze Star

Robert Edmund Walet was among those Jesuits who served his country as an Army chaplain during World War II. He distinguished himself by earning the Bronze Star, which is awarded for acts of bravery, praiseworthy service or meritorious achievement.

Born in New Orleans on Nov. 15, 1910, Bob followed the educational course of many other New Orleanians who became Jesuits. First he was educated at Holy Name of Jesus School and then at Jesuit High (1924-28). After graduation he joined the Society, entering the Novitiate on Aug. 14, 1928.

Everything was typical from then on: two years of Novitiate, two of Juniorate and three of philosophy. After earning an M.A. from St. Louis University, he taught at Jesuit High in Tampa, Fla., for three years. Back on track, he studied theology at St. Marys, Kan., from 1938 until 1942. He was ordained on June 18, 1941.

Initially serving at Jesuit High in Dallas for a year (1943-44) he spent much of his ministry in the Province's high schools. However, in the midst of World War II, his career was interrupted by two years of service as a chaplain in the U.S. Army. He was a captain in the 63rd Infantry Division in the European Theater, and when the war ended he remained with the Army of Occupation.

Following his discharge from the Army, he was sent to Jesuit High in Tampa for a series of jobs which culminated with his being named rector-principal (1948-53). This was followed by a stint at St. John's High in Shreveport, again as rector-principal (1953-59). Success breeds success, and so he became the rector of Jesuit High in New Orleans for six years (1959-65).

A great change in his ministry came about when he left school administration and – still in New Orleans – was assigned to Holy Name of Jesus Church for an extended period (1965-79). He then served in two more parishes as different as oil and vinegar: St. Charles Borromeo in rural Grand Coteau (1980-83) and Immaculate Conception in metropolitan New Orleans (1983-86).

Fr. Walet retired to Ignatius Residence, and after a brief illness he died on April 7, 1988, at age 77. He is buried at Grand Coteau.

John Thomas Walsh, SJ
1915 – 1989
The priest who got the third degree

John Thomas Walsh III enjoyed learning, as is evidenced by his three master's degrees in English, speech and education. He was also a man who, in his later years, was involved in many parish organizations and attended countless meetings – a service that some may think is grounds for sainthood!

Born on May 12, 1915, in Memphis, Tenn., John attended St. Bridget's Elementary School and Christian Brothers High School in Memphis (1929-33), after which he spent a year being taught by the Jesuits at Spring Hill College (1933-34).

He entered the Novitiate on Aug.1, 1934, to spend the obligatory two years in spiritual formation and two more years in the Juniorate. He returned to Spring Hill for philosophy, earning a B.A. in English. He was privileged to continue the study of English at Fordham University (1941-42), finishing with an M.A. John's Regency consisted of two years at Spring Hill College, after which he went to St. Mary's for theology. He was ordained on June 18, 1947.

Fr. Walsh was primed for a ministry in education. He returned to Spring Hill to teach English for 16 years (1950-66). Toward the end of this period he went to Northwestern University for an M.A. in speech.

He was appointed principal of Strake Jesuit College Prep in Houston, but soon suffered a heart attack that changed the direction of his ministry. He remained in education, but without the stress and pressure of the regular high schools. He joined the staff of Corpus Christi Minor Seminary and remained for 11 years (1967-78). During this period he earned his third master's degree, this time in education from Texas A&I University in Kingsville, near Corpus Christi (1976).

Fr. Walsh's ministry then turned to the parishes staffed by the Order. He was an associate at Our Lady of Guadalupe in San Antonio for eight years (1978-86), followed by a year at Immaculate

Conception in New Orleans, then two years at St. John's Cathedral in Shreveport, and finally mere months at Immaculate Conception in Albuquerque.

He was basically a gentle and tranquil man. Often his peers would comment on how pleasant it was to be in his company. Perhaps the best testimony to Fr. Walsh came from the remarks of his last superior:

> Here was a man 74 years old and in poor health, yet he undertook his ministry with a sense of humor and great courage.... He not only said a Mass or two each day and heard confessions; he became involved in all of the parish organizations and attended their meetings.... Fr. Walsh was a good community man and provided his brothers with wit and charm.

A hard-working priest, Fr. Walsh suffered a fatal heart attack on Sept. 23, 1989, and died at age 74. He is buried at Grand Coteau.

Joseph Michael Paul Walsh, SJ
1912 – 1990
The seafarer who
wore a Roman collar

Joseph Michael Paul Walsh was a character in an age when characters were common in the Order. Not only was he a talented musician, he was also a sailor from a family of sailors.

On Jan. 16, 1912, Joseph was born in Mobile to a seafaring family with close connections to Spring Hill College. His uncle, Joseph M. Walsh, SJ, was president of Spring Hill from 1928 to 1933 and Provincial after that.

After parochial grade school, Joe attended Spring Hill High School and started college at the University of Alabama. After a year, he transferred to Spring Hill College, where he earned a B.S. in 1932. After Joe's graduation, his father – also named Joseph Walsh – arranged for Joe to sail around the world on one of his boats, surely a learning experience unlike any other.

Joe entered the Novitiate on Aug. 19, 1933, for his Jesuit formation. Then he moved through the traditional priestly program: two years of philosophy at Gonzaga in Spokane, finishing with an M.A., three years of Regency at Jesuit High in New Orleans (1939-42), and finally theology at St. Mary's College (1942-46). He was ordained on June 17, 1945.

Fr. Walsh's priestly career began in education. He taught philosophy, first at Spring Hill College (1948-51) and then at Loyola (1951-52). Fr. Walsh – nicknamed "Porthole Joe" because of his own nautical passion and to distinguish him from his Jesuit uncle – pursued a doctorate at Fordham University, graduating with his PhD in philosophy in 1956.

Fr. Walsh taught at Loyola for seven years (1956-63) before he returned to Spring Hill College for a decade. While teaching in the college, he also taught briefly in the Jesuit Philosophate.

It is known that his enthusiasm for teaching waned, and he turned his priestly focus to parish ministry. In three years time he served in three places: the Gesù in Miami, St. Joseph's Church in Antigua, West Indies, and Immaculate Conception in New Orleans.

In 1979 the lure of salt water led him to St. Patrick's Church and the Holy Family Mission in Apalachicola, Fla., where he served until 1983. The first thing Joe did upon arrival there was to organize the youth of the parish into a troop of Sea Scouts to share his enthusiasm for sailing.

He then spent five years serving in two Pensacola, Fla., parishes: St. Stephen's and St. Joseph's, where this restless sailor had more time for his boats. In 1988, he returned to his hometown to work at St. Joan of Arc Church, where he remained until his death in 1990.

Fr. Walsh was a talented and somewhat famous musician. As a member of the marching band at the University of Alabama, Joe marched out on the field and took the starring position in the center of the "A" formation to play the *alma mater*. During his Regency, he conducted members of the Jesuit High Band in jam sessions, teaching them syncopated jazz. He could play trumpet, trombone, clarinet, piano and drums. However, in the Society as a full-fledged priest he found less time for music.

His peers commented on aspects of Joe's ministry mostly unknown to later generations. One stated:

> Nobody was (more) devoted to the works of mercy with the poor and the sick and the troubled than Joe.... During his years at Spring Hill he went on a regular basis to Pure Heart of Mary School and tutored the students in math.

During his final days at St. Joan of Arc, Fr. Walsh was diagnosed with a benign form of leukemia, which quickly became virulent. A stroke took his life on April 11, 1990. He is buried at Spring Hill.

Scott Youree Watson, SJ
1914 – 1989
'I heard he was a saint...'

Scott Youree Watson was greatly loved and respected for his charity and intellectual prowess. Shortly after his death, found among his effects were five 4 x 6 cards covered front and back with a brief account of his intellectual history – a noteworthy record indeed.

Born in St. Louis on Sept. 7, 1914, Youree grew up in Natchitoches, La. He knew tragedy as a child: His mother died when he was only two. Since his two older brothers were physically handicapped, he spent more time indoors reading than playing outside. He grew up among books, and one of them, Thomas Campbell's *The Jesuits*, inspired an interest in the Society of Jesus. After a year of college and just shy of his 18th birthday, he entered the Society at Grand Coteau.

Early on superiors noted not only his prayerful spirit but also his intellectual gifts, particularly his passion for history, poetry and philosophy. He and his close friend, Arnold Benedetto, went to post-war Rome in 1946 to study philosophy at the Pontifical Gregorian University. They were later to serve as colleagues on Spring Hill College's philosophy faculty.

Forty years of his life were spent teaching and researching, two-thirds of them at Spring Hill College and the last third at Loyola University. A competent writer, he authored a dozen articles. His masterpiece was to be a serious treatment of the philosophy of aesthetics, which was nearly finished when he died.

A voracious reader, Youree was unique in that he managed to read nearly all of the articles and books written by his Jesuit brethren. He also retained a keen interest in poetry, especially the poems of Gerard Manley Hopkins, a convert to Catholicism and a fellow Jesuit.

Fr. Watson was the kind of teacher who befriended both his students and his colleagues, and he was a spiritual mentor to many of them. Some said his greatest gift was as a counselor. He saw something precious or valuable in everyone and everything, even in the essays he required his students to write.

In a poll of Spring Hill alumni he was named among the best teachers. To commemorate and honor his work at Loyola, the Rev. Scott Youree Watson, SJ, Distinguished Professorship in Arts and Sciences was established.

He admired writers and carried on a lengthy correspondence with Flannery O'Connor, the great Southern fiction writer and apologist for Roman Catholicism, whom he had met when she gave a lecture at Spring Hill.

Earlier in his life, he had suffered with tuberculosis. When he was later hospitalized with heart disease, his TB returned and further weakened him. After a long hospitalization, Fr. Watson died on Sept. 26, 1989, at age 75. He is buried at Spring Hill.

He was the soul of charity, having a spiritual quality that was discernible by all. On the day of his funeral at Loyola, a student inquired of the cooks where Fr. Watson's body was laid out. The student explained:

"I heard he was a saint, and I wanted to see a saint."

Michael Aloysius Watters, SJ
1891 – 1969
A bilingual teacher,
a man of many letters

Michael Aloysius Watters was a devoted teacher and pastor who performed admirably throughout his career. And in the latter part of his life he was a prolific writer of letters, which he penned mostly at the desk by his sick-bed in Grand Coteau.

Born in Dublin, Ireland, on June 21, 1891, Michael must have had a rigorous education, since he had five years each of algebra, geometry, history, English and Latin. As a young adult, he crossed the ocean and traveled to San Antonio, Texas, where he attended the Oblates Apostolic School in 1908. However, he left the school and enrolled at Spring Hill College to pursue further studies.

John D. Foulkes, SJ, took Michael under his wing and was instrumental in advising him to enter the Novitiate at Macon, Ga., which Michael did on Aug. 14, 1912. After Novitiate, he stayed two years in Macon doing his college studies and then traveled to Mount St. Michael's in Spokane to study philosophy. During his Regency, he taught at Immaculate Conception High School in New Orleans, after which he studied theology for four years in Barcelona, Spain. He returned home to Milltown Park in Dublin for his ordination on July 31, 1926.

As is the case with many Jesuits of the New Orleans Province, his apostolic ministry was channeled in two directions: teaching high school and providing pastoral service in the Province's parishes. His teaching career began at Jesuit High in New Orleans, followed by three years at Jesuit High in Tampa and five years at St. John's High and Parish in Shreveport (1931-35), where he also served as pastor at Cedar Grove Mission Church. At the end of his teaching career he worked for one year at Jesuit High in Dallas, and from 1958 to 1966 he returned to St. John's Parish and school in Shreveport.

His fluency with Spanish influenced the parishes to which he was sent, including San Ignacio in Albuquerque, Our Lady of Guadalupe in San Antonio, Sacred Heart, Holy Family and Immaculate Conception in El Paso, and the Gesù in Miami.

During his last teaching assignment in Shreveport, his health began to fail. After being diagnosed a consumptive, he was sent to a hospital in Lafayette, La. His superiors thought it better to transfer him to nearby Grand Coteau, since he was very sick and needed the constant care of the infirmarian.

It is noted about his files in the Province's archives that they include "massive correspondence, mostly with women. His letters were very highly treasured and he really exercised an apostolate of the pen in his days at Grand Coteau."

On March 2, 1969, Fr. Watters died at age 77. He is buried at Grand Coteau.

One of his obituaries states:

"What estimate can we put on his life? There was nothing extraordinary about him, but he was one of those faithful and devoted priests who do well all that they do."

Hagema James Yamauchi, SJ
1920 – 1976
Japanese-American theologian and spiritual director

Perhaps Hagema James Yamauchi was so empathetic and compassionate to the people he counseled because he himself had been on the receiving end of sanctioned intolerance in the United States during the war years of 1941 to 1945.

He apparently rose above the prejudice and hatred directed toward Japanese-Americans since the bombing of Pearl Harbor on Dec. 7, 1941, and even now, years after his death, he remains well-regarded and respected as a teacher and spiritual director.

Born in New Rochelle, N.Y., on April 26, 1920, Jimmy was the only child of Hagema Yamauchi, a native of Japan, and Agnes McCarthy of Glasgow, Scotland. After high school, he entered the Novitiate at Grand Coteau and began his formation.

After his philosophy at Spring Hill (1941-44) and given the intense anti-Japanese feeling sweeping the country, it was of great concern where Yamauchi would do his Regency, and so he remained at Spring Hill. Despite the intolerance directed toward Japanese-Americans, he was a successful teacher for the young men who were enrolled in the armed services as well as for returning veterans.

Shortly after the end of World War II, James began his theology studies in Belgium and then studied in Rome for a doctorate in theology (1952-55).

Fr. Yamauchi taught theology at Loyola, where he was chair of the Department of Religious Studies (1955-66), and at Spring Hill for 10 years (1966-76). In fact, much later, in 1985, the Yamauchi Lectures in Religion series was begun at Loyola in memory of Fr. Yamauchi. The series seeks to perpetuate his work by bringing the results of religious scholarship to a wider audience.

Speaking of Fr. Yamauchi, Tom Clancy, SJ, commented on his teaching:

I would think that he was easily the outstanding teacher, both at Loyola and Spring Hill. He had a gift in the classroom which challenged and inspired a whole generation of students. He was not an easy mark for grades. Indeed, at Loyola he was the first teacher who made the students take theology seriously.

Living in the atmosphere of theology, it was no surprise that he began the ministry of spiritual direction. Those who came to him included dedicated laymen as well as students, priests, nuns and fellow Jesuits. It is said that as he matured he allowed his theological mind to include "less intellectual and more spiritual understanding in dealing with souls."

Joseph Vath, Bishop of Birmingham, noted that "people's problems were Father Jim's meat and drink. He was always counseling the doubtful, comforting the sorrowful, and instructing the ignorant." He was especially gifted in counseling priests, guiding many through difficult periods of discernment.

What a tribute it was to allow him in 1971 to establish a Tertianship at Spring Hill. His own mentor was Fr. Anthony Achèe, his master both in the Novitiate and in his own Tertianship. A peer observed:

"Like all good Tertian instructors, he was a doctor of the 'second conversion' and he could speak from experience, since his own gradual evolution from a dutiful and conscientious Jesuit to a man deeply united with God was apparent to his brethren."

From his early priestly days, he had suffered from a wide variety of debilitating illnesses: diabetes, cancer, high blood pressure and, worst of all, heart disease. Despite this, he truly had a zest for life, whether it was taking on difficult tasks or delighting in the telling of a new joke.

Bishop Vath offered this assessment of Fr. Yamauchi:

He was at home with God. He could speak about God, about prayer, about spiritual life as one who was quite familiar with every aspect of his subject.

On Jan. 18, 1976, Fr. Yamauchi suffered a massive heart attack and, despite immediate medical care, he died at age 55. He is buried at Spring Hill.

Patrick Henry Yancey, SJ
1896 – 1969
Biology with 'Butch'

Although he was named for one of the most famous patriots of the Revolutionary War, Patrick Henry Yancey much preferred to be called "Butch," and so he was.

Born on Oct. 20, 1896, in Tampa, Fla., Butch served as an altar boy in all four local Catholic churches. Traditionally educated in Catholic schools, including Jesuit High, he entered the Novitiate in Macon, Ga., in 1912, and after initial training he traveled to Spokane, Wash., for philosophy studies.

He spent his Regency at Spring Hill College (1919-23), where he was assigned to teach high school physics and Spanish as well as various science courses in the college. After teaching biology for three years, he founded the Mendel Club, a successful and prestigious student club focused on science.

Every regent had to be a jack-of-all-trades, and Butch was no exception. In addition to teaching, he was in charge of all music programs at Spring Hill.

Eventually his Jesuit course of studies took him to Oña, Spain, for theology (1923-28). Butch had studied French and Latin and was fluent in Spanish, so he was ready for Spain. Upon return to the U.S.A., he began doctoral studies in biology at St. Louis University Medical School.

One of the highlights of his doctoral program was a summer spent studying at Woods Hole, Mass., the premier site for marine biology. He participated in the American Association for the Advancement of Science, as well as the Catholic Round Table of Science. Despite his fear that he had spread himself too thin by taking such diverse courses, he passed his exams and completed his dissertation, "Some Physiological Effects of Experimental Cell Disorganization." He earned his PhD on June 3, 1931.

Fr. Yancey was again assigned to Spring Hill, where he taught biology, Spanish and anatomy. He taught physiology to the nurses at Providence Hospital and, for 16 years, served as chaplain for the hospital's nuns.

He resuscitated his old Mendel Club, metamorphosing it into the Mendel Biological Society, and he began a journal, *Mendelian*. In 1937 his biology club was eventually absorbed as a chapter of the Beta Beta Beta National Biological Honor Society, a goal he had chased for many years.

He taught biology to pre-med students and wore their successes like victory rings, delighted that he was helping them become doctors. He would take them to visit quality medical schools in the South and to converse with their faculties, who, in turn, received a preview of quality applicants. Everyone benefitted. With pre-med students in mind, he composed a handy "list of Greek and Latin roots of biological terms for the use of my students." It was later published as *Introduction to Biological Latin and Greek* in 1944.

As a professor, he maintained his presence in the scholarly world. He became secretary of the Alabama Academy of Science (1934), then twice its president (1937 & 1939). He made extensive trips abroad to converse with European scientists; similarly, he attended several conferences a year, often addressing them as a keynote speaker.

The post-war years saw an explosion of G.I. students filling the classes at Spring Hill, including biology with Butch. In 1950 President Harry Truman appointed him to the National Science Foundation, necessitating regular travel to the nation's capital. Biology at Spring Hill College was secure and appreciated.

In 1966, Fr. Yancey retired from teaching, at which time he was given the rank of professor and chairman emeritus. On this occasion the dean spoke of him:

From 1931 until 1966 Father Yancey has devoted his abundant energy and talent to establishing a biology department with high academic standards and to preparing about 500 students for medicine, dentistry and medical technology. Over the period of 35 years the biology department at Spring Hill has been a quality department. Fr. Yancey's reputation as a first-class educator received national recognition in 1950 when President Truman appointed him a charter member of the National Science Foundation…. As director of the Albertus Magnus Guild, Father Yancey has extended his influence into international circles. As author of 63 published papers and a member of numerous professional biological societies and officer in many of them, Father Yancey rightly merits the title "Distinguished Educator."

Fr. Yancey died on Oct. 22, 1969, at age 73. He is buried at Spring Hill.

Firmin Ybarrechevea, SJ
1868 – 1950

Born in St. Ignatius' homeland, he worked 45 years as a missionary in the U.S.

Of his pastoral work as a missionary, Fr. Firmin Ybarrechevea said, "I carried the Church in my hand." And, indeed, he did carry the Church and the Word of God to many souls during his 45 years of ministry.

Firmin was born in the homeland of St. Ignatius, in Beria near Bilbao, Spain, on July 7, 1868. He was one of three brothers who entered the Society of Jesus and labored in the New World. Firmin joined the Jesuits at Loyola in Spain, where he made his two years of Novitiate. He pronounced his vows on Sept. 24, 1887, in Macon, Ga.

Struggling with English, he did not advance in the Juniorate. He traveled to Woodstock for two years of philosophy (1889-91), followed by five years of Regency at different schools. In 1896, Firmin went to Montreal to study theology, but he suffered from the bitter cold. Therefore, he was sent to Grand Coteau, La., for two years of private tutoring in theology before being ordained on Dec. 3, 1899.

For 45 years he gave himself unsparingly to mission and parish work in Florida, Alabama and New Mexico. He labored in the scattered mission stations of Florida, enduring the poverty, indifference and ignorance of many – even the opposition and hatred of some. In the course of his 15 years in Florida, he worked in many places, such as Tampa, Ybor City, St. Petersburg, Fort Myers and Lakeland.

In 1915, he began 11 years of fruitful apostolate in Alabama, both in Selma and Spring Hill. At that time the term *missionary* meant many miles to cover on foot or in a buggy. It also meant much begging for the needs of the apostolate. It was fortuitous that Bishop Edward Allen subsidized Fr. Firmin's labors to build several churches.

In 1926 Fr. Firmin was sent to Albuquerque, where he worked for nearly 20 years. Toward the end of this assignment, he was severely injured in an automobile accident. Because of Fr. Firmin's injuries, Fr. Joseph Dardis brought him to Grand Coteau, where he was confined to bed for the next five years and gradually lost his eyesight.

Many lives have celebratory high points. For Fr. Ybarrechevea, two punctuate his infirm years. On Sept, 14, 1945, he celebrated his diamond jubilee as a Jesuit. His brother, Castor, was able to come over from Montezuma, N.M., for the event. On Dec. 3, 1949, Fr. Firmin marked his golden anniversary as a priest. To honor him, the community sang songs in Spanish.

Soon after, he became very weak and sank into a fatal coma. Fr. Ybarrechevea died on April 3, 1950, at age 81. He is buried at Grand Coteau.

MODERN ERA

1968 - 2014

While the Jesuits of the New Orleans Province entered the 1970s with noticeably declining membership, they continued to be recognized as top-flight pastors, preachers, builders and teachers.

As was the trend with other religious orders, vocations to the Society of Jesus decreased between the 1960s and the decades that followed. After peaking at about 600 members in 1960, the New Orleans Province entered this new era with approximately 200 members.

Adjusting to this global trend, the Jesuits invited lay men and women to become more involved in the work of the Society. The laity stepped up, welcoming the chance to participate in many of the Jesuit apostolates.

Meanwhile, in a particularly eventful time in U.S. history, Richard Nixon resigned his Presidency in the wake of the Watergate Scandal, the Vietnam War raged on and finally ended in 1975, and the U.S. was the first to put a man on the moon.

For the Jesuits, the age ended with the consolidation of the New Orleans Province with the Missouri Province to form the new U.S. Central and Southern Province, taking effect on July 31, 2014.

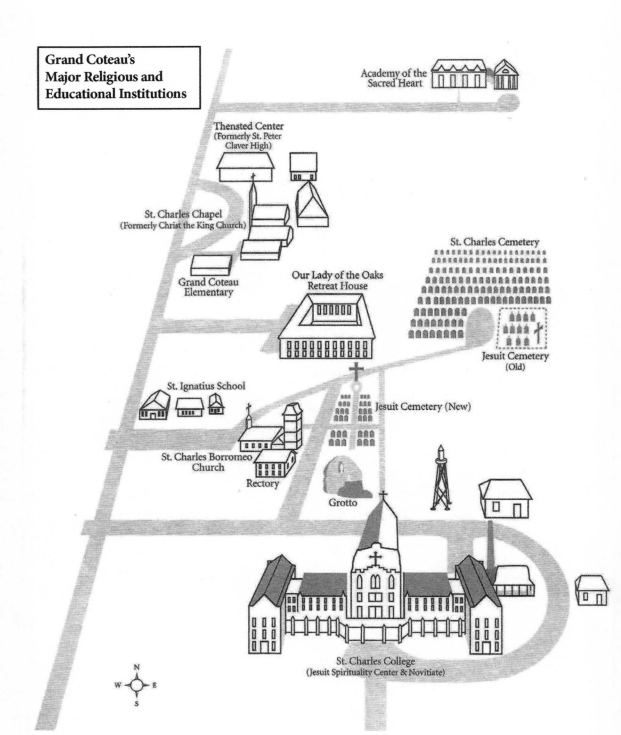

Grand Coteau's
Major Religious and
Educational Institutions

Academy of the
Sacred Heart

Thensted Center
(Formerly St. Peter
Claver High)

St. Charles Chapel
(Formerly Christ the King Church)

St. Charles Cemetery

Grand Coteau
Elementary

Our Lady of the Oaks
Retreat House

Jesuit Cemetery
(Old)

St. Ignatius School

Jesuit Cemetery (New)

St. Charles Borromeo
Church

Rectory

Grotto

St. Charles College
(Jesuit Spirituality Center & Novitiate)

N
W   E
S

Michael Alchediak, SJ
1935 – 1994
He helped to save Strake Jesuit

Michael Alchediak was born on June 28, 1935, in Tampa, Fla., in Sacred Heart Parish, where he was baptized, given his first communion, confirmed, ordained, and from which he was buried. He came from a loving Lebanese family of eight.

Even as a schoolboy he was drawn to the priesthood and so he entered the Novitiate at Grand Coteau in 1953 after graduating from Jesuit High in Tampa. He made the regular course of studies of the Society and was ordained in 1966.

The next year he was called out of graduate studies in mathematics to become principal of the new high school in Houston, Strake Jesuit. He guided the institution first as principal and then as president-rector.

In January of 1971 Strake Jesuit found itself in a serious financial situation which threatened the very existence of the school. Its bank, Sharpstown State Bank, was forced to close as a result of a stock scandal and Strake Jesuit lost $6 million. Fr. Alchediak rallied the Jesuits and their lay friends in the fight to save the school, and Strake Jesuit eventually came out of the crisis stronger than ever.

In 1981 he went to work for the provincial as head of the Jesuit Seminary and Mission Bureau in New Orleans, and then in 1987 he went to Jesuit College Prep in Dallas as its president.

Fr. Alchediak always had big goals and unrelenting enthusiasm, but after a year or so in Dallas his health began to fail. He had a series of medical tests which concluded in 1990 that he was HIV positive. His medical history revealed that long before the hazards of AIDS were known, he had had a blood transfusion with tainted blood.

He continued as president of Jesuit College Prep as long as he could, but the 6-foot-5 giant was very ill and getting worse. He stepped down in Dallas and went home to Tampa to face the end. His final months were spent at his childhood home, nursed and cared for by his parents and siblings.

He was cheerful to the end. A few months before his death, he talked to a reporter and recalled his first years as a Jesuit at Grand Coteau, when "the old Jesuits" were there. Now he was the one who was dying.

"I'm very content, happy, and in good spirits," he said. "I have put myself in the hands of God."

On April 29, 1994, Fr. Alchediak died, at age 58. He is buried at Grand Coteau.

Robert L. Anderson, SJ
1916 – 2005
He fought Franco in Spain
and rescued nuns in Mobile

While a student at the University of St. Thomas, Robert L. Anderson spent a summer in Europe. However, he did not study at a French university or tour the museums and cathedrals as so many college students do. Instead, he spent his time there fighting for the Republicans against Francisco Franco and his Nationalists during the Spanish Civil War.

Born on April 12, 1916, Anderson, a Midwesterner from St. Paul, Minn., took all of his pre-Jesuit education in his hometown. But drawn to warmer climes, he entered the Novitiate of the New Orleans Province in 1938. After the regular periods of Novitiate and of Juniorate, he studied philosophy at Spring Hill (1941-44); his Regency took him to the Jesuit high schools in Dallas, Shreveport and Tampa. He studied theology at St Marys, Kan., and was ordained on June 14, 1950.

Fr. Anderson spent 33 years in service at Spring Hill College and the Archdiocese of Mobile. His labors at Spring Hill were quite varied: He taught English (1952-58), scripture (1958-68) and photography (1969-75). Besides teaching, he had his hand in various publications as moderator of the student newspaper and the college yearbook.

Many of his photos found their way into college publications. Because he had suffered for years from hand tremors, his picture-taking was awkward, to say the least, but still he produced many wonderful photos. While most of his ministry was spent in photography, communications and publications, there is no record that he ever trained for them. He just seemed to be naturally talented in those areas.

For 25 years he served as chaplain to the Visitation Monastery across town. His devotion to the Visitation nuns was most on display in September of 1979 when for several hours he made his way over dangerous ground and dug through debris left by Hurricane Frederick to reach them. The Visitation Order honored him for his long devotion by making him an auxiliary member of the Order.

In 1975 his labors shifted from the college to the post of diocesan director of communications. At this time he assumed the editorship of the local Catholic paper, *The Catholic Week* (1977-85).

New Orleans was his next destination, and he took up residence at Loyola University, not as a faculty member but as the director of publications for the Province, a position he held from 1985 to 1999. His years there offered him the opportunity to work for social justice through involvement with Pax Christi and similar organizations dedicated to Christian nonviolence and creating a world reflective of the peace of Christ.

Fr. Anderson was an unassuming man, usually quiet by temperament, though he was known to lose his temper occasionally when provoked or frustrated. A good conversationalist with a wonderful sense of humor, he was basically a friendly person, more a spectator of life than a performer.

Clearly in physical decline, in late August of 2005, he was hospitalized in New Orleans, where he rode out Hurricane Katrina. He was so ill that five days later, he was evacuated to Lake Charles, La. In the post-Katrina chaos and confusion, the Jesuits in New Orleans had no word of his whereabouts and were unaware that he had been taken to Lake Charles. The silence about Fr. Anderson caused fellow Jesuits Larry Lundin and Danny Tesvich to go searching for him, finally locating him at Rest Haven Nursing Home.

Utterly exhausted from the relocation and from his chronic illness, Fr. Anderson died on Sept. 15, 2005. He is buried at Spring Hill.

James C. Babb, SJ
1914 – 2002
A head for business
and a heart for service

With a gift for business and administration, Fr. James C. Babb served his various communities in many positions of leadership during his seven decades as a Jesuit.

One of 11 children, he was born in Brockton, Mass., on Dec. 23, 1914. He entered the Novitiate of the New Orleans Province in 1933, following a regular course of formation: philosophy, Regency at Spring Hill, and theology at St. Marys, Kan.

In 1948 he traveled to Ceylon and served ten years, not so much as a missionary, but as the procurator charged with the financial affairs for the Ceylon Mission. After that, he was appointed rector of St. Charles College in Grand Coteau (1958-61), which groomed him for the same position at the Jesuit House of Studies in Mobile (1961-67).

These were years of great change and turmoil, which placed substantial burdens on any rector or superior. Not only was the Church implementing many changes mandated by Vatican II, but the United States was also in the midst of great social and political upheaval. He had a nearly impossible job. Performing admirably, he moved from rector of the college to retreat work at Our Lady of the Oaks in Grand Coteau, serving as assistant director for three years before becoming its director in 1971.

More administration positions awaited him. Fr. Babb was made rector of Jesuit High in New Orleans (1971-73) and then Vice Provincial for Pastoral Affairs (1973-77). He moved in 1977 to Montserrat Retreat House, eventually becoming its director (1978-85). Returning to Our Lady of the Oaks as director (1985-1991), he championed institutional responsibility for employee benefits, facilitating a retirement plan and health insurance for the workers. Fr. Babb was then posted to Ignatius Retreat House in Atlanta, where he served both as its superior and director (1991-2002).

What was James Babb like? He was, as they say, "a smooth operator." Well liked and well regarded, he was much appreciated for being a patient and attentive listener, as well as a competent administrator.

His primary ministry had always been that of director and superior, that is, internal ministry to communities and staffs. His provincial wrote to him on his jubilee: "I want to write my gratitude to you for the excellent service you have given for so many years in leadership positions in the retreat ministry."

His response says much about the man: "I have experienced great satisfaction in every assignment I have been given, and they include a wide range of things: mission procurator for Ceylon, ten years; superior of four places, 16 years; retreat work, six years."

While at the Oaks, his provincial wrote this to him: "You sometimes want more of a perfect response than reality is likely to give…. Please do not be too precipitous about changing things and judging the performance of people."

Fr. Babb replied to these admonitions in a positive way: "The feeling grew that our men needed encouragement more than correction. They need someone who listens rather than someone who talks…. It gives me great comfort to know that, despite my clumsiness, I have helped some of my brethren."

Worn out with good works and suffering kidney failure, Fr. Babb retired to Ignatius Residence in New Orleans, where he died on June 11, 2002. He is buried at Grand Coteau.

Lloyd A. Barry, SJ
1913 – 2002
Champion of education
and respect for the Jesuit Brother

Brother Lloyd Barry, born June 14, 1913, in Alexandria, La., had already earned a degree in mechanical engineering from Louisiana State University in 1941 before he joined the Order.

His was a career path that was rather unusual. At that time a candidate aspiring to become a brother in the Society was not required to have a college degree or specialized skills – and few, if any, did. Later, Bro. Barry would publicly campaign for appropriate education for the brothers.

Because of his range of skills, over the years Bro. Barry was assigned to various high schools and parishes in the Province: Grand Coteau, 14 years; Spring Hill, 10; Jesuit Dallas, 15; and Sacred Heart, El Paso, 7. Bro. Barry once wrote, "I didn't set out to be a teacher" and "I have never taught a class," but he was a born teacher who taught many Jesuit brothers.

It was not enough that he was a recognized leader who shared his knowledge and skills, he also returned to Grand Coteau in 1957 to take charge of the Brothers' Technical Training Program. The aim of this program was to ensure that each brother received appropriate training, status and respect in the Society. He remarked on the occasion of the final vows of Bro. Charles Doherty:

"Through the dedication to God of his prayers, works and sacrifices, he will share in all the rights, privileges and obligations of all the members of the Order."

Then, beginning in 1960, utilizing his knowledge and organizational skills, he supervised the projects and works of the Brothers' Maintenance Corps. One of his greatest contributions was his effort to inform others of the brother vocation:

What is a Jesuit Brother? He is the man who teaches art at Spring Hill.... Before any of these he is a Jesuit in the full sense of the word. The motivation in all Jesuits is the same: 'For the greater glory of God and for the Salvation of Souls.'... Their basic spiritual training is the same.... Their community exercises are the same.

In his study of the history of the brothers in the Society of Jesus, Bro. Barry found that in the early Society there was no separation of classes, although Rule 14 prohibited brothers from learning, if illiterate, when they entered the Order. But he found in Ignatius' writings three things of great interest

about the first brothers: 1) juridical equality, 2) religious identity in the full sense, and 3) commitment to serve the Society in those things in which others could not engage without detriment to the common good.

Two superiors general in the 20th century affirmed that for which Bro. Barry was laboring. Fr. Wladimir Ledochowski said, "Brothers should have quality education and training." Fr. Jean-Baptiste Janssens remarked, "We have only one 'social class,' that of the sons of the same Society."

Two periods of his life illustrate a strong pastoral bent. In 1965 Bro. Barry was posted to Campinas, Brazil, where from 1970 to 1973 he joined brothers of the New Orleans Province – Tony Coco and Robert Hollingsworth – at Centro Kennedy, a Jesuit vocational school, to teach the unemployed a trade. From 1988 to 1995 he was stationed at Sacred Heart in El Paso, where he engaged in direct ministry to the poor and needy.

Bro. Barry advocated always that the Province make the most and best use of its brothers, which meant appropriate education and training as well as elevation of the level of respect for and status of the Jesuit Brother.

Bro. Barry died shortly after sunrise on Easter Sunday, March 30, 2002 – God's exclamation point on the rich and zealous life of an outstanding Jesuit. He is buried at Grand Coteau.

Emmett Martin Bienvenu, SJ
1913 – 1998
'A truly great scholar,'
a Woodrow Wilson fellow

Fr. Emmett Martin Bienvenu was considered one of the brightest Jesuits of his time. Born July 29, 1913, in St. Martinville, La., he presumably attended the local grade school before completing secondary schooling at Spring Hill High School in Mobile.

He joined the Society of Jesus in 1930, spending two years of Novitiate and two years of college in Grand Coteau. His formation path was typical: philosophy, Regency, theology and ordination in 1944 at St. Marys, Kan. He earned a B.A. and an STL from St. Louis University and an M.A. in classics from Loyola in Chicago. For his excellence in teaching and innovation in education, he was awarded a Woodrow Wilson Fellowship in 1966.

He taught the classics at Jesuit High in New Orleans for nine years and was considered one of the best educators in the school for his Socratic method of teaching. Fr. Bienvenu also taught a special Greek class to older, non-traditional students wanting to read Homer. One of his students, a lawyer, commented:

"Father Bienvenu is the person who makes this class so interesting. Normally it is impossible to find a great scholar who is willing to teach a group. But he has the flair. I think he likes to teach, and he is a truly great scholar."

In 1957 he moved to Loyola to teach the classics, becoming chairman of the language department and leaving a legacy to Loyola students – the Rev. Emmett M. Bienvenu, SJ, Endowed Scholarship for the Classics.

He was a staunch conservative when it came to curriculum and most other things. For example, he vigorously opposed the opening of the Jesuit dining room to women. (But after it was voted in, he took advantage of the new rule to have coeds as frequent guests at his table, so much so that it was often the topic of jocular conversation among his fellow Jesuits.)

He retired in December 1997. Even after his transfer to Ignatius Residence, he commuted to Loyola for a few semesters to teach a course in Latin.

Fr. Bienvenu died on June 6, 1998, of congestive heart failure, and is buried at Spring Hill. He was 84 when he died. He was a Jesuit for 67 years and a priest for 54.

Joseph E. Browning, SJ
1920 – 2004
Traveling man

Fr. Joseph Browning was a man who was well-advised to keep his bags packed, since he did so much traveling in service to God and His people.

A native of Little Rock, Ark., Joseph E. Browning was born on March 30, 1920, and was baptized in St. Andrew Cathedral. He attended grade school there from 1926 to 1933 and graduated from Catholic High School in 1937. He studied at Spring Hill College (1937-38), but transferred to Loyola University in New Orleans, where he earned a B.A. degree (1938-41). He then entered the Jesuit Order and went to the Grand Coteau Novitiate for spiritual training (1941-43); he continued his education by returning to Spring Hill College to

study philosophy (1945-48). He spent his Regency teaching at Jesuit High in Dallas (1948-51). Like so many Southerners, he traveled to St. Marys, Kan., to study theology (1951-55) and was ordained in Mobile on June 16, 1954.

He was assigned to St. John's High School in Shreveport to serve in the counseling department (1955-59), but he transferred to pastoral ministry – his chief apostolic work for the rest of his life. In Mobile once more, he served as assistant pastor of St. Ignatius Church (1961-67), followed by his service in Shreveport, where he became assistant pastor at St. John's Church and then pastor (1968-80). He was next assigned as pastor to St. Ann's Church in West Palm Beach, Fla. (1980-83). And still the journey continued: He served as associate pastor of St. Rita's Church in Dallas (1983-85), then Sacred Heart Church in Tampa (1985-88), Immaculate Conception in Albuquerque (1988-91) and St. Charles Borromeo in Grand Coteau (1991-92). While stationed in Grand Coteau, he acted as the chaplain of Village du Lac, an assisted living facility for the elderly and persons with disabilities in Lafayette, La., his final service (1992-93).

He retired in 1994 to Ignatius Residence because of heart trouble. He died on May 2, 2004, at age 84 and is buried at Grand Coteau. His obituary in the Province newsletter provides additional insight into this good-natured Jesuit:

"A Jesuit 62 years and a priest 49 years, Joe was by nature a conservative in every way, but he never gave offense. He was always the gentleman.

"As a scholastic, Joe was the classmate most likely to be nominated for the 'Mr. Nice Guy Award.' Later, as a pastor who was famous for arriving late for every appointment or meeting, he was affectionately referred to as 'the late Father Browning.' But his simple kindness and sincerity covered his flaws."

John James Capelle, SJ
1916 – 2006
Chaplaincy was his signature ministry

Fr. John James Capelle's many years of service to the people of God took him from the youth and enthusiasm of high school students to the despair and hope of prisoners.

Born in New Orleans on Aug. 15, 1916, John attended Holy Name of Jesus School (1923-30) and then Jesuit High School (1930-34). After graduation he entered the Novitiate, on Aug. 1, 1934, and pursued a regular formation: Juniorate, philosophate, Regency and theology. Fr. Capelle was ordained on June 18, 1947.

His apostolic assignments fell into three categories: high school ministry, parish ministry and chaplaincy. He spent a decade on and off teaching at Jesuit High in New Orleans. His peers considered the peak period of his teaching career to be his years as athletic director for Jesuit High School (1958-63).

A new path opened for him when he became assistant pastor at St. Ignatius Church in Mobile (1965-68), followed by service at St. John's Church in Shreveport (1968-70) and at St. Joseph Church in Mobile (1970-71).

Then he began his signature ministry: chaplaincy. After he attended the Prison Chaplain Training Program at Orleans Parish Prison in New Orleans, he became the chaplain at Jefferson Parish Prison and the New Orleans House of Corrections (1971-77).

His chaplaincy ministry also included hospitals, and he spent two years as chaplain based at Sacred Heart Church in Tampa (1977-79) and one year in Miami while in residence at the Gesù. He returned to prison ministry as chaplain to the El Paso County Jail.

After a semester sabbatical, he served as chaplain in Las Cruces, N.M., at both its hospital and prison. His next six years were divided as pastor to St. Anthony Church in Artesia, N.M., and then at Gesù Church in Miami. John's last seven years of ministry were spent as chaplain at Touro Infirmary and Nazareth Inn, both in New Orleans (1993-2000).

Fr. Capelle served ceaselessly and devotedly in these three ministries. Judging by his success at chaplaincy and parochial ministries, he was surely a compassionate and understanding man.

In 2000 he retired to Ignatius Residence with the assignment that he "pray for the Church and the Society" (2000-04). As he came to need more medical care, he was transferred to Our Lady of Wisdom Health Care Center in New Orleans, where he lived for two years.

Fr. Capelle died of heart failure on Dec. 28, 2006, and is buried at Grand Coteau. He was 90 years old, 72 years as a Jesuit and 59 as a priest.

William Lionel Champagne, SJ
1920 – 1990
Simplicity and humility personified

William Lionel Champagne, born in Baton Rouge, La., on Feb. 8, 1920, was first attracted to the diocesan priesthood and so he studied at St. Benedict's in Covington. However, after three years, he entered the Society of Jesus, on July 30, 1940.

His education from then on was traditional: spiritual formation, first college studies, philosophy, Regency at Jesuit High in New Orleans, and theology. He was ordained on June 17, 1953.

His priestly career divided clearly into three parts: labors in Ceylon/Sri Lanka, service in the parishes staffed by the Province, and finally work in the mission in Brazil.

In Ceylon, after one year in language school at Yatiyantota to learn Sinhalese, he became an itinerant minister to various schools and mission stations: assistant at Hingurakgoda (1957), administrator at Tampalagam (1958-59), assistant and prefect at Ratnapura (1958), assistant at Ampara (1958-60), and minister at the Jesuit school in Trincomalee (1960-63).

One of the great attractions Fr. Champagne felt for the missions was the simplicity of the lifestyle there. He was uneasy with too many conveniences and disliked being waited upon.

Fr. Tom Clancy told how in 1957 "Champ" was serving in a tiny rural parish. A movie company was shooting *The Bridge on the River Kwai* in the vicinity. One day a chauffeured limousine drew up at Champ's front door, and he went out to see what the fuss was about. He looked at the passenger in the back seat and asked, "Are you someone I am supposed to know?" It was Sir Alec Guinness, the lead character in the movie!

In 1963 Fr. Champagne returned to the Province and began a long career in its parishes: Immaculate Conception in New Orleans (1964-68 and 1970-76), St. John's Church in Shreveport (1968-69), the Gesù in Miami (1984-87) and Sacred Heart in Tampa (1987-90).

His desire for the missions remained strong and so he studied Portuguese in order to work in Osasco,

Brazil (1976-78). Upon his return to the United States, he ministered to the sick, first as infirmarian at Grand Coteau (1979-81) and then at Ignatius Residence, the Jesuit retirement community in New Orleans (1981-84).

His indefatigable zeal is evident from his labors. He brought to his assignments the added value of being a competent maintenance man, gladly and humbly helping to maintain property and grounds. No one would ever accuse him of ambition or putting on airs. He was, in sum, an excellent priest.

Fr. Champagne had a quirky side, namely, riding a motorcycle during his sixties. It was a sight to see the helmeted Champ mounted on his cycle. He would take Murphy Ross, SJ, on the back seat to tool around the West Bank of New Orleans.

While laboring at Sacred Heart in Tampa, his last assignment, Fr. Champagne died at age 70 on Feb. 13, 1990. He is buried at Grand Coteau.

Fr. Tom Clancy wrote in Fr. Champagne's obituary an apt description of him:

"Champ was always known as a practical man. He loved to fix things, and he was a natural minister. He got along well with simple people."

Thomas Hanley Clancy, SJ
1923 – 2009
A man of letters

Thomas Hanley Clancy was the third Jesuit to come from Helena, Ark., where he was born on Aug. 8, 1923. He was surely one of that city's brightest stars.

He entered the Novitiate in 1942, and began his traditional Jesuit education, which was augmented by an M.A. from Fordham (1951), theology studies at Facultés S.J. Louvain (STL, 1956), and a doctorate from the London School of Economics (1960).

Fr. Clancy spent ten years teaching history and political science at Loyola University of New Orleans and eventually became chairman of that department (1966-69). After serving as academic vice-president for Loyola from 1968 to 1970, he edited *America* magazine for one year and then became the Provincial of the Jesuits of the New Orleans Province, which at the time covered ten states in the South and Southwest (1971-77).

As Loyola's vice-president for communications, from 1977 to 1989, he was responsible for the operations of WWL radio and WWL-TV. In this capacity he wrote the script for *Loyola: A Very Special Place*, as well as 269 one-minute spots, "Religious News Today." He was the mover behind the broadcast of "A Closer Walk," a 15-minute religious program narrated by Harold Cohen, SJ.

Clancy was the recipient of major scholarships: He was a Fellow of the Shakespeare Library and received a grant from the Society of Religion in Higher Education, which provided the opportunity for him to study at Oxford University (1965-66).

He showed considerable leadership in the area of race relations and social development during a tumultuous time in America. He served as a faculty advisor of the Southern Project of the National Student Association (1961-65) and organized the annual Southern Students Human Relations Seminar at Xavier University (1962-65).

Tom excelled at many ministries. He established a center for privately directed retreats at St. Charles College in Grand Coteau. He gave spiritual direction at Notre Dame Seminary. He himself had a regular pastoral ministry, namely, weekly Mass at "the Big Three": Orleans Parish Community Correctional Center, Orleans Parish Prison, and the House of Detention.

As a Jesuit, he preached hundreds of retreats to groups as diverse as nurses, theologians, religious, priests and seminarians. From 1952 to 1999, he reviewed 77 books and wrote 157 articles and a dozen short pieces which appeared in encyclopedias. He also wrote or compiled a number of books, including *Papist Pamphleteers* (1964), *An Introduction to Jesuit Life* (1976), *The Conversational Word of God* (1978), three editions of *Our Friends* (1978, 1989, 1998) and *English Catholic Books* (1996).

He was busy, but not too busy to get in a game of golf when he could.

Besides delighting in the jokes and clever one-liners of others, Tom's own *bon mots* were celebrated: "Jesuit colleges are like the isle of Manhattan. The only ones who can afford to live there are the very poor and the very rich."

Illustrating the virtue of "hope," he said of the widower Johnson, who was getting married again: "It's a triumph of hope over experience."

Fr. Clancy said of his friend, the social activist Lou Twomey, SJ, "The most striking paradox of his life was that such a kind man should have been embroiled most of his life in controversy."

In challenging the Province to greater zeal, he observed: "The members of AA have discovered that they can only stay sober when helping other people to stay sober."

He was a man in love with the Word and words.

Diminished by Alzheimer's, Fr. Clancy died at age 85, on April 13, 2009. He is buried at Grand Coteau.

Francis James Coco, SJ
1920 – 2006
A clarinet-playing Jesuit in the French Quarter of New Orleans

Few would expect to find a Jesuit priest – or any priest, for that matter – playing jazz in various bars and venues in New Orleans' famed French Quarter. But those who did and were lucky enough to hear Fr. Frank Coco play his clarinet were blessed indeed!

The musically talented Francis "Frank" James Coco was born on Oct. 6, 1920, in Helena, Ark., birthplace of at least two other Jesuits, including his younger brother, Bro. Anthony Coco, SJ. At a young age, he learned to play clarinet and saxophone, and by the age of 13 he was playing with his brother in several local bands on the clarinet his brother had bought from a pawn shop in Memphis.

Frank left home – and his clarinet-playing – to enter the Novitiate in 1938. He was educated in the ordinary course of studies: philosophy at Spring Hill College (1942-45) and theology at St. Mary's College (1948-52), where he was ordained on June 14, 1951.

After ordination he began a lengthy teaching career at Jesuit High in New Orleans (1954-70). Then, for the remaining 36 years of his life, he worked in retreat ministry, serving in most of the retreat houses staffed by the Jesuits of the New Orleans Province: Manresa House of Retreats in Convent, La., Montserrat Retreat House in Lake Dallas, and Our Lady of the Oaks in Grand Coteau, La.

If this was the sum of his ministry, then one should consider him a typical Jesuit, an ordinary priest. But right when the Church was modernizing itself by means of Vatican II, Fr. Coco answered a second call, or rather, a call that had been muted by notions of traditional religious life. He came back to his music and his clarinet.

Fr. Coco became acquainted with the royalty of the New Orleans Jazz scene: Ronnie Kole, Pete Fountain, The Dukes of Dixieland and Al Hirt, among others. Time allowing, Frank took his clarinet and gradually worked his way into the company of the greats, who quickly appreciated his talent; he was welcomed to play a set or two with the best bands in the French Quarter.

He had entered a world of jazz talent – the nation's best – which included quality friendships with quality performers. Pete Fountain laughingly told him to send his antiquated Albert-system clarinet to the Cabildo, a renowned museum next to St. Louis Cathedral. Fountain, the king of clarinetists, replaced it with one worthy of Frank's talent. He also designated Fr. Coco the chaplain of the "Half-Fast Walking Club," which required Frank to wear a theme costume each Mardi Gras (pirates, Indians, Minutemen, clowns, etc.).

From mid-life on, music figured in his ministry. Unfailingly, he dressed in "clerics," the ordinary clerical street dress, and he became known as "the Jazz Priest." He would play tunes like "A Closer Walk with Thee," "Amazing Grace" and "When the Saints Go Marching In" for groups on retreat, as well as for funerals and weddings. Once, after he finished a song in one of the clubs of the Quarter, a patron shouted: "Are you going to preach a sermon?" Frank responded, "I just did."

In his sixth decade, Fr. Coco started writing his memoirs and titled them *Blessed Be Jazz*, which explains why he was up at all hours of the night playing his music in the Quarter. The book was published posthumously in 2009. His music can be heard on two CD albums: *A Closer Walk with Three* (with the Ronnie Kole Trio) and *Live from St. Louis: An Evening of Jesuit Jazz*.

In 2005, his failing heart necessitated his transfer to Ignatius House infirmary. Fr. Coco died on Sept. 7, 2006, at age 85, and is buried at Grand Coteau.

Harold Francis Cohen, SJ
1928 – 2001
A bilingual Charismatic leader and broadcaster

Born in New Orleans on Nov. 29, 1928, Harold Francis Cohen attended Jesuit High School (1941-45), where a decision made on a retreat led him to the Jesuit Novitiate in 1945.

His formation was predictable until he began theology; because he was already fluent in Spanish, he went to study at Oña, Spain (1955-57), unlike most American Jesuit scholastics at that time.

Life in Spain was extremely hard at that time. Once, he knelt before the rector and begged to be allowed to buy some eggs. Many factors such as a lack of food and the very frigid climate led him to leave Spain and return to the States to complete his theology at St. Mary's in Kansas. Unlike the rest of the theologians, he thought the food at St. Mary's was excellent. Harold was ordained on June 18, 1958.

He was a teacher and counselor at Jesuit High in New Orleans (1959-66), a chaplain and teacher at Loyola University (1966-79), and helped in the formation of young Jesuits (1971-76).

In 1968 a Fordham student made him aware of the Catholic Charismatic movement and he immediately began organizing Thursday night Charismatic prayer services. Beginning in 1970, he participated in the annual Charismatic convention in New Orleans, which normally drew more than 2,000 people. From 1973 to 1981 he organized Charismatic conferences, retreats and workshops in North and South America, in Europe and Australia. In 1973 he gave the keynote address to the International Conference on Charismatic Renewal at South Bend, Ind.

In 1981 his first radio show, which was broadcast for 15 minutes nightly, aired on WWL radio in New Orleans. In 1983 he began broadcasting on local TV the "Closer Walk Ministry." He produced approximately 150 programs (26 in Spanish) which aired on WLAE in New Orleans, EWTN and 13 other national networks. He also produced TV programs like "Catholics, the Bible, and the Early Church," "Friends with Jesus: a Scriptural Ignatian Retreat," "Our Catholic Treasures," "Winners for Christ," "Mercy Our Mission," and *"Caminando Con Jesus."*

He worked strongly for pro-life causes, often picketing abortion clinics. Fr. Cohen promoted devotion to Mary and to God's Divine Mercy as found in the life of Saint Sr. Faustina Kowalska. He fostered Eucharistic adoration, often praying for hours himself each day before the Blessed Sacrament.

In 1999, Fr. Cohen developed pulmonary fibrosis. He continued to work until a few months before his death, on Jan. 15, 2001, at age 72. He is buried at Grand Coteau.

Edward Thomas Coles, SJ
1924 – 2003
Before he was a priest,
he was a prisoner of war

Fr. Edward Thomas "Bubba" Coles was a member of "the Greatest Generation," having served in the U.S. Army during World War II.

He summarized his service in the European Theater of operations from 1943 to 1945 in the following manner:

> *After induction at Camp Humbug in Shreveport, La., I moved constantly for advanced training ... arriving at southern France in Marseilles ... combat in the Vosges Mountains ... went further north to Mainz ... continued front-line fighting and relieved Patton's tanks so they could break circle around Bastogne ... moved south to Sessenheim ... was captured by Germans in trying to attack Sessenheim ... transported behind German lines.... We came to our permanent Stalag – Stalag VII – 18 miles northeast of Munich.... On April 30, 1945, the American tanks of the 45th Division rolled in and liberated us.*

Born on Dec.14, 1924, in Houston, Coles graduated from St. John's High School in Shreveport in 1942. He attended Loyola in New Orleans for one year (1942-43) before enlisting in the Army on June 28, 1943.

Coles entered the Novitiate on Sept. 25, 1946, and passed through the stages of Jesuit intellectual training, finally being ordained on June 17, 1959.

Fr. Coles was the founding principal at Strake Jesuit College Prep in Houston (1961-64). He earned an M.Ed. in educational administration from the University of Houston in 1964. He next served as principal at Jesuit High in Tampa (1964-69). Soon he was appointed Chairman of Loyola's Department of Education, but the next year he started doctoral studies at the University of Florida, one of the few things he did not finish. He was appointed principal of Jesuit High School in New Orleans, but he resigned after a severe heart attack.

Because of health concerns, he took a series of jobs in the Province's educational positions which afforded less stress: counselor in Shreveport, assistant to the principal in Tampa, director of finance and counselor in Tampa, treasurer and counselor in Dallas, and counselor in Houston.

In the early 1980s Bubba's apostolic labors turned to a new field: parish ministry. He began in Dallas as associate pastor at St. Rita's (1983-84) and then was assigned to St. Michael's Church in Houston (1984-87), followed by a year at St. Ignatius Church in Spring, Tex. After a two-year stay at Strake Jesuit, Fr. Coles returned to parish ministry at St. Rita's in Dallas (1991-96), St. Vincent de Paul in Houston (1998-2000), and finally to Holy Name of Jesus Parish in New Orleans in 2000.

His heath continued to deteriorate, so much so

that he had to be cared for in Our Lady of Wisdom Health Care Center, near Ignatius Residence, the Jesuit retirement home.

Admired and respected, Fr. Coles died on Oct. 21, 2003, at age 78, and is buried at Grand Coteau.

John Thomas Condry, SJ
1917 – 2006
Three ministries graced with humor

Fr. John Condry was blessed with a sense of humor by the grace of God. He spent his long life ministering to junior high students, parishioners, retreatants and his Jesuit brethren.

John Thomas Condry, born on July 13, 1917, in Eckhart Mines, Md., was educated in Miami and entered the Novitiate at Grand Coteau in 1936, following the hallowed path of Jesuit educational training.

After ordination, Fr. Condry was assigned to Jesuit High in New Orleans, where he taught for the next 20 years (1951-71). He taught only eighth-graders, the pre-freshmen students who, while intelligent, suffered from the acute social distress of transitioning to high school. His touch with these boys was masterful: He was teacher, scoutmaster, uncle and guardian angel to them – and for 20 years!

At mid-life, Fr. Condry left education to serve in sacrament and Word at the new Jesuit parish in Dallas for a four-year stint.

His third ministry shot up like a sapling as he began giving the Spiritual Exercises at Jesuit retreat houses. He started at Maryhill Retreat House in Pineville, La. (1984-85). But Fr. Condry was "called up higher" with an assignment to Manresa House of Retreats in Convent, La. (1987-92). He returned to Grand Coteau to work in Our Lady of the Oaks Retreat House, where he had two periods of directing retreats (1980-84 and 1992-2006).

What made Fr. Condry so effective? First, he had a delightful sense of humor, bringing it into his talks and homilies. At Grand Coteau he generously became part of the local parish ministry, saying the 6:15 a.m. Mass and hearing the confessions of the children attending nearby St. Ignatius School and the Academy of the Sacred Heart.

People commented on his gentle presence. He was noted especially for reminding the parishioners of the core of the Gospel: God's compassion toward them and God's hopes for them.

Fr. Condry wrote about his ministry in a short piece on the occasion of his 70th anniversary as a Jesuit:

> The Society of Jesus afforded me all the means necessary to have a full, happy, meaningful life of service in three different ministries.... Providence has probably decreed that I should end back at the beginning. But I can truthfully say it's been a wonderful life for which I most gladly render heartfelt thanks to God and to the best of caring brothers – the Society of Jesus.

Fr. Condry developed a form of leukemia that diminished him relentlessly. His last days were crowded with friends who came to say good-bye and plant one last kiss on his face. His gentle death is the dream of many. He received the Sacrament of the Sick and the Viaticum, and the Prayers for the Dying were recited by the entire staff of Our Lady of the Oaks.

At age 89, Fr. Condry died on Aug. 1, 2006, and is buried at Grand Coteau.

Harold Louis Cooper, SJ
1916 – 1997
Master of Ignatian retreats, champion of social justice

Attracted to the priesthood, Harold Louis Cooper searched for a religious order that he could embrace for his whole life. He eventually found the Society of Jesus.

Cooper was born on Sept. 25, 1916, and educated in Mobile, where he finished his secondary schooling at Spring Hill High School (1934). Initially attracted to the Maryknoll congregation, he attended Vernard College in Clarks Summit, Penn. (1931-32 and 1934-36) and St. Gregory's Seminary in Cincinnati, Ohio (1932-33).

After further discernment he entered the Society of Jesus in Grand Coteau on Oct. 21, 1936. His intellectual formation as a Jesuit included the Juniorate at Grand Coteau and philosophy at Spring Hill College (1940-43). He spent his Regency at Jesuit High in New Orleans (1943-44) and then at Jesuit High in Dallas (1944-46); afterwards, he studied theology at St. Marys, Kan., (1946-50) and was ordained on June 14, 1949.

Fr. Cooper was assigned to Loyola University, first to teach theology (1951-53) and then philosophy (1953-60, 1962-68 and 1973-81). From his earliest days at Loyola he was involved in counseling, inquiry classes and student retreats. In the midst of his teaching he served as the chaplain at Loyola University.

He left the university to found Ignatius Retreat House in Atlanta. After taking special studies in Adult Education in England (1968-69), he began service as the vice-provincial for pastoral ministries in January 1970. Indeed, his commitment to giving retreats matured with a long tenure at the Cenacle Retreat House in Metairie, La. (1973-81) and then at Montserrat House of Retreats in Lake Dallas (1981-83 and 1985-88).

After a brief stay at Sacred Heart Church in Tampa, Fr. Cooper was appointed superior of the retirement community, Ignatius Residence (1988-91). With his labors at Manresa House of Retreats in Convent, La. (1991-93), he achieved the distinction of having worked in all four of the Province's retreat houses. The catalogue of Harold's ministries warrants the judgment that he was an indispensable religious, ready and able to handle a wide variety of pastoral assignments.

In addition, he flowered as a champion of social justice. He spent many years in the desegregation movement in the 1950s and '60s, writing and lecturing against segregation.

Fr. Cooper conducted retreats for religious and instructed converts. In the late 1950s he was a regular correspondent for *America*. Time and again his colleagues heard people commenting that he was a "much loved and respected" person.

For the last four years of his life, Harold resided in Ignatius Residence. His acute illnesses included emphysema and a weakened heart. As death approached, Harold was attended by Fr. Jim Deshotels and a dear friend, Marie Louise Davidson, who remained with him to the end. He was so short of breath that he was unable to speak, until he traded this earthly breath for a breath of heaven.

Fr. Cooper died on Feb. 19, 1997, and is buried at Spring Hill.

Daniel Alexander Creagan, SJ
1928 – 2009
Painter, performer, teacher: A man of considerable artistic talent

Fr. Daniel Alexander Creagan used his artistic gifts and talents to glorify God through art and music. His creative expression earned him the opportunity to perform and to paint, as well as to teach those students lucky enough to be in his classes.

Born Dec. 13, 1928, in Boonville, Mo., Creagan moved with his family to New Orleans, where he eventually attended Jesuit High. On Aug. 14, 1945, he entered the Novitiate and followed the hallowed path of Jesuit priestly formation: philosophy at Spring Hill and Regency at St. John's High School in Shreveport. He sailed to France for theology, studying at *Maison St. Augustin Seminaire Missionaire*, Enghien/Chantilly from 1955 to 1959. Dan was ordained on July 30, 1958, at the historic Cathedral of Senlis in the quiet town north of Paris.

Upon his return to Spring Hill, Fr. Creagan was quickly made chairman of the Fine Arts Department in 1961, a position he held for 22 years. Dan's "fine arts" commitment spread in two directions: painting and music. He studied classical guitar with Manuel Lopez Ramos (1970-72) and became so proficient that he was invited to Mexico City as a performer in the Master's Class. He was also the choir director for the college church at Spring Hill, a patient but demanding instructor. Additionally, Dan produced several Spring Hill Fall Festivals of Fine Art in the early sixties.

His constant goal was continued self-improvement in all areas, especially in the arts. So to further develop his painting skills, he earned an MFA from the University of Colorado in 1967. He taught his students to paint in many genres and to appropriate the technique, vision and palette of the Masters.

Dan's own painting remained in the realm of realism. One of his watercolors was accepted in the International Watercolor Exhibit in the Betz Gallery in Houston. His last show, "A Celebration of Realism," was held on the campus of Spring Hill in January 2007.

He was courteous, clever, intelligent, pleasant and peaceful. His "high church" liturgical style was always reverent and enriching. Somewhere along the way Dan metamorphosed into a Kentucky Colonel, not just with the white beard, but with white suits, a most pleasant drawl and a passion for *Gone with the Wind*.

His interest and talents were eventually channeled toward parish ministry, three parishes to be precise. First he served for six years as acting pastor of Sacred Heart Church in Abbeville, S.C. (1985-91). After this, Dan was made the superior and pastor of Holy Name of Jesus Church in New Orleans (1991-97). Success at this prominent parish shaped him to be associate pastor at St. Ignatius Church in Spring, Texas (1997-2006).

When it became time to go home, in 2006, Fr. Creagan retired as artist-in-residence at Spring Hill, where he died March 6, 2009, and is buried.

Thomas J. Cronin, SJ
1920 – 2005
He possessed kindness and empathy –
and a strong independent streak

Thomas J. Cronin's parents, both born in County Kerry, Ireland, immigrated to Pennsylvania to seek a new life and advantages for their children. One of those children chose to be a man in service to God.

Tom Cronin was born on July 6, 1920, in Pittsburgh, where he was baptized, reared and educated. After a year at Duquesne University, he entered the Jesuit Novitiate in 1939. The rest is predictable: Novitiate and Juniorate; philosophy at Spring Hill College, where he earned a B.S. in physics (1943-46); Regency in Dallas (1946-49) and theology in St. Marys, Kan. (1949-53).

Fr. Cronin began his ministry teaching theology at Spring Hill (1954-62). A sea change occurred in 1962 when he began giving retreats in the retreat houses in the South: Our Lady of the Oaks in Grand Coteau (1962-64), Ignatius House in Atlanta (1964-65) and Montserrat in Dallas (1965-68). He then labored in various parishes which the Province staffed: St. Ann in West Palm Beach (1968-70), Gesù in Miami (1970-74), Assumption Parish in Houston (1974-76) and finally Immaculate Conception in New Orleans (1976-77).

Next, he returned to the retreat house circuit, working at Manresa (1977-87), then at Our Lady of the Oaks (1987-93) and finally back to Manresa (1993-2005).

Fr. Cronin was a complicated man who sometimes found living in community to be difficult. He had his share of life's burdens, and more than just a slight tendency toward stubbornness.

On the other hand, many of his students and retreatants appreciated him for his kinder, gentler nature.

Colman McCarthy of *National Catholic Reporter* fame and a graduate of Spring Hill wrote on learning of Fr. Cronin's death:

"… his first assignment in 1954 was running the counseling office and teaching theology at Spring Hill College…. My good fortune was to be among the many students Tom Cronin befriended."

McCarthy also referred to Tom's "kindness and innate gifts for empathy."

Another obituary mentions that "Retreatants loved the collection of stories that Tom used in his retreat talks and also his gentle way of proclaiming the gospel."

Some of those with whom he lived and worked claimed that Tom's signature song was Frank Sinatra's "My Way." His independent streak was distinct and undeniable.

The Jesuit career of Fr. Cronin came to its end on Feb. 24, 2005, early in the morning. He was 84 and had been a Jesuit for 65 years and a priest for 51. He is buried at Spring Hill.

Gregory F. Curtin, SJ
1927 – 2002
A teacher of tolerance and respect

Fr. Gregory F. Curtin earned respect and popularity as a teacher and counselor. His use of audio-visuals was novel for the times, and his Religion and Film course at Loyola University became a staple from 1972 on.

His colleagues found him encouraging to his students, joyful and serene. He taught tolerance and respect for the values of others and tried to learn from them. He challenged students to find out what they really believed and to arrive at some notion of the "truth" by comparing the relative merits of conflicting positions.

Born in Knoxville, Tenn., on May 11, 1927, he attended Catholic schools there until he entered the Society at Grand Coteau in 1944. After Juniorate he studied philosophy at Spring Hill College (1948-50), skipped Regency, did theology at West Baden, Ind., and was ordained in 1953.

His inaugural priestly ministry began at St. John's High School in Shreveport (1955-56), but after a year there he became the *socius* to the novice master at Grand Coteau (1956-57). A year later, he joined the staff of Immaculate Conception Church in Albuquerque (1957-61) and began teaching and counseling at Jesuit High in El Paso (1961-62).

His next assignment brought him to Atlanta as minister (1962-63), followed by a return to Albuquerque (1963-64). In 1964 he came to Jesuit High in New Orleans as teacher and counselor, one of his longest assignments (1964-72). In 1972 he joined Loyola University as an associate professor in theology at City College, Loyola's night school.

In the Jesuit community he served as the rector's admonitor for several years, as well as house consultor and confessor to many. City College celebrated his 20th anniversary in 1991.

Fr. Curtin always had significant health challenges. As a result of rheumatic fever he had developed a serious heart condition, and when he was 26 doctors informed him that he would not live very long due to his weak heart. But his long years of active apostolic work proved them wrong. Still, medical issues always shadowed his life.

Following a heart valve implant, Greg remained in a deep coma from which he was not expected to recover; however, eventually his body began to heal. But in the 1990s both the valve and his heart began to weaken again.

After years of struggle, Fr. Curtin died on March 31, 2002, at the age of 74. He is buried at Grand Coteau.

John Francis Deeves, SJ
1928 – 2010
The reluctant priest

While at Jesuit High in New Orleans, John "Jack" Francis Deeves starred on the varsity baseball team that won the state championship. Even though he probably could have played college ball, upon high school graduation in 1945 he entered the Society.

Born in New Orleans on Sept. 11, 1928, John desired to become a Jesuit brother because he was mechanically adept. He feared the public speaking that would be required of him as a priest.

"I felt no desire to preach or do anything that would place me in front of a crowd," he once said.

The novitiate staff persuaded him otherwise. Fr. Deeves wrote his thoughts on how he was pulled into priestly ministry:

The most satisfying and joyful experiences of my priesthood have been the forgiveness of sins. Karl Rahner (one of the most important theologians of the 20th century) stated that forgiving sins is the most important thing a priest does.... I did feel that it would be a wonderful thing, through God, to be able to forgive sins and offer absolution. I have found that ministry consoling and humbling. Priests are always impressed with the trust given us by penitents, as well as by their genuine love for God.

He spent the years 1949-52 at Spring Hill College studying philosophy and earning a B.S. in physics. In Regency at Jesuit High in Tampa, he taught physics and math for three years (1952-55) then studied theology at St. Mary's (1955-59).

Fr. Deeves was ordained on June 18, 1958.

He earned an M.S. in physics in an intense summer program at Purdue, and soon thereafter Fr. Deeves taught math and served as assistant principal at St. John's High School in Shreveport (1959-60). He was then posted to Jesuit High in El Paso to teach physics and math (1961-72) and served as the athletic director and czar of daily school bus transportation for Jesuit High and Loretto Academy. He left El Paso when Jesuit High closed.

After one year at Jesuit High in Dallas, Jack returned to El Paso to work at Loretto Academy and El Paso Community College (1973-77), again teaching physics and math. In 1978, he returned to Dallas to teach physics at Jesuit.

While serving as cheerleading sponsor, Fr. Deeves suffered a major heart attack on Oct. 24, 1988. He waited for a heart transplant, and several months later he received one, in June 1989. After a long recovery he went on to teach physics at Ursuline Academy in Dallas. On balance, Jack spent 47 years teaching in high schools.

Even with a new heart, his stamina and health declined. On Oct. 16, 2010, Fr. Deeves died at the age of 82 and is buried at Grand Coteau.

Alphonso Ignacio del Marmol, SJ
1922 – 2002
He bypassed West Point
to become a soldier for Christ

Alphonso Ignacio del Marmol was one of many native New Orleanians who became a Jesuit.

Born Dec. 8, 1922, he graduated from Jesuit High in 1939. While a high school student he won the city yo-yo championship, an accomplishment he used in later years to get the attention of youngsters he was attempting to instruct.

Declining an appointment to West Point, he chose instead to be a soldier for Christ. On Aug. 14, 1939, he entered the Novitiate at Grand Coteau, where his formation was routine. Part of the first group of Southern Jesuits to leave for foreign missions after World War II, Alphonso arrived in Ceylon in 1946.

Like most Jesuits in Ceylon, he did many things in various places. He was first sent to De Nobili College in Poona, India, for one year and then to Kurseong, India, for three more years of theology, after which he was ordained.

Alphonso was a jack-of-all-trades. During his career in Ceylon/Sri Lanka he was a teacher, a house minister and a parish priest. When needed, he directed choirs and instructed seminarians. Many a Sodality he moderated, and he excelled as the mission photographer. But like many other Jesuit missionaries, he struggled to learn Tamil, the language of that part of Ceylon, even though he was fluent in Spanish and French.

Periodically the Province sends out requests for information about a particular Jesuit. The following comments come from several of these inquiries about Fr. del Marmol:

He is obedient and docile, loving and affable, simple and without guile.

He is a very handsome man, which attracts many women. Thus, great prudence is required in his dealings with women.

He is still a youth. At this time he does not have any special talent. He is dedicated, such that many different positions could be assigned him.

A later report described him as a man of solid virtue, *optimum ingenium*, good judgment, adequate in prudence. In dealings with others, he was said to be flexible, open, strong, steady and prompt to act. Finally, a still later evaluation said of him that he was a spiritual man, an obedient and disciplined person. He is most noteworthy for his zeal for souls.

Returning to America, he experienced what most returning missionaries experienced: culture shock. In Sri Lanka, priests were highly respected, which was not always the case in the States. The sea change of Vatican II rearranged how Americans worshiped and prayed, which could be vexing to men used to a more predictable liturgical life. He had difficulty with many of the new changes in the Church, for at heart he was a traditionalist.

Eventually he returned to Sri Lanka, where on Feb. 12, 2002, he died in Batticaloa, at age 80. He is buried there.

William Thomas Dillon, SJ
1917 – 1988
A ministry marked by illness – and lots of drama

William Thomas Dillon was a man of service, humility and an uncomplaining acceptance of great illness in his life. While suffering partial blindness and chronic pain, he was preparing himself for his ultimate union with God.

Born in New Orleans on Nov. 7, 1917, William entered the Novitiate at Grand Coteau on July 17, 1934, after graduation from Jesuit High School. His course of studies was traditional: philosophy at Spring Hill, Regency at Jesuit High in New Orleans, then theology, and ordination on June 16, 1946.

Almost all of Fr. Dillon's ministry was spent in various parishes of the New Orleans Province: Sacred Heart Parish, El Paso (1948-51); Guadalupe Parish, San Antonio (1951-58); Immaculate Conception, New Orleans (1961-64); Immaculate Conception, Albuquerque (1964-65); St. Mary's, Key West (1966-67); Holy Name, New Orleans (1967-81); and Immaculate Conception, New Orleans (1981-88). His involvement in the retreat ministry lasted only three years, at Xavier Retreat House in Pass Christian, Miss. (1958-61).

Fr. Dillon was renowned for his dramatizing even the simplest things. One of his fellow Jesuits observed:

"He was on stage in the spotlight when he was describing a particularly difficult situation with dramatic emphasis, well-timed dialogue and plenty of gestures."

Illness often interrupted his ministries. While at Immaculate Conception in New Orleans, he lost sight in his right eye and suffered extreme fatigue. William was in pain during the last few years of his life and was rushed to the local hospital on many occasions. He convalesced at Manresa House of Retreats in 1965 and fulfilled light duties as the chaplain at the Cenacle Retreat House in New Orleans (1966).

His provincial, Edmundo Rodriguez, tells in his funeral homily how he spent a lot of time at Fr. Dillon's bedside during his many hospital stays. He goes on to comment that Fr. Dillon was quite aware of "the weakness of his heart and that he might die at any time, yet he was peaceful and ready to go to the Lord when He called."

When Fr. Dillon retired completely, he went to live at Ignatius Residence, and it was there, on Jan. 6, 1988, that he died. He is buried at Grand Coteau.

A close friend of Fr. Dillon's composed an insightful eulogy describing some of his actions which were known to only a few. He was a man of simple rituals, like sorting his mail. He would rapidly view the mail, discarding pitches that promoted "modern stuff." A letter from family was put aside to be enjoyed at leisure. Then he studied the return address, postmark and sender, trying to guess the contents.

One of Bill's favorite themes was "He must increase, I must decrease." He seemed never to care what others thought of him, only what God thought. Similarly, his favorite prayer was "Lord, you know all things; you know that I love you." One of his basic principles is found in John 21:22: "What does it matter to you (what others think and do), you follow me." One final principle: "God would rather have us humble than perfect."

Joseph Francis Doyle, SJ
1936 – 2008
An intuition for souls in need

Joseph Francis Doyle, born in New York City on Dec. 4, 1936, attended Fordham Prep and the Jesuit-run Fordham University, where he was class president in his graduating year. While at Fordham, he fell in love with a young woman and was even engaged.

But his fiancée handed him *The Imitation of Christ* as a gift, saying, "Everyone knows you're supposed to be a priest."

Joe entered the Society in 1958. The results of his Jesuit entrance exam scored him atop all applicants in the area of psychology, but not so well academically. Blessed in the spiritual life, he struggled with studies. But he made the grade. After philosophy, Joe began his first of many stints at Jesuit High in Tampa. In 1967 he attended Regis College in Toronto for theology. His compassion for and intuition in regard to souls in need became so evident that many colleagues and a few faculty members sought him out as a spiritual director. Joe was ordained in 1970.

No one doubted that Joe's ministry would be the care of souls, especially those of young Jesuits. He worked with Jesuit collegians for three or four years then served as master of novices from 1975 to 1981. After assignment to Strake Jesuit in Houston, he moved to other ministries. He was the superior to the retired Jesuits in New Orleans, and in 1988 Fr. Doyle was named pastor of St. Joseph's Church in Houston.

Despite the fact that organization was never one of Joe's recognized skills, he succeeded well. He was even celebrated as a city hero for collecting weapons and having them destroyed.

He returned to Tampa in 1996, this time as president of Jesuit High School. This unlikely administrator succeeded wonderfully. George Steinbrenner of New York Yankees fame had a grandson ready to take the entrance exam for Jesuit High and he offered to build an elaborate weight facility for the school. *Quid pro quo?* Fr. Doyle's answer: "If you really want to benefit the school, Mr. Steinbrenner, we are in great need of a better library."

Although Joe would deny that he manifested many virtues, his friends knew better. He could be called a priest's priest, because of all the counseling he did for local clergy. He was a designated guru, confessor and director; he practiced *cura personalis* (care for the entire person) long before it had a name.

Joe differed from his peers in two things: intuition and "the gift of tears." Preparations for a talk or liturgy were merely advisory to Joe, for anything could happen at Mass. Tears were a signature feature of Joe; his feelings, liberated by grace, could be seen streaming down his cheeks. His tears, often embarrassing to people, simply indicated that Joe thought more with his heart than his brain. What a greater love it is to cry with one's friends.

Shortly after retiring from Jesuit High in Tampa in 2008, Joe suffered a stroke, which required him to move to Ignatius Residence for rehabilitation. Sufficiently recovered, he returned to visit friends in Tampa, where he suffered serious heart complications.

On Dec. 6, 2008, Fr. Doyle died at age 72 and is buried at Spring Hill.

Robert Anderson
1916 - 2005

Michael Alchediak
1935 - 1994

James Babb
1914 - 2002

Lloyd Barry
1913 - 2002

Emmett Bienvenu
1913 - 1998

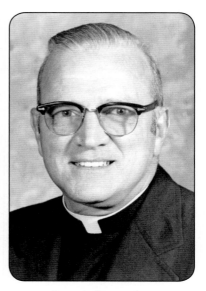

Joseph Browning
1920 - 2004

John Capelle
1916 - 2006

William Champagne
1920 - 1990

Thomas Clancy (1923 - 2009), at left, with New Orleans
Mayor **deLesseps "Chep" Morrison** (circa 1960)

Francis Coco
1920 - 2006

Harold Cohen
1928 - 2001

Harold Cooper
1916 - 1997

John Condry
1917 - 2006

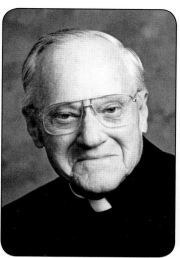

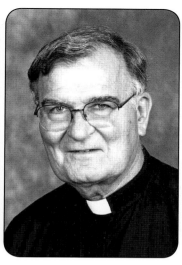

Daniel Creagan
1928 - 2009

Thomas Cronin
1920 - 2005

John Deeves
1928 - 2010

Gregory Curtin
1927 - 2002

William Dillon
1917 - 1988

Joseph Doyle
1936 - 2008

J. Fillmore Elliot
1930 - 2004

Alphonso del Marmol
1921 - 2002

Ignatius Fabacher
1909 - 2000

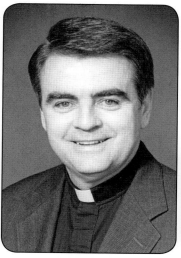

Gerald Fagin
1938 - 2012

Walter Furman
1913 - 2007

Robert Gafford
1916 - 1988

Donald Gelpi
1934 - 2011

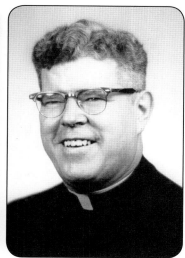

Thomas Gillin
1922 - 2010

Thomas Hatrel
1922 - 1988

Sidney Gilly
1920 - 1994

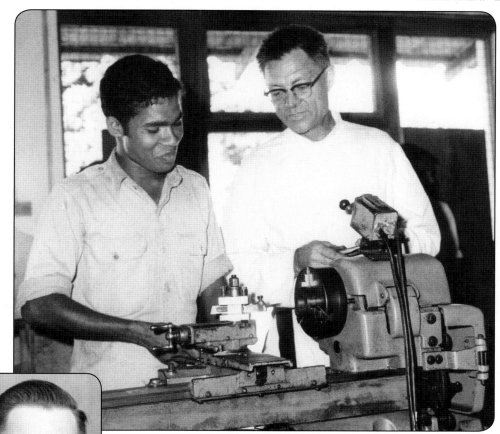

Eugene Hebert
1923 - 1990

Harry Heiter
1914 - 1991

Duval Hilbert
1923 - 1995

Robert Hollingsworth
1930 - 2005

M. V. Jarreau
1915 - 1998

Thomas Jenniskens
1926 - 2013

John Keller
1917 - 1999

Norbert Keller
1928 - 1990

William Kidwell
1924 - 2008

Michael Kennelly
1914 - 2011

Alfred Lambeau
1918 - 1993

Joseph Leininger (1924 - 2007)
leaves the classroom for the last
time as his students applaud him.

Lawrence Luettgen
1925 - 1998

George Lundy
1947 - 2011

Michael Majoli
1915 - 1996

Ransom Marlow
1934 - 2000

Harold Martin
1916 - 1995

Joseph McGill
1929 - 2009

Clement McNaspy
1915 - 1995

Joseph Meyer
1915 - 1997

Cyril Miesch
1918 - 1987

John Henry Millet
1915 - 1998

Henry Montecino
1918 - 2003

Michael Moore
1913 - 2000

William Moran
1925 - 1998

George Murphy
1922 - 2011

Anthony O'Flynn
1915 - 1992

Charles O'Neill
1927 - 2009

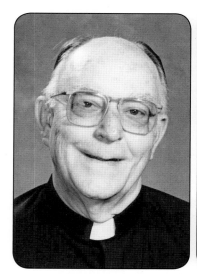

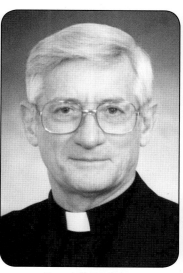

Daniel Partridge
1921 - 1992

Patrick Phillips
1927 - 1998

Frederick Ponder
1913 - 1995

Robert Ratchford
1924 - 2013

Joseph Reising
1941 - 2000

Robert Rimes
1922 - 2012

Francis Riedinger
1913 - 2004

Frank Hinze
1908 - 2004

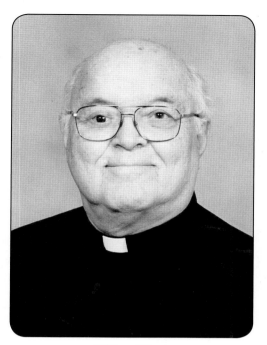

Hilton Rivet
1922 - 2007

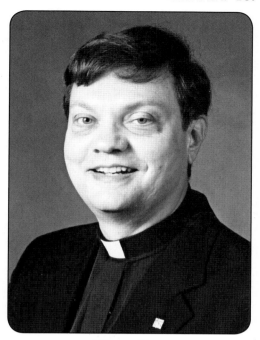

Wayne Roca
1940 - 1999

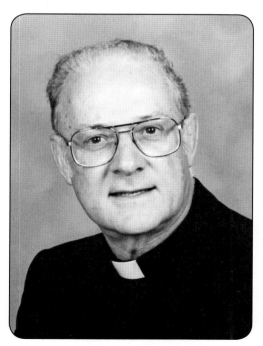

Edward Romagosa
1924 - 2009

Edward Schott
1928 - 2005

John Schroder
1919 - 2014

Thomas Stahel
1938 - 2006

Hilliard Stiegler
1926 - 1999

Harry Tompson
1936 - 2001

John Moore
1922 - 1968

Richard Thomas
1928 - 2006

Bernard Tonnar
1912 - 1996

St. Charles College in Grand Coteau, La., is an anchor of Ignatian spirituality in the Southeastern United States. It is the epicenter of a Jesuit community that includes a Jesuit novitiate, senior Jesuit pavilion, Jesuit Spirituality Center, and neighboring Jesuit parish (St. Charles Borromeo) and retreat house (Our Lady of the Oaks). A 2-year, $16 million renovation of the historic facility was completed in 2013.

Retreatants' dining room

Prayer and reading room

Bishop Michael Jarrell, Bishop of Lafayette, prepares to bless the cornerstone of the newly renovated St. Charles College as Fr. Mark Lewis, S.J., Provincial of the New Orleans Province, unveils it in September 2013.

HANC AEDEM
SUB TITULO S. CAROLI BORROMEO
AD INSTITUTIONEM CURAMQUE NOSTRORUM
DICATAM
PATRES FRATRESQUE SOCIETATIS IESU
AMPLIS AMICORUM DONIS ADIUTI
RENOVANDAM CURAVERUNT

ANNO DOMINI 2013

P. ANTHONY H. OSTINI, S.J., RECTORE
R. P. MARK A. LEWIS, S.J., PRAEP. PROV. NEO AUREL.
F. LAWRENCE J. HUCK, S.J., OPERUM NOTARIO

BLITCH KNEVEL, ARCHITECTIS
J.B. MOUTON, CONTRACTORE GEN.

Translation:
The fathers and brothers of the Society of Jesus, aided by the substantial gifts of friends, renovated this sacred building, which is dedicated to the education and care of those who come here, in the year of Our Lord 2013. Fr. Anthony H. Ostini, S.J., Rector; Fr. Mark A. Lewis, S.J., Provincial of the New Orleans Province; Bro. Lawrence J. Huck, S.J., Director of the Works; Blitch Knevel, Architects; J.B. Mouton, General Contractor.

Main chapel

Sidney Tonsmeire
1909 - 2001

Patrick Usina
1923 - 1981

Roy Vollenweider
1914 - 2005

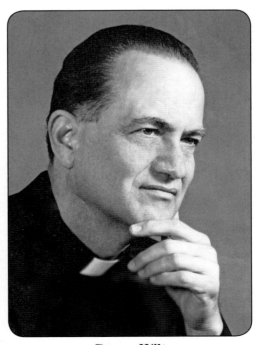

George Wiltz
1934 - 2007

J. Fillmore Elliot, SJ
1930 – 2004
The man never stopped!

J. Fillmore Elliot, born in New Orleans on Dec. 30, 1930, came from a family which produced two Jesuit priests (Clyde and Larion) and two Sisters of St. Joseph of Medaille. After graduation from Jesuit High, Fillmore continued the family tradition and joined the Jesuits in 1948.

He was a part of the generation of Jesuit brothers who did not study for professional degrees. Instead, he turned his focus toward medical care and served as the community infirmarian for more than 20 years, first at Grand Coteau and then at Spring Hill.

His disposition was as therapeutic as any medicines he proffered. Was there ever a Jesuit so continually cheerful, extroverted and helpful by nature? He was known for adjusting the Society's rules to improve the care of the sick. If he had a failing it would be that in his work he tended to run in all directions at the same time, trying to do everything for everybody.

From 1974 to 1977, he labored in Campinas, Brazil, as nurse and sacristan. After that, he undertook a similar ministry at Immaculate Conception Parish in Albuquerque (1978-84), in particular visiting those in the hospitals on a regular basis.

Fillmore suffered a near-fatal heart attack in Albuquerque, so he was moved to the infirmary at Ignatius Residence in New Orleans. It came to light that besides serious cardiovascular problems, he suffered from diabetes. But as much as his health allowed, he spent seven years in ministry to the residents, driving some to their medical appointments and collecting their medicines. Also, he helped the neighboring pastor with the distribution of communion and other services. But he was not finished yet.

In 1993 he received certification in hospital pastoral ministry, which he then practiced at Tampa General Hospital for ten years, even when he was reduced to a motorized wheelchair. But his own health problems required him to return to New Orleans to be cared for at Our Lady of Wisdom Health Care Center.

In his final years, he was renowned for making coffee for the people in his wing and bringing it to them first thing in the morning – the quintessential Fillmore. And on Feb. 24, 2004, just months before his death on June 25, he was crowned King of Mardi Gras at Our Lady of Wisdom, reigning with his customary benevolence over the chaos and mirth.

His vocation was that of Jesuit brother, and he was truly a brother to all Jesuits of the Province. He is buried at Grand Coteau.

Ignatius Maria Fabacher, SJ
1909 – 2000
'Faultless Fabby': A holy, nearly faultless man

A native New Orleanian, Ignatius Maria Fabacher was born on June 3, 1909, into a large family with close connections to the Jackson Brewing Company. While he could have entered the beer business, instead he entered the Jesuit Novitiate on Sept. 7, 1928.

Ordained on June 18, 1941, he spent his first 25 years of service in the internal ministry of his various communities. He served as the minister for Jesuit High in Tampa, then as minister, procurator and *econome* for St. Charles College in Grand Coteau (1944-57). In 1958 he moved to Jesuit High School in El Paso, where he served for eight years as minister and procurator.

His ministry took a new direction in 1968 when he was made associate pastor of Gesù Church in Miami and chaplain at the local Veterans Administration hospital. Soon he became the pastor of Gesù, a position he held for four years.

He exchanged his role as pastor for that of hospital chaplain at Lafayette General Hospital in Lafayette, La., where he served for six years, 1976-82.

He was then stationed in Grand Coteau as Diocesan Representative for Hospitals and as Diocesan Coordinator of Health Affairs (1982-86). He served two more chaplaincy assignments, first at Village du Lac in Lafayette (1986-92) and then at Mary-Joseph Residence in New Orleans (1992-2000).

His work was recognized by two important groups of his peers. He received a citation for his Contribution to Spiritual Growth of Brothers (1985) and an award from the U.S. Conference of Diocesan Coordinators of Health Affairs (1987).

During his tenure at St. Charles College, he noted on more than just one occasion that he had never been ill a day in his life, and he could not understand why other Jesuits were not as healthy as he. But as chaplain to many sick and dying people, he eventually learned that despite all best efforts, people deteriorated, were riddled with cancers and heart diseases, and died. His chaplaincy mellowed him and made him sympathetic.

Additionally, he had a well-merited reputation for holiness in his younger days, leading some to call him "Faultless Fabby." He outgrew this as well.

He died at age 90 on St. Patrick's Day in 2000 and is buried at Grand Coteau.

Gerald Matthew Fagin, SJ
1938 – 2012
Master of the Spiritual Exercises

The spoken word was Fr. Gerald "Jerry" Matthew Fagin's true medium, particularly presentations at innumerable conventions, conferences and retreats.

His mind was both fresh and fertile; he spoke wisely and with compassion. Consider these titles of some of his presentations: "The Spirituality of Aging," "Fidelity in the Church," and "The Theology of Exit."

Born on April 19, 1938, in Dallas, Jerry graduated from Jesuit High in Dallas and joined the Order on Aug. 14, 1956. His training was typical: Juniorate, philosophy, Regency in Dallas and theology in Willowdale, Ont., with ordination on June 7, 1969. Jerry remained in Canada for further studies, earning an STL in theology in 1970 and a doctorate from St. Michael's College in Toronto in 1974.

Fr. Fagin began his ministry in 1973 as instructor of theology at Loyola of New Orleans, where he briefly served as superior of the collegians. In 1976, he was whisked away from Loyola to Grand Coteau to be *socius* to the master of novices for two years. In 1978, he returned to teaching as an associate professor in the Religious Studies Department at Loyola, a position he held until 1989.

But the hand of administration kept landing on his shoulder. Jerry was named chairman of the Religious Studies Department and then rector of Loyola's Jesuit community, a stressful position for which he was not well-suited.

Then the worst possible thing for him happened: He was appointed provincial of the New Orleans Province. He served less than a year and resigned because he could not manage the stress of the office.

Back at Loyola, Fr. Jerry returned to teaching in the Religious Studies Department (1991-95), and then he joined the faculty of the Loyola Institute for Ministry (1996-2012). He also began to give spiritual direction to local seminarians, which was appropriate for him since he was adept at the *Spiritual Exercises*, both as a teacher and as a practitioner.

Because he could never refuse a request, he seemed to be relatively slow to produce his writings and publications: *A Dream Confirmed* (2003) and *Putting on the Heart of Christ* (2010). Another of his works, *Discovering Your Dream*, was published posthumously in 2013.

During treatment for prostate cancer, Jerry learned the disease had already spread rapidly through his body. Soon, he could no longer hear or speak. Many people gathered to say thanks and good-bye, so many that access to him had to be restricted. All wanted to touch the man they knew to be a holy Jesuit. His rapid decline and death shocked his friends.

He died on June 14, 2012, at age 74 and is buried at Grand Coteau.

Walter Laurie Furman, SJ
1913 – 2007
Master of mathematics

Walter Laurie Furman, born Nov. 30, 1913, in Charlotte, North Carolina, studied physics at The Citadel (1933), but he never lost his accent or stopped walking like a cotton farmer. He knew that his audience enjoyed his idiosyncrasies, a clever way to draw in a crowd.

He matriculated as a graduate assistant at the University of Florida (1934-36), earning an M.S. in physics. He then came to New Orleans to teach high school, where he was urged to talk with Fr. Sam Hill Ray, SJ, about the priesthood. Eventually Furman entered the Novitiate, in 1938, and followed a regular course of studies: philosophy and Regency at Spring Hill College, then theology in Kansas (1946-50). He also developed a deep love for praying the Liturgy.

He was awarded a mathematics scholarship to the University of Florida and swiftly completed preliminary work for his doctorate. The research topic for his thesis, basically what the Colombians were saying and writing about mathematics, required him to travel to Bogotá, where he catalogued books and journals in the libraries of the National Library of Colombia. Upon his return to the States he submitted his thesis and was awarded his doctorate in 1961.

Fr. Furman's entire professorial ministry was spent teaching mathematics at Spring Hill College, from 1961 to 1979. During many summers he taught math to juniors at Grand Coteau, where his heavy Southern accent evoked merriment among his students. Because university policy required that faculty retire at age 65, Fr. Furman had to give up teaching at Spring Hill.

Although a "professor emeritus" at Spring Hill, his "retired" teaching career took a new turn when the Alabama Academy of Science received a National Science Foundation grant that provided funding for scientists to visit and teach at high schools.

Fr. Furman was one of the first selected. His stipend included travel by bus to a town or city, plus meals and lodging. At the designated schools, usually African-American, he taught students in the morning and conducted workshops for faculty in the afternoon.

From his own notes one learns that cleverness and incorporating his idiosyncrasies were commonly used strategies for his successfully teaching mathematics.

As more educational personnel learned about Fr. Furman and his program, more invitations came his way. There was, indeed, life after Spring Hill College.

One act of generosity describes the heart of this exceptional Jesuit educator. He regularly spent his Sundays assisting priests near and far, making himself available to parishes all over Alabama; he would offer to stand in for a weekend, a week, or two weeks so that the pastor might make his retreat or take a well-deserved rest.

On July 22, 2007, Fr. Furman died at age 93. He is buried at Spring Hill.

Robert Francis Gafford, SJ
1916 – 1988
Serving the poorest of the poor on the U.S.-Mexico border

Robert Francis Gafford, born in El Paso, Texas, on April 5, 1916, was one of those rare Jesuits who served most of his ministry in his hometown. In all, he served the people of El Paso for more than 38 years.

When Gafford joined the Jesuits on Aug. 2, 1934, he moved from the arid Southwest to the utterly green Louisiana, definitely a change not only in climate but also in culture. He was moving into an area whose unofficial motto is *Laissez les bon temps rouler*, or "Let the good times roll." His progress in the Order was typical: Novitiate, Juniorate, philosophy and theology. He was ordained on June 18, 1947.

Fr. Gafford ("Zeke" to his friends) began his priestly ministry at Sacred Heart Parish in El Paso, a city which continued to be his home for most of the rest of his life. He served at Sacred Heart for six years before being transferred to St. Francis Xavier Church in Albuquerque. Eventually, he returned to his parishioners in El Paso and remained their pastor for 25 years (1956-81).

Just blocks from the U.S.-Mexico border, Sacred Heart Parish served the poorest of the poor. And Zeke imagined how he might help his parishioners. Along the way he built the parish gymnasium, a cafeteria and homes for the aged and for drug addicts. During much of this time, he and fellow Jesuit Fr. Harold Rahm were serving together in the parish.

In every sense, Fr. Gafford was a devoted "worker-priest." But even the best machines begin to age and wear out. In 1981 he became pastor emeritus of Sacred Heart and lived for seven more years with declining health. Fr. Gafford died on July 30, 1988, in El Paso, where he is buried.

Fr. Harold Rahm, his co-missionary in El Paso, wrote an "In Memoriam" upon his friend and colleague's death. He called Fr. Gafford "the greatest and humblest saint with whom I have had the pleasure to live." It was not because he and Zeke agreed on strategy or functioned as teammates. On the contrary, "We lived together like a mixture of oil and water." Harold described himself as "an unorganized extrovert – which went completely against Zeke's way of thinking." To Zeke's credit, "He never said no to my ideas and defended my mistakes before all who criticized. My name was in the local papers and on television every week. He hated publicity, never attended civic affairs ... but he loved me as a Jesuit and I admired and loved him."

Fr. Rahm described a typical day for Fr. Gafford:

After Mass, he went to his office and daily, all day long, attended the never-ending file of Spanish-speaking and English-speaking people who patiently waited their turn. Thousands and thousands of dollars in small sums passed through his hands for the poor, the crippled and also the "bums" waiting or sleeping at the church door, which opened at 5:00 a.m.

Fr. Rahm added:

He was always my saint and ideal, pri-marily because I knew that while he did not understand me ... he accepted, encouraged, looked at my better side, and maybe now and then was proud of me.

Donald Louis Gelpi, SJ
1934 – 2011
An 'Outstanding Educator,' a doctor of philosophy

Fr. Donald Louis Gelpi was an extraordinary educator, a founder of religious institutions and a prolific author. He also played the ukulele!

Born in New Orleans on May 30, 1934, he entered the Society in 1951. His formation was traditional: Novitiate and Juniorate at St. Charles College in Grand Coteau and philosophy at St. Louis University (1955-58), where he earned an M.A. and a PhL (Licentiate of Philosophy). After Regency at Jesuit High in New Orleans, he started theological studies at College St. Albert in Louvain, Belgium, but returned to the U.S. to St. Mary's College in Kansas to finish that part of his studies.

He completed his residency for a doctorate in philosophy at Fordham University in record time. He spent the following year writing his doctoral dissertation on American author and transcendentalist Ralph Waldo Emerson's notion of religious experience. He received his PhD in philosophy from Fordham in 1971.

Fr. Gelpi taught philosophy at Loyola in New Orleans for four years (1969-73), then joined the faculty of the Jesuit School of Theology at Berkeley, which later became a graduate school of Santa Clara University. There he helped found the Institute for Spirituality and Worship, a one-year theological renewal program. In 1974, he was voted an Outstanding Educator of America.

Five years later, he co-founded the John Courtney Murray Group, a post-doctoral research seminar focused on theological enculturation. In 1979, at Xavier University in Cincinnati, he delivered the Bellarmine lecture, part of a lecture series designed to bring Jesuit scholars to a public audience. He also delivered the Gorman-Garrett lecture at the University of Dallas in 1988, and in recognition of his excellence in theological scholarship, he was a Luce Fellow at the Graduate Theological Union in Berkeley, Calif., for the sabbatical year 1993-94.

He became an emeritus professor at Jesuit School of Theology at Berkeley in 1999 but continued both teaching and writing. In the spring of 2001, he held the Beckman Chair in Theology, an honorary position endowed by the family of brothers and Jesuits Robert and John Beckman at Xavier University in Cincinnati.

A prolific and scholarly writer, he authored more than 20 books, among them *Life and Light: A Guide to the Theology of Karl Rahner; Functional Asceticism: A Guideline for American Religious; Discerning the Spirit: Foundations and Futures of Religious Life;* and *Closer Walk: Confessions of a U.S. Jesuit Yat.* His articles were published in *America, The Current, Modern Schoolman, Theological Studies, Thought* and other publications.

Fr. Gelpi had many interests other than scholarship. He frequently led Saturday hikes in the parks of the San Francisco Bay Area. In all seasons he sponsored wilderness weekend trips for students of the Jesuit School of Theology at Berkeley. In addition to his passion for hiking and backpacking, Don played the ukulele, did needlepoint and sketched with oil pastels.

After developing a type of bone cancer, he moved to the Jesuit infirmary in St. Louis, where he died peacefully at age 76 on May 6, 2011. He is buried in St. Louis.

Thomas Marion Gillin, SJ
1922 – 2010
He introduced South Carolina to the Spiritual Exercises

If ever a life caught a second wind, it is that of Thomas Marion Gillin, born in New Orleans on Sept. 8, 1922.

The first wind blew him from Jesuit High in New Orleans into the Jesuit order (1939), where his training was standard: philosophy at Spring Hill College, theology at St. Mary's College, and ordination in 1952. The second wind blew him into areas that had not yet known a Jesuit presence.

Like many Jesuits, Fr. Gillin did a little bit of this and a little bit of that, always in different places. He taught at Jesuit high schools: Shreveport (1946-49), New Orleans (1954-56) and El Paso (1960-61). Then he started giving retreats: Manresa House of Retreats (1956-57) and Our Lady of the Oaks Retreat House (1964-66), quickly becoming its director, from 1966 to 1970. Many retreatants in Grand Coteau chanted his praises because of his responsibility for the new private baths and air conditioning installed in the retreatants' rooms. Influenced by Vatican II, Fr. Gillin was innovative: He initiated retreats for nuns, women, and married couples in a previously all-male retreat house. Later he served in two parishes: St. Ignatius in Mobile (1970-71) and Gesù in Miami (1972, 77-80).

Fr. Gillin's second wind came when he began to build churches and parishes in places that had not yet seen a Jesuit. He celebrated the recently canonized saints Elizabeth Ann Seton (1975) and John Neumann (1977) by making them patrons of his new churches since they were both American-born, pioneering Catholics. He went to Mauldin/Simpsonville, S.C., where in five years he oversaw the building of St. Elizabeth Ann Seton Catholic Church. In Columbia, S.C., he built St. John Neumann Church (1977-84), and after a posting to develop the parish of St. Ignatius in Spring, Texas, (1985-89), Fr. Gillin returned to South Carolina to serve as the pastor of St. Gerard Parish in Aiken (1992-2003).

Building upon his experience as a retreat master, Fr. Gillin began presenting the Nineteenth Annotation version of the Spiritual Exercises to his parishioners at St. Gerard as a way to help them strengthen their spiritual lives. The Spiritual Exercises of St. Ignatius, a form of contemplative prayer to bring people into closer communion with God, were designed originally by Ignatius to be given by a priest or director to another person over a certain period of time – a one-on-one directed retreat. The Nineteenth Annotation version is a little different since the reflection and prayer are done not at a retreat house, but at home or elsewhere.

He surely had a hand in their parish mission statement:

> To be "a People for Others." Together we strive to reveal the Christ we find in one another, we celebrate in the Liturgy, we share in the tradition in the Creed, and in the Living Word of God. Empowered by the revealed Christ, we are sent to build community and witness to the Word with the preferential love for the poor. (Excerpted from the St. Gerard Mission Statement, adopted by the Parish Council, 1993).

Fr. Gillin returned to New Orleans, not to retire but to become chaplain at Malta Square Retirement Community at Sacred Heart Church, the newly converted senior living facility on Canal Street. After the devastation to New Orleans caused by Hurricane Katrina in 2005 and being weary of years, he retired to the Jesuit infirmary.

On Sept. 17, 2010, Fr. Gillin died at age 88. He is buried at Grand Coteau.

Sidney Joseph Gilly, SJ
1920 – 1994
'A beautiful voice and a passion for preaching'

Fr. Sidney Joseph Gilly was a man who must have worn out several sets of luggage during his many years of ministering to God's people. He served in one capacity or another in 16 schools, parishes or retreat houses over a period of 40 years.

Gifted with a beautiful singing voice, Gilly, born in New Orleans on Nov. 1, 1920, graduated from Jesuit High and entered the Novitiate in Grand Coteau on Aug. 14, 1937. His formation was typical: two years of Novitiate, two years of Juniorate, and three years of philosophy. He returned to Jesuit High in New Orleans for his Regency (1945-49), and concluded his formation with four years of theology. He was ordained on June 19, 1952.

His first assignment was that of assistant pastor at Sacred Heart Parish in El Paso (1954-58), an appropriate assignment since Sidney was fluent in Spanish. He was transferred to another Spanish-speaking parish, San Felipe in Albuquerque (1958-63), but later returned to El Paso as director of social services at Our Lady's Neighborhood Center. For four years he was assigned to several retreat houses as a preacher of retreats, first at Xavier Hall in Pass Christian, Miss. (1966-69) and then at Manresa House of Retreats in Convent, La. (1969-70). A decade later, he returned to retreat ministry at Maryhill Retreat House in Pineville, La.

Fr. Gilly's ministry from 1970 to 1980 was directed to priestly, parochial service in eight different parishes. He spent 1970-72 at the Gesù in Miami, both as assistant pastor and head of the religion department of the grammar school. He spent the following year at St. Ann's in West Palm Beach (1972-73) and the next year at St. Charles Borromeo in Grand Coteau.

Things were a little more stable during his four-year appointment at St. Joseph's Parish in Houston, where he was appointed archdiocesan director of Cursillo, working to provide participants with methods and techniques to bring Jesus Christ to the world through evangelization.

He was then assigned to Immaculate Conception Church in New Orleans (1978-80), until he began helping in the priest-poor Diocese of Charleston, which comprises the entire state of South Carolina. First he was assigned to St. John Neumann's Parish in Columbia, S.C. (1981-82), and then to St. Andrew's Church at Myrtle Beach (1982-85). For nine years he served as pastor of St. Mark's Church in Newberry (1985-94), during which time he also took care of St. Mark's Mission in Chapin, which grew into a parish of its own under his care.

In the summer of 1994, he was diagnosed with cancer and was flown to New Orleans in the private plane of Carroll Campbell, South Carolina's long-time governor. On Nov. 9, 1994, Fr. Gilly laid down his burden and met the Lord. He is buried at Grand Coteau.

One Provincial said of him:

"Sidney Joseph Gilly's outstanding quality as a priest was his openness and kindness. Everywhere he went people loved him. He also had a beautiful voice and a passion for preaching."

Thomas Joseph Hatrel, SJ
1922 – 1988
Ministering in the ice and snow

Fr. Thomas Joseph Hatrel grew up in the steamy climate of south Louisiana but served much of his ministry in the ice and snow of Alaska.

Thomas was born in New Orleans on May 21, 1922, and was educated at Holy Name of Jesus (1928-35) and Jesuit High in New Orleans (1935-39). After high school graduation he entered the Novitiate on Aug. 14, 1939, following a predictable formation: Juniorate and philosophy at Spring Hill College, Regency at Jesuit High in New Orleans, and theology in Kansas. He was ordained on June 19, 1952.

His early years as a priest were spent in the high schools of the Province, namely Jesuit High in New Orleans (1954-57) and Jesuit High in Tampa (1957-74), where he taught math. He remained in Tampa, not as a teacher but as director of the community services program for five years (1974-79).

When his tenure in high schools ended, he began the second part of his ministry as a missionary in the Jesuit establishments in Alaska. He was posted to Immaculate Conception Grade School in Fairbanks, Alaska, where he taught math as well as served as athletic director and chaplain for the school (1979-83). The principal remarked upon his leaving: "We've never had a man like this." His final assignment was to a bare and bleak area in Alaska near the mouth of the Yukon River, to a people who had rarely ever seen a priest.

Fr. Hatrel, however, began to develop serious heart problems. He informed a close friend in the Province and asked him to keep quiet about it.

"I don't ever want to reach the point where I can't stay and work in Alaska. Don't tell anyone about this. Just pray for me."

But after he was assessed for heart surgery, he chose a hospital in Anchorage. However, the damage to his heart was irreparable, and Fr. Hatrel died on May 5, 1988, at age 65. He is buried at Alakanuk, Alaska.

Jesuit Father Frank Coco wrote the following on the occasion of Tom's death:

"I never had a better friend in or outside the Society of Jesus."

Fr. Coco credited Fr. Hatrel with three overarching virtues that guided his life: competitiveness, flexibility, and love of all of God's creation.

He was an athlete's athlete, a squad member of the great football teams at Jesuit High and an excellent hurdler. This competitiveness expanded into the doggedness and determination needed to become a Jesuit priest, since Fr. Hatrel was a somewhat mediocre student, which in an order dedicated to education was something of a handicap.

Flexibility was evident in the successful changes he made from school to school, from teacher to director, and from the Southern states to Alaska. Fr. Coco defines "love of all God's creatures" as love for "all people, especially the little children, the glories of nature, animate and inanimate." It would seem that Fr. Hatrel's posting to Alaska reflected all of these virtues.

Eugene John Hebert, SJ
1923 – 1990
The martyr of Ceylon

Did Fr. Eugene John Hebert's peace-making work in Ceylon lead to his death? How did he die?

The mystery of Fr. Hebert's disappearance and presumed death in the summer of 1990 still baffles and haunts his colleagues, friends and family.

Born in Jennings, La., on Oct. 9, 1923, Eugene was educated in several south Louisiana schools: St. Charles Academy in Lake Charles (1930), Mount Carmel in Lafayette (1931), Cathedral High School in Lafayette (1932-33), and Jennings

High (1933-37). Then he moved to Mississippi, where he finished his secondary schooling at St. Stanislaus in Bay St. Louis (1937-41).

He entered the Society of Jesus on Aug. 14, 1941, and spent two years in both the Novitiate and the Juniorate (1941-45). He studied philosophy at Spring Hill College (1945-48), earning a B.S. in mathematics and physics. He spent his Regency halfway around the world, in St. Michael's College in Batticaloa and in St. Joseph's College in Trincomalee, Ceylon. Finally, he went to De Nobili College in Pune (formerly Poona), India, for theology (1951-55) and was ordained on March 25, 1954. At this point, he was fluent in English, French and Tamil.

Stationed in Ceylon, he was assigned to the Province's schools, where he taught a variety of subjects, instituted a performing band and earned the respect of his fellow Jesuits and his students. A colleague once remarked:

"The boys loved him because he had no favorites…. His hands were always busy repairing everything from watches to motorcycles and lorries."

He established a Technical Institute, where as director he taught the boys what Americans call "shop." In the midst of this hubbub, Gene revived his skill with the clarinet and gathered boys to form a band.

Musical bands were unknown on Gene's side of the island, and when the band paraded and played, it caused near-riots by excited bystanders. Attired with outgrown uniforms from Jesuit High School of New Orleans, the band began playing regularly at the leper community of Mantivu, first to celebrate the opening of its library and afterwards regularly to enrich the lives of the lepers. The Prime Minister, Ceylon's first citizen, once paid a visit to the Eastern Province, which occasioned a "command performance" by the band. Fr. Hebert instructed the boys, "Play as you never played before – and make it loud."

Fellow Jesuits know of his dedication, indefatigability and striving for excellence. A colleague remarked in his obituary:

"I was impressed by his drive and his force of personality…. Because he believed so firmly that winning was expected and the natural fruit of all-out trying, he never had a boy who took his course in math to fail the OL exam."

His zeal was equally shared in his priestly endeavors.

"He would accept Masses, confessions and ceremonies in the Sinhalese fishing villages along the east coast even though he knew only the Sign of the Cross in that language," a colleague observed.

Occasionally internal evaluations are submitted to the Provincial; Fr. Hebert's two extant ones contain the judgments of his Ceylon confreres. As a Jesuit he was considered *optime*, that is, "excellent," and he always enjoyed praise and support from the Ceylonese Jesuits.

Fr. Claude Daly, SJ, identified Fr. Hebert's premier virtue – which could have led to his demise:

"He was a peace-maker. Gene never tired of telling the soldiers and police, many of whom were his good friends and who had played basketball in the schools, that only understanding and simple justice towards the families and the children not involved in the conflict could bring peace…. All three priests [Fr. Chandra Fernando, Fr. Selvarajah and Fr. Hebert] who died in the past two years were victims of their effort to bring peace between all the groups."

Alerted to a conflict among Tamils, Muslims and Hindus in the village of Valaichchenai, just 25 miles north, Fr. Hebert drove his motorcycle as fast as he could to mediate the conflict. He succeeded. After the meeting, he took a Tamil boy with him and set out for Batticaloa.

What happened next is a mystery except for the fact that Gene disappeared – no trace of him, his cycle or the Tamil boy. On Aug. 15, 1990, Fr. Hebert vanished from the earth, but not from the eye of God.

Harry Pillans Heiter, SJ
1914 – 1991
A priest in perpetual motion

St. Ignatius once likened a good Jesuit to a staff in a man's hand: It is constantly in motion. By that criterion, Fr. Harry Pillans Heiter was an exemplary Jesuit, ready for any task, anywhere and at any time.

A native of Mobile, born on Sept. 6, 1914, Harry attended Oakdale Grammar School (1919-26) and spent a year at Barton Academy (1926-27) before finishing at Murphy High School in Mobile (1927-31).

In 1937, after a period of six years that are unaccounted for, Harry entered the Novitiate, where he spent two years, followed by two years of Juniorate. He returned to Mobile to study philosophy at Spring Hill College, where he earned an A.B. in Latin (1941-44). Then he began his Regency, which started at St. John's High School in Shreveport (1944-45) and concluded at Jesuit High in

New Orleans (1945-47). As expected, he traveled to St. Mary's College in Kansas for his theology studies (1947-51).

His ministry was varied in terms of where he worked, what ministries he performed, and the frequency with which he was reassigned. He taught in many of the high schools of the Province as well as in its university and college, performing diverse tasks. At Jesuit High in New Orleans he was assistant principal and prefect of discipline (1952-56); and at Strake Jesuit in Houston, he was a teacher of Latin, English and mathematics (1963-64). He also taught theology and was minister of the house at Loyola University (1956-61) and then was a teacher at Spring Hill College (1964-75).

Much of his ministry was spent at retreat houses: Montserrat Retreat House in Lake Dallas, Tex. (1976-78), Ignatius House in Atlanta (1978-80), The Cenacle Retreat House in New Orleans (1981-82), Manresa House of Retreats in Convent, La. (1982-85), and finally at Our Lady of the Oaks in Grand Coteau (1985-88).

He taught seminarians, first at Grand Coteau instructing novices and juniors (1961-63), then Sisters of St. Joseph at St. Joseph College in Jensen Beach, Fla., teaching theology and philosophy (1966-67), and finally at Corpus Christi Minor Seminary (1980-81). He also served as chaplain to the Carmelite Monastery in Mobile (1988-91).

In 1990, Jesuit High School in New Orleans recognized his labors by designating him the recipient of the prestigious North American Martyrs Award, which is given to alumni.

The following year, on June 21, 1991, Fr. Heiter died at age 76. He is buried at Spring Hill.

Duval Joseph Hilbert, SJ
1923 – 1995
He did retreat work 33 years,
until ALS stopped him

One time while fishing, Fr. Duval Joseph Hilbert witnessed the capsizing of a skiff occupied by two men. One man surfaced, but the other man sank.

Without hesitation, Duval dove in, found the drowning man, towed him to shore and gave him mouth-to-mouth resuscitation for 20 minutes until Agis Journis, age 26, began to breathe. The exhausted Hilbert continued for another 40 minutes until a rescue squad arrived. Those who help save souls rarely have such an occasion to save lives as well.

Duval Hilbert, born in New Orleans on Oct. 8, 1923, graduated from Jesuit High School and entered the Society on Aug. 15, 1940, at Grand Coteau. There he learned to be a Jesuit. He progressed through philosophy (1944-47), Regency at St. John's High School in Shreveport (1947-50), and theology (1950-54).

With two exceptions, "Duvy" to his friends, was early on dedicated to the preaching of the Spiritual Exercises in the retreat houses of the Province: first at Xavier Hall (1955-58), next at Our Lady of the Oaks (1958-61), a return to Xavier Hall as superior (1961-64), then Manresa as director (1966-79), a time at Montserrat (1985-91) and finally, once again at Our Lady of the Oaks (1991-95). In all, 33 years of his priestly ministry were devoted to retreat work.

Fr. Hilbert will be remembered as the director of Manresa who chose the lesser of two evils. Men traveling to retreat were wont to stop for fortification to face their retreats, which led to many DWIs and some accidents. Duvy proposed this compromise: If the men would forego their libations en route, he would provide an open bar at the retreat house for the half hour before supper. Solomon could not be prouder.

Besides suffering from a bad back and legs – "I have been through 19 major surgeries" – Duvy was diagnosed with amyotrophic lateral sclerosis, better known as Lou Gehrig's disease. In the spring of 1995, he moved to Ignatius Residence, where the progressive and unrelenting disease destroyed the rest of his body.

During Fr. Hilbert's time at Ignatius Residence, Fr. Louis Poché interviewed this "strong man, in charge, the boss." Fr. Hilbert shared his thoughts:

"I can still move my left hand a little, but that's about it. Some people can't understand how I can be happy in these circumstances, but I have wonderful people around me. I want to get through this last part of my journey with as much happiness and joy as possible, as much for the sake of the people who love me as for myself."

The interviewer then asked, "Can you say where you were the happiest?"

"No, I can't rank the retreat houses in terms of where I was happiest. Wherever I happened to be! I never woke up saying, 'Oh, God, I have to go to work today.' It was always, 'What can I do today?'" the veteran retreat master responded.

On Dec. 18, 1995, Fr. Hilbert died at age 72. He is buried at Grand Coteau.

Herbert Francis Hinze, SJ
1908 – 2004
'Expert supervisor of construction and maintenance'

Herbert Francis Hinze was born Oct. 26, 1908, in the Baptist environs of Waco, Texas – to be precise, in Cego, a very small community in West Falls County. It seemed unlikely that Frank would have much exposure to the Catholic faith, but an inspiring story changed the direction of his life.

As a young man, Frank read about two Jesuits, Martial Lapeyre and George Feltes, who in 1932 landed their crippled aircraft on an ice-covered mountain in Alaska and survived six days in minus 40-degree weather. Frank was mightily impressed, not only with the event, but that both were Jesuit brothers. Inspired by their courage and tenacity, he subsequently converted to Catholicism in 1932, and after another year he entered the Novitiate to become a brother of the Society of Jesus.

This was a talented man who developed considerable skills after he took a course in architectural drawing in 1924. His trademark as a Jesuit brother was designing buildings and other related projects.

Bro. Hinze organized and planned the construction of two buildings at Loyola University and seven at Spring Hill College. He not only drew the plans for buildings, but equally important, he was dedicated to their maintenance. Indeed, he headed the maintenance department at Spring Hill College for nearly 25 years.

Who was Frank Hinze? He showed great courage in his environment to become a Catholic and a Jesuit brother. His fidelity to his vocation is evidenced by his many years of steady service. One colleague said of Frank:

"Mild-mannered and always pleasant to deal with, Francis was an expert supervisor of construction and maintenance."

As talented as he was in his chosen field, he also asked to labor in unrelated areas: sacristan, infirmarian, and supervisor of food services.

At age 84, Bro. Hinze was working as minister and treasurer of Ignatius Residence when a serious fall injured his back. This beginning of his physical decline was followed by a series of strokes that caused him to retreat ever so gently into deeper silence.

Bro. Hinze died on Feb. 17, 2004, at age 95. He is buried at Grand Coteau.

Robert Earl Hollingsworth, SJ
1930 – 2005
Corporal works of mercy: vocational training in Brazil

Although Robert Earl Hollingsworth was born a Baptist in Linton, Ind., he converted to Catholicism and was baptized in 1948.

Born on Jan. 27, 1930, little is known of his early years and elementary and secondary schooling. After a year working for Coyne Electric in Chicago and serving in the U.S. Army in a tank division from 1951 to 1953, Hollingsworth formed a construction company specializing in concrete in Corpus Christi, Texas.

While doing a job at Corpus Christi Seminary he met Fr. "Dutch" Jenniskens, SJ, and began to serve at Father's daily Mass. Bob and Dutch had frequent conversations about faith and spirituality, with the result that on Feb. 9, 1962, Bob entered the Novitiate at Grand Coteau. He was 34 when he pronounced his vows as a Jesuit brother in 1964.

In 1966 Bro. Hollingsworth joined the New Orleans Province mission in Brazil, where he would serve nearly 40 years. He began his mission work at the newly founded *Centro Social Presidente Kennedy*, which caters to poor and uneducated rural Brazilians coming to the large city of Campinas. Here they are taught social and professional skills to help them gain employment as skilled workers.

Besides serving as director and treasurer of the *Centro*, he wore many other hats. Ever the builder, he constructed *Nossa Senhora de Pompeia* Church, then *Bom Pastor* Church – surely with expert concrete work. Some said his most important construction project was bettering the lives of those in vocational training at *Centro Kennedy*.

In an interview, Bro. Hollingsworth spoke about the *Centro* and what it does.

"About 1,900 people come here every day for some kind of service. We estimate 456,000 persons per year…. We take care of many of them almost from birth to the grave. Seriously, we offer all kinds of services. We're helping all the immigrants who come to the big city with no preparation. A corporal work of mercy, eh?" he said.

Using skills learned in the Army and in his Jesuit training, Bro. Hollingsworth was a pious and dedicated leader, exuding competence and confidence. Even though he failed to learn Portuguese, his colleagues maintain that he truly communicated.

When listeners "would turn on their imaginations," they could figure out what he was trying to say. He spoke, they say, the "language of love," and his sense of humor was loud and clear.

The best way to measure the success of Bro. Hollingsworth's labors is to imagine the hundreds of thousands of students who studied at *Centro Kennedy*, trained there, and moved on to have successful professions, especially in the hospitals of the region.

The people whose lives he touched had kind things to say of him. One young man said, "He was always positive and never complained." A young woman said he was never able to pronounce her name, Zoraide, so he called her Dona; Bro. Bob was, she said, "my friend." Some knew him as "the suffering servant who did not open his mouth."

In his later years, he began to have health problems, but for him leaving Brazil was not an option.

On Sept. 25, 2005, Bro. Hollingsworth died at age 75 in Campinas, São Paulo, Brazil, where he is buried.

Rudolph Bernard Horstmann, SJ
1918 – 1993
Top-notch teacher
of math and science

Rudolph Bernard Horstmann was a fabled teacher of math and science in Jesuit high schools in Tampa, Shreveport and New Orleans. Parents wanted their sons to study under him because they had faith in his standards and teaching methods; they wanted the best.

Horstmann was born into a thoroughly German family in New Orleans on the Feast of the Assumption, Aug. 15, 1918. He attended Benjamin Franklin Elementary School (1923-30) and Warren Easton High (1931-35). After graduating from Loyola University with a B.S. in chemistry in 1939, he began a career as a chemist with Ethyl Corporation in Baton Rouge, where he did graduate work at Louisiana State University.

Perhaps influenced by his positive experience at Loyola, he entered the Society on Sept. 7, 1943, at Grand Coteau. After two years of formation, he remained in the Juniorate for two more years to attain mastery of Latin. Difficult though it may have been for a chemist, he spent three years studying philosophy (1947-50) and then theology at St. Marys, Kan. (1951-55). He was ordained on June 16, 1954.

His first 25 years of ministry were spent in the classroom, mostly in high schools. After one year of teaching at Jesuit High in Tampa, he settled down at St. John's High in Shreveport, staying from 1957 to 1974. His teaching career was completed with a stay of six years at Jesuit High in New Orleans (1974-80).

His remaining years of ministry were done in various Jesuit parishes: Holy Name of Jesus in New Orleans (1980-82), St. Ann's in West Palm Beach (1982-83), then 10 years at St. Joseph Church in Mobile.

His excellence was widely recognized. He was an active member and officer of the Louisiana Science Teachers' Association throughout the 1960s. In 1970 he was chairman of the American Chemical Society (Ark-La-Tex Section). He was recognized for superior service to the Advancement of Science in the Schools of Louisiana in 1967.

Fr. Horstmann died on Nov. 4, 1993, at age 75. He is buried at Spring Hill.

Martin Voorhies Jarreau, SJ
1915 – 1998
He liked Loyola and Jesuit High –
but he loved his N.O. Saints!

Fr. Martin Jarreau was a die-hard fan of the New Orleans Saints. It was said that if one watched the Saints' games on Sunday, a figure in clerics looking for all the world like Martin could be seen pacing on the sidelines. One has to wonder how this native New Orleanian would have celebrated the Saints' Super Bowl win in 2010 had he lived to see it.

Martin Voorhies Jarreau was born into the widely recognized, long-established New Orleans Voorhies family on Aug. 6, 1915. His elementary schooling was typical of most Catholic youngsters and was divided between Holy Name and St. Rita's schools. From 1928 to 1932, he attended high school at St. Aloysius, run by the Sacred Heart Brothers. "M.V.," as his friends called him, spent his college years at Loyola University (1932-36), earning a B.S. in economics while also serving in the Louisiana National Guard for three years.

On Sept. 22, 1937, M.V. entered the Novitiate at Grand Coteau, where he spent the first two years in Jesuit formation (1937-39) and two more years in the Juniorate, even though he had his degree from Loyola. However, because of his degree, his philosophy studies at Spring Hill College were shortened by a year (1941-43). He spent three years of Regency at Spring Hill and Jesuit High in Tampa, and like so many others he went to St. Marys, Kan., for theology (1946-50). He was ordained on June 14, 1949, by the Southern Jesuits' own Bishop Ignatius Glennie.

Like so many other Jesuits, he spent half of his ministerial life either teaching in schools or performing cabinet-level administrative tasks. He started teaching at Spring Hill College (1951-53) but was soon sent to Atlanta to found Ignatius House, the fourth Jesuit retreat house in the Province. It still operates, thanks to the seeds M.V. planted there.

Later he was part of the administration of Loyola University, spending four years in the development office (1966-70). After this he was briefly Loyola's Vice-President for Community Relations (1970-71). His labors in education included Jesuit High in New Orleans as a religion teacher (1971-72). He remained there, but his work turned to fundraising for the Province's retirement home.

Much earlier Fr. Jarreau had served at St. Ann's in West Palm Beach. Fla. (1953-57). Several years later, he traveled to Tennessee for a year as pastor of St. Ann's Church in Nashville (1974-75), followed by a year at St. Henry's, also in Nashville (1975-76), then returned to St. Ann's in West Palm Beach for eight more years (1976-84). At the end of this he became a member of the Tribunal Office in the Miami chancery (1984-98), where he served as case director and assessor for petitions of annulment.

Fr. Jarreau died in New Orleans on April 1, 1998, and is buried at Grand Coteau.

Thomas J. Jenniskens, SJ
1926 – 2013
The man called 'Dutch'

In the early years of the 20th century the pastor of a church on the West Bank of the Mississippi River across from New Orleans was in need of help to manage a dairy operation that provided milk for two orphanages. The priest, Msgr. Peter Wynhoven, was of Dutch extraction, and he invited dairymen from his homeland to come to Louisiana to work in the dairy.

Among those who responded were Thomas and Louise Jenniskens. A few years after they arrived and settled on the West Bank, Tom Jr. – a future Jesuit priest – was born in Marrero, on July 9, 1926. In all, there were five Jenniskens children, and they grew up on the family's dairy farm, which supplied milk not only to the orphanage but to other customers in the New Orleans area as well.

After attending Immaculate Conception grade school and graduating from Jesuit High School, Tom entered the Novitiate at St. Charles College in Grand Coteau on July 30, 1943. It is here that fellow novices gave him the nickname "Dutch." His progress through his formation was steady. He earned a B.A. in Latin at Spring Hill College in Alabama and did his Regency at Jesuit High in New Orleans from 1950 to 1953. After theology at St. Mary's College in Kansas, he was ordained on June 13, 1956. He attended Loyola University in Chicago and earned an M.Ed. in counseling in 1970.

He was first assigned as assistant pastor to St. John's Church in Shreveport and then as a teacher at his former high school in New Orleans. In 1960 he was posted to Corpus Christi Minor Seminary in Texas. It was like Regency once more: He wore many hats and performed many tasks. To the Jesuit community, he was the minister; to the seminary, he was a teacher of speech and drama, Latin and English, as well as the spiritual director, librarian and Sodality moderator.

A candid remark from Fr. Jenniskens on Oct. 22, 2010, revealed his lifelong commitment to his vow of obedience:

"I have been a Jesuit for 50 years, and never received an assignment that I wanted…. Superiors make mistakes, but God never makes a mistake in guiding us through our superiors."

But Dutch made it a point to fit in and cooperate and find satisfaction in the work to which he was assigned. He was finally allowed to do counseling work when he was assigned to Jesuit High in New Orleans in the mid-1970s; but he was also made rector of the community during this period. He was then appointed rector of St. Charles College in Grand Coteau (1975-78). Dutch was next assigned to Strake Jesuit in Houston, where he was director of pastoral activities, director of counseling and teacher of theology (1979-94).

Dutch was a skilled ceramicist and thoroughly enjoyed the hobby. Under many a Christmas tree were his nativity scenes or his Santa Clauses. He made ceramic crosses for his brothers celebrating jubilees. His handiwork was sold frequently to benefit the scholarship fund at Strake.

He still had one more important job: retreat director at the Spirituality Center in Grand Coteau, where he served from 1994 until 2004. Then he retired to Ignatius Residence, where he continued to share the fruits of his talent for ceramics.

Fr. Jenniskens died on May 22, 2013; he was 86 years old, a Jesuit for 69 years and a priest for 56 years. He is buried at Grand Coteau.

John Francis Keller, SJ
1917 – 1999
Educational leader
and social justice advocate

John Francis Keller had a talent for leadership, an activist's passion for social justice, and a genius for long-term friendships and peacemaking.

He officiated at the marriages of innumerable friends, baptized their babies, brought peace between enemies and reconciled differences among friends.

A native New Orleanian born on March 7, 1917, John graduated from Jesuit High in New Orleans and entered the Society on July 17, 1934. His Jesuit education was conventional except for his special studies in physics and mathematics at St. Louis University (1943-44; 1949-50). He was ordained June 18, 1947.

Fr. Keller taught for 15 years at Spring Hill College then migrated to Loyola in New Orleans, where he served in many capacities: chaplain, chairman of academic departments, and director of graduate studies and research grants. Eventually he became the university's treasurer and executive vice president.

Fr. Keller's excellent work in education resulted in his leadership in many professional organizations, such as the Louisiana Association of Independent Colleges and Universities; the Louisiana State Board of Regents' Special Advisory Committee on Public and Private Post-Secondary Education; and the Governor's Special Commission for Educational Services.

Fr. Keller was an advocate for social justice. He served on the Law Clinic staff, worked as director of Loyola Law School Minority Programs and as director of the Loyola Law School Minority Recruitment and Retention Program (1984-97). From 1991 until his death he actively served on the Louisiana State Commission for Financial Assistance to Post-Secondary Students.

Fr. Keller's career propelled him to the circles of power in the state capital. To equip himself better to navigate these new waters, John went to Loyola Law School and received his J.D. degree in 1982.

Along the way he received many honors, including selection as an Honorary Member of the Louisiana Senate (1975). In 1979, Loyola University awarded him an honorary LL.D.

Fr. Keller celebrated his share of jubilees: his 50th and 60th anniversaries as a Jesuit, and in 1997 the 50th anniversary of his ordination. He used these events to gather alms for the Jesuit Retirement Fund of the Province.

In the late 1970s, John developed cancer, which resulted in the loss of his left leg. With crutches and a wheelchair, he remained active and became an unofficial lobbyist for the handicapped in Baton Rouge. It was rumored that in 1977 he used the loss of his leg to influence Congress to vote for a bill to give money to private colleges – and therefore to Loyola.

On Jan. 28, 1999, Fr. Keller died at age 81. He is buried at Grand Coteau.

Norbert Alfred Keller, SJ
1928 – 1990
A late bloomer, he was
one of the Order's 'best men'

Norbert Alfred Keller did not always plan to be a Jesuit. In fact, after high school he worked for 11 years before he answered God's call to the Society.

Keller was born in New Orleans on May 26, 1928. It is presumed that he went to grade school at Holy Trinity, but it is known that he graduated from Holy Cross High School in 1944. He spent the years 1944 to 1955 in various jobs and finally in 1955 entered the Order in Grand Coteau for the obligatory two years of Novitiate and two years of Juniorate. He went to Spring Hill College for three years of philosophy (1959-62) and to Jesuit High in Shreveport for Regency (1962-65).

He was part of the theology class which moved from St. Marys, Kan., to St. Louis University (1965-69). In his formation he earned three degrees: M.A in philosophy (Spring Hill College, 1962), M.A. in theology (St. Louis, 1969), and an STL in theology (St. Louis, 1969).

Fr. Keller's first assignments were to high schools. He returned to Jesuit High in Shreveport to teach theology and English (1969-72), and then he spent six years at Strake Jesuit in Houston, basically teaching theology. Finally, he was assigned to Jesuit High in New Orleans, which was his *alma mater* Holy Cross's most bitter rival (1978-81). In addition to teaching English and Latin, he was designated rector of the Jesuit community there.

Perhaps it was because of his extensive work with high school students that he was made the master of novices of the New Orleans Province (1982-87), a position entrusted only to the Order's best men. His final ministry was to serve as an assistant to the provincial (1987-90), particularly as the assistant for formation.

On Labor Day of 1990, he and the new provincial, Fr. Ted Arroyo, attended the traditional Labor Day picnic at Ignatius Residence. Earlier that week, when Fr. Arroyo expressed doubts about being able to live up to expectations as provincial, Fr. Keller, who was Fr. Arroyo's spiritual director, tried to bolster his confidence.

"Don't worry about that, Ted, I'll be around here to help you," Fr. Keller told him.

Unfortunately, he was not able to fulfill that promise.

Back from the Labor Day picnic, the two men were watching the 10 o'clock news when Fr. Keller suffered a heart attack and died instantly, on Sept. 3, 1990, at age 62. He is buried at Grand Coteau.

Michael Francis Kennelly, SJ
1914 – 2011
A high-profile operator,
he opened Strake Jesuit in Houston

Michael Francis Kennelly was about as Irish-Catholic as one could be. People only needed to hear his Irish brogue to know he was the real deal. But he was also a powerful and effective man, someone who could, for instance, start a new school and raise serious money almost at will.

He was born on March 22, 1914, in Kilbaha, Moyvane, County Kerry, Ireland. At the urging of an uncle, the family immigrated to New York, where Michael began secondary school at Regis High in 1930. Another uncle, Rev. Patrick Ryan, invited Michael to finish his education at Spring Hill High School (1932-33). He then entered the Novitiate in 1933 and followed the traditional path of education common to Jesuits.

After ordination, he returned to Ireland to do studies in education at University College in Dublin (1947-49), where he earned two degrees in education. He also earned a B.A. in classics at Spring Hill College in Mobile and an M.A. (Honorary) in education at National University in Dublin.

Fr. Kennelly began his education ministry as a successful principal of St. John's High School in Shreveport (1949-53). Then he went to Jesuit High in Tampa as both rector and principal (1953-59), during which time he arranged to purchase land for a new school. And he raised the necessary money, not only for the land but to build the first building of the new school on North Himes Avenue.

To continue his successful work, he was sent to Houston to open a new high school, Strake Jesuit College Prep, named for George Strake, a generous benefactor. As founder, rector and president, he watched the school grow from one small classroom building on the Texas plains to the leading Catholic high school in the area (1959-70).

After serving as president and rector of Loyola University (1970-74), Fr. Kennelly was assigned to St. Catherine's Church in Didsbury, Manchester in the U.K., where he served in pastoral capacities.

Upon his return to the U.S. in 1980, he took up residence in Tampa for ten years, first as an assistant at Sacred Heart Church and then as pastor (1982-90). His final position was as assistant to the president at Jesuit High in Tampa.

One phrase expresses Fr. Kennelly's strategy, style and level of success: high profile. He served as chairman of the Board of Directors of Loyola (1968-73), Strake Jesuit (1959-70) and Jesuit High in Tampa (1953-59); he also served as a board member of St. Francis de Sales Grade School in Houston (1966-70). He was probably the only educator in America who was simultaneously a board member of a university, a high school and a grade school.

His high profile can be seen in the ways he was acknowledged for his civic service. One such example is the awarding of *Les Palmes Académiques*, given by the French government for significant academic, cultural and educational achievement. Houston, Texas, proclaimed Dec. 26, 1960, as MFK Day and made Fr. Kennelly an Honorary Citizen. He was also inducted into the ranks of "Honorary Senator of the State of Louisiana."

Who was this Michael Kennelly? He was indubitably an Irish Catholic, who never lost his brogue, which probably contributed to his success in fund raising. He knew at some point that he had the gift of building and endowing high schools and so he fostered it. He was loyal to his inner circle of benefactors and friends, as evidenced by his constantly sending them cards and other reminders. He sat in a seat of power just about all his ministerial life.

On Jan. 3, 2011, Fr. Kennelly died at age 96, the oldest living Jesuit in the Province at the time. He is buried at Grand Coteau.

William C. Kidwell, SJ
1924 – 2008
Unflagging promoter of the Sodality of Our Lady

Fr. William C. Kidwell was relentless and insistent in urging students and faculty to join or support the Sodality of Our Lady, later renamed the Christian Life Community (CLC).

He was often successful, as evidenced by his recruitment of two students to accompany him to the Shrine of Our Lady of Martyrs in Auriesville, N.Y., to do maintenance on the old building. This kind of anecdote could be repeated dozens of times. He never ceased trying to recruit people to the Jesuit apostolate, the Christian Life Community.

On Aug. 11, 1924, Kidwell was born in Montgomery, Ala., where he attended the local parish elementary and high schools. He entered the Society of Jesus in August of 1942, spending the traditional two years each of Novitiate and Juniorate (1942-46). He then returned to Alabama to study philosophy at Spring Hill College, where he earned a B.S. in chemistry (1946-49).

Fr. Kidwell taught three years at St. John's High School in Shreveport (1949-52), after which he went to St. Marys, Kan., for theology, finishing with an STL in 1956. After ordination he did special studies in chemistry, first at the University of Illinois (1957-58), where he earned an M.S. in chemistry, and then for three years at the University of Iowa.

After serving with the Jesuit team which staffed the Corpus Christi Minor Seminary (1961-62), he spent many years teaching chemistry to students in Jesuit schools. He taught a year each at Jesuit High in Tampa and then at Jesuit High in New Orleans, before working at Spring Hill College (1962-65).

Fr. Kidwell enjoyed the stability of a longer tenure at Strake Jesuit College Prep in Houston, where he taught classes and also fostered the Sodality (1965-72). He was moderating the Sodality when, in 1967, its name was changed to Christian Life Community.

He returned to Spring Hill College as the chaplain of its CLC (1972-75). He traveled to Shreveport to resume teaching and serve as counselor to the local CLC (1975-78). He again made high schools the base of his CLC ministry, fostering it at Jesuit High in Tampa (1978-84), where he was assigned as assistant pastor at Sacred Heart Church, with much of his time invested in the CLC (1984-86).

Fr. Kidwell took his labors to Miami, serving in various schools and institutions for nearly 20 years. He first worked at Belen High School, teaching and fostering CLC (1986-89), followed by campus ministry and moderating the CLC at St. Benedict/Pace High School (1989-90). He moved to St. Brendan High/Mercy Hospital as campus minister/chaplain and, of course, moderator of the CLC (1991-93). He then served at Lourdes Academy as chaplain and moderator of his beloved CLC (1993-97). He remained in Miami at Gesù Parish as pastoral minister and chaplain at Mercy Hospital, Mt. Sinai Hospital and others from 1996 to 2007.

When the health of this hard-working priest failed him, he was admitted to Our Lady of Wisdom Health Care Center in New Orleans in 2008. Shortly after this, Fr. Kidwell died of heart failure on Jan. 13, 2008, at age 83. He is buried at Spring Hill.

Alfred Oscar Lambeau, SJ
1918 – 1993
Kind and selfless, he taught at Spring Hill College 36 years

Alfred Oscar Lambeau's father, Peter, sought to enter the Society of Jesus as a brother after the death of his wife, Leonora. But the idea that a priest-son would work side-by-side with a brother-father did not win approval, so Peter Lambeau became a Franciscan brother and his son a Jesuit priest.

Al was born in Chicago on Dec. 20, 1918. After primary education in Chicago, he transferred from St. Viator College to Spring Hill and completed his undergraduate degree in 1940. The rest of Al's formation is familiar: Novitiate (1940-42), philosophy (1943-46), Regency at Spring Hill, and special studies in classical languages at Fordham (1948-49). Al began his theology at St. Albert de Louvain, Belgium, but returned to St. Marys, Kan., to finish it (1950-53).

After teaching for three years in the Juniorate, Al arrived at Spring Hill, where he would serve for the next 36 years, teaching French and chairing the Language Department. Little of the record survives, but one of his students proffered these observations:

> Me – the girl he used to roll his eyes over… in my freshman year because I wore ripped jeans. Me – who would torture him with so many questions and was never satisfied with his

answers. And me – the person who had somehow, finally, lived up to his expectations. And how high they were!

Despite his orderliness and perfectionism, students came to love him for his frequent and touching kindnesses to them. To the student body, Fr. Lambeau was "the cute little Jesuit with the cigar." Many of his students would remember his pronouncement: "I do not keep office hours for fear of succumbing to the Big H [heart attack] and going unnoticed until the third day." Jesuits passing through the college made the obligatory visit to Al for the latest *bon mots*.

Fr. Lambeau became the father minister, a role he played in the Jesuit community for 20 years. He had the makings of a good spy, for he noticed everything, as he headed off a "charging bull" or counseled a depressed Jesuit. Some called it yeoman service, but it was simply his exercise of Christian charity.

Fr. Lambeau died on Aug. 28, 1993, and is buried at Spring Hill.

At his funeral, former Spring Hill president William Rimes, SJ, said it best:

"Fr. Lambeau will always be remembered as a person who took care of everybody before himself – a quiet, hidden and respected man who did all his work behind the scenes."

Joseph Blessing Leininger, SJ
1924 – 2007
'A mathematical man for others'

Joseph Blessing Leininger and his twin Charles Andrew, born on May 22, 1924, in New Orleans, shared many things other than a birth date. (Blessing, by the way, was their mother's surname.)

The boys were educated in local parochial schools and graduated from Jesuit High in New Orleans. Bibliophiles, they would hold contests during the summers to see who could read the most books; eight books a week was the norm.

Joseph (known as J.B.), who graduated with honors, was unaware of what Charles (known as C.A.) was planning after their graduation, but it didn't surprise many that they both entered the Novitiate on the same day, Aug. 14, 1940. They remained for two years of Novitiate and two of Juniorate. They studied philosophy at Spring Hill College, with J.B. earning a B.S. in mathematics.

When it was time for theology, the Leininger twins traveled to Kansas; they were both ordained on June 17, 1953.

Appointed principal of Jesuit High in Dallas for two years, J.B. dedicated himself to the education of youth at Jesuit high schools throughout the South: Tampa, Shreveport, Dallas, New Orleans and Houston.

He was a math teacher's math teacher. He spent as little time as possible standing before the class; he preferred to stand in the back calling on students to go to the board and "do math." Whatever fear or dislike the students had when the course began, J.B. was regarded by them at the end of the course as their "best teacher" ever.

His math teaching was interrupted by his appointment as director of the Seminary Bureau. But he returned to teaching math at Strake Jesuit College Prep, which became home base for him.

After being granted a sabbatical and after contacting St. Aloysius and Riverview, the two Jesuit schools in Sydney, Australia, J.B. spent an enjoyable year teaching math there for one semester per school.

During this year, he wrote regularly to his twin, C.A., describing the exotic character of Sydney and Australia, but with the proviso that C.A. keep the letters and return them to him. In all of their years of ministry, J.B. and C.A. were together only once: C.A. was principal of Jesuit High in New Orleans when J.B. taught math there.

At a certain point in his career, J.B. taught himself to paint and do ceramics. His skill was widely recognized, although he could not imagine selling any of his works. In time he persuaded C.A. to teach himself painting and ceramics as he had done.

J.B. had other passions that would endear him to many. He was a great reader, especially of science ficton and fantasy; those summer reading contests with his twin must have solidified his love of literature. Surely aided by his math skills, J.B. loved to play cards, board games and vocabulary-building games.

But however much he enjoyed books and brain games, his energy and devotion were mainly focused on his students. Warm and fuzzy he was not, but he showed patience and persistence with them, serving them and giving them his best. One might say J.B. was "a mathematical man for others."

He died at age 83 on Oct. 27, 2007. He is buried at Grand Coteau.

Lawrence Joseph Luettgen, SJ
1925 – 1998
West Point graduate, paratrooper in Korea, priest and chaplain

Before Lawrence Joseph Luettgen was a priest, he served his country as a paratrooper in Korea.

After one year at the College of Engineering at Marquette University, he received a scholarship to attend the U.S. Military Academy at West Point, graduating in 1946 with a B.S. in civil and military engineering. Then he was sent to Korea, where he was part of the field artillery in the U.S. Army and a paratrooper in that same area for four years (1946-50).

Born in Milwaukee on April 17, 1925, Luettgen completed his primary and secondary schooling in his hometown. Immediately after his military discharge, he entered the Novitiate at Grand Coteau, on July 1, 1950. He spent the requisite two years in the Novitiate but only one year in the Juniorate since he already had a college degree. Then he was off to Spring Hill for three years of philosophy (1953-56), followed by one year of Regency at Jesuit High in New Orleans (1956-57). He went to St. Mary's in Kansas for theology (1957-61) and was ordained in his hometown on June 16, 1960.

For 20 years, starting in 1962, he served on the staff of Corpus Christi Minor Seminary, first as a teacher, then as assistant principal and then as treasurer. During this time he studied in summer school at Marquette University and was awarded an M.A. in American history in 1968.

Preparatory to Fr. Luettgen's change from teaching to a chaplaincy, he completed a semester of study in 1982 at Corpus Christi Memorial Hospital. And so he began his ministry as a chaplain. He served at the Texas Medical Center in Houston (1984-85), then at Baptist Hospital in New Orleans (1986), then moved to Lafayette General Medical Center in Lafayette, La., for four years (1986-90). His final assignment was to Sacred Heart Church in Tampa, from which base he served as chaplain at Tampa General Hospital (1991-95).

Fr. Luettgen's eight years in the U.S. Army certainly influenced his Jesuit life. From the beginning he did not appear to be a teacher; despite his sense of discipline, he never brought that into his classes. Although it seems counter-intuitive, given his engineering education, Larry was a voracious reader of current and military affairs, politics (ecclesiastical, state and federal) and history, as well as Scripture, theology and spirituality. All of this enlivened his conversations and discussions. Still, with his turn to chaplaincy work, he was able to listen, console and bless.

Eventually this robust, energetic priest began to decline in health. Larry had two coronary bypass surgeries, diabetes and then multiple mini-strokes. One such stroke occurred in January of 1997 when he was celebrating the community Mass at Ignatius Residence in New Orleans. Before the recitation of the Our Father he seemed to freeze, and then he sagged and fell to the floor.

On the Wednesday of Holy Week, April 8, 1998, Fr. Luettgen died. He is buried at Grand Coteau.

George Francis Lundy, SJ
1947 – 2011
He worked with Sr. Helen Prejean to ban the death penalty

Politics, labor issues, capital punishment and affirmative action are just some of the issues for which Fr. George Francis Lundy was a passionate and eloquent advocate.

His ministry as a Jesuit provided him with the tools and the platform to speak out against what he considered egregious injustices.

Born in Chicago on Jan. 26, 1947, he grew up in a politically active family, which likely prepared him for his life's work. After his Chicago education, George entered the Novitiate in Grand Coteau on July 30, 1966. His studies were predictable: college, philosophy and theology.

In an unusual flash of imagination, his superiors decided his Regency would be to work for affirmative action for high schools. Ordained in Chicago on June 3, 1978, he matriculated at the University of Chicago, where he was awarded a doctorate in education.

Fr. Lundy joined the faculty of Loyola in 1980 as director of the Institute of Human Relations and taught courses in the Institute's Labor Studies Program. He created a school which taught labor leaders and shop stewards how to be better union organizers.

Loyola's president Fr. James Carter picked Fr. Lundy in 1986 to be the provost and vice-president for academic affairs, a position he held for six years. In 1995 George became vice-president of Detroit Mercy University, an appointment followed in 2000 by his becoming the president of Wheeling Jesuit University.

This tells little about the energy, vision, passion

and endurance of Fr. George Lundy. His advocacy of justice meant that he was a fish swimming upstream. Together with Sr. Helen Prejean, CSJ (author of *Dead Man Walking*) and Rev. Joe Morris Doss, pastor of Grace Episcopal Church in New Orleans, Fr. Lundy started a coalition of religious leaders opposed to the death penalty. This issue remained so important to him that he sought support from the medical community as well. (If physicians don't participate, deaths in capital punishment cases cannot be declared legally.)

Fr. Lundy's advocacy was in print as well as in speech. Some of his best writings were recycled again and again, such as "The Three R's of Nonpublic Education in Louisiana: Race, Region and Religion." Similarly, important arguments kept re-appearing as chapters (e.g., "Death as Punishment") of important books.

But his health was not good. First, he suffered a severe stroke, which left him limp on his left side. Then on Dec. 20, 2011, Fr. Lundy suffered a more severe stroke – one that killed him. He was 64 years old. He is buried at Grand Coteau.

Fr. Lundy possessed a singular intellect and a steely dedication. Remarks from colleagues tell of the measure of this apostle of justice. Loyola president James Carter highlighted George's modern Jesuit virtue: "He was an educator who lived out the Jesuit commitment to social justice as central to our educational mission." A law professor praised him as a no-nonsense type of man: "He had a razor-sharp mind and no tolerance for bureaucratic double talk."

Michael Blaise Majoli, SJ
1915 – 1996
Humor and storytelling enhanced his effectiveness as a teacher and counselor

Michael Blaise Majoli is remembered fondly for using the Southern penchant for storytelling and humor in his counseling, teaching and retreat work.

He was born in New Orleans on Feb. 3, 1915, the son of an Italian father and an Irish mother. He was christened at Sts. Peter and Paul Church and attended its grade school (1922-29) and then Jesuit High, graduating in 1933. He attended Loyola University for one year (1933-34).

On July 3, 1934, Mike entered the Novitiate and spent two years in spiritual formation and two years in the Juniorate. He studied philosophy at Spring Hill College (1938-41), also earning a B.A. in Latin and English. Following a two-year Regency at St. John's High School in Shreveport (1941-43), Mike did special studies in sociology at St. Louis University (1944). From there he went to St. Mary's to study theology (1944-48). He was ordained on June 18, 1947, at Holy Name of Jesus Church in New Orleans.

The ministry of Fr. Majoli encompassed many assignments in the Province. He was first assigned to Jesuit High in New Orleans, where he taught sociology and was a student counselor (1949-51). Then he taught sociology at Spring Hill College and served as counselor for its students (1951-53).

He was named *socius* to the provincial (1953-59), an assignment requiring a patient, diligent person with good skills in Latin and wise judgment. After this he served as rector of St. John's High in Shreveport (1959-65), until he returned to Spring Hill to teach sociology (1965-68). Eventually he was assigned to Jesuit High in New Orleans, first as alumni director (1968-72) and also as teacher of sociology (1969-70). Then he was named minister to the Jesuit community (1972-75).

The second half of Mike's ministry was spent in retreat work. He traveled to Lake Dallas, Texas, to serve as assistant director of the facility (1975-81), and then was assigned to Manresa House of Retreats in Convent, La. (1981-87).

He became ill in 1987 and retired to Ignatius Residence in New Orleans for several years. On April 10, 1996, Fr. Majoli died at age 81. He is buried at Grand Coteau.

A press release on the occasion of Fr. Majoli's death pays this tribute:

"Fr. Majoli was full of stories and anecdotes. He liked to mix humor into his conversation. This made him popular in personal counseling and in hearing confessions. It also contributed to his lively style of writing. He was notorious for his endless supply of puns, mostly bad."

Addicks Ransom Marlow, SJ
1934 – 2000
World-renowned genius in mathematical physics

As a student "amateur" astronomer, Addicks Ransom Marlow, clearly showing a propensity for physics, built a large working telescope, ground the lenses, and constructed a structure to house it. And this was only the beginning of his amazing accomplishments, particularly in the areas of mathematics and physics, all in service to God.

Born in San Antonio on Oct. 3, 1934, Marlow entered the Novitiate at Grand Coteau in 1952. His formation was regular: Juniorate (1954-56) and philosophy at Spring Hill College (1956-59). Besides philosophy, he graduated with a B.S. in physics. Instead of Regency, he attended Georgetown University, earning a PhD in mathematical physics in 1964. After completing his studies in theology at Weston, Mass., he was ordained in 1966.

Fr. Ransom returned to Spring Hill in 1968 as associate professor of physics and mathematics. In 1973 he moved to Loyola University, where he served for 26 years as an associate professor of physics.

He was twice a member of the board of trustees (1977-83 and 1988-91) as well as a board member of the Loyola Corporation (1976-2000). He belonged to numerous university committees, celebrated Masses in campus ministry, and was a residence hall counselor for more than 25 years.

He was much loved by the students for his openness, his gift of counseling, his enthusiasm for chess, and even for planning the annual Christmas decorations.

He was known worldwide for his research in mathematical physics. Between 1977 and 1987 he organized six international conferences at Loyola University dealing with the topic. Each conference produced a volume which received national media coverage because of the attendance of world-renowned scholars like Edward Teller, the "Father of the Hydrogen Bomb."

Fr. Marlow also served as a guest editor for the *International Journal of Theoretical Physics*, a reviewer for *Mathematical Reviews*, and a member of the editorial board for the *American Journal of Physics*. Local radio and TV often utilized him as an astronomy consultant for various programs.

His own publications were many and varied and to some may seem to be esoteric. His books include *Mathematical Foundations*, *Quantum Theory*, and *Quantum Theory and Gravitation*. His articles appeared in the *Journal of Mathematical Physics*, *Quantum Logic*, *Quantum Theory* and *Structure of Time and Space*. He offered papers at conferences in 14 cities in Sicily, Germany, Mexico, England and elsewhere.

Fr. Ransom was a brilliant eccentric who loved and helped his friends. But in his early sixties his energy waned noticeably as his health declined. Lung problems and congestive heart failure threat-

ened his life, and in desperation he arranged for a special heart surgery in Berlin. The surgeon implanted a newly developed mechanical heart pump – a device not approved in the U.S. But Fr. Marlow's lungs were too weak, and he didn't survive the operation.

Fr. Marlow died in Berlin on Jan. 15, 2000. His body was cremated and returned for burial at Grand Coteau.

Harold Philip Martin, SJ
1917 – 1995
'Childlikeness' and simplicity characterized this effective priest

"And He said: 'Truly I tell you, unless you change and become like little children, you will never enter the kingdom of heaven.'" (Matthew 18: 3) The author of a collection of children's stories, Harold Philip Martin, who was called "Martincito" by his Hispanic parishioners, exuded an aura of childlikeness and simplicity of faith. He truly embraced the words of Christ in Matthew's Gospel.

Born Nov. 15, 1917, in Mobile, Ala., Harry attended local primary schools as well as McGill Institute, then operated by the Brothers of the Sacred Heart. After attending Spring Hill College for two years (1934-36), he entered the Society on July 30, 1936. As expected, he received spiritual formation and continued his collegiate studies at Grand Coteau (1938-40). He returned to his hometown for philosophy (1940-43) and spent his Regency at Jesuit High in New Orleans (1943-46). Eventually he studied theology in St. Marys, Kan. (1946-50) and was ordained on June 14, 1949. His pastoral career was punctuated by an M.A. in theology, which he earned in 1969 at St. Mary's University in San Antonio.

Fr. Martin's ministry for the first 20 years was directed to parochial work. He spent nearly a decade at Guadalupe Parish in San Antonio (1950-59), where his competence in Spanish served him well. He spent only a year at Immaculate Conception Church in New Orleans (1959-60) and was then sent to serve as chaplain to American Catholics in Caracas, Venezuela (1960-62). He returned to Guadalupe Parish (1962-69) and then spent a year at Christ the King Church in Grand Coteau (1969-70). He traveled to Brazil to spend ten years at the *Centro Kennedy* in Campinas, where he served in the role of superior of the Jesuit community.

Like a child, he was inquisitive and continued to learn new things even as he got up in years. He studied Kreyòl to help the many Haitians flooding into Miami; he kept his French and Spanish alive, and in his old age he even started to learn calculus.

For 14 years he served as a compassionate confessor at Gesù Parish in Miami. As children dream of the future, so Fr. Martin envisioned developing Gesù into a downtown center of spirituality, in addition to its established role as a provider of traditional liturgical services. He literally worked not only up to but through his last day of earthly life.

Harry coined the phrase "The Old Crock Society," which prompted another Jesuit to describe him this way:

"Harry was more than a writer who could crack wise and crock-wise. There was a gentleness of tone which revealed a delighted reverence for a God who would summon people into the Gesù."

If Jesuits were to have epitaphs on graves, Fr. Martin's would read, "We hold a treasure in earthen vessels."

Fr. Martin died on Aug. 23, 1995, 78 years old and 59 years a Jesuit. He is buried at Spring Hill.

The pastor of Gesù Church in Miami focused his sermon at Fr. Martin's funeral on the reason why Harry was such a popular person and an effective priest. He summed it up in one word: childlikeness.

"He was childlike in his simplicity, in his charm, in his displays of affection and in his easy approachability, in his humility and self-effacement, in his enthusiasm and his creativity."

Joseph Paul McGill, SJ
1929 – 2009
Ceylon missionary, retreat master and lover of books

Joseph Paul McGill was a man of many quirks, some of which involved money and books. Typically, Jesuits receive funds for vacations and annual retreats, but Joe, with permission, stayed in Grand Coteau for both, allowing him to spend those funds on books and journals. This went on for years, so that after his death, there were approximately 4,000 books in his quarters.

Sometime after he was born in New York City on Dec. 11, 1929, Joe's family moved to New Orleans in search of an environment more beneficial for his poor health. In the city later known as "the Big Easy," he was a popular teenager, renowned for his skilled dancing. But Joe felt something stronger

than popularity and parties tugging at him. So he entered the Society at Grand Coteau, on July 30, 1947, spending four years there.

After philosophy, he traveled to Ceylon as a missionary, spending his Regency learning the Tamil language and teaching at St. Michael's College in Batticaloa. When it was time, he went to St. Mary's Theological College in Kurseong, India (1958-61), and was ordained on March 19, 1960.

Joe waited in India for a visa allowing him to return to Sri Lanka (formerly Ceylon), which had since gained its independence and had made it clear that Europeans and Americans were no longer welcome. The visa never arrived, and Joe was eventually assigned to direct retreats at the Manresa Retreat House in Nyegezi, Tanganyika.

After a short stint at Jesuit High in New Orleans as a religion teacher and chaplain to the alumni, he was assigned to Loyola University as director of spiritual life (1975-79). Then he spent seven years at Immaculate Conception Church in New Orleans (1981-87).

His chief ministry of directing retreats continued with his appointment to Our Lady of the Oaks Retreat House in Grand Coteau (1988-92). He returned there in 1999 and remained until his death in 2009.

Fr. McGill, considered by some to be a perfectionist, once declared he was "incompatible" with the world as it was. He was also an intensely private person, avoiding most social gatherings and not readily sharing personal information. Therefore, most colleagues were ignorant of how severe his diabetes was, and even fewer knew of his heart problems.

One of Joe's friends observed:

"Fr. McGill was 'not of this world' for many, many years before his death. He showed dignity, manliness, humility, unflinching clarity and understanding (and an occasional white hot flash of the Irish)."

Never comfortable with the hustle and bustle of modern American life, he was strongly attracted to the peace and quiet of the Ceylon mission and the retreat house environment. He spoke with fondness of the tempo of life in the missions, where, he said, the people "live at a human pace" – not at the break-neck speed that characterizes much of the Western world.

Retreatants who were aware of Fr. McGill's brittle health would ask him occasionally, "How ya doing, Father?"

"Well, I'm standing and I'm breathing," he would say with a smile, knowing full well that might not be the case the following day.

Because of worsening heart disease and diabetes, Joe had to resign from preaching retreats. When it became clear that he needed assisted living, it was planned that he would soon transfer to Ignatius Residence. But before any action could be taken, 79-year-old Fr. McGill died at Our Lady of the Oaks on Dec. 2, 2009. He is buried at Grand Coteau in the Jesuit cemetery near the retreat house.

Clement J. McNaspy, SJ
1915 – 1995
Prolific author and movie
consultant for The Mission

Fr. Clement J. McNaspy was so renowned a Jesuit author, historian, musicologist and linguist that his obituary was printed in *The New York Times*.

Fluent in a dozen languages, including French, Dutch and Spanish, he contributed to many periodicals, was an authority on liturgy, served as an editor of *America* and wrote 29 books. Also, he consulted for the movie *The Mission*, which was loosely based on his book, *The Lost Cities of Paraguay*.

"C.J.," as he was called by almost everyone who knew him, was born in Lafayette, La., the heart of Cajun country, on March 22, 1915. His father was a professor and coach at Southwestern Louisiana Institute (SLI), now called University of Louisiana at Lafayette. His mother, Agnes Thibodeaux McNaspy, began his education at home when he was very young.

He attended the Christian Brothers school in Lafayette starting at age nine, and before he was 12 he had written a book on astronomy. His other special interests were music and languages. He was frequently seen auditing courses at SLI.

In 1931, at the age of 16, he joined the Jesuits in nearby Grand Coteau. After his ordination in 1944 he returned to Grand Coteau to teach the young Jesuits for two years. During the following year he made his Tertianship in Canada, picking up his doctorate in music along the way.

The next 33 years of his life were divided into three nearly equal parts: teaching at the Juniorate in Grand Coteau, administering as dean of the Music School while teaching at Loyola, and serving as associate editor of *America*. During these heady years before and after the Second Vatican Council, C.J. did a great deal of lecturing and writing to explain the new thinking in the Church.

Perhaps his greatest influence was as a counselor and mentor of young clerics and other promising writers and artists. He played a key role in the founding and development of the Jesuit Institute for the Arts, which began in 1970 at Holy Cross College in Worcester, Mass., and continued for several summers thereafter, attracting Jesuit and non-Jesuit artists from all over the world to locations as varied as Rome, Santa Clara and New York.

When he was in his mid-sixties, Fr. McNaspy began a new career as a missionary in Paraguay, where he taught young Jesuits once more and wrote about the early Jesuit achievements in that country. He spent his last years as a teacher at Loyola. His memoirs were published posthumously by Loyola University Press in 1996 with the title *Play On*.

On Feb. 3, 1995, Fr. McNaspy died, at age 79, and is buried at Grand Coteau.

Joseph H. Meyer, SJ
1915 – 1997
Director of minor seminary
in the Ceylon / Sri Lanka Mission

The internal evaluation of Joseph H. Meyer following his Jesuit formation was excellent. He was judged *insigniter* (outstanding) in spirituality, obedience, discipline and zeal for souls. As one person wrote:

"He is a good religious who works diligently…. He is loved by all of ours (i.e., Jesuits). He is filled in a superior manner with charity, which is displayed in his labors…. He would make an excellent director of a minor seminary."

Born in Albuquerque, N.M., on Jan. 13, 1915, Joseph matriculated at the local Catholic school, St. Mary's. In time, he migrated from the bare New Mexico landscape to the green, humid world of Grand Coteau, entering the Society on Aug. 30, 1932.

His formation followed the normal pattern for young Jesuits: four years at Grand Coteau; three years of philosophy at Spring Hill College; Regency at Jesuit High in New Orleans; and four years of theology at St. Marys, Kan. He was ordained on June 16, 1946.

Fr. Meyer's first assignment after ordination was St. John's High School in Shreveport, La., until 1952. In that year Joe's request to be sent to Ceylon was granted. Upon arrival, he was immediately made the director of the minor seminary of the Diocese of Trincomalee. This fit well with Bishop

Ignatius Glennie's plans to foster native vocations. Joe was a solid choice for director because he was known for his piety; his charges loved and respected him; and although he was a bit shy, he was always friendly.

One ancillary work was to write copy for *Lanka Mail* and *Esjays*, two little bulletins which were sent to benefactors of the mission in the U.S.A. He also served in the Jesuit house of formation in Dalugama, Ceylon.

In 1997 he suffered a serious physical and mental decline and fractured his hip in a fall. Eventually he was sent to a convalescent home run by the Sisters of Charity in Kegalle. In his last days he insisted that he wanted to go home. When asked whether he meant Kandy in Sri Lanka or the U.S.A., he said, "No, to Heaven."

On June 12, 1997, God answered his prayer and Fr. Meyer died, at age 82. He is buried in Sri Lanka.

Cyril Charles Miesch, SJ
1918 – 1987
He taught math in Dallas, Shreveport and El Paso

The priesthood must have been like a flower growing in his family's garden, for Cyril Charles Miesch's brother also became a priest. The brothers dedicated their lives to ministering to God's people.

Born in Texarkana, Tex., on Sept. 11, 1918, Cy was educated at Sacred Heart School in Texarkana and graduated in 1937. After graduation, he entered the Jesuit Order on Aug. 14, 1937, and remained in Grand Coteau for four years, two in the Novitiate and two in the Juniorate.

He moved to Spring Hill College for his three years of philosophy (1941-44) and earned a B.S. in math. His Regency began at Jesuit High in Dallas (1944-45), but finished at Jesuit High in Tampa (1945-47). Cy studied theology at St. Marys, Kan. (1947-51), finishing with an STB in theology. He was ordained on June 14, 1950.

His first assignment was as minister at Assumption Hall, the Jesuit House of Studies on Spring Hill's campus (1952-57). His next field of apostolic work was as math teacher in various Jesuit high schools: in Shreveport (1957-59), in Dallas (1959-65) and in El Paso (1965-70).

Shortly after arriving in El Paso he was assigned also as the community treasurer – after all, he was a math teacher. Much later in his life he spent one more year at Jesuit College Prep in Dallas (1985-86).

His apostolic work became exclusively pastoral when he served as chaplain at Schumpert Hospital in Shreveport from 1970 to 1985.

Unfortunately, he was a heavy smoker, a habit that eventually caused him to have lung cancer. He moved to Ignatius Residence in New Orleans, where he died at age 68 on New Year's Day of 1987. He is buried at Grand Coteau.

John Henry Millet, SJ
1915 – 1998
The gnome of Grand Coteau

A story went around that while studying philosophy, John Henry Millet was sailing on Mobile Bay and got lost. When the Coast Guard found him, he was asked, "Who are you?" His response: "I'm a philosopher."

Born on Aug. 31, 1915, in Dallas, Texas, John Henry graduated from Spring Hill High School and entered the Novitiate on Aug. 29, 1933. He followed the regular course of studies. After a traditional Regency, he studied theology and was ordained on June 18, 1947.

His first two decades of priesthood were spent at St. Peter Claver Church in Grand Coteau. This facility, built in the times of racial segregation, sought the protection of its patron, St. Peter Claver, SJ, who labored for the salvation of thousands of African slaves.

As associate pastor under Cornelius Thensted, SJ, Fr. Millet enjoyed the distinction of being the first associate to last beyond a year working with the volatile Fr. Thensted. The two men agreed on very few matters. It was common to hear Fr. Thensted return home and shout *"Father Millet!"* to inaugurate the newest argument. Fr. Thensted shouted because John Henry had a serious hearing defect.

While out at supper, Fr. Millet would launch into animated blow-by-blow accounts of his battles with Fr. Thensted. Everyone in the restaurant was entertained, and one person told the owner that he should pay Fr. Millet to come back every Sunday.

A contemporary once described him:

"John Henry, stooped even then, and wrapped in a worn cassock, splattered with remains of the good earth, strode through an admirably simple life with an inscrutable smile. His language was sprinkled with studied, earthy archaisms that sparkled his conversation."

This diminutive priest was a large, eccentric figure. He loved square dancing and often called the steps at a dance. He devised a scheme to collect duck stamps by putting a box with appropriate information in every store he could. Total success: His boxes supplied hundreds of stamps, which produced substantial funds for the Jesuit Seminary and Mission Bureau. To better aid his Black farmers-parishioners, he attended the University of Southwestern Louisiana in nearby Lafayette to earn a B.S. in Vocational Agricultural Education.

Fr. Millet found another calling: hospital chaplaincy, a role he played for 20 years. He served as chaplain at Lafayette General Hospital (1967-72); the V.A. Hospital and Jackson Memorial Hospital in Miami (1972-75); the V.A. Medical Center in Bath, N.Y., (1975-86) and finally at Our Lady of Lourdes Hospital in Lafayette, La. (1988-89).

He was eventually listed as "retired," but when translated accurately this meant that for the next several years he served as chaplain to a series of local nursing homes (1989-97).

Fr. Millet died on Sept. 16, 1998, a Jesuit for 65 years and a priest for 51. He is buried at Grand Coteau.

Fr. Thomas Clancy's obituary for Fr. Millet observed:

"He was a crusty character, and most of his life a hearing defect made him converse at high volume. His clothes were rarely neat or clean and he became more gnomelike with each passing year. A holy man, a zealous priest, and a very special Jesuit."

Henry Raymond Montecino, SJ
1918 – 2003
Loyola philosophy teacher,
missionary and retreat director

Fr. Henry Raymond Montecino was a highly regarded philosophy teacher, foreign missionary and director of the Spiritual Exercises.

In New Orleans on June 13, 1918, Montecino, usually known as "Monty," was born into a religious family of six sisters and one brother. Monty attended a Catholic grade school in Baton Rouge (1925-32), after which he was a student at Spring Hill High School in Mobile (1932-34).

At 16, he entered the Novitiate in Grand Coteau, on July 3, 1934. His priestly education was typical: undergraduate studies at Spring Hill College (1938-41); Regency first at Spring Hill College (1941-42) and then two years at St. John's High School in Shreveport (1942-44); and theology at St. Marys, Kan. (1944-48). He was ordained in New Orleans by Archbishop Rummel on June 18, 1947.

He did special studies in philosophy at St. Louis University (1951-53). He earned three degrees: an A.B. in French from Spring Hill College and an STL in theology and an A.M. in philosophy from St. Louis University. After Tertianship, he was assigned to the philosophy department at Loyola, where for more than 30 years he taught and counseled students. In the often-hostile cultural climate of the 1950s he was among the few early faculty members to promote racial integration of the university.

Fr. Montecino made many lifelong friends at Loyola, so it was the natural choice that he be named alumni chaplain (1979-84). He was a competent, gracious leader whose good qualities were appreciated. His peers elected him president of the Jesuit Philosophical Association (1964-65). He served as the superior of the Jesuit community at Loyola for three years (1969-72), and rector of the same (1973-78). Finally, he served as chairman of the Province Commission on Aging (1981-84).

He helped guide the early charismatic prayer meetings in the Archdiocese of New Orleans in the 1970s and early '80s.

In 1984, at the age of 66, he answered the call to teach in Africa, and for three years he taught philosophy there at the National Alokolum Seminary in Gulu, Uganda (1984-87).

Back in the States, he was assigned to the ministry of directing retreats at the Jesuit Spirituality Center in Grand Coteau (1987-99). This assignment may have been his finest hour. After his retirement in 2002, the staff of the Spirituality Center as well as the retreatants he directed continued to seek the advice and wisdom of this holy and learned old Jesuit priest who was slowly going blind.

Macular degeneration stole his eyesight, emphysema weakened him, and heart failure took away his life. Fr. Montecino died on Dec. 8, 2003, at age 85. He is buried at Grand Coteau.

Michael Joseph Moore, SJ
1913 – 2000
A life of 'exquisite simplicity'

Brother Michael Joseph Moore did everything as well as possible and as frugally as he could. His responsibilities went as low as maintaining St. Charles College's boiler and as high as its water tower. Whatever the system, Bro. Moore kept it working.

Born July 6, 1913, in Mobile, Ala., Michael graduated from McGill Institute, as did his younger brother, John F. Moore, SJ, and then attended Spring Hill College briefly. Four years later, he entered the Novitiate, on Feb. 2, 1940, as a temporal coadjutor, i.e., following the vocation of a brother.

He served with a work crew of skilled brothers to renovate the Jesuit residence at Loyola University and then returned to St. Charles College in Grand Coteau as its inventive chief maintenance man. He also taught math and technical skills to young Jesuit brothers. He assigned individual projects, monitored and corrected them. If there was an error, he never said where, but required his student to find it on his own.

Bro. Terry Todd related that when he asked Bro. Michael to teach him three-phase electricity, Bro. Michael said he did not know this. But a few days later he handed Bro. Todd a single sheet of paper with an accurate, precise treatise on three-phase electricity.

Bro. Michael's personal papers contain endless lists: Roman emperors, ancient measures and their modern equivalents, and modern and Irish saints, among other interests. He had lists of the Province's brothers: by age, by seniority, and by date of birth.

Bro. Michael continued to educate himself by working through the progressive stages of serious mathematics. His brother John stated that Michael was an autodidact: he taught himself everything he needed to know.

Only because of Bro. Michael's many lists is there a report of his health. He always had many serious aches and pains – about which no one knew. He had the prudence to consult a doctor about the acute arthritic condition of both shoulders and a compression fracture of his lower spine. But observing him, one would never imagine the pain with which he lived.

Bro. Michael lived an ordinary life in which he was never the center of attention. Simplicity, frugality and humility best describe him. His brother John stated that he entered the Jesuits with the same ascetical habits and attitudes characteristic of a mature Jesuit.

Yet he liked to "make funny," so that those close to him found "a monk who was cheerful, recollected and good-humored." When Michael took vows in 1950, the rector asked him to speak.

"I have nothing to say," said he, and sat down.

Later, when asked to speak, Michael stood.

"Last year I had nothing to say; this year the grandeur of the occasion renders me speechless," he stated.

Photos of his room testify to the exquisite simplicity of his life: no air conditioning, only a fan (think Grand Coteau in the summer!); essential desk and chair; a medicine cabinet – empty; a six-shelved bookcase with only prayer books, *Our Friends* and his copy books. No pictures on the walls, no carpet on the floor. His armoire contained only four work shirts, underwear, a coat and shoes (work boots and day shoes).

He was authentic in his Jesuit life – which is why so many admired and respected him.

Outliving his brother John by more than three decades, Bro. Moore died on Sept. 15, 2000, at age 87. He is buried at Grand Coteau.

William H. Moran, SJ
1925 – 1998

Ceylon Provincial during turbulent times

William H. Moran became the house minister in Colombo, Ceylon, then *socius* and later Provincial at a time when several problems had already developed or were developing in the volatile nation.

An unstable new government, a heavy threat of expulsion of foreign missionaries, a government takeover of schools, a transition from Jesuit mission to Province status, and a visit from the New Orleans Provincial, Fr. Larry O'Neill – all of these things challenged Fr. Moran.

Born in Omaha, Neb., on July 30, 1925, William took his elementary education at local schools. He joined the Society on Aug. 14, 1942, and began his formation at Grand Coteau. After studying philosophy at Spring Hill College (1946-49), he sailed to Ceylon for Regency, teaching at the Jesuit schools in Batticaloa and Trincomalee (1949-52). He traveled to Poona, India, and was ordained on March 24, 1955. He studied in Machilipatnum, India, where he spent the period between theology and Tertianship in parish work and Tamil study.

Upon his return to Ceylon in 1957, his first assignment was as minister to the Jesuit house in Colombo for the Trincomalee and Galle missions. (At that time, the two Jesuit missions were in the process of becoming a vice-province.) From 1960 until 1972, Fr. Moran was given greater and greater administrative responsibility: minister (1959-60), *socius* to Mission Superior (1960-62), *socius* to the Provincial of the Ceylon Vice Province (1962-68), and finally Provincial of the Ceylon Vice Province (1968-72).

During this time, the government began to take over all private schools, which caused the Jesuits to close all but three of the upper grade schools. This was a bitter decision, but Fr. Moran saw the issue clearly and argued forcefully:

"We are hanging ourselves in holding on to the schools."

He petitioned for their closure and won approval.

Although Fr. Moran had been missioned to Ceylon in 1962, he went to India in 1972 to work in Jamshedpur doing a variety of tasks in aid of the Xavier Labour Relations Institute. In 1978, he was assigned to the new Sri Lanka Province. After he left both Sri Lanka (formerly Ceylon) and India and returned to the States, the next decade of his service was as associate director of the Jesuit Jamshedpur Mission Society, based in Baltimore, Md. (1981-90).

He moved to the New Orleans Province, and the last years of his Jesuit ministry were spent in three different parishes in Arkansas: St. Peter's Church in Mountain Home (1990-91), St. Agnes Church in Mena (1991), and finally St. Mary's Church in Siloam Springs (1991-97).

His health began to deteriorate rapidly, causing him to move to the Province infirmary in New Orleans. Within a few months, at age 72, Fr. Moran died, on March 27, 1998, 56 years a Jesuit and 45 years a priest. He is buried at Grand Coteau.

Merlin Mulvihill, SJ
1931 – 1991
'A good son of St. Ignatius'

Fr. Merlin Mulvihill was not necessarily a great scholar, a great saint, a great apostle, nor in most ways extraordinary. But he was a great man.

Born in New Orleans on April 19, 1931, he attended St. Rose of Lima and St. Stephen schools. In 1948, he graduated from Jesuit High in New Orleans and entered the Novitiate at Grand Coteau the same summer. In his studies as a Jesuit he was a better-than-average student; as a scholastic he returned to his *alma mater*, Jesuit High, to teach. In 1961 he was ordained a priest at Spring Hill College in Mobile.

Shortly thereafter he settled down to a lifetime of work as a high school teacher. He taught for 19 years at Strake Jesuit in Houston – during which time he earned a master's degree in religious education at St. Thomas University. All his life he had a consuming interest in theology and was unusually well read on the subject.

In 1982 he moved to Jesuit High in New Orleans, where he continued to teach and for three years served as rector of the school community. He was an excellent teacher of religion for the pre-freshmen at Jesuit High and a highly sought-after spiritual director for nuns, his fellow Jesuits and laypersons. He did quality work with Beginning Experience, a ministry of the archdiocese for separated, divorced and widowed Catholics.

For most of his life Fr. Mulvihill had a speech defect as well as poor eyesight, which gradually grew worse. Despite these physical obstacles, to the very end of his life he lived up to the description from an official report filled out on him early in his religious life by a Jesuit superior. He is "a fine religious – a good son of St. Ignatius – reliable, sincere, capable, and zealous."

On Oct. 20, 1991, at age 60, Fr. Mulvihill participated in the first part of the annual 1K walk and 5K run sponsored by Jesuit High in Audubon Park in New Orleans. After finishing the walk he posed with his arms uplifted in the victory sign. Immediately after, he collapsed and died, felled by a heart attack.

The respectful and appreciative crowd at his funeral filled the Martyrs' Chapel at Jesuit High to overflowing. He is buried at Grand Coteau.

George Anthony Murphy, SJ
1922 – 2011
The soul of hospitality

As both a librarian and guestmaster, Brother George Anthony Murphy was much-beloved and much-appreciated. Many considered him to be a most gracious and hospitable man.

Born Oct. 11, 1922, in Columbus, Ga., George was the only child of a skilled textile worker who had emigrated from England to Lowell, Mass., in search of employment. Shortly after his arrival in Massachusetts, Mr. Murphy was sent to the Macon, Ga., headquarters of the company that employed him. There he settled and started a family.

Few records of George's early childhood and education are available, so little is known of his early life, except that after high school he was sent to Spring Hill College. After George entered the Novitiate on Aug. 14, 1941, he pursued the path for ordained ministry. He was educated in the humanities in the Juniorate and in philosophy at Spring Hill; he spent his Regency in Shreveport. After studying theology at St. Mary's for two years, he returned to the Province to teach for three years. During this time of discernment, George was told he did not have a priestly vocation, so he asked to become a Jesuit brother. He was accepted and he made a second novitiate.

In 1960 Bro. Murphy earned a certificate in library science from Loyola University, a degree which determined the direction of his ministry for years to come. When a Jesuit high school was opened in El Paso, Bro. Murphy became its librarian for 11 years (1961-72). When the school closed, he brought its library to the Jesuit high school in Houston and served as librarian there. He moved east to Grand Coteau and its library, and then to the Provincial's residence in New Orleans. When Loretto Academy in El Paso needed a librarian, Bro. Murphy returned to that city to engage in his signature ministry.

While in El Paso, he became associated with Richard Thomas, SJ, and helped Fr. Thomas in his work with the neediest. In 1977 Bro. Murphy was missioned to Corpus Christi Minor Seminary, where he served as assistant librarian. During this time he made a fast friend of Tom Egan, SJ, who had been assigned to the Shrine of the North American Martyrs in Auriesville, N.Y. Since George had no particular assignments during the summers, he spent them with Tom at the Shrine.

In 1982, Bro. Murphy was posted to St. Charles College in Grand Coteau as librarian, assistant treasurer and guestmaster. Many notable Jesuit brothers have been porters, receptionists and guestmasters, and Bro. Murphy belongs in their company. Frequently he would fetch weekend retreatants from the airport or train station in nearby Lafayette and then take them back after the retreat was finished. Moreover, as guestmaster he greeted arrivals when they showed up at the retreat center and escorted them to their rooms, often detouring to give them a tour of the historic facility. He was the soul of hospitality, a grace for which many kept up their friendship with him. This glorious harvest lasted 22 years.

Threatened with a major illness, Bro. Murphy went to Ignatius Residence in New Orleans. Fortunately he did not need treatment, but he remained there in a new assignment: to pray for the Church and the Society.

A tall, thin and gentle man with ageless facial features, Bro. Murphy was always soft-spoken and prayerful. When he was in Grand Coteau, he could be seen walking the grounds of St. Charles College quietly praying his Rosary. When he lived in Ignatius Residence, after visiting with guests who had come to see him, he would invite them to join him in the on-premises chapel for a brief time of prayer before they got back on the road.

Bro. Murphy died on Nov. 19, 2011. He was 89 years old and 70 years a Jesuit. He is buried in Grand Coteau.

Anthony Duffy O'Flynn, SJ
1915 – 1992
Serving as Zimbabwe missionary satisfied his heart's desire

Anthony Duffy O'Flynn traveled from America to Europe to Africa and enjoyed a second conversion during his life of service as a Jesuit.

Born in Washington, D.C., on Oct. 12, 1915, Anthony entered the Society at Grand Coteau in 1935. His mother provided the reason why he entered in the South rather than Maryland:

"Tony's great ambition was to serve the people of God as a missionary – whether Native Americans, Hispanics or Blacks – apostolates very dear to the New Orleans Province."

He passed through the normal course of studies, studying Latin at Catholic University and theology at St. Mary's (1946-49).

Fr. O'Flynn started at Loyola as Dean of Students and teacher of theology in 1952. In 1967, he began a doctoral study in moral theology at the Dominican School of Theology in Rome, known as the *Angelicum*. Returning to Loyola, he served as associate director of the night school, known at the time as the Evening Division, as well as assistant to the president of the university.

He still dreamed of being a missionary, and so Tony was sent to the seminary in Harare, Zimbabwe, where he taught moral theology, canon law and ethics. He was quickly selected as superior of the Jesuit community, a position he held for 15 years. He remained linked to the Province through his submissions to its newsletter.

In an interview with Tom Clancy, SJ, for *Jesuit Studies in Spirituality*, Fr. O'Flynn spoke of what came to be called his "second conversion":

In the spiritual life there was definitely a turning point. It came when I was transferred from Loyola to Jesuit High in Dallas in 1956. Up until then I had been content to take things as they came and reluctant to speak to superiors about problems, hoping things would get better by themselves. I knew change was possible. Since that time I realize that one must accept responsibility for one's life, must not depend on superiors to be mind readers, must state the case clearly, and must ask for and even suggest a remedy.

These realizations became marching orders, and Tony's efforts to change blossomed with his lengthy appointment to the seminary in Harare.

Fr. Joseph Hampson, provincial of the Province of Zimbabwe, wrote of Tony:

He was a much-loved member of the mission and Province for 18 years, available in the true Ignatian sense, combining personal care and affection, wit, wisdom and humor…. He always missed Zimbabwe.

These remarks were echoed by the vicar general of Harare:

The memory of Fr. O'Flynn's long and dedicated years of cheerful and assiduous service, both at the seminary and in his frequent assistance to the clergy, religious and faithful of the Archdiocese, at parish and community level, was an inspiration.

In 1990 Fr. O'Flynn returned to the New Orleans Province, where he taught theology in the City College for two years.

He retired to Ignatius Residence and died on July 13, 1992, at age 76. He is buried at Grand Coteau.

Charles Edwards O'Neill, SJ
1927 – 2009
An enthusiastic scholar, an animated teacher

Perhaps being a native New Orleanian inspired Charles Edwards O'Neill's area of study for his doctoral dissertation: French Colonial Louisiana. In the pursuit of historical research, he acquired a reputation for his intellectual acumen and scholarship.

Born Nov. 16, 1927, Charlie attended schools in New Orleans and after graduating from Jesuit High, he entered the Novitiate in 1944. His formation was typical: Juniorate (studying languages, literature and history) and philosophy at Spring Hill College, where he earned a B.A. in history.

Back at his *alma mater*, he taught the humanities – Latin, English and history – for three years. He began theology, first at the *Institut Saint-Augustine* in Enghein, Belgium (1954-57), and then at *Institut Saint-Louis* in Chantilly, France (1957-58). A year later, Charlie began doctoral studies in history at the Gregorian University in Rome (1959-61).

After his course work, he returned to Loyola to teach history and begin to write his dissertation. Needing to do further research on his dissertation, he sequestered himself in the archives of the *Collège de France* in Paris. He was awarded his doctorate in 1963.

Returning to the States, Fr. O'Neill taught history at the Juniorate, and in 1965 he was hired by Loyola as assistant professor of history. He was promoted to associate professor in 1967 and soon Fr. O'Neill was honored as a full professor.

But new duties crowded in on his teaching and research. He became vice-provincial for the education of Jesuits (1970-73), and then Father General appointed him as Superior of the House of Writers in Rome, where he served for seven years (1976-83). Concurrently he became the director of the Jesuit Historical Institute in Rome.

Finally escaping administration, he devoted his time to writing (1993-2004). His most respected book was the outgrowth of his dissertation, *Church and State in French Colonial Louisiana*. He wrote other books and dozens of articles.

Fr. O'Neill was an accomplished man who made the most of his Jesuit education by learning languages, refining his writing skills, displaying curiosity and devotion to research. He was welcome in the major European archives, an indication of his reputation in continental circles.

Many groups bestowed awards on him, such as the French *"Chevalier, l'Ordre des Palmes Academiques"* (1968), Outstanding Educators of America (1970), and Outstanding Teacher of American History (1977).

Various bishops of the New Orleans Diocese requested that he serve on the diocesan commission to do proper historical research on Henriette Delille, the 19th century founder of the Sisters of the Holy Family, a New Orleans religious order of African-American women. Her cause for canonization was then being promoted in Rome (1989), and Archbishop Alfred Hughes appointed Fr. O'Neill "an official notary for the historical documents" to be included in the official archdiocesan acts concerning Henriette Delille (2003).

Charlie O'Neill was a man who was witty, clever, surprising and learned. For example, he began one letter to Father *Socius* thus: "After months of waiting for a single answer to a twice-repeated question. . ." To insiders his quips and barbs were humorous and entertaining.

He tirelessly encouraged young Jesuits to embrace an academic career, giving personal testimony through his excitement over his own work. He worked unceasingly and diligently because he loved what he did.

After he was diagnosed with Parkinson's, the disease took a steady and relentless toll on his body. On Dec. 19, 2009, Fr. O'Neill died at age 82. He is buried at Grand Coteau.

Daniel Winslow Partridge, SJ
1921 – 1992
Master of management, finances and fund-raising

Daniel Winslow Partridge was one of those indispensible men with great managerial skills who served in many capacities in numerous Jesuit institutions.

Born in New Orleans on Dec. 2, 1921, he began elementary school in Mobile, but finished in New Orleans, where he graduated from Jesuit High School in 1938. This was followed by one year at Spring Hill College and one year at Loyola University.

Daniel entered the Jesuit Novitiate twice, and it is possible that during the year between Spring Hill and Loyola he made his first application. He re-entered the Society in 1941, spending two years of Novitiate and two years of Juniorate at Grand Coteau and three years of philosophy at Spring Hill College. Then he earned a B.A. in sociology at Spring Hill and later pursued an M.S. in education from Fordham. He taught both in Tampa (1947-49) and in Shreveport (1949-50).

His first assignment after ordination indicated the direction of his ministry. He proved to be excellent at finances, organization and fund-raising when he became the minister of St. John's High School in Shreveport (1955-58). Then he was made the *econome* (i.e., treasurer) for the Ceylon missions (1958-65).

For several years he fulfilled many duties at Loyola University, as dean of students (1965-66); at Jesuit House of Studies in Mobile as minister (1966-67), and at Jesuit High School in New Orleans, in the alumni and development office and as *econome* (1967-69).

His managerial skills were demonstrated in his directorship of Our Lady of the Oaks Retreat House in Grand Coteau (1970-74). He returned to Jesuit High in New Orleans in charge of public relations and as director of development (1974-76).

In 1976 he was asked to open Ignatius Residence in midtown New Orleans, a facility for retired Jesuits and for Jesuits working in diverse apostolates in the city. His service at Loyola University as assistant to the president for development and public relations (1976-79) was followed by a stint at Ignatius Retreat House in Atlanta, as much to assist with the finances and management as to give retreats (1979-82). Finally he returned to Jesuit High in New Orleans as assistant to the president, teacher and minister (1982-86).

Suffering from congestive heart failure, Fr. Partridge retired. His final year was highlighted by the reception of the North American Martyrs' Award, an honor bestowed by the Jesuit High School administration.

Fr. Partridge died on Nov. 21, 1992, at age 70. He is buried at Spring Hill.

Alfred Patrick Phillips, SJ
1927 – 1998
An outstanding educator and retreat director

A recognized educator, Fr. Alfred Patrick Phillips appeared in *Outstanding Educators of America* (1973), *Who's Who in Religion* (1975-77, 1980), and the *American Catholic Who's Who* (1979).

Appropriately named for Saint Patrick, he was born in Mobile on March 16, 1927, just a day before St. Patrick's feast day. He attended the local Catholic schools and then joined the U.S. Army.

Because World War II was coming to an end, Phillips served in Europe for only a brief time (1945-46) and returned to Spring Hill College in Mobile, from which he graduated with a B.S in history in 1952.

He entered the Novitiate in Grand Coteau on July 30, 1952. His course of formation was untypical: just one year of Juniorate, three years studying philosophy in St. Louis, and only one year of

Regency, teaching at Jesuit High in Tampa, after which he studied theology at St. Marys, Kan., earning an STL (1959-63).

He was ordained on June 13, 1962, and attended Regis College in Willowdale, Ontario, to study for a master's degree in theology. Although he became a candidate for the STD degree from the same school of theology, the degree was never granted.

Fr. Phillips' ministry was initially focused on university level teaching and service. He taught theology at Loyola University in New Orleans at various times from 1963 to 1976. From 1967 to 1969, he was a special lecturer in theology at Carleton University in Ottawa. Upon his return to New Orleans, he once again taught at Loyola and was dean of campus ministry until 1976.

In 1976 his career shifted to retreat ministry. He was appointed director of the Jesuit Spirituality Center in Grand Coteau and eventually became the superior at St. Charles College, where he worked from 1976 to 1985. He served as rector of Jesuit College Prep in Dallas (1985-91), and then he was assigned to Manresa House of Retreats, where he preached retreats and served as both the superior and director.

Fr. Phillips served at Manresa until he suffered a heart attack and died on May 13, 1998, at the age of 71. He is buried at Spring Hill.

Fr. Phillips was a much-beloved and -respected priest. When asked what he hoped men would know when they finished their retreats at Manresa, he said:

". . . that they know God loves them unconditionally."

Frederick Bromberg Ponder, SJ
1913 – 1995
Ceylon missionary, pastor, minister to the Royal Navy

A strong calling to be a missionary led Frederick Bromberg Ponder to consider life as a Jesuit priest.

Born in Mobile, Ala., on Dec. 14, 1913, Ponder was educated in local parochial schools and graduated from Spring Hill High School in 1932. Entering the Novitiate after graduation, he followed the traditional formation program and took philosophy at St. Louis University, where he earned a B.A. in English. For his Regency he taught at Jesuit High in New Orleans and then studied theology at St. Marys, Kan.

After ordination he taught in college and high school. But still he wanted to be a missionary, and finally his yearning for the missions was fulfilled in 1948, when he embarked for Ceylon. He was assigned to St. Michael's College in Trincomalee, the Jesuits' flagship school in the area, where he taught and served as spiritual father (1948-53).

After a year's study of Sinhalese, he left education for pastoral ministry, first as pastor in Sorikalmunai (1954), and then in Hingurakgoda. Following those appointments, Fr. Ponder was named principal of St. Joseph's College in Trincomalee (1956-65), where he later joined the staff of St. Mary's Catholic Church.

It pleased him to serve the Queen as an Officiating Minister to the Royal Navy and the Royal Ceylon Navy (1960-67). He was also quite proud of two other things: As District Commissioner of the Trincomalee District Boy Scout Commission, he was awarded the Medal of Merit on Feb. 4, 1964, for "specially good services to scouting," and in Colombo at the close of the Marian Year, he preached to a crowd of more than 100,000 people. Fr. Ponder brought back to the States a British accent, to the delight of many.

When he returned from Ceylon in 1967, he began a career in parish ministry: Holy Name of Jesus Church in New Orleans (1968-71), St. John's Church in Shreveport (1971-79), Immaculate Conception Church in New Orleans (1979-81), and Sacred Heart Church in Tampa (1981-82). He moved to Holy Cross Church in Natchitoches, La., where he also engaged in campus ministry at Northwestern State University (1982-86). Later he served for six years at the Nativity of the Blessed Virgin Mary in Campti, La., near Natchitoches (1986-92), before returning to Holy Name Church in New Orleans.

After a life full of labors, Fr. Ponder retired from active ministry to Ignatius Residence, where he died on Nov. 3, 1995, as the community was gathered in the chapel saying the prayers for the dying.

A modest man, he confessed to "doing a little good" – an understatement, to be sure. And after a long and satisfying life, he reflected, "This has been a most wonderful life."

He is buried at Spring Hill.

Robert J. Ratchford, SJ
1924 – 2013
Airman, administrator,
teacher of chemistry – and
student of Karl Rahner

Robert Ratchford followed an unusual career path before and after entering the Jesuit Order, one that took him from an obscure community in South Dakota to a university town in Austria, where he was taught by one of the most renowned theologians of the 20th century.

He was born in Firesteel, S.D., on Nov. 16, 1924, and reared there. He studied chemistry at the University of Indiana, spent time in the U.S. Army Air Corps as a gunnery instructor from 1943 to 1946, then returned to the university to continue studying chemistry.

In 1947, he transferred to Spring Hill College in Mobile and while there was inspired to enter the Jesuit Order, which he did on July 30, 1948.

After the routine study of philosophy, he was sent to Catholic University in Washington, D.C., to earn a doctorate in chemistry, which was awarded in 1958. He went to Jesuit College (*Jesuitenkolleg*) in Innsbruck, Austria, for his theology courses (1958-62) and while there he became fluent in German. Karl Rahner, SJ, one of the most important theologians of the 20th century, was one of his professors. After ordination at Innsbruck on July 26, 1961, Fr. Ratchford did post-doctoral work at the eminent Max Planck Institute in Götingen, Germany.

Upon return to the States, he was assigned to Loyola University in New Orleans, where he began teaching chemistry in 1964. While still teaching during the '70s, he also served in several administrative roles in the university: alumni and development director (1971-74); acting academic vice-president (1974-75); Dean of Arts and Sciences (1975-79); and assistant academic vice-president (1979-80).

The danger of showing administrative ability is that the successful administrator cannot escape more of it, as was the case with Fr. Ratchford. Twice more the Province asked his assistance, including a stint as the Provincial's executive assistant from 1980 until 1987. But the world of chemistry was never far away, as he returned to Loyola to teach for seven years (1987-94).

Every Jesuit has or should have a hobby. Fr. Ratchford's was aviation. Perhaps this goes back to his Army Air Corps work in World War II. He was a chaplain in the Civil Air Patrol from 1970 until 2008. In 1985 he received a commendation for flying an ill two-year-old child to Philadelphia.

He also had other ministries which required feet on the ground. He served as chaplain for the Jefferson Parish Correctional Center and as alumni chaplain at Loyola.

When he experienced a decline in his health and needed assistance, he moved to Ignatius Residence, where he lived for a number of years. Fr. Ratchford died on Good Friday, March 29, 2013. He was 88 years old, 64 years a Jesuit and 51 a priest. He is buried in Grand Coteau.

Joseph Herman Reising, SJ
1941 – 2000
He played a major role
in the formation of young Jesuits

Fr. Joseph Herman Reising was a much-admired priest. A senior Jesuit wrote this to him on the 25th anniversary of Fr. Reising's priesthood:

"I wanted you to know how much I appreciate your priestly example, which I have observed through the years we have been friends. Your zeal, compassion and your prayerful approach to the celebration of the sacraments, fortified by your deep faith, have impressed me greatly…. Thank you, too, for being my friend."

Born Jan. 27, 1941, in Monroe, La., Joseph took all of his schooling in New Orleans, including Jesuit High (1953-58). He entered the Novitiate in 1958 and followed the traditional course of formation: Juniorate, philosophy, Regency at Jesuit High in New Orleans, and theology at Woodstock College in Maryland and New York City. Along the way, Joe attended Catholic University, earning a master's degree in psychology.

His priestly ministry began as teacher and chaplain in Louisiana Jesuit schools, serving in New Orleans from 1972 to 1980 and in Shreveport from 1980 to 1984. When the Jesuits withdrew from Jesuit High in Shreveport, Fr. Reising crossed the street to become assistant pastor of St. John Berchmans Church (1985-86). He was then posted to the Novitiate to be the assistant master of novices (1986-91).

His next jobs were those of internal ministry, such as assistant to various bureaus of the provincial staff, including provincial assistant for formation and province assistant for retreat houses. In 1998 Fr. Reising was assigned to Manresa House of Retreats.

A report about what transpired there speaks to Fr. Reising's manner of doing things:

"Joe immediately began to involve himself in local speaking engagements and the ministries of the neighboring parish, St. Michael's. He helped prepare second-graders for First Communion; and in a quite different vein he became a weekly visitor to the local youth detention center."

Fr. Joe was what Jesuits call *disponible*, a person whom it was easy to move and who would grow wherever planted. At times, his ministry focused on counseling youth and visiting the detention house for youth. Moreover, his roles as associate master of novices, as *socius* to the formation director and as provincial assistant for formation speak to his earnest commitment to the best interests of young Jesuits. Not one to assume leadership positions, Fr. Reising's talents lay in being a cooperative member of the team and in contributing to the group's labors.

Fr. Reising wrote an exhortation for retreatants at Manresa, which sums up his spirituality:

The happiest people are the "thank you" people. They take nothing for granted. They appreciate every gift received – from God, from others – and make the effort to express their gratitude in some way…. And do I appreciate the gift that I am? That has been a real struggle for me. One thing that helped me was hearing the statement: "God made me, and God does not make junk."

In his fifties, Fr. Reising developed thyroid cancer and then a fatal lung disease associated with esophageal cancer. He died, on Dec. 29, 2000, at the relatively young age of 59. He is buried at Grand Coteau.

If Jesuits had epitaphs, the following remark of St. Thomas of Villanova might be found on Fr. Reising's tombstone: "One who is humble easily obeys everyone, fears to offend anyone, is at peace with everyone, is kind with all."

Francis J. Riedinger, SJ
1913 – 2004
The brightest guy in Loyola's Physics Department

Because of the direction of the political changes in Germany and the imminent threat of Adolf Hitler, Francis J. Riedinger immigrated to Chicago with his family. That move enabled him to spend the World War II years in New Orleans, employed in radio-electronics.

Frank was born Jan. 2, 1913, in Rotenfels, a small village near Baden-Baden, Germany,

Because he was observed to be mechanically inclined, his parents enrolled him in a technical school, where radio-electronics grabbed his attention. He took a year-long course at the RCA Institute to obtain both the FCC Radiotelegraph and Radiotelephone commercial licenses. By 1941 Frank was working in New Orleans.

He applied to be a Brother in the New Orleans Province in 1946. During his Novitiate in Grand Coteau, he met Frank Benedetto, SJ, who was being assigned to Loyola. Together they determined that Frank Riedinger, too, would be an excellent fit for Loyola because of his radio-electronics skills and his machine shop experience.

In 1958 Bro. Riedinger joined Tony Maurillo, the machinist in Loyola's Physics Department, where low-temperature research was getting under way. Fr. Benedetto asked Bro. Riedinger to learn as much as he could about cryogenics, because he wanted the Loyola lab to liquefy helium. So Bro. Riedinger took a tour of all the companies and universities which made liquefied helium.

With a trunk load of knowledge, he returned to Loyola to join with a new machinist to design and build a helium liquefier. Their older machine, donated to the department in 1953, was itself later donated to the Smithsonian Museum. Although only 16 years old, that liquefier was considered as significant in its field as the McCormick reaper and the Wright Brothers' airplane.

Bro. Riedinger's new helium liquefier worked with such success that Loyola was able to supply surplus liquid helium to others. But when the demand for liquid helium weakened, the project at Loyola softened. Another Jesuit Brother, Terry Todd, learned from Bro. Riedinger how to manage the helium machine, thereby freeing Bro. Riedinger to pursue other projects.

When Bro. Riedinger answered an advertisement for a man to repair a small island-hopping ship in the Jesuit missions in the Caroline Islands, he made the ship functional for years. Later he volunteered to work in a Jesuit-operated warehouse in Fremont, Calif., where another Jesuit had stored radio equipment for use in the missions in the Pacific. Bro. Riedinger began to repair this equipment and even to develop it for specific uses in the missions.

The last months of Bro. Riedinger's life were

marked by an inability to rest and a state of confusion that found him trying to communicate with his caregivers in German, his native language. Near him was Bro. Terry Todd, Frank's longtime friend, co-worker at Loyola, and fellow missionary in the Pacific.

It was fitting that Bro. Riedinger died in Bro. Todd's arms, on Sept. 16, 2004. He was 91 years old and a Jesuit for nearly 60 years. He is buried at Grand Coteau.

Bro. Todd described Bro. Riedinger as a man of a gentle and kind nature. He noted Frank's quiet and extremely profitable habit of converting every scrap of leftover metal into funds for the missions.

Robert B. Rimes, SJ
1922 – 2012
A Jesuit of singular integrity and holiness

Even though some thought he could have pitched for the Red Sox, Robert B. Rimes followed in the footsteps of his older brother, William, and joined the Jesuits.

Bobby, as he was known by most, was born in Monroe, La., on Nov. 30, 1922, and entered the Society on Aug. 14, 1942, at St. Charles College in Grand Coteau, after attending Spring Hill College (1939-42). He received his B.A. in philosophy from Spring Hill in 1949. For Regency he taught at St. John's High School in Shreveport (1949-52), and he took theology at St. Mary's College in St. Marys, Kan., receiving an STL in 1956. He was ordained in June 1955.

After ordination Fr. Rimes was missioned to Grand Coteau as *socius* to the master of novices for eight years. In 1965 he was appointed master of novices and served in that role for ten years. An excellent baseball player, he pitched for the novices' team when they challenged the juniors who lived across the building. He could have pitched for the Red Sox!

He was then assigned to Strake Jesuit in Houston as a member of the faculty and as campus minister. In 1977 he was appointed rector of the Jesuit community at Spring Hill College, where he taught and worked in campus ministry. In 1978 he was also appointed director of tertians.

In 1983 he returned to Grand Coteau as associate pastor at St. Charles Borromeo Church for one year and then returned to Spring Hill in 1984, where he again taught theology, was a campus min-

ister and served as rector of the community from 2001 to 2003. He also served the Archdiocese of Mobile as a Vicar for Religious.

In the last years of a long and fruitful ministry he continued to offer spiritual direction to many and assisted in various pastoral ministries in the Archdiocese of Mobile.

He was a through-and-through spiritual director. Most of his ministry was spent preaching to Jesuits and to the people in the parishes where they served. He studied the Scriptures long before it was fashionable and found insights and stories to enliven his speaking. Fr. Rimes was a Jesuit of singular integrity and holiness. All of his life he made fast friendships with good people, such as his fishing buddy, Fr. Ed Romagosa.

Eventually, age crept up on Fr. Rimes, who had seemed never to age. He began having difficulty with his memory, leading to a nearly total loss of memory; the eternal youth became increasingly feeble.

On May 30, 2012, at age 89, he died while in the hospital, 70 years a Jesuit and 57 a priest. He is buried at Spring Hill.

Hilton Landry Rivet, SJ
1922 – 2007
'Hey, Lord...Can You Give Me a Minute?'

Fr. Hilton Landry Rivet was an excellent writer and a master woodworker. Examples of his woodwork grace various Jesuit recreation rooms, and his writings on social justice issues remain easily accessible.

Born in New Orleans on Aug. 21, 1922, Hilton attended Jesuit High and spent two years at Loyola before he entered the Order in 1941. During the next decade his life unfolded in typical Jesuit fashion: Novitiate, Juniorate, philosophy and sociology (1945-48), special studies in sociology (1948-49), and then theology (1951-55).

The first half of his ministry orbited around Spring Hill College in Mobile: Regency (1949-51), sociology teacher (1956-57), then dean of students (1957-68).

New Orleans was the axis of the second part of his ministry: prison chaplain (1969-75), director of the ministry to the poor at the Colombiere Counseling Center (1975-78), pastor of Immaculate Conception Church (1976-79), rector of the Loyola Jesuit community (1979-84), and pastor of

Holy Name of Jesus Church.

Fr. Rivet also wrote, first about prison and prisoners and then about justice in Christian discipleship. He is renowned for *Hey, Lord. . .Can You Give Me a Minute?*, a book of 30 vignettes, with titles such as "God is no dummy" and "I fail in everything." He published *Songs for Use in Catholic Services*, a song book for the Hunt Correctional Center in St. Gabriel, La.

As pastor at Holy Name of Jesus, Hilton wrote "Word from Our Pastor" for the weekly church bulletin. He often wrote about the changes brought about by Vatican II, addressing a congregation many of whom thought that the word "change" was poison. Titles of some of these writings are worth noting: "Reformability of the Church," "Social Mission of the Church," "Collegiality," and "Openness to the Modern World."

His ministry was strongly focused on racial problems, especially during his six-year tenure in the Orleans Parish Prison and the Hunt Correctional Center, whose inmates were overwhelmingly African-American. He wrote a modest pamphlet on black saints, such as Martin de Porres, the Martyrs of Uganda, and Josephine Bakhita. His last ministry was as pastor of the black parish, Immaculate Conception, in Baton Rouge.

What was he like? Candid, some say blunt. Many Jesuits would say he exemplified the Ignatian "*magis*," a Latin word meaning "more" and referring to the practice of doing more for Christ and therefore for others. He never backed away from difficult challenges, either in the parish or the prison. He could not resist talking about controversial topics. As one Jesuit said:

"Hilton was not particularly diplomatic. He taught many Jesuits to say 'I don't know.'"

Because Fr. Rivet never saw a doctor, he had no idea that a serious cancer was growing in his stomach until the pains arrived. There was nothing to do for him but to accompany him on his final journey.

Fr. Rivet died peacefully on Nov. 8, 2007, and is buried at Grand Coteau. He was 85 years old, 66 as a Jesuit, and 52 as a priest.

William Wayne Roca, SJ
1940 – 1999
He taught government using Plato's Republic *as the foundation*

William Wayne Roca is best described as a man of passion: He loved being a priest, he loved being a Jesuit, and he loved the students he taught.

Born March 21, 1940, in mid-town New Orleans, he attended Crossman Public School (1945-51) and then Jesuit High, both within a block of his home. He entered the Novitiate at Grand Coteau on July 30, 1957, and followed the traditional path for formation.

As a regent, he taught at Jesuit High in Tampa, where his dramatic intuition and hard work made his student-performed plays celebrated in the area. He studied theology at Regis College in Willowdale, Ontario (1967-71), and even learned to ice skate. In addition to his M.Div from Regis College, he earned an M.A. in political science from the University of Toronto.

His ministry was spent in the classrooms of the schools of the New Orleans Province. He was assigned to Jesuit College Preparatory in Dallas as teacher and assistant principal. Following a position in administration at Jesuit High in Tampa, he was posted to Jesuit High in New Orleans, where he spent 25 years teaching government.

His was a unique approach: His students read and discussed Plato's *Republic* as a foundation for further study. Evaluation from his students was always positive, and usually enthusiastic. His lay teaching peers were his allies; they elected Fr. Roca to the Faculty Senate at Jesuit High (1987-88), and likewise at his next school, Archbishop Rummel High (1992).

Fr. Roca's parents lived a mere block from Jesuit High, and after his father's death, he pondered what his filial duties were to his ailing mother. He decided to care for her in her own home, acting as her daily nurse. If his peers had not noticed it before, they noticed it now: Fr. Roca's resolve was like concrete; once he made a decision about what was demanded of him, no amount of reasoning or reproach could change his mind. If determination is a virtue, he was exceptional in his care for his mother.

One spring, when his services at Jesuit High were no longer needed, another door immediately opened at Archbishop Rummel, a Christian Brothers high school. There, Fr. Roca served as chaplain and teacher of political science. His colleagues commented that they had never seen him so satisfied, energetic and happy.

But death was not far away. A persistent sinus problem was finally diagnosed as cancer. Fr. Roca took chemotherapy, but just as he was certified to resume his work, the cancer returned.

Spending his last days at Ignatius Residence, Fr. Roca died on Dec. 6, 1999, at age 59. He is buried at Grand Coteau.

Edward Joseph Romagosa, SJ
1924 – 2009
A master communicator,
a prayerful, eloquent man

Edward Francis Romagosa was respected by his students and even loved by some. Many would attribute their love of language and literature to him and his impassioned teaching. Some even went on to emulate him in their own classrooms.

Born on Sept. 22, 1924, in Thibodaux, La., Edward's family arranged for him to attend Jesuit High in New Orleans. Upon graduating in 1941, he entered the Novitiate in Grand Coteau and followed the traditional formation path for young Jesuits. All was typical until theology, for which he traveled to Louvain, Belgium, because he was fluent in French (1951-55). He was ordained on Aug. 15, 1954.

With an M.A. in English from Marquette University, Fr. Romagosa, or "Roma" to his friends, returned to the Juniorate to become its stellar professor (1957-67). Students acclaimed his teaching; every young Jesuit whom he taught had nothing but praise for his insightfulness and his urgency to help them speak well – and to find fresh and effective ways of communicating.

In addition, Fr. Romagosa taught an evening course on art appreciation at a time when the best machine available for illustration of great works of art was an overhead projector. During this time Roma began work on a doctorate in English at LSU and eventually accumulated 30 graduate hours

toward it. But reaching deep into his soul, he wrote to his Provincial:

I've concluded that I do not have the requisite temperament or respect or ambition for the doctoral degree in English literature. I do not feel that I could maintain through the few years that would be required for it the purity of intention that would allow for holiness or happiness.

After the Juniorate closed in 1967, Roma turned his piety and eloquence to parish ministry and to the pulpit. How blessed the parishioners of St. Rita's Parish in Dallas were to hear four years of Roma's sermons! At his *Arrivederci, Roma* fete in 1973, the parish president said:

"You only need listen to one of his homilies when he brings the Gospel message down to everyday practice, in words that have meaning and touch the core of human expression."

Beginning in 1974 he became pastor for four years at Our Lady of Prompt Succor in Coteau, La., near New Iberia. Roma then returned to Grand Coteau, serving two years as rector of St. Charles College. During this time he offered his services to various pastors in the diocese so that they could make their retreats and take a holiday.

Next, this prayerful, eloquent man took up a new ministry: preaching retreats. He began at Maryhill Retreat House in Pineville, La. (1982-84) but soon the Society inserted him into its own retreat houses: Montserrat in Dallas (1984-88); Our Lady of the Oaks in Grand Coteau (1988-91); and finally Manresa House of Retreats in Convent, La. (1991-2009). By all accounts, he preached quality retreats and became a sought-after confessor.

In the waning years of his career, he was diagnosed with Parkinson's disease, which took a slow, debilitating toll on him. Despite all efforts to keep him at Manresa, he eventually had to be taken to Our Lady of Wisdom Health Care Center, where he died April 4, 2009. He is buried at Grand Coteau.

One of Fr. Romagosa's brightest students, who himself became a professor, paid this tribute to him late in Roma's life:

My mental DNA is directly traceable to you.... You introduced me to a world of imagination captured in words of interlocking beauty and wonder. I have never left that world. I take much too much for granted that you will always be here. Your voice is always behind my voice as I open the same door to generations of bright university students.

Edward W. Schott, SJ
1928 – 2005
*Chemistry teacher
of the first order*

With three degrees in chemistry, Fr. Edward Schott made his mark in the classroom for more than three decades as a top-notch teacher around the Province – in New Orleans, Tampa and El Paso.

Born in New Orleans on April 30, 1928, Ed attended Redemptorist High School and Loyola University, from which he graduated with a B.S. in chemistry in 1947. From there he matriculated at the University of Illinois at Urbana and received an M.S. in chemistry.

He fell into the orbit of the Society of Jesus and entered the Novitiate on Sept. 7, 1950. After his first vows, he stayed only one year in the Juniorate and moved to Spring Hill College for his study of philosophy. At this point he did four years of doctoral study at St. Louis University, a degree he seems not to have finished. For his theology courses he traveled to Austria, where the Jesuits of the Austrian Province held the professorships in the Faculty of Theology at the University of Innsbruck. He was ordained in Innsbruck on July 25, 1963.

Fr. Ed Schott began his ministry with several degrees: a B.S. and an M.S. in chemistry, an STL in theology and an ABD (all but dissertation) in chemistry. Fr. Schott was assigned to Spring Hill College to teach chemistry and remedial reading (1965-73), also serving as chaplain to the students. In 1973 he taught chemistry at Xavier University in New Orleans, and then for the next nine years he taught chemistry at Jesuit High School in Tampa, where he also served on the faculty of Hillsborough Community College (1977-80).

The last 17 years of his active ministry were spent in El Paso, Texas. This included teaching computer science and mathematics for the Ysleta Public School District, St. Charles Seminary, Cathedral High School and particularly Loretto Academy. For many years Fr. Schott also served as chaplain at Loretto.

In 2001 he retired to Ignatius Residence in New Orleans. For two years he taught computers, and for the last two years of his life he was the community sacristan.

After a ministry filled with good works, Fr. Schott died on Dec. 2, 2005, at age 77. He is buried at Grand Coteau.

John Frederick Schroder, SJ
1919 – 2014
*Big man on the
mission band*

John Frederick Schroder was a big man in more ways than one. He was big in physical stature and long on energy and stamina, and he spoke from the pulpit with a big, booming voice.

He was also very big in his belief in the value of the Province's mission band.

John was born on Jan. 11, 1919, in Atlanta, one of five children. He was educated at Georgetown Prep (1933-36) and then at the University of Notre Dame (1936-40). With the beginning of World War II, he enlisted in the U. S. military for four years of service. After discharge, his intention was to study for the bar, but he felt a calling to the Society of Jesus.

He entered the Novitiate on Aug. 14, 1944, and moved quickly through the typical formation process. He had one year of Regency at Regis-Loyola in Montreal (1947-48) and two years at Jesuit High in Tampa (1948-50). He studied theology at St. Marys, Kan., and was ordained on June 17, 1953.

His first assignment was to the Province mission band, the pastoral ministry wherein several Jesuits decide on an apostolic center, such as Augusta or Selma. This band of priests would set up headquarters in a given city and catechize the people there, as well as radiating from the central place to surrounding villages and towns. The priests would regularize marriages, baptize and confirm children, hear confessions and celebrate the Eucharist.

In 1955, Fr. Schroder began his mission band ministry in Augusta, Ga., and in 1963 he moved to Jesuit High School in Tampa. From 1974 to 1976, he served at Blessed Sacrament Parish in Harriman, Tenn. His work as "Shepherd of the Harriman Missions" was featured in a 1975 issue of *Extension* magazine.

Records in the Jesuit archives show he traveled regularly to present his patented weeklong parish missions. At one point, for instance, he led back to back missions at Blessed Sacrament in Jonesboro, Ark., St. Francis in Houston, St. Cyril in Houston, St. Joseph in Beeville, Tex. and St. Mary's in Gainesville, Tex.

Fr. Schroder served as superior of Ignatius Retreat House in Atlanta from 1976 to 1980. Then he started a new ministry in Belize, first serving at

Sacred Heart Church in Dangriga. From there, he moved to St. Francis Mission in Corozal Town, where he labored from 1981 until 2003. This mission served many small, poor villages.

Worn down by age and decades of working very long hours, this big man's energy and stamina waned. So, he went first to Jesuit Hall in St. Louis in 2003, then to Ignatius Residence in New Orleans in 2008 and finally to Grand Coteau, where he died on Jan. 25, 2014. He was 95 years old, a Jesuit for 69 years, and a priest for 61 years. He is buried at Grand Coteau.

Thomas Herbert Stahel, SJ
1938 – 2006
Pastor, Provincial, Paraguay missionary – and editor of America

Thomas Herbert Stahel was born in New Orleans on Jan. 4, 1938, and when he was 10 he moved with his family to Greenwood, Miss., where he went on to graduate from high school in 1955. From there, he left the South to study in the East, graduate from Georgetown, earn a master's degree from Yale, and eventually serve in the U.S. Army.

He was doubly honored for his collegiate studies with memberships in the Gold Key Society and Alpha Sigma Nu.

Stahel entered the Novitiate in 1961, and because of his prior education he advanced quickly through philosophy and theology studies. He received his PhD from Johns Hopkins in 1968, where he was honored with several fellowships, including a Woodrow Wilson Fellowship and a Johns Hopkins University Fellowship, among others. He was "a Jesuit exquisitely trained."

His ministry involved three parts: publications, province administration and overseas missions. Fr. Stahel was appointed associate editor of the Jesuit-run magazine *America* in 1972 and later became its managing editor. During this time he contributed the weekly column "The Word," as well as a wide variety of editorials, articles and reviews. The core of his priestly career involved 13 years at *America* and 12 years in governance for the Society of Jesus, including six years as the provincial of the New Orleans Province.

In 1977 Fr. Stahel was appointed provincial of the Province, a job he held until 1983 and found challenging. Given his qualifications, it is no surprise that he also served on several college boards, and notably three full terms at Georgetown University. His direct involvement in matters of social justice was evident in his attempts to involve Jesuits in ministry to black Catholics, such as staffing black parishes.

He returned to *America* as associate editor, but was quickly made executive editor. In the course of his work there he was awarded the Catholic Press Association's "Best Interview" (1986) and two similar awards in 1994. He returned to province administration for four years as the *socius* to the provincial to handle routine matters as well as others of great delicacy.

Finally, Fr. Stahel was assigned as pastor simultaneously to the two Jesuit churches in New Orleans, something he did well until he was stricken by cancer.

Despite his exceptional academic talent, Fr. Stahel also held elementary jobs, such as working as *socius* to the novice master in Paraguari, Paraguay. His Spanish was good enough for him to write articles for *Accion*, the magazine of the Jesuits in Paraguay. Later he served as the director of novices for the New York Province mission in Benin City, Nigeria (1995-99).

For those who knew him, Fr. Tom Stahel is remembered as a man of exceptional integrity, loyalty and dedicated service. He was a man of keen perception, quality thoughts and solid knowledge about many matters. A mother of a priest once said to Fr. Stahel in the presence of Tom's own mother, "Tom, dear, I raise my glass to *the finest priest* I know."

Fr. Stahel died of cancer on July 5, 2006, and is buried at Grand Coteau.

Hilliard F. Stiegler, SJ
1926 – 1999
He worked for the betterment of New Orleans public schools

A born organizer with a social conscience, Brother Hilliard Stiegler contributed his managerial skills and passion for social justice to his community and to the people he served. Even while battling formidable health issues, he worked hard to develop better schools for Louisiana's African-American population.

Born in New Orleans on Aug. 4, 1926, Hilliard was educated at Holy Name Grade School and St. Aloysius High School, where he won academic honors and was editor of the school newspaper. Passionate about jogging, he was a determined though not especially skillful athlete.

After entering the Order as a candidate for the priesthood at Grand Coteau in 1943, he began his Novitiate and then spent two years of undergraduate studies at Spring Hill College. He distinguished himself as a model religious and an excellent student.

He took his first year of Regency in 1948 at Jesuit High School in Tampa, where he taught Latin and English. He returned to Spring Hill for philosophy studies (1949-51) and had a second year of Regency in 1952 in Shreveport, where he taught English and history, as well as serving as moderator for several student activities.

At this point Hilliard changed his goal from the priesthood to Jesuit brother. Returning to Grand Coteau in 1953, he began his work as a brother by serving as librarian at St. Charles College. However, when his organizational talents were recognized, he was appointed buyer for the house, czar of its kitchen, custodian of the wine cellar and assistant treasurer (1954-58).

Later, at Spring Hill College, he performed the same tasks. Then he moved across campus to the Jesuit House of Studies, where he was assigned the jobs of buyer and refectorian.

Returning to Grand Coteau, he served as subminister, treasurer and house consultor (1967-75). During his various times at Grand Coteau, he was also active in community development, especially in the area's public schools, where he served as a volunteer and substitute teacher. He did much to improve their physical plants as well.

When he was posted to the provincial's residence in New Orleans, he was charged with duties utilizing his managerial and accounting skills: brother minister and assistant treasurer for the Province (1977-78). He was later missioned to the community at Loyola University as its minister (1979-83). He took classes at Loyola's College of Business Administration, earning an MBA in 1980.

At Loyola, he was an advocate for social justice, especially in regard to the inadequately supplied African-American public schools. He focused on the run-down Alcée Fortier High School and recruited students interested in painting and repairing it. His work at Fortier was recognized in a full-page spread in the New Orleans newspaper. He was also active in civic affairs, serving on the Citizens' Oversight Committee for New Orleans Public Schools.

However, Grand Coteau was never far from his mind, and he returned as its brother minister and maintenance director (1984-90). Continuing his social justice advocacy, Bro. Stiegler was renowned for helping the workers at the college when their finances were tight; "generous" is the word regularly used to describe him.

He returned to New Orleans to work at Ignatius Residence, where he did various jobs, including working with music therapy interns and giving voice lessons. Though he was slowing down due to age and health issues, these conditions did not impede his service to the underprivileged while at Ignatius Residence. On the contrary, he resumed his work of renovating poor schools. And he even became a special instructor in Orleans Parish schools (1994-99), where he coached students in reading and helped in fundraising events.

Indeed, he continued to share his time and talents with those in need until, due to deteriorating health, he was no longer able to work.

Bro. Stiegler died on March 3, 1999, at age 72. He had been a Jesuit for 56 years. He is buried at Grand Coteau.

Richard M. Thomas, SJ
1928 – 2006
A candidate for sainthood

Testimonies and statements that would verify miraculous occurrences through the intercession of Fr. Richard M. Thomas have been collected to expedite the application for sainthood of this holy man. Some of his many parishioners have contributed stories about miracles in his name.

Born in Seffner, Fla., a country town east of Tampa, on Feb. 29, 1928, Richard was a leap year baby. He entered the Novitiate at Grand Coteau on Aug. 14, 1945, when the world celebrated Victory-in-Japan (V-J) Day. Dick spent two years in the Novitiate and then two challenging years in the Juniorate. He studied philosophy at Spring Hill College and taught at Jesuit High in Dallas, after which he began theology in St. Marys. Because of acute allergies, he transferred to the California Theologate in Alma, Calif., and was ordained in San Francisco on June 13, 1958.

Fr. Thomas taught at Jesuit High in New Orleans (1960-64) before being missioned to work with the Hispanic poor in El Paso. Even though he had very large shoes to fill when Fr. Harold Rahm, SJ, moved to Brazil, Fr. Thomas succeeded many times over, making some strategic moves, many of which pleased people in El Paso and some of which did not.

Fr. Thomas terminated the daily "bread line" for the poor on the belief that people should learn to fish rather than being given the fish. He facilitated the sale of El Paso's Old Youth Center building and acquired a larger building he named *Las Alas*. The Wednesday night prayer group grew, expanding to include catechism classes for children, individual prayer counseling, and increased hours of confessions.

He dreamed of a place where parishioners could grow food, a place that would be an oasis of peace. In time Fr. Thomas established such a place, The Lord's Ranch, east of Vado, N.M. Over the years the ranch provided recreation and rehabilitation to needy youth, housed hundreds of visitors from all over the world, sponsored retreats for young and old, and became the home of KJES International Shortwave Radio Station.

His energies bubbled up constantly: Our Lady's Youth Center grew so that it included food banks, medical and dental clinics, prison and mental health ministries, and a school. His concerns for the poor also spread to Juarez, Mexico.

To support all of these ministries, Fr. Thomas sent numerous solicitation letters with very blunt exhortations. He observed to his audience that the Church unfortunately does not give the appearance of being "poor-in-spirit." His audience, too, hardly knew the needs of the poor "because few of us ever meet the poor." He concluded:

"May I recommend multiple, prolonged visits to your city's slums. I say multiple and prolonged because until one gets on a first-name basis with more than one family, he won't begin to absorb their attitudes and comprehend their needs."

Many people in El Paso consider him a holy man. Miracles have been documented, in particular the one which occurred on a Christmas morning at the Juarez city dump. Fr. Thomas had brought a truckload of food, and as the people came and received this gift, the food never ran out. Testimonies came from lepers, cancer victims and others.

The provincial of the New Orleans Province authorized a modest prayer card with a prayer for the poor through the intercession of Fr. Thomas. In a letter dated Feb. 2, 2012, the provincial urged El Paso citizens to collect documentation of graces received, which the Province would add to other materials related to Fr. Thomas. Members of the Province were urged to send in memories, concerns, and examples of holiness that might be useful in the canonization process.

Fr. Thomas died after an extended illness, at The Lord's Ranch on May 7, 2006, at age 78. He is buried in El Paso.

Harry William Tompson, SJ
1936 – 2001
He served the poor of downtown New Orleans

Fr. Harry William Tompson was renowned for his loud voice and teasing manner, but he was also notorious for his explosive temper. Most of all, he is remembered for his zeal, vision, productivity and dedication to the people he served as a teacher, administrator and pastor.

Born in New Orleans on July 13, 1936, Harry graduated from Jesuit High in 1954 and soon entered the Novitiate in Grand Coteau. He studied philosophy at the Jesuit House of Studies on the campus of Spring Hill College, earning a B.A. in secondary education and an M.A. in philosophy from Spring Hill. After a three-year Regency in Shreveport, he studied theology (1964-68).

Fr. Tompson's ministry was divided into three parts: high school teaching and administration, preaching retreats at Manresa House of Retreats, and re-founding the Immaculate Conception Parish in New Orleans. His apprenticeship in the ministry of high school education began at Jesuit College Prep in Dallas (1968-70) and continued at Strake Jesuit in Houston (1970-74). He served in administration at Jesuit High in New Orleans, first as principal (1974-79) and then as president (1979-87).

Testimonies at his retirement paint a picture of a noble Fr. Tompson. He motivated parents to participate in their sons' education and to support the institution which provided it. They loved Harry, as noted by one parent who declared, "We never refused you anything."

Many placed Fr. Tompson in the pantheon of past Jesuit presidents. One admirer wrote:

"History will show that very few have left so much behind as you…. Your years at Jesuit High School were probably the most productive in all aspects in the history of the school."

In 1989 Fr. Tompson went to Manresa House of Retreats in Convent, La., where he spent four years using all his communication skills and his ability to speak simply and tersely to retreatants. Appreciation of Harry grew at the retreat house just as it did at Jesuit High.

But Father was not finished. He became pastor of the nearly defunct Immaculate Conception Church in downtown New Orleans. With the exodus of professional and commercial services from the Canal Street area, the Jesuit church had lost most of its parishioners, its support, and its spirit. Quickly Fr. Tompson increased the attendance and participation in the liturgy.

Then he considered a different kind of downtown ministry. Since the church was surrounded by poor, homeless people, he remodeled the first floor of the building next door to the rectory to provide street people with showers and machines to launder and dry their clothing. And since many young poor people had no job skills whatsoever, Harry undertook to construct a restaurant (*Café Reconcile*) staffed by people wanting to learn the hospitality skills necessary to become waiters, table setters, receptionists, busboys and short-order cooks.

Fr. Tompson fostered the building of a Nativity school – The Good Shepherd School – just blocks from the church. These schools recruit minority children, whose attendance requires intense parental participation. The aim is to form students who can move to quality high schools after elementary school. The program requires considerable financial support, which was no problem for Harry.

Fr. Tompson displayed many virtues: zeal, indefatigable labor and dedication, but he was also notorious for his explosions of anger and shouting. One senior Jesuit said of him:

"He could make me mad one minute and glad the next…. Few stayed mad at him, and then they would come back to work with him and for him, because his goodness far outweighed his spurts of temper and impatience."

Fr. Tompson was operated on for prostate cancer, but the disease had already spread throughout his body. In spite of his illness, his last wish was fulfilled when he paraded with a Mardi Gras krewe in the St. Patrick's Day Parade, his personal nurse at his side.

On April 5, 2001, Fr. Tompson died, a mere 64 years old. He is buried at Grand Coteau.

Bernard Anthony Tonnar, SJ
1912 – 1996
A 'late blooming' writer, he served Loyola 29 years

Among Bernard Anthony Tonnar's distinguished achievements at Loyola was his establishment of Loyola's Mexican Summer School in 1958 and then its International Program of Studies.

Born Dec. 21, 1912, in Greenville, Miss., Bernie graduated from Spring Hill High School in Alabama then immediately entered the Novitiate in Grand Coteau, on Aug. 30, 1932. His formation began with college studies and philosophy, after which he did special studies in mathematics at Catholic University, receiving an M.A. in 1941. He taught mathematics at Spring Hill College and traveled to St. Mary's College for theology. He was ordained on June 17, 1945.

His first priestly assignment was to St. Francis Xavier Negro Mission in Miami, where he served for four years. In 1951 he was posted to Loyola University in New Orleans, where he remained for nearly 30 years, until 1980 – roughly a Jesuit's apostolic lifetime. Initially he taught mathematics, but later served as assistant dean of arts and sciences for 11 years.

In the late 1950s he was made director of international studies, then dean of the College of Arts and Sciences for one year, and finally he was elected to the university's board of directors. He left the university world to become the superior of Ignatius Residence for six years.

His peers called him a "late bloomer" for it was not until around 1980 that Fr. Tonnar began writing for publication. His articles began appearing in the local *Times-Picayune*, *National Jesuit News*, *The Catholic Digest* and *America*. He often wrote on the ecumenical hope that Catholics not take literally "no salvation outside the Church;" his conviction on this matter was strong and personal since his mother was Protestant.

Fr. Tonnar denied that his thinking was derivative of that of John Courtney Murray, SJ, a co-author of the Vatican II document *Dignitatis Humanae*, which affirmed religious freedom as an inalienable right. Fr. Tonnar found it curious that he was considered "pre-Trent" by some, since his articles would place him as "post-Vatican II."

After his stint as superior of Ignatius Residence, he was appointed to Immaculate Conception Church in downtown New Orleans (1986-90) and then worked for six years at Holy Name of Jesus Church.

In 1996, Fr. Tonnar retired to Ignatius Residence, where he died on April 1, 1996, at age 83. He is buried at Spring Hill.

On the occasion of Fr. Tonnar's death, the Jesuits received many letters expressing praise for this significant educator and generous servant. One described him in these words:

> *During his entire apostolate Fr. Tonnar attracted fans and followers. Students loved him and he had a host of friends…. He had a friendly approach that attracted many to seek his counsel in and out of the confessional. He was a zealous priest whom people loved.*

Similar sentiments were expressed by a former student:

> *He was what a Jesuit should be, a thorough gentleman, a fine priest, a wise counselor, and a loyal friend; he was, indeed, A Man For Others.*

Sidney Albert Tonsmeire, SJ
1909 – 2001
Longtime pastor, minister, Seminary Fund solicitor

Sidney Albert Tonsmeire was an indefatigable solicitor of funds for various Jesuit needs, especially for endowments for the Seminary Fund. His archival file is half-filled with correspondence pertaining to receipt of moneys that he solicited.

"Sid," as he was called, was born in Mobile, Ala., on April 19, 1909, one of four sons. He was educated in parochial grade schools and went to Spring Hill High School, from which he graduated in 1926. He matriculated at Spring Hill College from 1926 to 1930, took a year off to work, and then entered the Novitiate on Oct. 31, 1932. He took his first vows on Christmas Day in 1934.

Because of his Spring Hill diploma, Tonsmeire spent only one year in the Juniorate and then went to St. Louis for two years of philosophy. Not surprisingly, his Regency was spent in his hometown at Spring Hill College (1937-40). He studied theology at St. Marys, Kan., for four years and was ordained on June 22, 1943.

His priestly ministry began with an assignment to Loyola University as a student counselor, after which he was transferred to Spring Hill College as the Jesuit minister for ten years (1947-57). After he returned to Loyola as its minister for two years, his apostolate immediately took a new direction when he was assigned as pastor of Holy Name of Jesus Church, next door to Loyola (1959-67).

At St. Ann's Church in West Palm Beach, Fla., he ministered as pastor for nine years (1968-77) and then served a long tenure as pastor of St. Joseph's Church in Mobile (1977-94). He remained at St. Joseph's until he went into semi-retirement at Spring Hill College in 1994, but only because the decline in his powers made the move necessary. He was then 85 years old.

Four years later, when walking became too difficult for him, Sid made a graceful transition to Ignatius Residence.

On Nov. 18, 2001, Fr. Tonsmeire died at age 92. He is buried at Spring Hill.

Oscar Patrick Usina, SJ
1923 – 1981
Keeper of the books

Oscar Patrick Usina exhibited qualities of gregariousness, self-effacement, and excellence in accounting and financial management in three decades of service to the Province and its institutions.

Usina, born in St. Augustine, Fla., on May 14, 1923, received his elementary and secondary education locally at the Cathedral Parish School (1928-36) and at St. Joseph Academy (1936-40).

On Aug. 14, 1941, Pat entered the Society of Jesus at the Novitiate in Grand Coteau as a candidate for the priesthood. He spent two years in the Juniorate (1943-45) and three years at Spring Hill College studying philosophy, during which he earned a B.S. in physics (1947). Regency followed with one year at Spring Hill and one year at Jesuit High in Dallas.

During this time he discerned that the priesthood was not his vocation, but being a Jesuit was. Hence, he transferred to the grade of temporal coadjutor on Aug. 18, 1950, and officially became a Jesuit brother.

Bro. Usina went to work immediately in the treasurer's office at Grand Coteau and stayed for four years (1950-54), then he joined the Provincial's Curia at Jesuit High in New Orleans as assistant treasurer (1954-57). From there he went to Xavier Hall Retreat House in Pass Christian, Miss., for two years as its bookkeeper. He spent one year at Grand Coteau before settling down in 1960 at Jesuit High in Dallas as its treasurer for 21 years.

When his health began to fail, he was assigned to the Province infirmary in New Orleans. On Aug. 10, 1981, Bro. Usina died at age 58. He is buried at Grand Coteau.

Bro. Usina is remembered as one of those people easily accessible to others. It is not known just how his lisp affected his life, but he was fearless in trying to communicate. He was genuinely good to be with; he made friends easily. As a bookkeeper and as a Province financial examiner, he was superb.

Roy William Vollenweider, SJ
1914 – 2005
'Chief' was Spring Hill's
living, breathing history book

Roy William Vollenweider, born in New Orleans on Nov. 9, 1914, knew from a young age that he wanted a life in service to God and His people. Roy wrote about those early days and his certainty of a vocation to the priesthood:

In second grade I told Sister I wanted to be a priest. My pastor advised me to talk to the priests at Jesuit High. I didn't know anyone so I visited with the principal, Fr. Percy Roy; I shocked him by telling him that I wanted to become a Jesuit. He was very kind and told me to see the provincial, Fr. Salter, and in the meantime to enroll in the school. Fr. Salter went to see my father, a painter at Charity Hospital, and arranged for me to go to Jesuit High School on a scholarship.

After graduation he attended Loyola for one year and then entered the Novitiate in 1933. With one exception, Roy progressed through the traditional Jesuit formation: philosophy and history, as well as Regency, at Spring Hill College, and theology at St. Mary's. After philosophy, he was given the exceptional and rare permission to earn a master's degree in history at St. Louis University, which he completed in 1942. He was ordained in 1947.

Fr. Vollenweider taught Latin and history in the Juniorate for three years and then was posted to Spring Hill, where he taught for the next 43 years. He taught his life's love, history, as well as political science. Before his hearing failed, he also served as a student counselor. Eventually he lent a hand in the alumni office, since he was the living memory of the college.

Fr. Roy Vollenweider was often called "Chief" because during World War II waves of military students swept through the college, and he could never remember their names, so he called all of them Chief. One of these chiefs asked if he could call Fr. Vollenweider Chief. After that, there was only one Chief.

The anecdotes about Fr. Vollenweider are many and pleasant. By mid-life Chief was totally deaf, yet he was the proctor of Mobile Hall. About life in the dorm he said:

"I don't see anything! I don't hear anything! And I won't say anything."

His was the steady presence of a caring adult for the undergraduates, their Chief. After May graduations, Chief would make the rounds of the dumpsters. He would retrieve unreturned library books – he rescued hundreds! – as well as wardrobes of perfectly good, quality clothing, acres of bed linens, and other discarded but still useful items. He returned the library books and laundered the clothing and the linen, folding and stacking it in the room which became known as "The Cave." Next year's students had access to these found items and could take what they needed – *gratis*.

He was asked if he missed having children.

"I don't worry about not having children because all of these kids are mine," he replied.

On July 24, 2005, Fr. Vollenweider died at Ignatius Residence in New Orleans; he was 90 years old. He is buried at Spring Hill.

George Francis Wiltz, SJ
1934 – 2007
Leadership
was his calling

An effective and much sought-after leader, George Francis Wiltz was blessed with considerable skills in administration and fundraising – talents which he used with great success in several schools and institutions of the Province.

A native New Orleanian born on Aug. 3, 1934, George was baptized at St. Ann's Church and later attended its parish grade school from 1940 to 1948. Upon graduation from Jesuit High in New Orleans, he entered the Society in Grand Coteau in 1952. After completing two years of Novitiate and two years of Juniorate, he moved to Spring Hill for his college studies and philosophy. He spent his Regency at Jesuit High in New Orleans (1959-62), and studied theology at St. Marys, Kan. (1962-66).

It would seem that George Wiltz was born to be

a president or a minister or a director or a superior – all positions he held at various times in his apostolate. His first assignment was at Spring Hill College as the minister of the House of Studies (1967-69); then he was promoted to the position of superior of the Jesuit philosophy students. He served as superior of the Spring Hill philosophy program (1969-70), then as superior of the philosophy program at Loyola in New Orleans (1970-72).

He began a long love association with Jesuit High in Tampa, first as its minister and as a counselor (1972-74). After four years as the superior of Montserrat Retreat House in Lake Dallas, he returned to Tampa to serve again as counselor (1978-80). But a greater managerial role was given him when he was made president of Jesuit High in Tampa for a term of six years (1980-86).

He returned to New Orleans as director of the Jesuit Seminary and Mission Bureau, surely because of his proven administrative skills and his ability to raise funds. He shifted cities and apostolates when he became superior of Ignatius House in Atlanta (1988-94). He returned to Loyola University to serve as an assistant to the president for development.

Finally, another position was assigned, this time as associate pastor of St. Rita Parish in Dallas (1996-97), then, for the second time, as director/superior of Montserrat Retreat House at Lake Dallas.

George was on sabbatical from 2003 to 2004 at Ignatius Residence in New Orleans and served as superior there from 2004 to 2005. He was a retreat director at Manresa House of Retreats from 2005 to 2007. His last assignment, made in 2007, was as associate pastor at Holy Name of Jesus Parish.

However, soon after beginning this mission, Fr. Wiltz died, on Oct. 26, 2007, at age 73. He is buried at Grand Coteau.

Glossary

"Baronne Street" – A commonly used term to refer to Immaculate Conception College (1849-1911) and/or Immaculate Conception Church, located at 130 Baronne Street in New Orleans. The church and the college were adjacent to one another and formed a compound.

For instance, a Jesuit might say, "I spent the first 20 years of ministry at Baronne Street." This could mean as a pastor, assistant pastor, teacher and/or administrator.

Biennium – A two-year course of study toward a doctorate. This was standard procedure for those seeking doctorates in philosophy and theology at the Gregorian University in Rome.

Consultor – A person designated to consult with and offer advice to a Rector or Provincial.

Degrees –
> **Canon Law**: JCB – Bachelor of Canon Law; JCL – Licentiate of Canon Law; JCD – Doctor of Canon Law.
> **Ecclesiastical**: PhL – Licentiate in Philosophy
> **Sacred Theology**: STB – Bachelor of Sacred Theology; STL – Licentiate of Sacred Theology; STD – Doctor of Sacred Theology.

Denver Mission – Jesuit parishes and other apostolates in Denver, Oklahoma, New Mexico and west Texas prior to 1919; staffed in part by Jesuits who came from the Naples Province. This Mission was dissolved in 1919 and its apostolates were divided between the Missouri and New Orleans provinces.

Econome – The Jesuit responsible for the finances of a community, i.e. a treasurer.

Ignatius Residence – The New Orleans Province's home for aging and infirm Jesuits in Algiers, La., across the Mississippi River from New Orleans. The facility functioned in this manner from 1981 until 2013, when a pavilion for aging Jesuits was opened in the newly renovated St. Charles College building in Grand Coteau, La.

Jesuit Volunteer Corps (JVC) – Offers women and men opportunities to work in Jesuit apostolates full time for justice and peace, serving the poor directly, working for structural change in the United States, and accompanying people in developing countries.

Juniorate – A course of study following Novitiate when vowed Jesuits made their "first studies," i.e. basic college courses, with emphasis on ancient languages and humanities. This course is referred to today as First Studies. Juniorate is also the facility in which Juniors resided and did their course work.

Junior – A Jesuit who is enrolled in the program of studies offered in the Juniorate.

Magis – A key component in Ignatian spirituality, *magis* is a Latin term for "more." It calls for a spirit of excellence and generosity in which ministry should be carried on and for a depth and quality in what one does. It invites us to consider how we can serve the world better, with deep commitment and zeal.

Mission Band – A group of Jesuits, not attached to any particular church or parish, who traveled to various communities in an evangelistic manner, preaching, giving retreats and administering the sacraments.

Novice – A candidate for the Jesuit Order who spends two years in spiritual formation, discernment and orientation to the goals and charism of the Order.

Novitiate – A two-year period of training and preparation in which candidates for the Society of Jesus discern whether they are truly called to religious life in the Order. It is a time in which candidates become familiar with the constitutions of the Society and are introduced to the various ministries characteristic of the modern Order.
Novitiate is also the facility in which Novices live, pray and study.

Philosophate – A college or part of a college with a strong department of philosophy where Juniors went to study philosophy, usually for three years.

Philosopher – A Jesuit student studying philosophy – one of the stages of priestly formation.

Provincial – The person whom Father General appoints to lead the Province, usually for a term of six years.

Rector – The person in charge of an institution or ministry, usually for six years.

Regency – The period of formation after First Studies during which a Jesuit engages in apostolic works, frequently as a teacher at one of the Province's high schools.

Regent – A Jesuit in the stage of formation known as Regency.

Restoration – After half a century of living under the Suppression of its apostolates and institutions in Europe, North America and elsewhere, the Society of Jesus re-emerged and began the long process of restoration of its numbers and its various ministries, churches, colleges, etc.
The Restoration followed the Napoleonic Wars, which ended in 1815, and the deaths or loss of power of the monarchs who had instigated the Suppression. The Restoration was ordered by Pope Pius VII in 1814.

Scholastic – A Jesuit in formation for the priesthood, i.e., continuing to take the courses which are necessary for priestly ministry after his Novitiate.

Socius – Executive assistant to the Provincial or to the Master of Novices, attending to administrative matters, correspondence, and the like.

St. John's College in Shreveport – Founded on Nov. 3, 1902, as St. John's College; called St. John's High School 1941-1960, then changed to Jesuit High School; since 1982, known as Loyola College Prep.

Spiritual Exercises of St. Ignatius – A collection of of spiritual activities including prayer, meditation, Scriptural readings, examination of conscience, and acts of self-denial – all designed to strengthen one's spiritual health, thus drawing the person into closer communion with God.

 The Exercises were written in the Sixteenth Century by Ignatius of Loyola, founder of the Society of Jesus. He was inspired to write them after experiencing the presence of God in a profound way while praying on the bank of the River Cardoner at Manresa, Spain, in 1522.

 Ignatian retreats at Jesuit retreat houses around the world are based on the Exercises.

Suppression – In the mid-1700s, enemies of the Jesuits alleged the Society of Jesus was engaged in political and economic exploitation and influenced European governments to punish the Society and suppress its extensive influence throughout the land. The Society had been a thorn in the side of European monarchies that wanted greater control over their national churches, following the example of the English Reformation.

 Subsequently, beginning with Portugal and France, in 1763 European monarchies confiscated or destroyed Jesuit colleges, churches and libraries. They banished the Jesuits from their countries and colonies using Decrees of Suppression.

 Jesuits met the same fate in Louisiana when a similar decree was issued by the local government on July 9, 1763. Their property was put up for auction and most Jesuits were forced to return to France.

 Adding to their shock, in 1773 they were notified that Pope Clement XIV had issued a Decree of Suppression of the Jesuits around the world. The decree not only suppressed the Society but "dissolved...and abolished" it.

 The Suppression would last for half a century.

St. Mary's College – In the town of St. Marys, Kansas, a school dedicated to the study of theology, i.e., a theologate.

Temporal Coadjutor – A Jesuit Brother whose work is in temporal matters.

Theologate – An institution or part of a college where Jesuit scholastics learn the history and content of theology and make their final preparations for priestly ordination.

Time Line

Focusing on the establishment and development of the Jesuits' New Orleans Mission and Province in the Southern United States

1540   St. Ignatius Loyola establishes the Society of Jesus, the Jesuits. Pope Paul III signs a papal bull approving the creation of the Order.

1566   Francis Borgia, Fr. Gen. of the Society, sends Jesuits to Florida.

1673   Fr. Jacques Marquette arrives in North America as explorer and missionary.

1700   Fr. Paul DuRue accompanies explorer Pierre Le Moyne d' Iberville on a trip to Mobile; Fr. DuRue becomes the first resident priest in Mobile.

1722   Fr. Pierre Francois-Xavier de Charlevoix, teacher and author, visits New Orleans.

1723   Fr. Joseph Francois de Kereben becomes superior of the fledgling Louisiana Indian mission.

1726   Colonial governor Bienville transfers a large tract of land at New Orleans to the Jesuits.

1727   Fr. Nicholas de Beaubois escorts Ursuline nuns from France to New Orleans.

1763   King Louis XV's Decree of Suppression banishes Jesuits from Louisiana.

1773   Pope Clement XIV decrees international Suppression of the Society of Jesus.

1814   Papal Bull of Pope Pius VII restores and vindicates the Society of Jesus.

1830   Spring Hill College at Mobile, Ala., is founded by the Bishop of Mobile.

1836   Bishop Antoine Blanc of New Orleans invites Jesuits to return to Louisiana.

1837   St. Charles College in Grand Coteau, La., is founded.

1847   New Orleans Mission is restored; Fr. Jean Baptiste Maisounabe is named Mission superior.

         State of Louisiana grants charter for incorporation of the Jesuits' New Orleans Mission, with the corporate title of *La Société Catholique d'éducation religieuse et littéraire*. (Catholic Society for Religious and Literary Education).

         Jesuits assume control of Spring Hill College at Mobile.

1849   College of the Immaculate Conception opens in New Orleans, on Baronne Street. (Later it would split off into Loyola University and Jesuit High School.)

1869   Spring Hill College students and teachers transfer from Mobile to St. Charles College in Grand Coteau, La.

1872   Novitiate is established at Grand Coteau, La.

1874   St. Stanislaus College in Macon, Ga., is founded.

1879   Novitiate in Grand Coteau is transferred to Macon.

1880   Independent Mission of New Orleans is named.

1897   Yellow fever ravages Louisiana.

1899   Sacred Heart College in Tampa is founded. (Its name would change to Jesuit High School in 1940.)

1902   St. John's College in Shreveport is founded. (Its name would change to Loyola College Prep in 1982.)

1907   New Orleans Mission is awarded the status of a Province; Fr. John O'Connor is named the first Provincial.
        Fire destroys St. Charles College.

1912   Loyola University of New Orleans is founded. (It had been the college division of the College of the Immaculate Conception, then split off in 1911 and moved to St. Charles Avenue.)

1919   New Mexico becomes part of New Orleans Province.

1921   Fire destroys St. Stanislaus College in Macon, Ga.; Novitiate is forced to move elsewhere – to Grand Coteau, La.

1926   Jesuit High School in New Orleans relocates to Carrollton Avenue. (It had been the high school division of the College of the Immaculate Conception, since 1849.)

1931   Manresa House of Retreats in Convent, La., is established.

1933   New Orleans Province Jesuits arrive in Ceylon to serve as missionaries.

1938   Our Lady of the Oaks Retreat House opens in Grand Coteau, La.

1942   Jesuit High School of Dallas is founded. (Its name would change to Jesuit College Preparatory in 1969.)

1947   Fr. Ignatius Glennie of the New Orleans Province becomes bishop in Ceylon.

1952   New Orleans Province passes resolution formally rejecting racial segregation.

1959   Montserrat Retreat House in Lake Dallas opens.
        El Paso Jesuit High School opens. (The school would close in 1972.)

1960   Strake Jesuit College Preparatory in Houston opens.
        Ignatius House Retreat Center in Atlanta opens.

1972   Jesuit Spirituality Center in Grand Coteau is founded and begins offering
        directed retreats based on the Spiritual Exercises of St. Ignatius.

2014   New Orleans Province merges with Missouri Province to form the USA
        Central and Southern Province.

Sources

**Note on primary sources –
Jesuit Archives and *Our Friends***

The main source of information for the biographies in this book is the New Orleans Province Archives in the Monroe Library at Loyola University New Orleans. Some 60 of these biographies originally appeared in *Our Friends* (three editions were published, in 1978, 1989 and 1998) and were edited further for re-publication in this volume.

Anderson, R. Bentley. *Black, White, and Catholic: New Orleans Interracialism, 1847- 1956*. Nashville: Vanderbilt University Press, 2005.

Angers, Trent. *Grand Coteau: The Holy Land of South Louisiana*. Lafayette, Louisiana: Acadian House Publishing, 2005.

Biever, Albert H., SJ. *The Jesuits in New Orleans and the Mississippi Valley*. New Orleans: New Orleans Province of the Society of Jesus, 1924.

— , *Reminiscences of a Southern Jesuit*. New Orleans: New Orleans Province of the Society of Jesus, 1930.

Clancy, Thomas Hanley, SJ. "The Ante-Bellum Jesuits of the New Orleans Province, 1837-1861." *Louisiana History: The Journal of the Louisiana Historical Association* Vol. 34, No. 3 (Summer 1993), pp. 327–343.

— , *Our Friends*. New Orleans: New Orleans Province of the Society of Jesus, 1st ed., 1978; 2nd ed., 1989; 3rd ed., 1998.

Delanglez, Jean, SJ. *The Jesuits in Lower Louisiana: 1700-1763*. New Orleans: Loyola University, 1935.

Hawkins, Donald A., SJ. "Pioneer Jesuits in the South – 1566 to 1763." www.loyno.edu. New Orleans: Loyola University, 2008.

Jesuits of the South Celebrate: 75 Years as a Province (1907-1982), Apostolic Ministry in the South since 1837, Early Jesuit Missions in the South (1566-1763). The Southern Jesuits: Vol. 2, No. 1. New Orleans: Jesuit Seminary and Missions Bureau, August, 1982.

Kenny, Michael, SJ. "Jesuits in Our Southland 1566-1946: Origin and Growth of New Orleans Province." New Orleans, 1946. (Unpublished Manuscript)

Lange, John W., SJ. *Palm Fringed Coast: History of Trincomalee-Batticaloa Diocese (1895-1967)*. Batticaloa, Sri Lanka: Guy F. Rajendram, SJ, 2007.

O'Neill, Charles E., SJ, and Joaquín M. Domínguez, SJ. *Diccionario histórico de la Compañia de Jesús: Vol. 1-4*. Roma: Institutum Historicum, Society of Jesus. Madrid: Universidad Pontificia Comillas, 2001.

Poche, Justin D. *Religion, Race and Rights in Catholic Louisiana: 1938-1970*. Ann Arbor, Michigan: ProQuest Information and Learning Company, 2008.

"Proceedings and Reports, 1916: Volume IX." *Publications of the Louisiana Historical Society*. New Orleans, Louisiana, 1917. Books.google.com, Nov. 3, 2014.

Index

Note: The names of the 220 men whose biographies are featured in this book appear in **bold**; their stories can be found on the page numbers showing in **bold**.

Italic page numbers refer to photographs and the captions accompanying them, and also to maps and the legends accompanying them.

The names of the men in the large photographs printed on the end sheets of this volume are included in the index. Their locations are listed as either *FES* (Front End Sheet) or *BES* (Back End Sheet).

Acknowledgements

Every book project that I know of represents the labor of not only the author but also a cast of others who are committed to its success. This book, too, enjoyed the careful attention of several such contributors.

The father of this collection of Southern Jesuit biographies is Thomas Clancy, S.J. (1923-2009), who researched and wrote three smaller books that were the forerunners of this expanded volume. He composed about 70 bios for *Our Friends*, which was first published in 1978, then updated and re-published in 1989 and 1998. Most of these writings are repeated in this volume.

Fr. Clancy's work was supplemented by additional bios written by Leo Nicoll, S.J., and Donald Hawkins, S.J., which appear in this edition. Fr. Nicoll contributed profiles of four Loyola University faculty members while Fr. Hawkins wrote about several colorful Jesuits of the 19th century.

I'd like to recognize Joan Gaulene, who worked with me searching the Jesuit archives to help select the men featured in this volume. Joan is the curator of the New Orleans Province Archives, which are located at Loyola University New Orleans. My work in the archives would have been practically impossible were it not for the proactive labors of this gracious lady.

Thanks also to the panel of readers who reviewed the galley proofs of this book with a critical eye to help assure accuracy: fellow Jesuits John Armstrong, Billy Huete, Mark Lewis, Tom Madden and Leo Nicoll; also, archives curator Joan Gaulene and Brooke Iglesias of the New Orleans Province staff.

We have Fr. Vince Orlando, S.J., to thank for the photos that add a unique element of life to this otherwise text-heavy volume. Besides photographing some of the men of the more recent generations, he surveyed hundreds of archived pictures, organized them, and worked to enhance their quality where needed.

Thanks, too, to the staff of Acadian House Publishing, who went above and beyond the call of duty to assure the accuracy and quality of this work. These include Trent Angers and Darlene Smith, co-editors; and graphic artist Robert Clements, who did the pre-press production of the body of the book. As editor-in-chief, Trent is a perceptive, detail-oriented and dedicated practitioner of his craft. He didn't let anything suspicious get past him, though this book is packed with a thousand details of date, time, place and the like.

Finally, my compliments to graphic artist Glenn Noya, who designed the book's cover. Glenn has a long history of working with the Jesuits of the New Orleans Province on numerous projects requiring an artist's touch, and I commend him again on behalf of the Province.

– J.N.

About the Authors...

REV. JEROME NEYREY, S.J., is a renowned scholar and a prolific author, having earned seven college degrees and published more than a dozen books and scores of articles.

His books include *Give God the Glory: Prayer and Worship in Cultural Perspective; Honor & Shame: Matthew and the Great Code; The Resurrection Stories;* and *The Passion Narrative in St. Luke.*

He holds degrees in the Classics from St. Louis University, Theology and Scripture from Regis College, and a PhD in Scripture from Yale. He taught at Weston Jesuit School of Theology in Cambridge, Mass., for 14 years before moving on to teach at Notre Dame in South Bend, Ind. Later, he was a retreat director at Our Lady of the Oaks in Grand Coteau, La., from 2007 through 2013.

Born and reared in New Orleans, he graduated from Jesuit High in 1957, entered the Jesuit Order that summer, and was ordained to the Catholic priesthood in 1970.

REV. THOMAS H. CLANCY, S.J. (1923-2009) was a man of many ministries, including retreat director, pastor, educator, prison minister, writer, editor and director of a radio and television station.

Born in Helena, Ark., he entered the Jesuit novitiate at Grand Coteau, La., in 1942. In addition to traditional Jesuit studies, he earned an M.A. from Fordham, an STL at *Facultés S.J. Louvain,* and a PhD from the London School of Economics.

In the 1960s he was a teacher of history and political science at Loyola University in New Orleans. He edited *America* magazine for a year in the early 1970s and was Provincial of the New Orleans Province from 1971 to 1977. He was responsible for the operation of WWL Radio and TV in New Orleans from 1977 to 1989.

Between 1952 and 1999 he reviewed 77 books and wrote 157 articles, including a dozen that were published in encyclopedias.

The books he wrote or compiled include *Papist Pamphleteers, An Introduction to Jesuit Life, The Conversational Word of God,* and three editions of *Our Friends.*

A leader in the on-going quest for improved race relations in the 1960s, he organized the annual Southern Students Human Relations Seminars at Xavier University from 1962 to 1965.

Inspiring Books
from
Acadian House Publishing

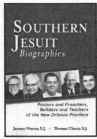

Southern Jesuit Biographies

A 256-page hardcover book containing brief biographies of 220 Jesuit priests and brothers who served the people of the Southeast and Southwestern U.S. Spanning a period of some 300 years, their work included teaching in schools and colleges, preaching the Gospel, building churches and schools, administering the sacraments, leading retreats, working with the poor, and promoting peace and justice. The book is well-illustrated with photographs, both historic and contemporary, as well as maps. (Authors: Rev. Jerome Neyrey, S.J., and Rev. Thomas Clancy, S.J. ISBN: 0-925417-92-0. Price: $40.00)

Blessed Be Jazz

The 192-page hardcover autobiography of Rev. Frank Coco, SJ (1920-2006), a Jesuit priest who served for more than 50 years in south Louisiana as a retreat director, high school teacher and jazz musician. Using his clarinet, he performed extensively in New Orleans nightclubs, sitting in with some of the best-known jazz musicians of his time, including Ronnie Kole, Al Hirt and Pete Fountain. (Author: Rev. Frank Coco, SJ. ISBN: 0-925417-89-0. Price: $19.95)

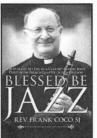

Getting Over the 4 Hurdles of Life

A 160-page hardcover book that shows us ways to get past the obstacles, or hurdles, that block our path to success, happiness and peace of mind. Four of the most common hurdles are: "I can't / You can't," past failures or fear of failure, handicaps, and lack of self-knowledge. This inspiring book – by one of the top motivational speakers in the U.S. – is brought to life by intriguing stories of various people who overcame life's hurdles. (Author: Coach Dale Brown. ISBN: 0-925417-72-6. Price: $17.95)

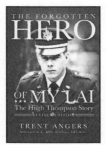

The Forgotten Hero of My Lai
(Revised Edition)

The 272-page story of the U.S. Army helicopter pilot who risked his life to rescue South Vietnamese civilians and to put a stop to the My Lai massacre during the Vietnam War in 1968. Revised Edition shows President Nixon and some of his political allies in the House of Representatives interfered in the judicial process to try to prevent any U.S. soldier from being convicted of war crimes. (Author: Trent Angers. ISBN: 0-925417-90-4. Price: $22.95)

Grand Coteau
The Holy Land of South Louisiana

A 176-page hardcover book that captures the spirit of one of the truly holy places in North America. It is a town of mystery, with well-established ties to the supernatural, including the famous Miracle of Grand Coteau. Brought to life by dozens of exceptional color photographs, the book focuses on the town's major religious institutions: The Academy of the Sacred Heart, Our Lady of the Oaks Retreat House and St. Charles College/Jesuit Novitiate. The book explores not only the history of these three institutions but also the substance of their teachings. (Author: Trent Angers. ISBN: 0-925417-47-5. Price: $44.95)

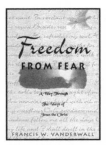

Freedom From Fear
A Way Through The Ways of Jesus The Christ

Everyone at one time or another feels fear, guilt, worry and shame. But when these emotions get out of control they can enslave a person, literally taking over his or her life. In this 142-page softcover book, the author suggests that the way out of this bondage is prayer, meditation and faith in God and His promise of salvation. The author points to certain parables in the Gospels as Jesus' antidote to various fears. (Author: Francis Vanderwall. ISBN: 0-925417-34-3. Price: $14.95)

Dying in God's Hands

A 152-page hardcover book that provides keen insights into the hearts and minds of the dying. It is based on a dozen or more interviews with terminally ill hospice patients, in which they share their hopes, dreams, fears and needs. The majority of the interviews provide evidence that faith in God and belief in the hereafter are the greatest strengths of the dying. Designed to comfort the dying and their loved ones, the book also contains a section of prayers and prose from all major world religions. (Author: Camille Pavy Claibourne. ISBN: 0-925417-64-5. Price: $16.95)

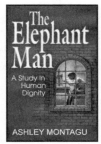

The Elephant Man
A Study in Human Dignity

A 138-page softcover book whose first edition inspired the movie and the Tony Award-winning play by the same name. This fascinating story, which has touched the hearts of readers throughout the world for over a century, is now complete with the publication of this, the Third Edition. Illustrated with photos and drawings of The Elephant Man. (Author: Ashley Montagu. ISBN: 0-925417-41-6. Price: $12.95.)

TO ORDER, list the books you wish to purchase along with the corresponding cost of each. Add $4 per book for shipping & handling. Louisiana residents add 8% tax to the cost of the books. Mail your order and check or credit card authorization (VISA/MC/AmEx) to: Acadian House Publishing, Dept. SJB, P.O. Box 52247, Lafayette, LA 70505. Or call (800) 850-8851. To order online, go to www.acadianhouse.com.

K.
9.
167.
II.

Provincial Congregation
New Orleans Province of the Society of Jesus at Grand Coteau, La., April 7-9, 1961

Jesuit priests from five states came together in Grand Coteau, La., for a Provincial Congregation in the spring of 1961. At the time, membership in the Province was at its peak, with some 600 Jesuit priests and brothers.

Front row, left to right: *William G. Coyle (Asst. Pastor, St. Ann's, W. Palm Beach), Henry F. Tiblier (Superior, Jesuit High, El Paso), Malcolm P. Mullen (Prof. of Ontology, Jesuit House of Studies), Emmanuel Crowther (Superior, Reg. Mission, Trincomalee), E. Cecil Lang (Rector, Jesuit House of Studies), Andrew C. Smith (Vice-Provincial), Harry L. Crane (Prof. in Juniorate, Grand Coteau), Joseph B. Bassich (Spiritual Father, Jesuit High, New Orleans), John A. Toomey (Loyola, writer), Gabriel J. Barras (Pastor, St. Rita's, Dallas), John M. Moreau (Prefect of Studies, Jesuit House of Studies) and Joseph A. Butt (Regent, School of Economics, Loyola).*

Middle row: *John J. McCarthy (Asst. Pastor, St. Ignatius, Mobile), John V. Deignan (Spring Hill College, chemistry), Patrick H. Yancey (Spring Hill, biology), James F. Whelan (Head, Division of Education, Loyola), John A. Gasson (Prof. of philosophy, House of Studies), Samuel H. Ray (Teacher, Jesuit High,*